WOMEN WRITERS OF HUIZHOU

WOMEN WRITERS OF HUIZHOU

Imaginaries of Space and Place in Qing China

BINBIN YANG

UNIVERSITY OF WASHINGTON PRESS
Seattle

Women Writers of Huizhou was made possible in part by a grant from the Traditional Chinese Culture and Society Book Fund, established through generous gifts from Patricia Buckley Ebrey and Thomas Ebrey.

The Small Research Fund for faculty members in the School of Chinese, University of Hong Kong, provided support for indexing.

This book will be made open access within three years of publication thanks to Path to Open, a program developed to bring about equitable access and impact for the entire scholarly community, including authors, researchers, libraries, and university presses around the world. Learn more at https://about.jstor.org/path-to-open/.

Acknowledgments for previously published materials appear on pp. ix–x, which should be considered an extension of the copyright page.

Design by Katrina Noble   Composed in Minion Pro

UNIVERSITY OF WASHINGTON PRESS
uwapress.uw.edu

LIBRARY OF CONGRESS CATALOGING-IN-PUBLICATION DATA
Names: Yang, Binbin author
Title: Women writers of Huizhou : imaginaries of space and place in Qing China / Binbin Yang.
Description: Seattle : University of Washington Press, 2025. | Includes bibliographical references and index.
Identifiers: LCCN 2025004387 | ISBN 9780295754024 hardcover | ISBN 9780295754031 paperback | ISBN 9780295754048 ebook
Subjects: LCSH: Women authors, Chinese—Political and social views | Women and literature—China—History | Chinese literature—China—Huizhou Diqu—History and criticism | Chinese literature—Qing dynasty, 1644–1912—History and criticism | LCGFT: Literary criticism
Classification: LCC PL2275.W65 Y36 2025
LC record available at https://lccn.loc.gov/2025004387

♾ This paper meets the requirements of ANSI/NISO Z39.48-1992 (Permanence of Paper).

To new anchorings

CONTENTS

ACKNOWLEDGMENTS

I HAD THE fortune of receiving very generous help from my mentors and friends during the long journey I took in exploring and experimenting with the topics related to this book. I would like to thank Professor Robert Hegel for reading my book proposal again and encouraging me to complete this project, and Professors Beata Grant and Grace Fong for their mentorship and rich inspiration. Several conference panels and workshops helped me reframe my project: the AAS panel "Gender, Family, and Locality," organized by Professor Xiaorong Li in 2018, the AAS panel "The Family in Qing Personal Narratives," organized by Professor Clara Ho in 2022, the workshop titled "Rethinking Authorship and Agency," organized by Professors Grace Fong and Guojun Wang in 2022, the AAS panel "Traveling Women, Imagining Space," organized by Professor Yuanfei Wang in 2024, and the workshop "China Seen from a Locality," organized by Professor Xin Yu in 2024. I owe the direction that my book is now taking particularly to the stimulating questions and suggestions from Professors Yongtao Du, Maram Epstein, Grace Fong, Xiaorong Li, Weijing Lu, Manling Luo, Steven Miles, Guojun Wang, Yuefan Wang, Ellen Widmer, and Harriet Zurndorfer. I also appreciate the lively discussion with the other participants. Special thanks go to Professor Tobie Meyer-Fong for reading my revised conference paper in 2019 and offering her help and insights on Yangzhou, and to Professors Grace Fong and Guojun Wang for helping me develop a workshop paper in 2022. These papers were published as articles in *CLEAR* in 2022 ("Anchoring Identities in Yangzhou: Xú Deyin [1681–after 1760] and the Re-Invention of the Huizhou Legacy," *Chinese Literature: Essays, Articles, Reviews* 44 [2022]: 141–73) and in *JCLC* in 2023 ("Yangzhou Revisited: Spatial Imaginaries and Women's Literature during the Qing," *Journal of Chinese Literature and Culture* 10, no. 1 [April 2023]: 57–80). Those two journal articles laid the foundation for the present book. I also thank the journal editors, Professors Haun Saussy and Zongqi Cai, for revisions and support. I appreciate the permission of the copyright holders, *CLEAR* and Duke University Press, to incorporate and adapt parts of those articles in chapters 1 and 3 of this book.

This book also grew out of several inspirational research experiences. In the summer of 2019, Professor Xiaorong Li invited me to join her research trip to Anhui and graciously introduced me to new projects on Huizhou conducted or launched at Anhui University, particularly those by Professors Zhang Xiaopo and Geng Chuanyou. During our first day in Huizhou, I found material evidence of the family I studied for chapter 1 and began to get a real sense of the spatiality of the places I had read about. There I had the chance to learn from her fascinating study of the anthologizing projects on women's poetry in Anhui during the Republican period. In the winter of 2019, Professor Tobie Meyer-Fong invited me to her workshop at Johns Hopkins University and hosted me as a visiting scholar. I am grateful for her hospitality, the Library of Congress resources she introduced me to, and the memorable time I had in her department. I would like to thank Professor Marta Hanson for being a hospitable host and for sharing her research on Huizhou publishing of medical texts. In the summer of 2021 and the spring of 2023, when the COVID travel restrictions to mainland China were relatively relaxed, my husband, Fang Liu, urged me to resume my project and take self-funded research trips to Zhenjiang and Huizhou. My completion of chapters 2 and 4 relied on those experiences. Fang Liu took the two photographs of Huaitang Village incorporated in chapter 4. Just before my trip to Huizhou in March 2023, I received messages from Professor Harriet Zurndorfer, who very supportively and generously shared with me her research expertise on Huizhou. Her insights and encouraging words motivated me to complete this book. I greatly appreciate the support from Professor Louise Edwards during this time too.

This is my second time working with the wonderful team at the University of Washington Press. I owe the publication of this book to the support of Lorri Hagman and to the efficient and professional help of Caitlin Tyler-Richards and her colleagues Emily Feng, Beth Fuget, Dandi Meng, Joeth Zucco, and the copyeditor Elizabeth Berg. I am greatly indebted to the enthusiastic recommendations and constructive comments made by the two anonymous readers. The remaining mistakes are mine.

This book is a further development from a project awarded the 2018–19 Humanities and Social Sciences Prestigious Fellowship in Hong Kong, which provided me with teaching relief for the year 2019. The completion of this book straddled the entire COVID period, and my perspectives on its central thesis have been reshaped by that experience. I am grateful for the support and patience of the fellowship panel members. I deeply appreciate the support and inspiration over the years from Professors Derek Collins, Ronald Egan, Martin Huang, Huan Jin, Guotong Li, Pei-yin Lin, Kam Louie, Meijie Shen, Wei Wang, Yanning Wang, Shengqing Wu, Yulian Wu, and Yu Zhang. I would also like to take this opportunity to pay tribute to the late Professors Nanxiu Qian and Maureen Robertson, whose works continue to inspire exploration of women's literary and cultural history in China.

For the images and maps used in this book, my thanks go to the Palace Museum of Beijing, the Peking University Library, the Shanghai Library, and the US Library of Congress for granting me access to and permission to use reprints from their collections.

NOTE TO READERS

FOR THE SAKE of consistency and clarity, I refer to historical figures by their family and given names. I mention their style names, sobriquets, or honorific titles only when necessary for my discussion.

Due to limited space, I needed to summarize or briefly refer to a corpus of works while providing the original texts and translations of those that are crucial to my arguments. Readers may refer to the appendices for a list of relevant themes and selected original texts summarized or referred to in the chapters. I have likewise kept the glossary of Chinese characters to a minimum.

All translations not otherwise specified are mine.

WOMEN WRITERS OF HUIZHOU

INTRODUCTION

THIS BOOK TRACES the key moments when two trends converged in Qing (1644–1911) China as never before: the internal diaspora of mercantile lineages from Huizhou, in southeast Anhui, and women's rise to literary prominence. In the broadest terms, my aim is to foster a fruitful interplay between two areas of investigation that continue to generate new paradigms for understanding the sociocultural transformations in Qing China.

The book draws, first, from the insights in studies of Huizhou lineages regarding social mobility and patterns of change and continuity before and during the Qing.[1] Second, it engages with increasing scholarly inquiries into women's literary ventures and networks primarily from the Qing period, as well as efforts to retrieve their publications through reprinting and digitizing projects.[2] A recent sourcebook excavates rich literary and biographical sources for 617 women writers from Anhui, over one-fourth of whom were affiliated with the Huizhou area.[3] For my purposes, these sources situate women from Huizhou lineages in local cultural developments in Anhui and view them in dynamic interplay with women's literary networks in the lower Yangzi or Jiangnan region, the cultural heartland. They raise questions of geographical affiliation in transregional contexts, as well as of the degree of agency possessed by women of Huizhou lineages.[4]

Paradigmatic shifts in studies of social change before and during the Qing spurred the growth of what is now known as Huizhou scholarship. Ping-ti Ho's pioneering study highlights the perceived antithesis between institutionalized social stratification and a highly competitive system of social mobility. Despite the persistence of a hierarchical Chinese society, boundaries between the four major social groups—scholars, peasants, artisans, and merchants—became easily blurred due to the absence of effective legal barriers preventing upward or downward mobility. Opportunities for government service—offered primarily by an examination system implemented starting in the Tang dynasty (618–907)—and wealth hence became determinants of social stratification.[5] As a ladder of success, civil service examinations nevertheless provided only a small fraction of the population with opportunities for upward mobility. According to Benjamin Elman's estimates, peasants, traders, and artisans—who made up 90 percent of population in late imperial China (ca. fifteenth to nineteenth centuries) China—had no more than marginal success in the examination system. In his words, the "ironically larger 'success story' of the millions of failures in the civil examinations" lay elsewhere.[6] With the power of money increasingly felt during this time, merchants rapidly translated their fortune into social and cultural capital—so much so that at the local level and empirewide, literary and artistic production, intellectual trends, and social and political leadership became permeated with the presence of these "gentry merchants." Merchants from Huizhou emerged as a formidable transregional social force and accounted for the "splendid cultural and intellectual developments that characterized the lower Yangtze area during the eighteenth century."[7]

Transregional refers primarily to the penetration of the Huizhou merchants into the cultural heartland and across the empire. Those in the book industry gained influence in Jiangnan cultural centers during the late Ming, producing the finest publications, which brought them both profit and artistic fame.[8] The transregional aspect highlights early Qing elite networks connecting Yangzhou—a favored destination for sojourning and migrating merchants and a city with an ambivalent Jiangnan identity—with the Jiangnan region in a stricter geographical sense, namely, the area south of the Yangzi River.[9] The wealth and geographical reach of Huizhou merchants peaked during the High Qing, an era spanning around a century and a half between 1683 and 1839, often characterized as at once the zenith of Qing rule and a time of great shifts in social and gender relations.[10] To cope with challenges arising from their changing geographical affiliations, these merchants invented strategies to maintain their native-place ties while creating new identities in a multiplace arena of economic opportunities and social networks.[11] Rather than simply emulating the elite, as suggested in earlier paradigms of their social metamorphosis, they created a constellation of networks connecting the court in Beijing, cultural centers in the Jiangnan region, and their native place in Huizhou through the movement of material objects they produced and consumed.[12] A recent study goes so far as to characterize the transregional movements of the Huizhou merchants as internal diasporas, in the sense of networks of merchants linking their home communities to specific destinations within China and creating a common sense (or claim) of belonging, which paralleled the Chinese diasporas to destinations outside China.[13] These diasporic Huizhou families and communities "epitomized the era's spatial restlessness."[14]

Innovative as it is, Huizhou scholarship has been critiqued for leaving a major lacuna in its inquiry into the sociocultural transformations in late imperial China—namely, women and gender relations. The criticism concerns not so much leaving women completely out of the scope of studies as generating a particularly repressive picture of women's lives in Huizhou.[15] The Huizhou trade diaspora led to trafficking of women in its favored destinations, particularly in its symbiotic place, Yangzhou. And back in its native place, the changed family structure—wives left at home while husbands traveled or sojourned elsewhere for business—put women under moral scrutiny.[16] Huizhou became the epicenter of the cult of female chastity in what has been termed "a new gender regime" for the Qing.[17] In the mapping of women's literary activity during the Qing period, Huizhou is associated with intensified lineage control over women's lives and is deemed unlikely to nurture female talents like those active in the Jiangnan heartland.[18]

The chastity cult, however, must be understood as being embedded in ideological, psychological, cultural, and economic complexities beyond lineage or state control.[19] For elite families to win out in intense social competition outside the examination hall, their pursuit of social honor through the chastity cult and pursuit of cultural luster through women's (and men's) publications often figured as two sides of the same coin. This book places the women of Huizhou in transregional contexts and in women's literary ventures and networks that flourished during the Qing. Huizhou as a place identity was closely tied to diasporic communities in the Jiangnan heartland and across the Qing empire. Just like the men who transformed into gentry-merchants—or who took on a spectrum of identities combining traits of both social groups—women from Huizhou mingled with luminaries of the cultural centers and in time became indistinguishable from their peers among the educated gentry. Their writings survive in a diverse array of genres that are increasingly being uncovered in recent decades through reprinting and digitizing projects dedicated to Qing women's writings.

This book examines how changing relations between people and place catalyzed these women's literary creativity and imaginaries of space and place—or the spatial ordering of the world they imagined and wrote about to articulate their multiplace affiliations and cultural identities. For these women, to write about a place was to perceive it in a world dominated by the rapid social and spatial mobility that came to define the Huizhou impact, and to transform this impact into opportunities for cultural ascendancy. Their writings range from claims of belonging and literary or cultural ownership to broader visions of a cosmic and political order known as Jiuzhou (the Nine Lands) or Tianxia (All under Heaven) and ways of mapping and engaging with it. This book thus posits a spatial analysis of these writings as a lens to approach Huizhou and its women.

Spatiality

Spatiality as a critical lens has reshaped humanities studies across disciplines in recent decades, sparking new modes of thinking that lead to what is often referred to as the "spatial turn." In Edward Soja's succinct recapitulation, recognizing the "inherent spatiality of human life" as being no less important than, and interwoven with, life's temporal and social dimensions constitutes one of the most important intellectual and political developments of our time.[20] In China studies, Manling Luo has recently emphasized a methodological awareness of spatiality as a productive way to bring new insights to Chinese source materials and, at the same time, open a rich potential for broader intellectual dialogues not peculiar to the Chinese context. Luo suggests that "our engagements with theories outside the field should be not a one-way but a two-way street."[21] For her, medieval Chinese textual representations of spatiality foreground the role of text, or textual mediation, in the social production of space in civilizations with a writing tradition, and thereby call into question the lack of attention to textualization in theorizing about spatiality.

Importantly, discussions of place identity have stimulated new angles and questions integral to the spatial turn. Archaeological and sociological inquiries into how people and place are co-defined, for example, interpret people's spatial experience as a process of social and sensual anchoring in place and the related process of place-making as the humanization of place. Drawing from Heidegger's idea of worlding—the world-creating process through human agency—these studies emphasize the production of particular senses of place through social engagement. Questions examined span social codes and relations (including gender relations), worldviews, temporality and memory, and material culture.[22] Literary studies of people and place, by contrast, echo Heidegger by interpreting the world-creating process as essentially the "human impulse to own and *create* the world via language"—namely, through linguistic and literary representations.[23]

This book takes as its point of departure spatiality as a socially constructed and experienced idea, whereby human actors acquire social codes to craft identities. Spatiality as a critical lens allows the social texture of the texts I examine to emerge and enables me to understand the pinnacle of diaspora writing and imagination in Qing China in the broader human experience of place-making and anchoring. Specifically, I am interested in the culturally meaningful ways in which female authors engaged with and transformed, by the act of writing, the places they called home and those that determined the spatial ordering of their rapidly changing world. Insofar as a discussion of such engagement brings into play a literary approach with cross-disciplinary insights into place identity, scholarly inquiries made in the Chinese context have much to contribute to the expanding dialogue on spatiality.

Interest in describing places in China can be traced to early historiography that charted the terrains of the sage kings through geographical and mythological accounts.[24] The term *fangzhi*, or local gazetteers, derived from the responsibility of the Zhou (1027–770 BCE) historians for "keeping records of [the land] in all directions" (*zhang sifang zhi zhi*) and became synonymous with local histories during the late imperial period. The prominence of accounts, maps, and sometimes pictures of places in local histories led a group of Qing historians to identify these records as the defining feature of the local.[25]

Travel accounts and poetry by literati authors from as early as the Tang dynasty (618–907) incorporated personal experience and individual poetic vision into a narrative framework developed from historiography. Works by Liu Zongyuan (773–819), among others, signaled the mature phase of a form of autobiography that inscribed landscapes with encounters among place, nature, history, and the perceptions of the self.[26] One means for transmission or achieving literary immortality was to engrave the texts at the sites they described. The popularity of the practice—termed *moya*, or cliff-polishing—transformed the natural terrains at myriad historic or scenic sites in premodern China into "landscapes of words."[27]

From the mid-Tang on there emerged an intense interest in staking claims of literary ownership of sites and landscapes, while poets, as Stephen Owen famously argues, constantly reminded the legal owner of the impermanence of ownership. Bai Juyi (772–846?) poetically took territory away from its legal owner in the voice of someone who truly knew how to appreciate it: "Ever the most splendid sites lack a permanent owner: by and large the mountain belongs to the person who loves the mountain." Inherent in these claims were assertions of individual style and emergent literati identities for display, as well as the acquisition of cultural capital for the aggrandizement of the poets and their posterity.[28] Xiaoshan Yang posits a political reading of Bai's poetic claims: garden estates that aristocrats of the Tang capital owned but rarely visited or knew how to appreciate were, in Bai's political critique, reflections of their excessive lifestyle and symbols of the deterioration of public order.[29] Owen's latest study of literary ownership focuses on the changing social world of the Song (960–1279) and the contact zone of a new money economy and a key ethical turn. Developing a crisscrossing approach to the changes taking place in this contact zone—rather than a linear, cause-and-effect narrative—Owen offers refreshing readings of the best-known Song writers and the ways they spoke to the conflicting values of their time.[30]

In its expanded sense of the human habitation of places, Ao Wang argues in *Spatial Imaginaries in Mid-Tang China*, the mid-Tang marked the beginning of cross-fertilization between geographical knowledge and spatial imaginaries in literature. Cartographical production and geographical advancement fed into literary representations of the empire and its landscapes and frontiers. And conversely, literary production and innovation centered on place played a distinct role in empire building and imagination. In particular, Wang's rereading of classic landscape essays by Liu Zongyuan captures an otherwise neglected geographical awareness—namely, the domestication of the frontier that drove social and political transformation in the south.[31] For my purpose, the significance of these methodological developments revealing the centrality of human-place ties in the Chinese literary canons lies in their cross-disciplinary vigor and the potential they open for study of Qing women writers' transformative impact on *all-male* canons.

In her methodological reflections on studies of women and gender in late imperial China, Grace Fong highlights concepts such as the gaze, voice, agency, subjectivity, and authorship as useful critical angles. Having entered a shared critical vocabulary, these concepts suggest alternative modes of reading that deconstruct the victimization of traditional Chinese women and illuminate, instead, women's creation of multiple social and cultural identities through the act of writing. Such concepts continue to drive scholarly debates over "broader questions of the applicability of modern/postmodern feminist theories to literature of earlier periods and other cultures before the globalization of the twentieth and twenty-first centuries."[32] Spatiality brings new momentum to these scholarly efforts, given that gender relations are part and parcel of the social relations and human experience that are co-defined with spatiality. As Doreen Massey suggests, "Particular ways of thinking about space and place are tied up with . . . particular social constructions of gender relations."[33]

I am not suggesting that space and gender are mutually alien concepts in studies of Chinese literature and history. Gender distinctions during the Song period have been examined precisely in terms of how the ideal of the separation between inner and outer spaces provided a means of sexual segregation advocated by Confucian ritual and ethical teachings. Because this ideal relied on wealth by necessitating large homes with elaborate architectural structures that were only affordable for the well-to-do, gender and spatial distinctions were intimately connected to class distinctions. Patricia Ebrey astutely observes that "one way the upper class made its distinctiveness visible was by making its women invisible."[34] Expanding educational opportunities for gentry women during the late imperial period, roughly from the seventeenth to the nineteenth century, had the effect of blurring these spatial boundaries. Dorothy Ko's pioneering study of women's literary communities at various levels and across places in the Jiangnan region unveils the "expanded geography" of these women.[35]And travel poetry and writings by women from this time lent ample evidence and vividness to how women ventured beyond the inner quarters.[36] For Susan Mann, by contrast, the fact that women often chose to frame their travels in terms of virtue or family duty heightened the importance of the domestic space rather than indicating adventures away from home. In this sense, the domestic space "constituted a site for the continual reproduction and reinvention of ideas about gender difference and gender performance" in late imperial China.[37] The domestic space, fictionalized or problematized by the garden as an interface between the inner and the outer, gives rise to scholarly interest in family and gender ideologies of this time and women's changing relations to them.[38] Ellen Widmer further reveals, through a woman's travelogue and three novels from the late Qing, that free travel for women remained contested and that even reformist schemes for women needed to compromise between women's performance of gentility and the exigencies of a changing world.[39]

This book is not specifically about women's travels or networks in convoluted connection with the domestic space, although I take these factors into account in my discussion of the place identities and enhanced cultural visibility of women writers from Huizhou diasporic families. My interest lies rather in the bigger claims that the trade diaspora and enhanced social and spatial mobility enabled the women writers to make, and their literary as well as sociopolitical implications. These claims addressed the problematics of women writers' assertion of literary ownership of places or their families' legacies inscribed onto places, and formulated what may be called world-creating visions amounting to a changing worldview. By *worldview*, I refer not only to women writers' apprehension of the world they inhabited as a whole but also an awareness of their place in it and ways of engaging with the changes taking place in it.[40]

In Huizhou studies, the native-place identity of the Huizhou merchants is found to be closely tied to a cosmic and political order known as Tianxia, or "All under Heaven": first, an understanding of localities as microcosms and building blocks of Tianxia; and second, the invention of a Huizhou local identity as the model Confucian place among localities. Simply put, Huizhou was at once similar to other localities and distinct in its relation to Tianxia—here meaning the Qing imperium. The "translocal practices" of the Huizhou merchants, in the phrase of Yongtao Du, unveil a third aspect of the Huizhou-Tianxia connection. As Huizhou merchants traversed the Qing empire and established affiliations with localities of all kinds, they invented a range of social practices in managing resources, solving conflicts arising from changes of residence or household registration, and negotiating between different claims of belonging. These practices brought rural place ties and institutions in Huizhou into interaction with urban developments throughout the Qing empire. Du further suggests that the changing geographical imagination resulting from these practices paved the way for the rise of a national community in the late Qing era.[41] Du's thesis on the "order of places" concerns primarily the relationship between localities and the polity.[42] My reference to a larger cosmic or political order builds on these localities-polity dynamics, with a focus on their assimilation into the women writers' world-creating visions and spatial and cultural claims.

The concept of Tianxia, or "All under Heaven," has recently instigated debate and critique, not least because of the experimental space it opens for reimagining the contemporary world order and hence its bearing on realpolitik.[43] It also throws into question the political and linguistic polarities defining the early Chinese empire, such as self/other, intrinsic/extrinsic, and center/periphery.[44] Though this book is not about contemporary world politics or empire building in China, it echoes a revived interest in Tianxia with connotations ranging from the early ideal of cultural competence and ritualistic governance to late Qing cosmopolitanism.[45] In particular, the ways a woman envisioned and engaged with Tianxia, or the cosmic and political order associated with it, draw emphatic attention to her forays into a male-dominated domain.

Huizhou Scholarship and Women's Literature: Spatiality as a Nexus

It has perhaps by now become too obvious to observe that, overall, studies of changing human-place ties and the corresponding sociocultural transformation need to take into account women as agents of change. The efflorescence of studies following the pioneering works of Dorothy Ko and Susan Mann, among others, has shown that women's literary production needs to be approached socially and culturally, and often through a cross-disciplinary lens. Nonetheless, the turn to a spatial focus speaks to new directions in defining the nexus between Huizhou scholarship and broader terrains of research.

Underlying the latest project for reprinting and digitizing the *bieji*, or personal collections of poetry and prose, from Huizhou is a set of questions regarding what constitutes the nexus between Huizhou and Qing literature. Huizhou's encyclopedic collections of local sources easily omit literary sources such as those included in the *bieji*. Geng Chuanyou attributes this omission to clear-cut disciplinary boundaries, as modern concepts fail to capture the complexity of the Huizhou sources. Huizhou's historical and philosophical traditions—lineage and Neo-Confucianism, in particular—are believed to have eclipsed its literary achievements. On that basis too, Huizhou literature is rarely mapped onto Qing literature in current Chinese literary histories. Geng's approach in redressing this omission is not only to retrieve a repertoire of *bieji*, but more importantly, to question the very standards for evaluating them. What connected Huizhou literature with Qing literature lay in the quotidian, rather than canonical, nature of literary production in general during this time. Literary and historical studies share the "downward-looking" perspective, in Geng's phrase, in including minor or marginal figures into the scope of research, rather than focusing only on prominent or heroic figures.[46] Here again, clear-cut boundaries collapse: though the *bieji* are often relegated to the elite, hence perceived in opposition to the interests of the ordinary or common people, Geng's analysis suggests a decentering of cultural power often observed during this period.[47] While the *bieji* can be mined across genres for historical evidence, Geng emphasizes that literary studies contribute to the broadening impact of Huizhou scholarship with their peculiar attention to generic attributes interwoven with different forms of cultural production.[48]

Geng echoes, perhaps inadvertently, one of the key concepts that has for the past few decades stimulated English-language scholarship on women writers from late imperial China, namely, women's literature as a minor literature. Maureen Robertson's widely cited definition of the literary authorship of late imperial Chinese women draws from Gilles Deleuze and Félix Guattari to foreground the destabilizing effect these women exerted over the majority's canon, precisely through their strategic use of male-dominated forms of expression.[49] Robertson is among those who took the initiative in broadening the scope of historical and literary research on China by including minor or marginal figures.[50] In Fong's ground-breaking study on women's *bieji* as life histories—which she finds to closely resemble the "keeping of a diary or a journal"—the quotidian nature of *bieji* enabled female authors to craft identities beyond their domestic roles and to write themselves into history.[51]

In recent Huizhou studies, with the momentum brought by Fu Ying's sourcebook, more attention has been directed to the presence of the women of Huizhou in arenas beyond lineage control or the chastity cult. Literary works and figures now receive detailed analysis.[52] Literary sources are also being mined—in conjunction with other Huizhou sources—for evidence of women's managerial skills and business acumen on the one hand, and their political and historical insights on the other.[53] These studies lead to an emerging vision of the women of Huizhou as part of the broader canvas of women's rise to literary and cultural prominence in Jiangnan and elsewhere. Insofar as women's economic contributions are concerned, they confirm what has been put forth as evidence for women's role as "domestic bursars" through their shrewd use of dowry wealth as private funds.[54] A recent study identifies traces of Huizhou women's direct involvement in commercial activities and calls for more exploration in this direction.[55]

Now poised to bring greater understanding to women and gender relations in Huizhou, the studies sketched above also generate further questions, such as "Why Huizhou?"[56] One may wonder, for example, what distinguished women writers from Huizhou who were active in Jiangnan from their peers in Jiangnan, if they were assimilated into a common writing culture flourishing in Jiangnan? Is there any difference between those staying in their native Huizhou and those spreading out into diasporic communities, in terms of literary or cultural production? Women's political and economic acumen are topics that hold lasting appeal for those studying women and gender in late imperial China. And yet, how exactly Huizhou mattered as a place identity of the women concerned is not self-evident. Women's writings in times of chaos have been discovered in abundance in war-afflicted areas and are not limited to Huizhou. Nor is there any definitive evidence to date for Huizhou's peculiar role in nurturing women's interest in the state. Even regarding women's direct involvement in commercial activities, comparative studies with women in other commercially vibrant areas or merchant groups, such as in Shanxi and Guangdong, are necessary to demonstrate Huizhou's distinctness as a place identity. Moreover, the umbrella term "women of Huizhou" may itself raise questions about a localist agenda in staking claim to eminent figures affiliated with the area in ways indirectly related to native-place ties.[57]

This book does not claim to fully explore these questions, but place identity matters when it becomes an issue for those who find themselves in problematic relation to it. In distinction to the more usual literati writings on yearning for home when traveling or sojourning to take on posts or in exile, place identity matters in situations where home itself becomes questionable. The Huizhou trade diaspora and the corresponding complexity of the sojourning status gave rise to a range of arrangements concerning the change of registration and home not experienced by the earlier sojourners.[58] Efforts to craft place identity in response to such complexity reveal the Huizhou impact on authenticity claims made in competing for cultural resources, grappling with displacement, and—when catastrophe befell—making sense of a collapsed spatial and political order.[59] More importantly, by taking up the issue of women's place identity, this book problematizes assumptions about the homogeneity of women's writing culture as a byproduct of Jiangnan elite culture.

Women in diasporic families from Huizhou no doubt acquired the same literary language for social bonding and membership to clubs or networks of poets that enabled women in the Jiangnan heartland to stake literary and cultural claims. And yet, as I illustrate in this book, an acquired literary language served different purposes when literary and cultural claims inherent in that language became closely tied to spatial claims essential to diaspora writing. A female talent with Huizhou origins who was lauded for her Qiantang (Hangzhou, in the Jiangnan heartland) background yet who was closely affiliated with Yangzhou, for example, may well have inserted spatial codes into her writing in ways different from peers affiliated primarily with the Jiangnan heartland. Or, for that matter, she may have employed these spatial codes to craft her personal and family history in ways more sophisticated than hitherto imagined (see chapter 1). In the case of a woman who grew up in Yangzhou and returned to her native place in Huizhou, spatial claims provided a means of reanchoring place identities. They were, moreover, crucial to understanding her place in the lineage culture for which Huizhou was so well known, revealing how broader concerns—which aligned her writing with statecraft thinking—grew from her local experience (see chapter 4). Thus, spatiality as a critical lens that allows me to think of Huizhou scholarship in relation to Qing women's literature also highlights how Huizhou mattered as a place identity for the women discussed in this book.

The Example of Yangzhou

While I illustrate the diversity of spatial claims in the writings I examine and hence reach a more nuanced understanding of the umbrella term "women of Huizhou," Yangzhou figures prominently in the spatial ordering of the places I refer to. This is due not only to its symbiotic relation with Huizhou. Rather, the city known as "a place of women" lends itself in no small way to a discussion of spatiality and women.

Yangzhou was known for its women but not for women's literature. The "jade-white beauties" who played flutes by the Twenty-Fourth Bridge fueled literati fantasies from the Tang on and became omnipresent in poetry and anecdotal writings related to the city. Beginning in the late Ming, salt wealth turned Yangzhou into a city of women: entertainment quarters expanded and young women were groomed as "thin horses" (*shouma*) for sale as concubines for wealthy households.[60] The city's notoriety as a destination for the trafficking of women peaked in proportion to Huizhou dominance during the eighteenth century.

Though various historical sources often generated paradoxical stories of Yangzhou—contrasting the wealth of the city with the poverty of the broader

Yangzhou region, for example—one story seems definitive: "Yangzhou [the city and the prefecture] was not among the great producers of women's writing in the late imperial period. . . . The definitive 'accomplished woman' of Yangzhou in the late sixteenth and seventeenth centuries was the thin horse." The pattern of gender relations embedded in this story remained unchanged from the late sixteenth to the mid-nineteenth century, "in which major disruptions finally amounted to no more than minor fluctuations over time."[61] Implicit in this story is a clear-cut boundary between the realms of the "secluded and virtuous wives and daughters" from gentry families and the "beautiful women" for whom Yangzhou was known.[62]

Yangzhou's apparent lack of prominence in women's literary achievement during the late imperial era has been attributed to the fact that, unlike Changzhou and Hangzhou—the heartland of women's literary activities—it did not boast "strong, stable gentry societies."[63] It was not, however, as peripheral as it may appear. Susan Mann identifies it as one of the five "microregions" or "satellite zones" surrounding women's literary center—"areas where women writers were important but not so highly visible." The number of recognized Qing women writers in Yangzhou, based on what Mann gathers from Hu Wenkai's (1899–1988) sourcebook, range between 86 and 106—equal to that in Nanjing and around one-third of that in Changzhou.[64]

Dai Jian raises the number to 288, based on Shi Mei's addition to Hu Wenkai's sources on Jiangsu, as well as her own collection of sources from regional anthologies. Within Jiangsu, Yangzhou was second only to Suzhou and Changzhou.[65] Shi Mei and Dai Jian expand the geographical concept of Yangzhou in slightly different ways, but both draw from a demarcation of the area that can be traced to the Qing scholar Ruan Yuan (1764–1849): a broader Huaihai area that included the twelve counties in Yangzhou, Tongzhou, Rugao, and Taixing. These counties were all "formerly within Yangzhou [as an administrative area]" and provided the economic and cultural homogeneity in the area.[66] Dai Jian further attributes the vibrancy of literary activities in this broader area to the cultural homogeneity of the Jiangnan region, even though it was located north of the Yangzi River. There is nonetheless no clear connection between such vibrancy and what she terms a "culture of entertainment" dominating Yangzhou.[67]

Ruan Yuan was the first to draw attention to poets from the area during the Qing, including women, as part of his anthologizing projects to celebrate a genealogy of literary achievements in his native Yangzhou area while confirming its status as a cultural center in Jiangnan. *Courageous Spirits of Huaihai* (Huaihai yingling ji) and its sequel identified forty-six and eighty-seven women poets, respectively. The numbers grew in the *Collected Poetry from Jiangsu* (Jiangsu shizheng), initiated by Ruan Yuan and completed by his close friend Wang Yu (1768–1826).[68] My interest, however, does not lie in how many more women writers can be identified as being from the area. Ruan Yuan's editorial principles throw light on the vibrancy of literary activity, which was not limited by the number of poets he included.

There were simply too many poets affiliated with the area, he asserted. First, Yangzhou was a favored destination for sojourning poets (*liuyu shiren*). Second, Wang Shizhen (1634–1711), Lu Jianzeng (1690–1768), and Ma Yueguan (1687–1755) had hosted grand gatherings in Yangzhou as tributes to the Orchid Pavilion tradition, and since it was beyond the scope of his anthologies to include all those who had joined the events, he had to "reserve those poets for other anthologizing projects." *Courageous Spirits of Huaihai* did remain open to the poets who had changed their registration from other provinces to Yangzhou, but Ruan Yuan specified that "only those who had been born and died in Yangzhou could be included."[69]

Ruan Yuan's editorial principles reveal what Tobie Meyer-Fong refers to as Yangzhou's significance in the formation of a "transregional and transdynastic" literary center during the early Qing. The poetic series Wang Shizhen composed for elite gatherings at the cultural sites of Yangzhou became extremely popular. In time, his tribute to the Orchid Pavilion tradition during these gatherings became the predominant form of cultural emulation in Yangzhou. Poets used the sites as markers for a new elite identity affiliated at once with the city in recovery and with transregional cultural endeavors.[70] The other two names mentioned by Ruan Yuan, Lu Jianzeng and Ma Yueguan, testified to the continuation of cultural trends in emulation of Wang Shizhen and his coterie of poets. Lu Jianzeng was known for hosting an event at Red Bridge in 1757, when serving as salt controller in the Lianghuai salt administration located in Yangzhou. Ma Yueguan, by contrast, reminds us of the cultural ascendancy or "metamorphosis" of Huizhou merchants, which stimulated "splendid literary developments" in Yangzhou and across the Jiangnan region even as accounts of their extravagance pervaded the much-cited *Chronicle of the Painted Barks of Yangzhou* (Yangzhou huafang lu; 1795).[71]

When compiling the *Courageous Spirits of Huaihai*, Ruan Yuan came across anecdotes and events related to those who had exerted crucial influences on literary developments in Yangzhou. Although, as he had asserted earlier, it was beyond the scope of his anthologies to include all the poets affiliated with the area, accounts of the key figures brought to life the trends that had shaped the area's cultural repute. Thus did the *Collection of Anecdotes of Poets from Yangzhou* (Guangling shishi) come into print, three years after the *Courageous Spirits of Huaihai*. An early Qing figure, Wu Qi (1619–94), appeared frequently in this collection. A member of Wang Shizhen's coterie of poets and a Huizhou descendant who attained renown as a scholar-official, Wu Qi left numerous records about his literary activities. Women poets from his family were among the earliest to be recognized for their poetic talent in early Qing Yangzhou.[72]

Wu Qi's wife, Huang Zhirou, also a Huizhou descendant, was remembered for her song lyric on the Tower of the Luminous Moon (Mingyue Lou) in Yangzhou, in which she adopted a poetic language associated with the sudden reversals of fortune imbricated in the city's history to recapture the tower's former luster. Her last couplet related the destruction of the tower during the Ming-Qing dynastic transition to devastation across the land: "How can there be only one tower like this? / All lie quietly in ashes."[73] This piece placed her among the poets active in early Qing Yangzhou who commemorated the city by invoking historical references related to its sites. The literary reputation attained by other women in this family—the couple's two daughters, Wu Tan and Wu Wu, and daughter-in-law Bai Yusheng (all ca. 17th c.)—to varying degrees also testified to the factors enhancing the visibility of women poets in the area during and after this period. These included access to broader elite networks, exposure to key cultural trends, and in this case, the mobility and success of a Huizhou family that survived the dynastic transition.[74]

Yangzhou as a transregional cultural center prompts me to connect the dots between separate studies that either associate it primarily with the trafficking of women or retrieve rich data about the visibility of women writers in the area yet nonetheless attribute such visibility to the city's "entertainment culture." Status was an important factor underlying the two sides of the story: courtesans and concubines were trafficked, whereas wives and daughters from a higher social status—in gentry and merchant families alike—became writers, with the educational opportunities made available by their families. But even status need not be understood in absolute terms.

Concubines of Ruan Yuan acquired membership in literary communities in Yangzhou by acquiring a literary language about the city's sites. Among them was Tang Qingyun (1787–1832), a Huizhou native who grew up in Suzhou. Tang learned to compose poetry when Ruan Yuan invited Zhang Yin (1741–1807) and Zhang's husband Huang Wenyang (1736–?) to teach the younger brother of his wife Kong Luhua (1777–1832).[75] Discussions of social mingling in the city often refer to the presence of courtesans or concubines as entertainers at elite gatherings, drawing from poetic and artistic records of these gatherings.[76] By contrast, Tang's personal collection, *Nüluoting gao* (Manuscripts from the Pavilion of Cascuta; 1814, 1831), kept track of her presence as a participant in the rich repertoire of poetry produced by participants in gatherings that celebrated Yangzhou's famed sites—including the Tower of Literary Selection, which Ruan Yuan reconstructed and took symbolic possession of in light of his native-place identity and his family's legacy.[77] Most of all, Tang's poetic compositions on the Pavilion by the Qu River (Qujiang Ting) gathering confirmed her participation in what has recently drawn scholarly attention as a prime example of women's literary activities in mid-Qing Yangzhou.[78] When Ruan Yuan transplanted his cultural projects to Guangdong, Tang—in Ruan's company—quickly picked up the dominant cultural symbol Ruan created there, namely, the Hall of the Sea of Learning (Xuehai Tang).[79]

One wonders to what extent Tang Qingyun was exceptional among women of her social status, or how her status may have affected her spatial claims concerning Huizhou, Yangzhou, or Guangdong.[80] For those wives and daughters in Yangzhou—to whom this book now turns—the question remains: Were they writing under the pressure of the city's notoriety for extravagance and women when crafting their place identity?

Organization of This Book

I do not intend this book to be a comprehensive study of the around two hundred women writers who originated from Huizhou. Cases stand out when searching through the biographical and literary sources with relevant geographical factors, and matching this to collections of women's writings made available by large reprinting and digitizing projects in recent years. Those finding more records are more likely to provide a sense of the renown they attained or the literary networks or communities in which they were active. Eminent cases thus allow me to navigate a massive corpus of sources and isolate major trends. Inquiries into select cases can also resolve complications concerning the exact nature of the mobility of the women's families. For example, though around one-third of these women have been identified as descendants of Huizhou families that migrated to the Jiangnan heartland, their change of residence through temporary or longer-term arrangements and their self-identification in relation to a changed location were much more complicated than unidirectional migration.

More refined selection revolves around the extent to which a particular case can illuminate the Huizhou impact and women's literary developments as converging trends at a particular moment. The six chapters below identify six key moments, respectively, from the early to late Qing. The chapters also develop a spatial frame that foregrounds the sites and places at which the converging trends were anchored. This structure allows me to trace change in the spatial ordering of the world as imagined and written about by these women over time.

Chapter 1, "Anchoring Identities," begins by examining how transregional dynamics following the Ming-Qing dynastic transition created a female cultural identity as an early Qing exemplar of women's literary achievement. Xú Deyin (1681–after 1760) was an exceptionally talented woman writer usually associated with the Jiangnan cultural heartland, but Huizhou sources reveal the highly mobile history of both her natal and marital families as Huizhou descendants. The social success of her families built on a series of strategies for cultural anchoring and metamorphosis in early Qing Yangzhou, as the headquarters of salt administration and as a transregional and transdynastic literary center recovering from the devastation of war. The ways she attained fame in Yangzhou and beyond speak to literary trends encoded with political and spatial references. It was only when framed with her family's cultural aspirations formulated on the basis of the sites in Yangzhou, I argue, that Xú Deyin's effort to craft her cultural identities came to light. As she successfully carved out a cultural space for herself and reshaped her family histories and legacies, tributes paid to her by eminent figures ushered in a new era for the celebration of female talent.

Chapter 2, "Owning the Landscape," enters a phase of phenomenal expansion of both the Huizhou diaspora and women's literary activity and networks during the mid-Qing. This chapter approaches these expanding trends in Dantu (Jiangsu), a major port and gateway to the Jiangnan heartland that was separated from Yangzhou by the Yangzi River but, quite like Yangzhou, had ambivalent connections with the Jiangnan heartland. The landscape of

Dantu as represented and imagined by Bao Zhihui (1757–1810) and her family of poets and painters brings to life the encounter between the making of a new local Dantu identity and a Huizhou diasporic family's changing claims of belonging. Accelerated social and geographical mobility notwithstanding, the acquisition of a new identity was not taken for granted, and the Bao descendants called to their aid key localist cultural initiatives in overcoming hostility and authoring a family history of both displacement and success. It was up to Bao Zhihui, the most ambitious among this family of poets, to resolve the problem of naming home through what can be called a daughter's self-claimed ownership of family legacy and local landscape.

Chapter 3, "Traversing the Nine Lands," approaches a paradoxical juncture when cultural emulation centering on place reached a new zenith right before it gave way to the war and devastation of the mid-nineteenth century. Having spent decades in Guangdong, the southern frontier, a Huizhou diasporic family became active in the elite society of metropolitan Yangzhou during the 1820s and 1830s. A newly acquired literary language enabled He Bingtang (ca. 1770–?) and his daughters to create retrospectively their cultural identity and use Yangzhou as the nexus connecting imaginaries of space and place arising from their migration and travel history. Though writing about sites and places for cultural anchoring (or reanchoring) had become stereotypical, it was a bold move for the daughters to write themselves into a cosmic order, with claims of free traverse and thorough knowledge of that order. The cosmic order known as the Nine Lands, envisaged by the woman playwright He Peizhu (fl. 19th c.) from this family, casts her well-known drama in the fresh light of literary imagination cleverly interwoven with cartographical knowledge and human apprehension of the world as if "in one's palm."

Chapter 4, "Rectifying the Native Land and 'All under Heaven,'" tackles the impending crisis by shifting the focus from the outward-bound Huizhou families to a case where the native land—namely Huizhou, along with the increasing financial and social problems it suffered—received primary attention. Wang Ying (1781–1842) has attracted scholarly attention as a salt merchant's widow and a virtuous mother with Huizhou-Yangzhou roots, but much remains to be explored about her role in reshaping Huizhou in relation to the spatial order of the time.[81] Her literary, political, and genealogical writings unveil this role primarily in two respects: first, dispensing lessons on wealth, trade, and risk in her effort to safeguard the lineage and local community against conflict and financial ruin; and second, drawing on these lessons to formulate statecraft thinking. Instead of embracing native pride unconditionally and valorizing Huizhou as a model for all localities, she advocated local governance as the testing ground for improving the livelihoods of "All under Heaven." Wang Ying's case reveals the other side of the widow chastity cult, or the "new gender regime" posited in recent Huizhou studies—namely, the authority she obtained in speaking to the lineage and local community, even addressing the challenges besetting Qing governance on all levels.

Chapter 5, "Reimagining Huizhou across War and Devastation," spans the historical watershed that Sun Caifu (1825–81), a woman poet with Huizhou-Yangzhou roots, referred to as "new warfare" during the First Opium War (1840–42) and the Taiping War (1850–64). The literary and cultural production of Sun and her family resonated broadly with wartime writings and postwar endeavors in commemoration and cultural reconstruction. But Sun's favored strategy for writing and surviving the war was to embed trauma in cultural activities that kept alive her community of poets and friends—what was left of it and what she found anew while fleeing war. Following the war, Sun authored a long sequence of poetic biographies to commemorate the war dead and delineate a history of the war as experienced by each of the twenty-five female relatives and friends she wrote about. She then expanded this women-focused war history into a project for canonizing women's poetry from all ages. Infused into her ambitious, though never completed, project were her marital family's claimed link to a Song history of poetic canons and her effort to use this Huizhou legacy and its messages about dynastic trauma to grapple with the war trauma of her own time. In thus setting down her terms for commemoration—who acted as the historian of the war, who deserved to be commemorated, and what cultural legacy must be preserved—Sun placed both Huizhou and female talents in Chinese history at the center of a reimagined order.

Chapter 6, "Projecting Utopia/Dystopia," addresses the question of Huizhou's supposed decline following the troubled nineteenth century and recent challenges to this familiar story.[82] Unlike studies focusing on the epicenters of sociopolitical transformation during these decades, such as Beijing, Shanghai, and Tianjin, this chapter foregrounds shifts in centers and peripheries nationwide. The fictional experiment of Shao Zhenhua (fl. early 20th c.), a late Qing female novelist and Huizhou native, provided a sophisticated response to the literary and political trends enthralling Chinese reformers and thinkers at the tumultuous turn of the twentieth century. My focus in the last chapter of this book is a spatial frame that Shao adapted from late Qing narrative innovation to serve as a vehicle for political commentary. In projecting a dyad of utopia/dystopia through this spatial frame, Shao challenges the reader to ponder the utopian visions for China in an emergent national as well as international order.

In examining these select cases, I draw from Clifford Geertz's idea of "thick description" as an interpretive activity that searches for meaning in the totality of social life.[83] How female authors wrote in spatial terms needs to be understood in light of how they wrote their life histories and formulated family and local histories—even as their lives were being shaped by family and local sources. My discussion focuses in particular on the micro/macro links embedded in the selected cases, including personal history preserving or constructing the otherwise obscured facets of family history; local history unfolding in family history; and finally, personal history building on family and local histories for broader engagement.

1

Anchoring Identities

By walls painted in gold dust stands the home of [Xie] Daoyun.
金粉墻邊道韫家。

—*Xú Deyin*

Money was not what I favored;
I relied on brush and ink to dispense admonition.
我重非錢刀，我規惟翰墨。

—*Xú Deyin*

THE OFTEN MENTIONED symbiotic relationship between Huizhou and Yangzhou began in the later sixteenth century, as a result of the outpouring of Huizhou natives driven by increasing tax and levy burdens to take up the salt trade. The calamitous Ming-Qing dynastic transition destroyed some of the most powerful Huizhou diasporic families in Yangzhou but did not erase their imprint on the social and cultural fabric of the city. As very much a Huizhou colony in the eighteenth century, Yangzhou felt the reasserted power of the Huizhou merchants and what has by now been thoroughly examined as their impact on the cultural and intellectual life of the Qing elite.[1]

Yangzhou in the early Qing interval, particularly 1660–1700, had yet to see a commercial reflorescence of Huizhou merchants. The defining spirit of this moment was rather the quest for a new literary canon that catered to the aesthetic and power discourses at the beginning of a period of peace and reconciliation. Wang Shizhen's "Autumn Willows" (Qiuliu shi) poetic series spoke to that spirit with its "gentle and moderate expression"—as Kang-i Sun Chang summarizes—"with a sense of lingering emotion that was thought to be most appropriate for the new age."[2] Wang had originally composed this poetic series in Jinan (Shandong), but its sensational popularity continued well into the years when he served in Yangzhou. The autumn willows became a token of Yangzhou, rather than Jinan, as Wang and his emulators wrote Yangzhou into a "city of willows."[3] In Meyer-Fong's pioneering study of early Qing Yangzhou, it was Wang and his coterie of poets who used their cultural events and gatherings at various sites in Yangzhou as markers for the reconstruction of the city and its legacy. Through physical demarcation of space and culturally meaningful action, they reinvented the relationships among sites, historical references, and social structure. Their literary creativity epitomized the effort to create a new elite identity affiliated at once with the city in recovery and with transregional and transdynastic cultural endeavors.[4] At least two recent monographs show Wang Shizhen's centrality to the formation of an early Qing "arena of poets" (*shitan*) in Yangzhou and across the empire.[5]

The early Qing offered brilliant Huizhou examination candidates almost immediate access to officialdom. Twenty-three Huizhou descendants who changed their registered residence to Yangzhou served as officials in the Kangxi reign.[6] Sixteen Huizhou descendants earned the metropolitan graduate or *jinshi* degree with the "registered status of a merchant's household" (*shangji*) in Zhejiang during the Shunzhi and Kangxi reigns.[7] Among the latter group was Xú Xuling (1630–87; *jinshi* 1655), father of the female protagonist of this chapter, Xú Deyin (1681–after 1760). The practice of setting up the *shangji* as a path to examination candidacy began during the Ming Wanli reign (1573–1620). The Qing salt trade regulations specified the purpose of continuing the practice as selecting talents from among even the "peddlers selling fish and salt" (*yuyan fanfu*) and noted that a large number of merchants from Anhui had been living in Zhejiang to practice the salt trade. Their descendants were allowed to take civil service examinations in Zhejiang with this registered status rather than returning to their native place in Anhui—so that "non-native talents have the same opportunities as natives" (Yidi zhicai yu tuzhu wushu; 異地之才與土著無殊).[8] Xú Xuling was among the earliest Huizhou descendants during the Qing who achieved social "metamorphosis" through the *shangji*.

Xú Deyin is usually identified as a woman poet whose natal family was from Qiantang (Hangzhou), Zhejiang.[9] Her connection with the Banana Garden Poetry Club (Jiaoyuan Shishe) placed her among the early Qing women poets whose literary community figured prominently in the cultural landscape—and indeed the very cultural identity—of their native place, Hangzhou.[10] In hindsight, the Banana Garden poets were also setting the stage for the second high tide of women's literary creativity, which in the eighteenth century turned the Jiangnan cultural heartland into an incubator for female talent.[11] Nevertheless, local histories yield a plenitude of entries about the Huizhou origin of Xú Deyin's family. Her father, Xú Xuling, originated from Xiuning County and changed his registered residence to Qiantang for examination candidacy. His much-acclaimed career in the decades following 1655 involved extensive periods of service in the Lianghuai salt administration in Yangzhou.[12] Xú Deyin was born in Yangzhou. At fifteen she was married to Xǔ Yingnian (1682–?; *jinshi* 1700), a young scholar from a family with dual Huizhou-Yangzhou roots. She spent the better part of her life in Yangzhou, attaining fame as an exceptionally talented poet, especially late in life.[13]

Yuan Mei (1716–98)—from a later generation—looked up to Xú Deyin as the foremost among women with poetic talent (Bilai guixiu nengshizhe, yi Xǔtaifuren wei diyi; 比來閨秀能詩者，以許太夫人為第一).[14] Thus she set the benchmark for later women poets in Yangzhou. Zhang Yin (1741–1807), for example, became known as the best woman poet in this area after Xú. In turn Zhu Lan (ca. 18th–19th c.) became the best.[15] Xú Deyin assumed an array of geographical affiliations as her poetic works were included in major anthologies featuring poets from Qiantang, Yangzhou, Huaihai (a broader area covering Yangzhou and Tongzhou prefectures), Zhejiang, Jiangsu, Anhui, and across the Qing empire. In time she became the prime exemplar of Huizhou female talent. The late Qing and Republican scholar Xǔ Chengyao (1874–1946), himself a Huizhou descendant, identified Xú Deyin as "first and foremost among eminent women of our native land" (Wuli diyi mingfu; 吾里第一名婦).[16] Anthologists had their agendas of bolstering regional repute, and relations between the regional and the transregional in anthologizing projects require more in-depth investigation. For the present study, these anthologies provide a glimpse of Xú Deyin's posthumous fame and identity accretion.[17]

It is important to emphasize Xú Deyin's value to a discussion of how transregional dynamics created female cultural identity as an early Qing exemplar of women's literary achievements. Her case also suggests that the converging tides of the Huizhou diaspora and women's writing culture changed women's sense of human-place ties—not least their self-creation in spatial and cultural codes—to a degree previously unknown.

The Xǔ Family Publications

The discovery of the entire corpus of *Xǔ Family Publications* (*Xǔshi jiaji*, 1707, ca. 1746) provides an opportunity to trace Xú Deyin's life history within her marital family's history.[18] The Xǔ lineage originated from Gaoyang, Henan, and settled in She County of Huizhou during the Ming period. Xǔ Mingxian (ca. 17th c.), great grandfather to Xǔ Yingnian, was a successful merchant and moved his family to Yangzhou to join the salt trade during the late Ming. The family thus became known for its dual Huizhou-Yangzhou identity, while Gaoyang figured as its symbolic place of origin.[19] Xǔ Mingxian and his sons, Xǔ Chengzong (ca. 17th c.), Xǔ Chengyuan (ca. 17th c.), Xǔ Chengxuan (ca. 17th c.), and Xǔ Chengjia (b. before 1625; grandfather to Xǔ Yingnian), survived the tumultuous Ming-Qing dynastic transition. The wealth that Xǔ Mingxian had accumulated largely survived as well, enabling him and his sons to continue engaging in cultural projects and charitable works during the early decades of the new dynasty. Xǔ Chengxuan and Xǔ Chengjia earned the Qing *jinshi* degree in 1676 and 1685, respectively. Both served in the Hanlin Academy and a few other posts. In 1686 they obtained a court award to erect an arch in their native Tangmo village in She County, as a token of their social prestige. The arch, known today as the Arch for the [Xǔ] Brothers Who Both Entered the Hanlin Academy (Tongbao Hanlin Fang), remains a landmark in this area (fig. 1). Other material evidence for the family's prestige included their ancestral shrine, a bridge built in their honor, and a shrine for local worthies (*xiangxian*), including Xǔ Mingxian and his sons.[20]

Publication of the *Xǔshi jiaji* in 1707 was a celebration of the family's prestige, as attested by Xǔ Yingnian's latest success. This edition includes four personal poetry collections: Xǔ Chengjia, *Lieweige shiji* (Poetry collection from the Tower for Searching the Infinitesimal, 6 *juan*); Xǔ Changling (ca. 17th c.; father of Xǔ Yingnian), *Bimoting ji* (Collection from the Pavilion on Green Peaks, 1 *juan*); Xǔ Yingnian, *Huaishu shichao* (Poetic drafts from the House of Japonica Trees, 4 *juan*); and Xú Deyin, *Lüjingxuan shichao* (Poetic drafts from the Studio of Pure Green, 5 *juan*). In about 1746, decades after the death of Xǔ Yingnian, Xú Deyin authored a preface for a collection added to a reprint edition of the *Xǔshi jiaji*. It was a collection of poetry by her affinal grandson Xǔ Tianqiu (ca. 18th c.; adopted as heir to the Xǔ family), titled *Biyushanfang shichao* (Poetic drafts from the Mountain Cottage in Green

FIGURE 1. Arch in honor of the Xǔ brothers in Tangmo village, August 2019. Photo by the author.

Rains, 1 *juan*). In her preface, she predicted that the family legacy—of which she now perceived herself to be a custodian—would fall to Xǔ Tianqiu to further glorify.[21] In 1752, she published a sequel to her own personal collection, titled *Lüjingxuan xuji* (Sequel to [collection] from the Studio of Pure Green, 1 *juan*). Her publication received funding from two Yangzhou merchants, Ma Yueguan (1687–1755) and Wang Tingzhang (ca. 18th c.).[22]

Family publishing (*jiake*), as Dorothy Ko has shown, grew in popularity in late imperial China as a result of a publishing boom that decentralized the production of knowledge from a government monopoly to more diffuse and private channels. For families with social and cultural aspirations, publishing collected works of their talented descendants provided an effective means of showcasing their cultural achievements and using these achievements as cultural capital. One direct effect the popularity of family publishing had on women lay in the "incorporation of women's talent into the family's repertoire of cultural capital" through publication of their works.[23] For my purpose, publications of a Huizhou diasporic family preserved in the *Xǔshi jiaji* trace the family's history of changing geographical affiliations and the very process of its cultural anchoring and metamorphosis. They allow me to locate the mutually illuminating aspects of the creation of a family's elite identity and a woman's self-creation—especially where she perceived her family legacy as being assimilated into a changing culture in Yangzhou. What may seem a backdrop to Xú Deyin's rise to renown—namely, family metamorphosis over time—highlights the increasingly dominant role she played in reinventing her family legacy and her own cultural identity. The epigraphs offer a quick glimpse of how such reinvention grew out of the pressure to demarcate a cultural space separate from that dominated by wealth.

Searching the Infinitesimal (1707): Spatial Codes and Cultural Anchoring

Searching the Infinitesimal (Liewei) was the name the Xǔ family gave to one of their estates in Yangzhou, and Xǔ Chengjia incorporated it as the title for his personal collection of poetry. The phrase drew on a line by none other than Li Bai (701–762): "Eliminating my vision quiets down all disturbances; searching the infinitesimal leads to the utmost essence [of the Way] " (Miejian xi qundong, liewei qiong zhijing; 滅見息群動，獵微窮至精). Annotators interpreted the lines as a reflection of Li Bai's pursuit of non-action promoted by Laozi and Zhuangzi, and also as an allusion to Tao Qian's (352–427) celebration of hermit life in one of his "Drinking Wine" poems: "In twilight sun all disturbances quiet down" (Riru qundong xi; 日入群動息). Li Bai's original poem fell within the time of his political responses to the Li Lin (?–757; a Tang prince) incident during the An Lushan Rebellion (703–57). He composed the poem in the guise of religious reflections when fleeing south in the autumn of 757. Through thorough dedication to the ways of non-action, he claimed, he would be able to attain ultimate peace and freedom from outside turmoil. Most importantly, he would be able to preserve his life ("bao wusheng," otherwise interpreted as "attain immortality") in a haven comparable to Peach Blossom Spring, the land for refugees in Tao Qian's classic political allegory.[24] In 756, Li Lin had launched a military action in Yangzhou. Li Bai, then serving in Li Lin's administration, composed a series of poems to glorify the action. When the military action failed and was interpreted as a treacherous act by the authorities, Li Lin was exiled and died soon afterward. Li Bai took refuge in the mountains in Anhui before he, too, was exiled in 758.[25]

Political and geographical factors in this historical episode fed into Xǔ Chengjia's perception of himself as a refugee fleeing from the shifting political powers of his own time. He wrote profusely about such experiences and about the catastrophic effects of war.[26] These factors took a significant twist, however. He did not seek refuge in the mountains near his native Huizhou, as Li Bai did. Xǔ Chengjia described Yangzhou as a city devastated by war yet rebuilt into a haven. A tower for "searching the infinitesimal" appeared among the Xǔ family's estates, providing a physical and cultural haven for the Xǔ descendants as they became new residents of the city—and transformed themselves from a family of Huizhou merchants into *jinshi* degree holders and luminaries. Incorporated into the title for Xǔ Chengjia's poetry collection, the name of the tower is emblematic of his cultural aspirations. He composed voluminous poetic works affirming his affiliation with the very center of a new elite society in early Qing Yangzhou.

A sequence of fifteen poems dated before 1659 opens this voluminous collection. Under the title "Reflecting on the Past in the Weed-Covered City" (Wucheng huaigu), each poem evokes a historical site and mourns the destruction of its cultural legacy. Together they depict the city's vicissitudes at full scale. The ninth poem, for example, concerns one of the best-known sites, Twenty-Fourth Bridge (Niansi Qiao), beside which a beauty "white as marble" (*yuren*) used to play the flute.[27] Whatever literati sentiments or past prosperity of commerce and pleasure quarters is imbricated in these stock images, for Xǔ Chengjia the "winds and mists" over the bridge have changed, and the landscape is lost in the wide, unbounded river (Niansi fengyan gai, cangmang bishui xun; 廿四風煙改，蒼茫碧水潯).[28] Poems like these placed Xǔ Chengjia among the early Qing poets who shared a vocabulary of nostalgia and loss when writing about Yangzhou across the dynastic transition.

The first identifiable effort Xǔ Chengjia made in finding safe haven among the new elites who, in Tobie Meyer-Fong's study, rebuilt Yangzhou into a transregional literary center was to establish ties with Wang Shizhen. The poetic series Wang composed for events at Red Bridge (Hongqiao) in Yangzhou in 1662 and 1664 became "wildly popular," thereby turning the bridge into a new mecca for elite gatherings. Xǔ Chengjia and his elder brother Xǔ Chengxuan were present at the 1664 gathering.[29] In fact, they figured in one of Wang's compositions as two talents comparable to the illustrious Lu brothers, Lu Ji (261–303) and Lu Yun (262–303). Wang's original line, "the two talents rising to fame equally in Yunjian and Luoyang" (Yunjian Luoxia qimingshi; 雲間洛下齊名士) became a virtual title for the Xǔ brothers, recurring in anthologies and local histories valorizing the city's luminaries.[30] In the same year, on the Double Seventh Festival in 1664, Xǔ Chengjia was present at a farewell party hosted in Wang's honor at the Temple of Chan Wisdom (Chanzhi Si). He composed four poems to express his feelings at parting and, even more importantly, his wish that Wang's new post in the capital would bring resources for disaster relief to Yangzhou. Three days earlier, the counties of Gaoyou and Baoying had suffered a severe storm, and thousands had died in the flooding. All those present at the party implored Wang to report the disaster to the court.[31] When Wang received a promotion in the capital, Xǔ Chengjia reinforced the ties between the Yangzhou elite and Wang by sending congratulatory poetic compositions. He exalted these ties in hyperbolic terms, claiming that Wang's personality and erudition had attracted three thousand disciples in Yangzhou, including himself. The refined taste and gatherings of Wang and his followers had rebuilt the city's legacy and left a profound imprint on urban landmarks, particularly Red Bridge and the remains of the Sui palaces (Sui Gong).[32] Wang later referred to the Xǔ brothers as the foremost among those whose reputations he had promoted in Yangzhou. Achievements of the Xǔ brothers in turn demonstrated Wang's loyalty to the court. It was he, Wang suggested, who had discovered this cohort of talents and advanced their careers in service to the court (*tuixian jinda*; 推賢進達).[33]

These cultural as well as sociopolitical dynamics transformed Yangzhou during the early Qing and allowed Huizhou descendants such as the Xǔ brothers to create their cultural identities. Earlier, in 1660 and 1663, Xǔ Chengjia had taken the Qing civil service examinations at the provincial level. Although it would take over two decades for him and over one decade for his brother to pass all levels of the exams, opportunities for social metamorphosis opened along the way. Xǔ Chengjia's poetic compositions during the 1660s to 1690s recorded decades of elite gatherings: he did not miss any key event defining the city's new elite.

Around 1678–87, Xǔ Chengjia joined events celebrating the renovation of the Garden for Retirement (Xiuyuan), a private garden belonging to the Zheng family. Zheng Xiaru (?–before 1665), an official serving on the Board of Works, built the garden around 1659–65. After Zheng Xiaru and his son Zheng Weiguang (1628–65) passed away, Zheng Weiguang's son Zheng Maojia (provincial graduate [*jinjuren*], 1678) renovated and expanded the property into one of Yangzhou's finest private gardens in the 1680s. Zheng Xiaru was an affinal uncle of Xǔ Chengjia, Zheng Weiguang a cousin, and Zheng Maojia a son-in-law. Xǔ Chengjia composed several essays and poetic works to commemorate the renovation while at the same time reaffirming bonds between the Zheng and Xǔ lineages. No other two lineages, he wrote passionately, were as closely connected through intermarriage across several generations. He would most gladly see these affinal ties continue for the next hundred generations.[34]

Genealogical information gleaned from Xǔ Chengjia's commemorative essays reveals that the two lineages had similar Huizhou-Yangzhou backgrounds and social strategies. Xǔ Chengjia's grandfather Xǔ Shican was a close friend of Zheng Xiaru's father, Zheng Dongli. Intermarriages between the two lineages began with Xǔ Chengjia's father, Xǔ Mingxian, the salt merchant, marrying Zheng Dongli's daughter (fig. 2). Thus Xǔ Chengjia's mother was a Zheng.

The Zheng family attained the pinnacle of the Yangzhou elite during the late Ming. Parties and poetry contests held in their private gardens had attracted leading literati Qian Qianyi (1582–1664) and Mao Xiang (1611–93), foreshadowing the early Qing elite gatherings in Yangzhou. They epitomized the successful integration of Huizhou merchants into the gentry class.[35] The construction and renovation of the Garden for Retirement during the 1660s to 1680s no doubt served the Zhengs' effort to reassert their cultural power. These decades further witnessed successful careers of the Zheng and Xǔ descendants and frequent intermarriages. In decades to come, the Garden for Retirement would go through two more renovations, and gatherings in the garden would grow into a network of the most powerful gentry-merchants, including Cheng, Jiang, and Ma descendants.[36] But at this moment of renovation completed by Zheng Maojia, Xǔ Chengjia was celebrating a major milestone in the social ascendancy of the Zheng and Xǔ lineages following the dynastic transition.

Over the decades, the Xǔ family legacy also underwent a metamorphosis. Xǔ Chengjia traced the Xǔ lineage to the Ming grand academician Xǔ Guo (1527–96), a Huizhou descendant. He also bonded with a luminary, Xǔ Qingyu (ca. 17th c.), whom he addressed as an uncle and "our lineage's worthy" (*zongzhe*).[37] He attributed his achievements to access to his father's collection of books in a "blue chest," claiming that it was such family education that distinguished him from the "vulgar" scholars (Ziyou qingxiang fei suxue; 自有青箱非俗學). The "blue chest" alluded to an illustrious legacy of historical learning running in the Wang lineage during the Jin era (265–419).[38] In this

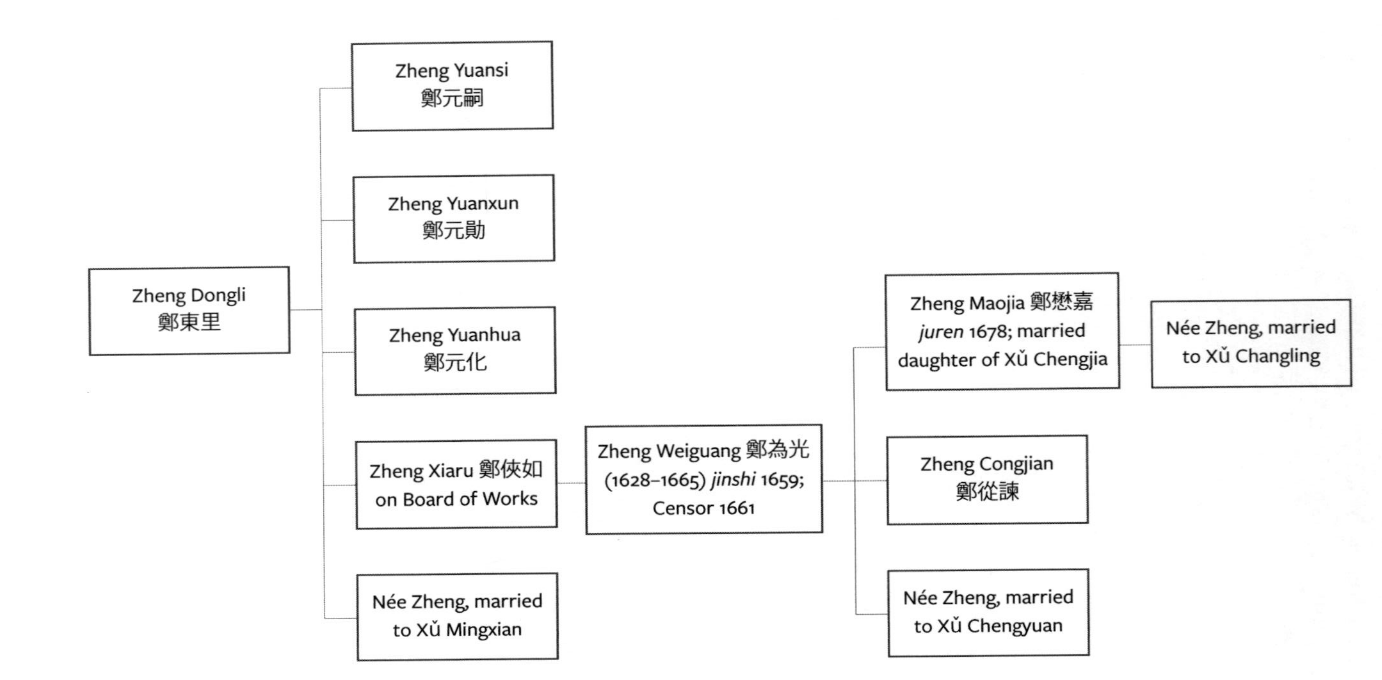
Zheng Dongli 鄭東里
Zheng Yuansi 鄭元嗣
Zheng Yuanxun 鄭元勛
Zheng Yuanhua 鄭元化
Zheng Xiaru 鄭俠如 on Board of Works
Née Zheng, married to Xǔ Mingxian
Zheng Weiguang 鄭為光 (1628–1665) jinshi 1659; Censor 1661
Zheng Maojia 鄭懋嘉 juren 1678; married daughter of Xǔ Chengjia
Zheng Congjian 鄭從諫
Née Zheng, married to Xǔ Chengyuan
Née Zheng, married to Xǔ Changling

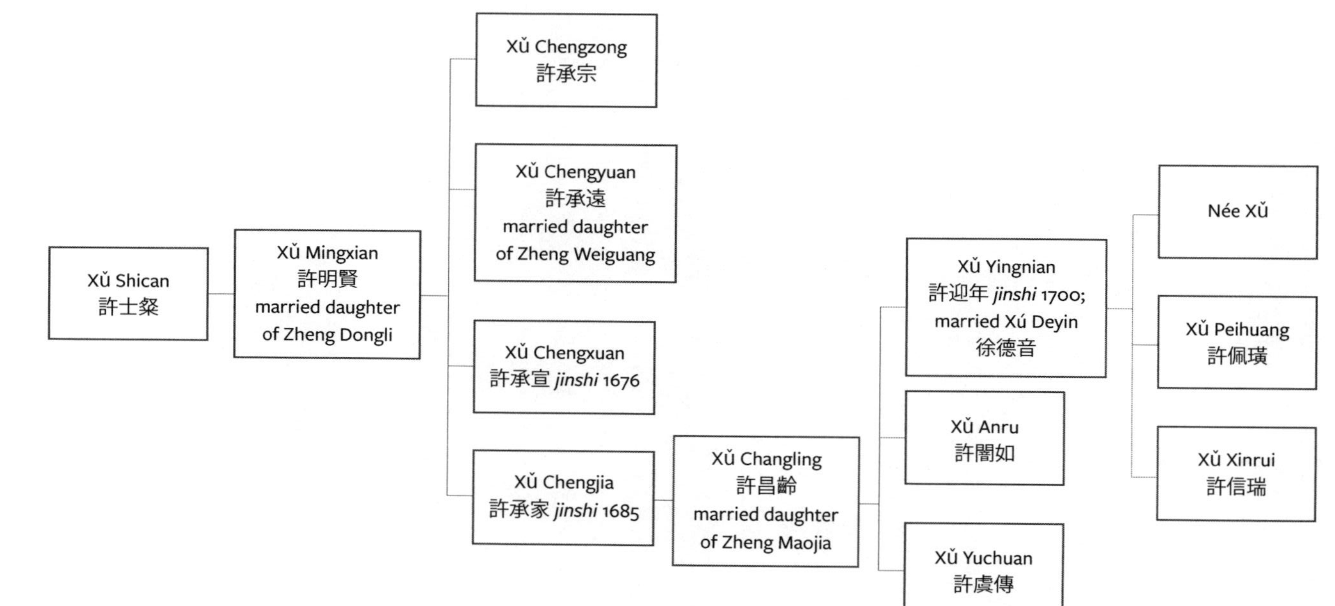

FIGURE 2. Zheng and Xǔ intermarriages in Huizhou and Yangzhou during the seventeenth century. For generations preceding Zheng Dongli, see Zheng Qinghu, *Yangzhou Xiuyuan zhi*, "Shixi" 1a.

light, his father, Xǔ Mingxian, transformed himself from a merchant into a scholar who laid the foundation for the Xǔ family's cultural legacy.

Xǔ Yingnian earned the *jinshi* degree in 1700, at the age of nineteen, thus marking a new milestone for the Xǔ family's social ascendancy. He celebrated his family's cultural achievements across three generations with publication of the *Xǔshi jiaji*. He also made Searching the Infinitesimal into his family's signature estate. At the beginning of his collection, Xǔ Yingnian claimed that the name of his studio, the House of Japonica Trees, originated from the trees that had grown for over a thousand years in the courtyard of the Tower for Searching the Infinitesimal. The tower had by now been transformed into a "thatched cottage" (*caotang*), though with no record of renovation or reconstruction.[39]

The name derived its prestige from the thatched cottage in Chengdu where Du Fu (712–70) had taken refuge from war.[40] Xǔ Yingnian celebrated the long-lived trees as potent symbols of his family, which he hoped would continue thriving for another hundred generations. He identified the thatched cottage as the location for the pastimes of his grandfather Xǔ Chengjia and his father, Xǔ Changling, while they were not serving in the administration (Zumi xiumu di; 祖禰休沐地). He now used it as a site for parties. By the time the eminent mid-Qing scholar-official Ruan Yuan took up anthologizing projects to reshape the elite culture of Yangzhou, the Xǔ family had caught his attention as one of the most successful families in the area, and their Thatched Cottage for Searching the Infinitesimal became a new site for refined gatherings.[41]

The Changing Story of an Estate

The Xǔ family already enjoyed unparalleled prestige in Yangzhou (Jiamen dinggui, yishi wupi; 家門鼎貴，一時無匹) when Xú Deyin married Xǔ Yingnian in 1696.[42] Xú Deyin's natal family had Huizhou origins, too. Her father, Xú Xuling, had earned the *jinshi* degree in 1655 with the registered status of a merchant's household. Although Xú Xuling did not have a copious literary output, there are abundant records of his rapid upward mobility. In 1670 he served as a salt control censor in the Lianghuai salt administration located in Yangzhou. His success in eliminating administrative defects earned him a significant promotion to the post of vice minister of works. In 1685 he was reassigned to Yangzhou to oversee the Lianghuai salt administration. The Huizhou local gazetteers praised him for his integrity in this post: he left his family poor when he passed away in 1687. It was probably during one of his tenures in Yangzhou that Xǔ Chengjia became a disciple or follower. Xú Xuling found Xǔ Yingnian to be an ideal match for his daughter Xú Deyin despite the generational discrepancy arising from his mentor-disciple relation with Xǔ Chengjia. It was Xú Xuling's deathbed wish that Xú Deyin be married to Xǔ Yingnian.[43]

Thus a marital bond was cemented between the two successful Huizhou families, except that the bride had taken on a Jiangnan identity, and the bridegroom, a Yangzhou identity. Decades later, this marriage would symbolize the convergence of the old Jiangnan culture with the new Yangzhou. As one leading literatus, Chen Wenshu, described it, "On bright moonlit nights [in Yangzhou] stands a new pavilion by the water; among expanses of plum blossoms [in Qiantang] appears the old river village" (Mingyue erfen xin shuixie, meihua shili gu jiangcun; 明月二分新水榭，梅花十里故江村).[44]

Xú Deyin had received a fine education in her natal home. Her mother, grand lady Lou, was a Qiantang native and highly literate. In 1707 Lou authored a preface for Xú Deyin's collection of poetic works, clearly taking pride in the education her daughter had received and the prestige her education brought to the new Yangzhou family. Although Xú Deyin was not a member of the Banana Garden Poetry Club at this point, she had drawn attention from its central figure, Lin Yining (1655–after 1730). She had also learned the style of cultural elites. Studying and dressing like a young scholar, she met her father's guests.[45] Lou lived with the couple in Yangzhou, and Xú Deyin represented the mother-daughter bond as continuing through scholarly pursuits in her new home.[46]

Xú Deyin soon picked up the keynotes of status performance in her husband's family. The couple was busy composing and exchanging poems both at Yangzhou's landmarks and at their family's several thatched cottages. They were known among the Yangzhou elites as an ideal "companionate couple."[47] While Xú Deyin continued to write about the glamour of Jiangnan and infused its symbolic capital into her new home, she also capitalized on her husband's family legacy in Yangzhou. First of all, she appropriated the thatched cottage to craft her own poet-hermit persona. An example concerned the Studio for Listening to [Falling] Blossoms (Tinghua Shuwu), a family estate that had served as Xǔ Changling's base for study and socializing. Xú Deyin described it as a thatched cottage for those living in the wilderness—that is, for hermits—and idealized the simple and secluded life therein. Despite its vaunted seclusion, however, the thatched cottage was located next to another household. The lady in that neighboring household, according to Xú Deyin, was utterly ignorant of the value of hermit life and therefore could not appreciate the "morning mists and sunset glow" in the wilderness, as she herself did.[48]

Neighbors with crude tastes were among Xú Deyin's favored themes. She referred variously to those on the south (*nanlin*), on the west (*xijia*), and across the east wall (*qiangdong*). She carved out a cultural space identified with the home of Xie Daoyun—the "model par excellence of a woman poet"—and spoke belittlingly of the neighboring house with its walls painted with gold dust (Jinfen qiangbian Daoyun jia).[49] The phrase "gold dust" was a stock metaphor of the extravagance associated with the Six Dynasties (222–589).[50] Just as Xie Daoyun distinguished herself by her poetic talent despite the extravagance of her time, Xú Deyin claimed literary distinction against the backdrop of what appeared to be a Yangzhou culture increasingly dominated by wealth. But sometimes it is difficult to tell whether she is referring to the neighbors or, in fact, to those in her own household. An early example suggests that she had a thatched cottage of her own where she enjoyed seclusion even while she frequently mourned over the changed generations of her time and had to pawn her clothes to buy drinks. Her life as a poet-hermit contrasted dramatically with that "next door" (*linshi*), where partying went on with boisterous songs.[51]

In 1705, Xú Deyin stayed in the capital while Xǔ Yingnian served as imperial secretary. Upon returning to Yangzhou in 1706, she composed a poem of twenty-four lines on how her former residence had changed, with a preface:

COMPOSED UNDER THE CRAB-APPLE TREE
IN MY FORMER RESIDENCE

Since I departed to the north, my former residence has been taken over by my brother-in-law Yuchuan [younger brother to Xǔ Yingnian] and his family. There grows a crab-apple tree by the courtyard and it has a style that could be a fine subject for painting. This spring I came back to the south. As I dropped by, I saw the tree in bloom and could not help lingering and viewing it, and memories came unceasingly to my mind. Thus I took a sprig of blossoms back home and composed the following poem to record my feelings.

In the poem, she recalled how she and the crab apple had kept each other company as if in a secluded valley for a decade, until she took her chest of books with her on her journey to the capital. Since then, the crab apple was "adorned in brocades," and her studio "suddenly turned into a room of gold" (Qingzi qiezuo qiluozhuang, yunchuang hugai huangjinwu; 清姿且作綺羅妝，芸窗忽改黃金屋). Addressing the crab apple like an old friend, she expresses her admiration of its hermit-like style and immortal beauty and fiercely condemns those who ruined it all: "Village boys danced and spun and stepped on fragrant petals in the mud; elderly women wore sprigs of blossoms that looked like weeds in their buns" (Cuntong xuanwu taxiangni, lao'ao chuiji charucao; 村童旋舞踏香泥，老媼椎髻插如草). With no adequate words to vent her pain, she took a sprig of blossoms to her thatched cottage, where she poured out wine and chanted poems to honor this fine guest.[52] Her poem later caught Ruan Yuan's attention and was quoted in his writings about the Yangzhou poets.[53]

No information is available concerning Xǔ Yingnian's family business in Yangzhou or the means by which they continued to live in abundance and expand their estates. But in Xú Deyin's representation, the Xǔ family enjoyed immense wealth and glittered with gold. Clearly it was not the village boys or elderly women but rather her brother-in-law whom she blamed for ruining her studio and the crab-apple tree. Through such gestures, she converted the family estates—both her former residence and her current thatched cottage—into her own cultural space. Immediately following was a poem in which she described how she received her uncle Lou Xiaozhai in her thatched cottage. She proudly told him about the modest meal she had prepared from vegetables emblematic of hermit life.[54] These examples suggest that Xú Deyin was beginning to play a role in shaping the Xǔ family's cultural legacy and identity in relation to her own.

As markers of identity, Xú Deyin's thatched cottage and the Thatched Cottage for Searching the Infinitesimal are not to be confused. She did not refer to the latter as a site for refined gatherings, as her husband, Xǔ Yingnian, emphatically did. On one occasion, she wrote about how a beautiful woman appeared in a neighboring garden to the east of the Thatched Cottage for Searching the Infinitesimal. The woman and the garden evoke romantic sentiments of a poetic style identified with the Song-era song lyricists. Xǔ Yingnian was known to excel at this style, especially that associated with Wen Tingyun (812?–866?).[55] Xú Deyin parodies this style by representing the woman tapping on all the balustrades in the garden—a stereotypical gesture of longing exaggerated for comic effect—with the intention of having an encounter. She further mocks someone (just who is unclear) in the Thatched Cottage for Searching the Infinitesimal. The woman must have a husband already, she conjectures, and there is no use looking sorrowfully to the east of the wall.[56] In similar tones she describes the seductive beauties seen on spring excursions. By the islands in the suburbs, for example, one saw nothing but "painted boats" (Shicui zhoubian, jiewei huafang; 拾翠洲邊，皆維畫舫).[57] She even explicitly mocks her husband's infatuation with a courtesan who was unfortunately taken by someone more powerful.[58] It appeared that a culture of wealth and sensual pleasures had by now overtaken the refined gatherings of earlier decades. According to her representation, the family's finest legacy was merging with these changing trends.

Red Bridge also took on a different character as it became primarily a pleasure quarter for the wealthy. Although the couple continued to draw from the bridge's prestige, their self-identifications in relation to the bridge and the painted boats diverged significantly. Xǔ Yingnian did not hesitate to write about the good times he had by the bridge. He enjoyed, for example, gazing at the glowing faces and "willow-slender" waists of singing girls. From a distance, too, through the window shade of another boat, he perceived a beauty and listened to her teaching girls to sing. He compared their voices to pearls rolling on jade plates.[59] Xú Deyin's matching composition contains no such sensual details. She keeps the beauties out of her sight, deep in their chambers.[60] The couple's boating experiences differ in other ways as well:

I took a new volume of lyrics to the boats crowding [at the bridge];
Wines were green, lamps red, I was in the mood to enjoy all.
If even the luminous moon could feel regrets—
Who would not recall the jade-white beauty playing the flute?[61]

—*Xǔ Yingnian*

新詞一束載輕船，綠酒紅燈逸興饒。若使明月翻有恨，誰人不憶玉人簫？

On a neighboring boat, pearl songs harmonized melodies from a
jade flute;
I felt uneasy that I enjoyed nothing but simple meals and collected poems.
All I wanted was to steal a view of the spring clouds.
I shall meticulously portray [its beauty] in poetry.[62]

—*Xú Deyin*

隔舫珠歌和玉簫，自慚苜蓿伴詩瓢。惟偷一幅春陰景，記在奚囊著意描。

Xǔ Yingnian placed himself in the midst of a party among the crowded boats, ready to enjoy good wines and new lyrics sung by singing girls. He did not hesitate to express his desire for the "jade-white beauty playing the flute," who had become an icon for the city's history of pleasures. He, not the moon, craves the beauty. In contrast, Xú Deyin places herself at a distance from the party. In the same way that she referred to her neighbors, she casts those on a "neighboring boat" in roles contrary to her own poet-hermit persona. Such contrasts raise questions about the companionate nature of the couple's poetic exchanges, even though the occasions and rhymes seem to match exactly.

Moreover, Xú Deyin sets her thatched cottage in opposition to the bridge. She calls the bridge Little Qinhuai, a name derived from the late-Ming capital of pleasure quarters, the Qinhuai area in Nanjing:

AUTUMNAL THOUGHTS, FIFTEEN COMPOSITIONS. #1

I had a thatched cottage built like that on the east bank of Rang River;[63]
Overlooking waters of the Little Qinhuai against the skyline. [Note: Red Bridge is alternatively named "Little Qinhuai."]
The moon at midnight keeps company with this person sitting in sorrow;
The sound of winds blowing over a leaf matches the rhymes of my chanted poem.
Even falling dew can startle wild cranes;
The spread net traps swan geese in flight.
Do not say that, because of her eccentricity, she indulges in strange outfits;
The [abandoned] woman wearing green sleeves rests her arms upon the slim bamboos.[64]

秋懷十五首 其一

小葺茆堂似瀼東，小秦淮水望連空 紅橋一名小秦淮。 伴人愁坐三更月，和我微吟一葉風。墜露卻能驚野鶴，張羅由此弋高鴻。謾言性癖耽奇服，翠袖閑憑修竹中。

Rangdong, the east bank of the Rang River in Sichuan, was across the river from the former site of Du Fu's thatched cottage. Xú Deyin's allusion to this prestigious tradition differentiates her thatched cottage from its actual location near Small Qinhuai, the pleasure quarters. By contrasting these markers of identities, she again highlights her poet-hermit persona. The poetic tradition of Du Fu further allows her to portray herself in the role of the abandoned woman. In Du Fu's classic representation, the abandoned woman lives a secluded life and relies on herself to repair her thatched cottage. The attire and posture of the abandoned woman—"green sleeves" and leaning on "slim bamboos"—become the defining attributes of what Xú Deyin portrays as her own "eccentricity" or "strange outfits," namely, what distinguishes her from her environs.[65]

In addition to these allusions, Xú Deyin fills her poem with disturbing images such as the startled cranes and trapped swan geese, as well as references to loneliness and sorrow. The remaining fourteen poems in this sequence develop a full range of allusions to foreground the contrast between, for instance, the household filled with gold and the weed-covered residence of an ill-fated scholar; refined yet unappreciated melody and vulgar licentiousness; the rich partying next door and the starving scholar; or the revellers next door and the exiled official who resists vulgar ways (*weisu*).[66]

Tensions prevailing in these poems can be attributed to the pressures Xú Deyin may have felt when moving to a city that had become increasingly identified with wealth and sensuality. By consigning the Thatched Cottage for Searching the Infinitesimal and Red Bridge to a changing Yangzhou culture, Xú Deyin represents her own thatched cottage as the reserve of the finest legacy. It figures elsewhere as her Studio of Pure Green, among the family's ever-expanding estates:

"[BIRD CHIRPING] BRINGS FORTH VERDANCY [OF MOUNTAINS] IN TWILIGHT SUN," WITH PREFACE

In the past I lived by Mount Wu [in Qiantang] and, one time, I heard the birds chirping among the mountains and a line came to my mind: "[Bird chirping] brings forth verdancy [of mountains] in twilight sun." Though it did not make much sense, the emotions and views it evoked fit well. I felt as if the line had originated from nature itself. Now I sit in my Studio of Pure Green; I see grass growing by the springtime pond, I hear orioles singing in the summertime woods, I watch swan geese stirring green leaves on sprigs high above [in autumn], and I listen to the cry of cranes as winds blow across pine trees [in winter]. The four seasons go by in turns. *Although the views are not like the famed ones by clear rivers and flourishing woods, the feelings they arouse are no different from those I had by Mount Wu.*[67]

喚起斜陽綠 並引

昔在吳山，聞山中鳥聲，偶得句曰："喚起斜陽綠。" 雖不可索解，而情與景合適，若得之自然。今坐綠淨軒中，草長春池，鶯啼夏木，雁驚危綠，鶴唳松濤，四時推奪，雖非清川長薄之勝，而況味不殊在吳山時也。

The preface is followed by a sequence of four poems describing these views. Xú Deyin draws from a poetic style idealizing hermit life, and the views bear no specific geographical references. The effect is to transpose the landscape of her natal home near Mount Wu and blend it with that at her studio in Yangzhou. She concludes this sequence by describing how she watched in twilight "all disturbances quieting down gradually" (Jiankan qundong xi; 漸看群動息), and listened to the woodcutter (the hermit) singing from afar.[68] The "disturbances quieting down" echo the family legacy Xǔ Chengjia had built. We may recall his allusion to the lines by Li Bai: "Eliminating my vision quiets all disturbances; searching the infinitesimal leads to the utmost essence [of the Way]." In this light Xú Deyin's studio becomes a parallel Thatched Cottage for Searching the Infinitesimal. It is the converging point of the legacies of her two homes.

Authoring Family Histories through Mourning Poetry

Xú Deyin foregrounds her natal family's legacy in more ways than by alluding to the landscape of Mount Wu. As recent scholarship reveals, from the Ming onward more women took up the function of biographer for their family members by composing mourning poetry.[69] Sometime after 1707 Xú Deyin's mother, Lady Lou, passed away, and Xú composed forty poems to lament her loss.[70] She structured these poems around Lady Lou's roles as an exemplary wife and mother and, consequently, conveyed her memories of both her mother and father and life in her natal home. She also used profuse interlineal notes to fill in the gaps left by poetic brevity.[71]

The majority of these poems (#2–31) revolve around an exemplary family biography. Although they draw largely from conventional language used to mourn the deceased, in the light of Xú Deyin's efforts to reshape the family legacy, they convey messages about the Xú family's status defined by ideal female and male qualities. Most striking among these messages is the poverty of the Xú family—in contrast to the flourishing Xǔs and their expanding estates. Such poverty is inconsistent with the extraordinary success of Xú Xuling's career, to which Xú Deyin repeatedly draws attention. For example, he was twice granted the authority to rule a vast area of the empire and brought peace to it (Liangchi jieyue jing fengjiang). Whether serving in the south or in the central administration, he played a key role in implementing laws and regulations (Nansheng zhongtai wo xian'gang). These accomplishments corresponded with Huizhou local gazetteers' accounts of his effectiveness in managing the Lianghuai salt administration and serving as the vice minister of works. Having been in positions of power for decades, Xú Xuling nonetheless had no savings or property; after his burial in Qiantang, Lady Lou purchased a house by selling her jewelry (#7 and 8). The message becomes clear: the poverty of the Xú family is a testament to Xú Xuling's integrity and diligence as an official who sought no personal gain.

A few more examples illustrate how Xú Deyin's representations of the ideal female and male qualities in her parents build on each other. Poem #11 starts with the dedicated service of Xú Xuling—on his deathbed he was sealing his last report to the emperor—and then mourns the fact that he had no heir and that only a nephew guarded his tomb, performing the mourning rites befitting a son. A note follows to add detail: "My late father did not seek to establish an heir for himself because he had been busy with the emperor's business, and also because he had not yet reached an advanced age. After he passed away, my mother, Lady Lou, chose from among his nephews the one worthy to continue his family line. That was my elder brother, Jifang."

Thus, the lack of an heir in the family demonstrates the sacrifices Xú Xuling made in performing his duty to the emperor. In selecting an heir for him, Lady Lou made a crucial contribution to the Xú family. Slightly later (Poems #15, 16, and 17, with notes), Xú Deyin represents how, due to Lady Lou's personal instruction, her brother Jifang was already establishing a scholarly reputation at twenty and continuing the Xú family's learning. She also remarks that her late father, who had always been just in dispensing legal judgment, finally had an heir to save his line from declining as repayment for his virtuous deeds.[72]

Similarly, in glorifying Lady Lou as a female exemplar comparable to the wife of Liuxia Hui (720–621 BCE), Xú Deyin coveys the message that Xú Xuling had the qualities for which the historical figure Liuxia Hui had been known, including in particular providing advice and assistance to the ruler. As recorded in Liu Xiang's (77–6 BCE) hagiography of female exemplars, Liuxia Hui earned the posthumous title Hui (Wisdom) because of the mourning verses his wife composed to commemorate his virtuous deeds.[73] Xú Xuling, too, enjoyed posthumous glory; according to Xú Deyin, Lady Lou carefully preserved all her life the mourning verses she composed for him (#12, with a note). Moreover, Lady Lou went to great lengths to collect and preserve Xú Xuling's memorials to the throne—writings that recorded his loyal and dedicated service (#13). A note again adds details: "My late father's memorials to the throne amounted to several hundreds. As he avoided using his loyalty and integrity to seek fame, he always burned his drafts. My late mother would watch him writing and secretly copy down into volumes what he wrote. Most of what has now been published as his draft memorials came from writings collected in this way."

Examples such as these served to highlight a range of admirable qualities in both Lady Lou and Xú Xuling. While serving as commemoration, they supplied the details necessary to preserve a family history. By contrast, though Xǔ Yingnian composed eight mourning poems for Lady Lou, he represented her virtues in much more general terms. He did not refer to any of the details of family history that Xú Deyin filled in. Once he mentioned Xú Xuling but only in connection with burial arrangements, describing the imperial gift of a tomb where Lady Lou was to be buried with her late husband.[74]

The gap between 1707 and 1733 suggests a reduction in the literary activity of the Xǔ family.[75] Biographical sources record that Xú Deyin gave birth to two sons, Peihuang and Xinrui. The elder son, Peihuang, passed the exam to select men of exceptional erudition and literary talent (*boxue hongci*) in 1736.[76] According to Xú Deyin, Peihuang was assigned to supervise river works and flood control in Henan in that year. He died of exhaustion and a sudden onset of illness during the winter, after managing floods and famines in his new post. Xú composed a forty-eight-line poem to mourn his death and addressed it to both her sons.[77] At exactly the midpoint (line 25), mourning becomes autobiographical:

When I was married into your [Xǔ] family,
Your father was living in dazzling wealth.
Money was not what I favored;
I relied on brush and ink to dispense admonition.
At twenty he mastered the sage's works,
And his name was registered under the golden gate [of the court].[78]
Not only did he bring glory to his native place,
He also continued the achievements of his family.
Who would know that he would die early?
All alone I lived in distress afterward.
I raised you both,
Giving my personal instructions for you to establish your reputation.[79]

嗟我嬪汝家，汝父正煊赫。我重非錢刀，我規惟翰墨。弱冠登賢書，遂通金閨籍。非徒光閭里，差不墜門業。孰云中道捐，獨處恆茹戚。顧復汝兩孤，丸熊冀成立。

Xú Deyin's mourning poem for her son fills the gap left by the family's reduced literary output between 1707 and 1733. As in the cases of Bo Shaojun and Qian Shoupu, mourning inevitably gives rise to autobiographical recollection. Bo pushed the boundary of this poetic genre to "raise a monument to herself as a devoted wife": while mourning her late husband she wrote her own life into a hagiography of a female exemplar.[80] In her elegy, Xú Deyin emphasizes again how dazzling the Xǔ family's wealth was, specifying that it was not for money that she married Xǔ Yingnian and suggesting that his success should be ascribed to her assistance and admonitions. She also portrays herself as an exemplary mother raising and educating her sons to continue the Xǔ family's reputation. In the rest of the poem she laments Peihuang's sudden death but sees hope in Xinrui, who by 1736 had been studying in the capital for three years.

A sequence of eight more mourning poems follows, these autobiographical to an even greater extent.[81] The second in the sequence stands out as a coherent account spanning two family histories. Because it provides complete histories of Xú Deyin's families intertwined with her own life history and adds important facts and dates, I translate it in full:

A scholar living in poverty and isolation,
My late father changed registration to Qiantang to enter the county school.

At the time my late grandfather traveled west of the Yangzi River [Jiangxi],
And bandits ravaged the land.
My grandmother eagerly anticipated his return,
When suddenly news of his death reached Hangzhou.
My father, determined to fulfill his filial duty,
Went on a journey alone, with no provisions.
A long way he treaded, carrying the bones [of my grandfather] on his back,
By Mount Vulture he found a proper tomb site.[82]
In the year Yiwei [1655] he became a *jinshi*,
Embarking on a career to host imperial rituals.
In the ninth year of the Kangxi reign [1670] he was bequeathed a new post,
To oversee the salt trade, he made visits across Huai Yang.[83]
Through much hardship he rectified all kinds of wrongs,
Enriching the state while protecting the trade.
He served as a censor over the years,[84]
And I was born in the year Xinyou [1681].
When he was assigned to govern broader regions in the east,
He took me—an infant then—to his post.
Journeying to the east he served by the side of the emperor,[85]
Who, by clear rippling waters, composed poems to give him as a gift.
By a special edict he was assigned to supervise river transportation,
Yet in two years he passed away suddenly.[86]
His spirit looked longingly toward the east of the Yangzi River,[87]
At that time I was only at a tender age.
My late mother was gentle by nature,
And yet she was determined to fulfill the principle of chastity.
She established an heir according to the [Xú] genealogical sequence,
And moved my father's coffin back to their home [in Hangzhou].
In bringing up her son and daughter,
She taught them principles to adhere to.
At fifteen I obeyed her order,
And married into the Xǔ family from Gaoyang.
My husband had lost fatherly protection at a tender age too,
We had each other's support and read together by the lamp.

He had the fortune of signing on the walls of the Swan Tower,
And received salaries by the Phoenix Pond.[88]
While he drafted imperial edicts,
He shed tears over filial concerns.
Illness excused him from his post, and he returned home,
Using scant earnings to serve his mother.
His sister married into an eminent family,
And earned praise for abiding by rules of the inner quarters.
Her husband was exceptionally talented,
Together the couple chanted the *Rainbow Dress Rhapsody*.[89]
In the year Xinmao (1711) my younger brother-in-law became *jinshi*,
Blessings and misfortunes, however, came in turns.
To see their sister [on her deathbed], my husband and his brother
    rushed to her side by night,
And they wept for her during her last moments.
From then on my husband suffered from paralysis,
For nine years he was bedridden.
Medicines cost much,
Gradually they exhausted the family means.
Not yet a widow then, I nonetheless had to manage all family affairs,
And design plans for the future.
When my two sons entered the National School,
I prepared their betrothal gifts with pearls and jewels.
For my daughter's wedding I sold off all my jewelry,
Her dowry dazzled the eyes of beholders.
My mother-in-law passed away suddenly,
My ailing husband could take nothing but congee.
I almost died of grief,
Regretting that I could not replace them in death by my own life.
I did my best to bury them properly,
And fulfilled their deathbed wishes.[90]

先考窮巷士，采芹籍錢塘。先祖游江右，山賊逞陸梁。王母望刀環，凶問忽達杭。吾父志殉孝，獨行不裹糧。跋涉負骨歸，安窀靈鶩旁。乙未成進士，始仕祠祭郎。康熙九年命，巡鹾蒞淮揚。三苦與六弊，裕國兼恤商。歷官棲烏第，辛酉吾以降。大東作填撫，襁褓隨啓行。東行侍御幄，清漪賜天章。特簡督漕帥，兩載忽云亡。秭歸江東顧，薄祐始扶牀。溫溫先恭人，峻節凜冰霜。按譜立冢嗣，丹旐返舊鄉。提携孤子女，教之以義方。及笄奉母命，遠嫁于高陽。良人亦少孤，燈窗時勉勗。雁塔幸題名，鳳池沾寸祿。簪筆掌絲綸，思親淚相續。引疾歸故鄉，蘭陔供半菽。妹適四姓家，閨範稱賢淑。逸少興方回，同詠霓裳曲。辛卯弟登科，福兮禍所伏。依妹夜載馳，兄弟牽衣哭。由此患風痺，九年臥牀褥。參苓費不貲，家計嗟日促。未寡先持門，啟後需布局。二子入成均，委禽炫珠玉。嫁女罄釵鈿，妝奩頗耀目。君姑忽棄養，病夫唯啜粥。滅性過哀傷，百身悲莫贖。兩代力安窀，謹受彌留囑。

We learn from this poem that the Xú family's strategy for upward mobility following the war was no different from what we have seen in the cases of the Xǔ brothers (Chengxuan and Chengjia)—namely, cultural anchoring and reinvention of family identity through changed residence, success in the civil service examination, and service to the new regime. In this case, new identities were rooted in the cultural heartland, Qiantang, whereas in reality Xú Xuling spent the key phase of his career in Yangzhou, where Xǔ Chengjia took the opportunity to become his disciple. We also learn the important fact that Xú Deyin was born in Yangzhou and lived at her father's official abodes in the area. It was not until after her father's death in 1687 that she and her mother returned to Qiantang. Clearly she acquired her Jiangnan identity during the nine years when she lived in Qiantang, before she and her mother moved into the Xǔ family's Yangzhou property in 1696.

In the ensuing story, Xú Deyin paints an idealized picture of her marriage, the successes of her husband and his siblings, and his filial concerns—glossing over the tensions she otherwise reveals about her new home. We learn about the ill fortune besetting the family after 1711, including illnesses, deaths, and expenses that exhausted family means. The key to this story lies in how she—in a way echoing Bo Shaojun—"raise[d] a monument to herself" through mourning and glorifying the deceased. She portrays herself coping with hardship and family affairs, including preparing abundant betrothal gifts and dowries for her children and fulfilling the wishes of the deceased.

Other mourning poems in this series provide details about her sons' lives and careers, but the key message remains that she was the sole pillar of the household (Dasha yibu zhi; 大廈一木支) throughout the decades of the 1710s to 1730s. It is unknown how she managed family affairs despite financial constraints. Her reference to "earnings from other than tilling the fields" (*daigeng*) used for her sons' education suggests income from what remained of the family business.[91] Alternatively, the phrase can be associated with "using the brush to till the fields of the inkstone" (*bigeng, yantian*), standard bywords for earning a living by selling works of poetry or painting. It was not uncommon for a talented gentry woman like Xú Deyin to put her fine education to this end in times of need.[92]

A Poet-Hermit in Transregional Networks

Xú Deyin returned to Yangzhou in 1736, having spent two years in Peihuang's residences in Henan.[93] She spent the rest of her life in Yangzhou and became known as a leading woman poet in transregional elite networks.

Her life as a poet-hermit was never a secluded one, as she would have us believe. Her studio provided cultural space for joint compositions, and Xǔ Yingnian perceived himself to be a host too.[94] Beyond the studio the couple busily allied themselves to Yangzhou's cultural landmarks and events. As much as Xú Deyin mocked the seductive beauties on spring excursions, she also envisioned the season as a time for poetry contests. She expressed her ambition to join in an "arena of poets" competing for the first prize (Citan zheng duozhi; 詞壇爭奪幟).[95]

The decades around 1737–60 witnessed Xú Deyin's phenomenal success as a woman poet. The thatched cottage where she claimed to live the life of a poet-hermit became a social space. Here she received visitors from across the Jiangnan region and beyond. According to local history, Yangzhou, located at the crossroads of the lower Yangzi and Huai Rivers, attracted travelers and sojourners, and "female talents from all directions" (*sifang cainü*) would pay their respects at Xú Deyin's home. Scholars of younger generations who knew her through family connections also looked up to her as an erudite female scholar like Ban Zhao (45?–117?) or Lady Song (283–?), seeking her out to discuss the art of poetry. Such renown was attributed to her solid scholarship, "unmatched by ordinary women who [only knew how to] paint their faces" (Fei xunchang nüliu tuzezhe keni).[96]

Among her visitors were two eminent literati, Shen Deqian (1673–1769) and Yuan Mei. They paid their respects whenever they traveled through or sojourned in Yangzhou.[97] Shen attributed his visits to his connections with Xú Deyin's two sons. He passed the *boxue hongci* exam in the same year as Xǔ Peihuang, and the provincial exam in the same year as Xǔ Xinrui. During one visit he received Xú Deyin's encouragement to pursue the "ancient Way" (*gudao*).[98] Xú Deyin mentioned in several poems Shen's visits around 1747–52, when he served as vice minister of rites. As a token of his respect, Shen brought her a board inscribed with his own calligraphy honoring her as a "Female Exemplar following the Expositor of Civilization [i.e., lady Song]" (Xuanwen yifan). Xú Deyin announced her intention to hang the board high up in her thatched cottage (Maotang yuan gaojie; 茅堂願高揭), in recognition of the renown it brought her. She referred to this fact again in a response to another official who similarly brought her an inscribed board and expected the boards hung in her thatched cottage to set standards for her descendants (Xuanxiang maowu shi zisun; 懸向茅屋示子孫).[99] In 1752, at the age of seventy-two, Xú Deyin put together poetic works composed after 1707 to be printed as a sequel to her poetry collection. In a preface, Shen celebrated both her virtue as a widowed mother and her erudition as a female scholar. He perceived these qualities as foundational to her achievements as a poet.[100]

Yuan Mei likewise made the connection through Xǔ Peihuang, with whom he took the *boxue hongci* exam. He was twenty-one in that year (1736), and it would take several decades for him to establish elite networks across Yangzhou and Jiangnan. His connections later included the Huizhou descendants Cheng Jinfang (1718–84), Jiang Chun (1720–89), and the Ma brothers. (Ruan Yuan was an affinal kin of Jiang Chun.[101]) In 1757, he attended a Red Bridge gathering that Lu Jianzeng hosted in emulation of Wang Shizhen. In 1758 he gave his cousin Yuan Tang (1734–71) in marriage to Wang Mengyi (1712–73), another powerful Yangzhou salt merchant. Starting in the 1760s, he frequently visited the Level-Mountain Hall, and those who wanted to meet him gathered in Yangzhou "like clouds."[102] It took even more time for his female disciples, such as Luo Qilan (1755–1813) and Bao Zhihui (1757–1810), to establish their repute and join or initiate elite gatherings in Yangzhou. During the decades between 1737 and 1760, however, it was Xú Deyin whom Yuan perceived as the exemplar of women's poetic achievement.[103] Like Shen Deqian, he praised Xú Deyin's poetic works for their erudition and moral strength.[104] His celebration of female talent—best known from his mentorship of younger generations of women poets—can be seen as inspired by Xú Deyin's example.

Matching the social ties yielded by Xú Deyin's sequel, *Lüjingxuan xuji*, with sources on contemporary Yangzhou elite culture provides further clues to her success. Her connections included the most powerful and best-connected Huizhou descendants, such as Jiang Yu (1706–75), Ma Yueguan (1687–1755), Ma Yuelu (1701–61), Wang Tingzhang (ca. 18th c.), Cheng Mengxing (1678–

1747), and Cheng Lingyan (ca. 18th c.). The Jiang, Ma, and Cheng descendants are best known for creating new cultural splendors in the city through their phenomenal wealth and active social and cultural engagement. Jiang Yu's family and the Xǔ family were affinal kin (*yinjia*). Jiang Yu's wife, Chen Pei (1707–28), was known for her poetic talent. When she passed away, Xú Deyin composed several mourning poems and authored a preface for her posthumously collected drafts.[105] The Ma brothers played leading roles in reshaping the urban landscape through major construction and cultural projects, and their private gardens became new landmarks in the city. Ma Yuelu and Xǔ Peihuang passed the same *boxue hongci* exam in 1736. Wang Tingzhang was a merchant whose wealth was said to have reached "ten million [taels of silver]." Ma Yueguan and Wang Tingzhang funded Xú Deyin's publication of her sequel.[106] Cheng Mengxing was an affinal grandson of Wang Maolin. He took the initiative to renovate the West-of-Bamboo Pavilion, though for some reason the project did not succeed. Xú Deyin's sequel ends with a poem in which she portrays herself as continuing Cheng Mengxing's efforts and resurrecting the cultural legacy of Du Mu (803–52) from the ruins of the pavilion lying beneath weeds and mists (Chongpi hanyan mancao zhong; 重闢寒煙蔓草中).[107] Cheng Lingyan, a nephew of Cheng Mengxing, is remembered for his painting about Red Bridge and for his commemorative essay, "An Account of Famed Gardens in Yangzhou" (Yangzhou mingyuan ji). Xú Deyin inscribed one of his paintings.[108] She also composed a poem about her visit to the East Garden (Dongyuan)—one of the famed gardens recorded by Cheng—and literally signed the site during a gathering where inscriptions were collected from the participants.[109]

These sources indicate the visibility Xú Deyin attained in the cultural landscape and among the web of powerful merchants in Yangzhou in her later years. The last fact, in particular, attests to a degree of social mingling previously unimaginable in the city: it was not the courtesans the city was known for but rather a celebrated woman poet who attended an elite gathering at a famous site, and who documented her presence through a joint poetic event. There is evidence that Xú Deyin continued to take an active interest in literary and scholarly pursuits after 1760, beyond the age of eighty.

The fact that Xú Deyin, a female talent usually associated with Qiantang, in the Jiangnan cultural heartland, had Huizhou origins and attained fame in

Yangzhou paints a highly mobile picture of women's rise to literary prominence and creation of new cultural identities during the Qing era. It draws particular attention to Huizhou and Yangzhou as previously understudied geographical factors in mapping women's literary productivity. This chapter reconsiders these geographical factors in the frame of a Huizhou family's history in early Qing Yangzhou.

Patterns emerge from the rich corpus of the Xǔ family's literary output. "Searching the infinitesimal," a phrase encoding political and geographical references and evocative of the prestige of Li Bai, became a form of symbolic capital driving the family's social and cultural ascendancy after the tumultuous dynastic transition. Used as a name for a family estate and the title for a family publication, the phrase signaled the strategies that descendants of this Huizhou family employed to create and anchor their cultural identity among the Yangzhou elites. For Xǔ Chengjia, these included taking up the opportunities in a new regime and entering the very center of the city's elite society through public service, cultural events, reconstruction projects, and intermarriage with another powerful Huizhou lineage. We have seen above all how his collection, *Searching the Infinitesimal*, crafted a landscape for elite bonding at the major landmarks and how he positioned his family estates in this landscape. By the time of his grandson Xǔ Yingnian, the Tower for Searching the Infinitesimal had become a new landmark in the city. Refined gatherings that Xǔ Yingnian in turn hosted at the site—now a thatched cottage deriving prestige from Du Fu—continued to enhance the family's cultural legacy.

Xú Deyin's efforts to craft her identities were similarly framed by attention given to physical sites. She carved out a cultural space identified with the home of Xie Daoyun, located by "walls painted in gold dust," in the face of an increasingly commercialized culture in Yangzhou. The partying rich next door or across walls on all sides, and by the same token those in neighboring boats by Red Bridge, contributed to her demarcation of space as the basis for identity formation, as she created her persona as a poet-hermit with refined taste. Tensions embedded in these demarcated spaces further reveal her effort to be as much about reinventing the legacy of her marital family, "dazzling" with wealth, as about joining its status performance. Even as her husband's family continued to enjoy high social and cultural standing in Yangzhou, she perceived its legacy as being assimilated into trends of sensuality and extravagance. By consigning the Thatched Cottage for Searching the Infinitesimal to these changing trends, she foregrounded her own thatched cottage as the reserve for the finest legacy.

While Xú Deyin played an increasingly dominant role in reshaping her marital family's history, she also became the biographer for her natal family. A corpus of her mourning poetry offers insights into her natal family's social strategies, particularly its creation of an elite identity out of what had originally been registered as merchant status. This family history added much to her self-appointed role as cultural curator. She transplanted to her studio not only a view evocative of Jiangnan culture but also the key attributes defining elite status during this time. Her mourning poetry for her son filled in the interval between 1707 and 1733, characterized by the reduced fortune and literary activities of the Xǔ family, supplying rich details of how she raised a monument to herself. Finally, with her rise to renown at a later stage of her life—when her thatched cottage became a symbolic cultural center embedded in elite networks across Yangzhou and the Jiangnan region—tributes paid to her by eminent figures ushered in a new era for the celebration of female talent.

This chapter establishes the case that transregional dynamics among Huizhou, Yangzhou, and Jiangnan generated strategies for cultural anchoring and identity formation—and above all a female cultural identity as an early Qing exemplar of women's literary achievement. For female talents like Xú Deyin and those to come in this book, Huizhou did not suggest a fixed identity defined by increasing lineage control over women's lives. Rather, it precipitated the transformation (and accretion) of their cultural identities and, in turn, their transformative impact on their families.

2

Owning the Landscape

The swan goose from the central island has lost its home.
中洲鴻雁已無家。

—*Bao Gao*

What a joy to spend our lives growing old together in our home mountains!
此生喜共家山老。

—*Bao Zhihui*

SUCCESS STORIES OF Huizhou merchants concentrated in the prosperous eighteenth century, when their monetary and cultural power peaked. Because success through the civil service examination was attainable for no more than a tiny fraction of the population, the success stories of these Huizhou merchants often lay elsewhere, primarily in the accumulation of wealth and cultural resources. As Benjamin Elman remarks, "We must look beyond the official meritocracy to see the ironically larger 'success story' of the millions of failures in the civil examinations."[1] The *Chronicle of the Painted Barks of Yangzhou* documents the imprint of Huizhou wealth on the city's infrastructure, institutions, gardens, entertainment, and cultural and intellectual production in almost all aspects—in addition to providing egregious details of the Huizhou merchants' extravagance.[2] Geographically, the Huizhou impact had reached far beyond Yangzhou, and even beyond the lower Yangzi or Jiangnan region. Huizhou scholarship has recognized that there was no part of the Qing empire where Huizhou merchants had not set foot, and that its diasporic communities had developed elaborate strategies for maintaining their multiple geographical affiliations.[3]

Success stories aside, with the expansion of the Huizhou diaspora came unprecedented fluidity of human-place ties. And certainly, many Huizhou diasporic families did not have good fortune even slightly comparable to the powerful Jiang, Ma, and Cheng merchants dominating Yangzhou—in terms of both wealth and the control they exerted in their host places. The epigraphs to this chapter illustrate the enormously rich repertoire of what I would call the diaspora writings of Huizhou descendants who were preoccupied with displacement and hence the desire to name home—even during a time commonly associated with their peaking impact.

The fluidity of human-place ties arose not only from the movement of people but also from the shifting relations between localities—not least concerning which were to be lauded as centers and which were to lie on the peripheries. Even within Jiangnan, the Jiangnan identity indicative of prestige or status associated with the cultural heartland could not be taken for granted. Dantu, which set the stage for the history of the diasporic Huizhou family examined in this chapter, had to define its place in Jiangnan geographically and culturally.

Dantu

Dantu was the prefectural seat of Zhenjiang in Jiangsu. A major port on the lower Yangzi River, Dantu was the gateway to the Jiangnan heartland. Across the Yangzi lay Yangzhou (fig. 3). As the Song statesman Wang Anshi (1021–86) famously wrote, "Jingkou and Guazhou are set apart by the [Yangzi] River; Mount Zhong is only a few hilltops away." Jingkou and Guazhou are used here as synecdoches for Dantu and Yangzhou, respectively. The former refers to the area by Mount Jing in Dantu, and the latter, a gourd-shaped island (hence the name Guazhou, meaning Gourd Island) located in the southern suburbs of Yangzhou. Mount Zhong was located to the southwest of Zhenjiang, in Jiangning (Nanjing). Expressing his wish to return to his estate by Mount Zhong, Wang Anshi succinctly captures the spring view he yearns for: "The spring breeze again tints verdant all along the bank, to the south of the [Yangzi] River." Dantu offers the spring view typical of Jiangnan as seen from his boat moored at Yangzhou.[4]

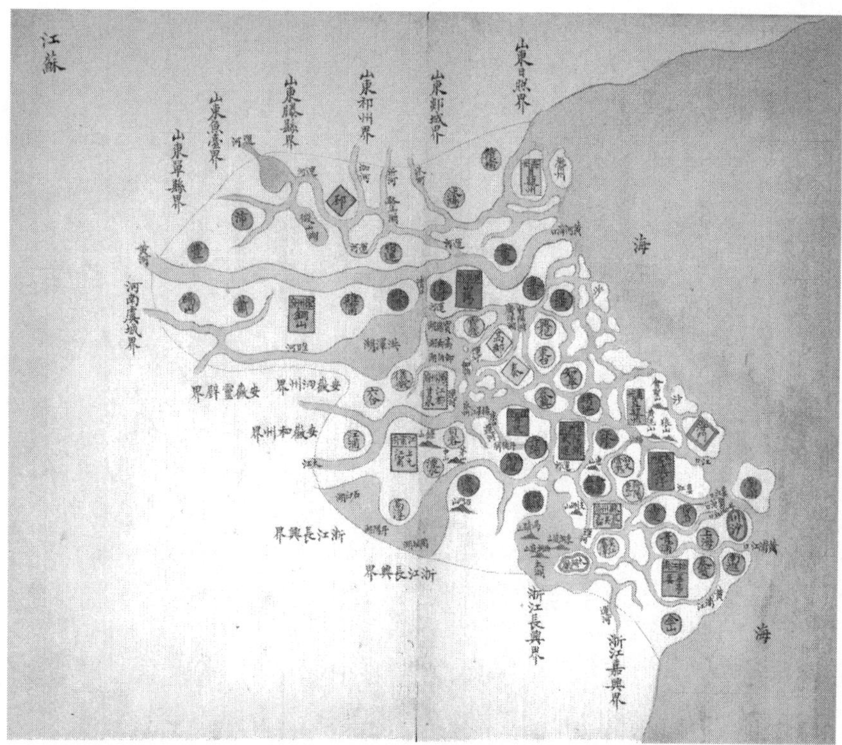

FIGURE 3. Dantu in a Qing map, *Guochao tianxia yudi quantu, Jiangsu* (1759–63). Used by permission of the Peking University Library.

Despite its geographical location south of the Yangzi River, Dantu had long taken on a northern identity. Warfare in the fourth century, during what had been known as the Great Turmoil of the Yongjia reign (307–11; Jin dynasty), brought to Dantu many refugees fleeing the north and, along with that population, northern dialects and lifestyles that turned Dantu into a migrant city. Contests between places driven by localism, coupled with vibrant transregional commerce during the late imperial period, fueled anxiety over its cultural identity. In particular, local Dantu officials complained that they had to attend exclusively to commercial needs that bound Dantu with the vast expanses of the Qing empire. Its port was always bustling, so much so that no one could spare a moment for “moistening brushes with ink for writing” (*ruhao chihan*; 濡毫摛翰). Localist cultural initiatives arose in response to anxieties over local identity, with the explicit aim of reviving a tradition of belles lettres in celebration of Dantu's magnificent landscape south of the Yangzi River (*Jiangzuo xingsheng*; 江左形勝).[5] Among the leading figures for these localist initiatives was the Bao family (fl. 18th–19th c.), including the female protagonist of this chapter, Bao Zhihui.

The Bao Family

The Bao family is generally considered native to Dantu, nurturing the foremost poets and painters in the area during the early to mid-Qing era: Bao Zhihui (1757–1810), a prized female disciple of Yuan Mei connected broadly with women's literary communities flourishing in Jiangnan during the High Qing. Bao Gao (1708–65), Bao Zhizhong (1740–1802; son of Bao Gao), and Bao Wenkui (1765–1828; nephew of Bao Zhizhong) strongly influenced what came to be known as the Jingjiang school of poetry.[6] Recent studies attribute their renown to their Jiangnan cultural heritage.[7] The three daughters of Bao Gao—Bao Zhilan (1751–1812), Bao Zhihui, and Bao Zhifen (1761–1808)—published a joint collection, *Jingjiang Baoshi san nüshi shichao* (Poetry by the three lady scholars from the Bao family of Jingjiang), and their names appeared in numerous entries in the Qing anthologies of women's poetry. A volume of Bao Zhihui's poetic works was included in the *Suiyuan nüdizi shixuan* (Selections of Poetic Works by the Female Disciples of Suiyuan; ca. 1796–1850).[8] Their mother, Chen Ruizhu (1714–78), a Dantu native, left only a thin volume of poetry but was said to have played an important role in their education.[9]

A lively history of the Bao family's changing geographical and cultural affiliations can be found in Huizhou sources. Bao Gao was recorded in the local gazetteers of Huizhou as a native of She County who contributed numerous titles to the gazetteers' sections on belles lettres.[10] A well-preserved Bao genealogy identifies Bao Gao's ancestors as being from the Chengfeng line, which moved to Yangzhou during the late Ming. Among them was Bao Daru (ca. 17th c.) and his son Bao Yi (ca. 17th–18th c.). Bao Daru or Bao Yi moved the family farther from the Yangzi River and settled in Dantu. Bao Yi made a living as a painter in Dantu and Yangzhou. He was known for his figure paintings and was said to demonstrate the "style and strength" (*geli*) of the Ming painter Qiu Ying (1498?–1552?). His son Bao Gao learned his profession and became well versed in such popular themes as flowers, birds, bamboos, and rocks. When sojourning in Yangzhou, Bao Gao made an effort to cater to the local Yangzhou art market, where patrons preferred more abstract, individualistic styles to verisimilitude (Gao zhi Guangling, gaiwei xieyi; 皋至廣陵，改為寫意). Bao Yi and Bao Gao were active among the professional painters broadly known as the Yangzhou school of painters.[11] Distinguished by his classical learning and poetic talent, Bao Gao took up tutoring jobs with wealthy households in Yangzhou. He spent his life crisscrossing the Yangzi River between Dantu and Yangzhou.[12]

According to Bao Qingxi (1852–1920), editor of the Bao genealogy, the Bao lineage's migration history provided important lessons. Despite the fact that the Bao family had flourished in Huizhou and its descendants had spread widely, Bao Gao's line, which moved to Dantu, was thin. The purpose of the genealogy was to remind Bao descendants of the many hardships that had jeopardized the line's survival during migration. Most of the Bao descendants in this line, he emphasized, earned only a meager living from pursuing Confucian studies or trading (*yeru xigu*). During the Qing era, there were only three descendants who succeeded in the civil service exams. He then highlighted the literary and scholarly achievements of Bao Gao and his family as key factors in enhancing the line's social status—urging later generations to emulate them so as to avoid "suffering from hunger in a poverty-stricken place and dispersing in all directions" (*donglei qiongxiang, lisan sifang*; 凍餒窮巷，離散四方).[13] Bao Qingxi exhaustively searched the local histories and an array of literary and biographical sources to showcase their achievements (fig. 4). With this "literary focus," several volumes of the Bao genealogy bore a close resemblance to collections of belles lettres in local gazetteers.

In Xin Yu's study of Huizhou publishing, the practice of including literary writings in genealogies can be traced to the mid-Ming. Yu refers primarily to works commissioned for farewell parties, birthday celebrations, ceremonies, funerals, and the like. From around 1500 on, these commissioned writings were increasingly collected into the literature (*wenhan*) sections of family genealogies in Huizhou.[14] What distinguishes the Bao genealogy is its lists of women's literary publications as an integral part of its legacy of belles lettres. Though a comprehensive study of records about women in Huizhou genealogies has yet to be conducted, the genealogies examined in recent studies highlight the women's moral conduct.[15] More often than not, readers find scant information about female lineage members, sometimes only wives' natal surnames.

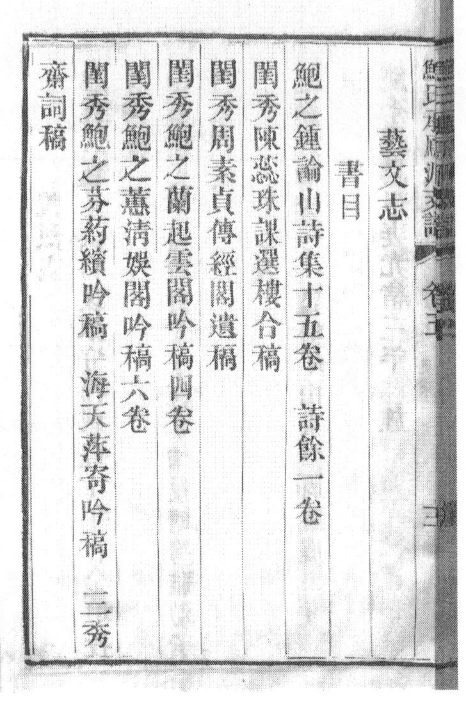

藝文志
書目
鮑之鍾論山詩集十五卷 詩餘一卷
閨秀陳蕊珠課選樓合稿
閨秀周素貞傳經閣遺稿
閨秀鮑之蘭起雲閣吟稿四卷
閨秀鮑之蕙清娛閣吟稿六卷
閨秀鮑之芬葯續吟稿 海天萍寄吟稿 三秀齋詞稿

FIGURE 4. Women in the Bao lineage's legacy of belles lettres. Bao Qingxi, *Xin'an Baoshi Chengfengpai zhipu*, "Yiwenzhi." Used by permission of the Shanghai Library.

The Bao genealogy editor no doubt had an agenda. Writing centuries later, after war and revolution had toppled the Qing empire, he found in the cultural achievements of Bao Gao and other Bao descendants a legacy to define his lineage and prevent it from dispersing due to the seismic changes taking place in his own time.[16] Still, the Bao women's presence in that legacy is noteworthy. Their prominence needs to be understood in light of Bao Gao's and others' investment in joining localist initiatives in Dantu.

The Landscape

The Song painter Mi Fu (1051–1107), who invented the abstract ink strokes of literati paintings featuring mists and clouds, was said to have based his signature misty hills on the landscape of Dantu. Hills near the city also gave rise to a peculiar cultural landscape juxtaposing the rural and the urban, as captured by the phrase "hills and woods by city and marketplace" (*chengshi shanlin*). The phrase celebrates a literati ideal of the hermit who seeks peace and seclusion at natural sites close to a bustling marketplace.[17] A Ming copy of Mi Fu's calligraphy on this phrase survives today in the stone inscriptions displayed at one of the Zhenjiang city's major tourist sites. Dantu gazetteers incorporated pictures of the hills as the town's defining geographical feature. In the pictures, the hills are usually represented as surrounded by or overlooking expanses of water and boats, thus indicating Dantu's identity as a major port on the Yangzi River.

I have provided in the introductory chapter a brief summary of the "encounters" between landscape, history, and the perceptions of the self in travel accounts and practices of cliff-polishing from the Tang period on. In *All Mine!* Stephen Owen describes how Song writers inscribed onto places and things an awareness of a changing social world permeated with money and conflicting values. When anxiety over local Dantu identity during the High Qing tied into a Huizhou diasporic family's search for home, the landscape of Dantu offered the cultural and affective ties desired by locals and migrants alike.

Several generations of poets formed groups to promote a style that painstakingly named and described Dantu's "magnificent landscape." These groups include Jingjiang Sanzi (Three Masters of Jingjiang, which included Bao Gao); Jingjiang Qizi (Seven Masters of Jingjiang, which included Bao Wenkui); and Songxi Wuyou (Five Friends of the Pine Tree Spring; including Bao Wenkui, Zhang Xuan [1756–?; husband of Bao Zhihui], Zhang Yin [1768–1829; cousin of Zhang Xuan], and two other local poets). The Zhang family, affinal kin to the Bao family, came from Jiangxi and settled in Dantu to take refuge from the calamitous Ming-Qing dynastic transition. Its family enterprise, Zhang Sheng Dabuzhuang (Zhang Sheng's Grand Fabric Store), soon became successful in the area and accumulated wealth for investment in elite networks and tastes. In addition to landscape poetry, their private gardens were known for demonstrating such tastes. Zhang Xuan, husband of Bao Zhihui, inherited the family business and further expanded the family's estates. His studio, Yinlü Shantang (Mountain Hall for Drinking Green [Wine]), became a focal point for groups of local luminaries.[18] Through affinal and social ties, furthermore, Bao and Zhang poets were connected with elites across the Yangzi River. A leading figure among them was Wang Wenzhi (1730–1802), a Dantu native who resided in Yangzhou.[19]

In painting, too, groups of painters developed unique styles for portraying the local Dantu landscape, later known as the Jingjiang school of painting.

These painters revamped an artistic tradition transforming Mi Fu's ink style into a more realistic representation of the local hills Jin, Jiao, and Beigu—alternatively known as the Three Hills (Sanshan). Whereas Mi Fu's misty hills remained anonymous, Jingjiang school paintings were permeated with identifiable details. Zhang Yin was among the first to highlight these details.[20]

There was further an overlapping interest in using poetry and history for localist initiatives. Bao Gao authored voluminous landscape poetry and local geographical and historical writings. His writings include *Huayang "Yiheming" kao* (Evidential research on the "Inscriptions for Burying Cranes" by the hermit of Huayang), *Jingkou wenxian lu* (Records of sources on Jingkou), and *Jiaoshan zhi* (A history of Mount Jiao). The "Inscriptions for Burying Cranes" remains on the polished cliffs, a massive "landscape of words"—to borrow Robert Harrist's term—on Mount Jiao today.[21] According to Bao Zhilan, landscape poetry by Bao Zhihui was based on history, and the reader should not take them as ordinary "sketches on travels" (Qishi kebei zhicheng, qibi kedang zhushu, wuzuo xunchang youcao duye; 其詩可備志乘，其筆可當著書，勿作尋常遊草讀也).[22] Personal expression through poetry thus acquired the prestige traditionally associated with historiographical writing.

A rich corpus of the Baos' and Zhangs' personal collections has survived, offering more opportunities for tracing their diasporic history and social and cultural strategies in the context of localist initiatives:

Bao Gao, *Haimen shichao*, 1739, 8 *juan*.[23]
Bao Gao, *Haimen shichao waiji*, 1739, 4 *juan* (with appendices).
Bao Gao, *Haimen erji*, manuscript with preface dated in 1753, 10 *juan*.
Bao Gao, *Haimen sanji*, manuscript ending in 1765, 6 *juan*.
Bao Zhizhong, *Lunshan shichao*, 1832, 15 *juan*, appended with *ci* 1 *juan*.
Bao Wenkui, *Yeyun shichao*, 1839, 12 *juan*.
Chen Ruizhu, *Kexuanlou yishi*, 1882, 1 *juan*.
Bao Zhilan, *Qiyunge shichao*, 1882, 4 *juan*.
Bao Zhihui, *Qingyuge yingao*, 1811; 1882, 6 *juan*.
Bao Zhifen, *Sanxiuzhai shicichao* , 1882, 3 *juan*.
Zhang Xuan, *Yinlüshantang shiji*, 1814, 16 *juan*.
Zhang Yin, *Taochan'ge ji*, manuscript with preface dated 1849, 4 *juan*

My discussion below draws predominantly on the collections of Bao Gao and Bao Zhihui. The former set the patterns and *topoi* that were to recur throughout the poetic repertoire of other family members. The latter was the most explicit in the two families in expressing literary ambition and incorporating such expression into the families' search for home and cultural anchoring. Bao Gao's preoccupation with displacement—as a result of the family's highly mobile history—brings into focus Bao Zhihui's favored strategy for phrasing mobility in terms of feeling at home and taking ownership of local landscape.

The Bao Cultural Elites: Writing Diaspora

A thirty-eight-line verse in the ancient style (*guti shi*) that Bao Gao sent to his former study mates in Dantu when sojourning in Yangzhou is a typical personal story embedded in his highly mobile family history.[24] The verse opens by praising Dantu from the perspective of a newcomer and a "scholar of obscure background" (*hanxiang shi*; lit., "scholar from a poor land"). Bao Gao looked up to Nan Xu, using the ancient name for Zhenjiang, for its historical legacy, beautiful landscape, and most of all, the illustrious families (*gaomen*) it had been known for since the Western Jin (265–317).[25] Whereas he identifies his own native home (*gujia*) as a place named East Pool in She County (She Dongtan), he emphasizes that he too (i.e., like other local Dantu families) has been living in Dantu for a long time. Growing up there required establishing connections with the local: first he paid tribute to nearby tomb sites (for ancestral worship) and built harmonious relations with his neighbors; then he bonded with local worthies distinguished by their literary talent; and finally, he gained gentry status (*jinshen chi*) by training in writing (*caogu xue*). Life at a young age involved much partying while pursuing literary and scholarly interests with friends—until, at some point, he found no further career opportunities opening for him. Driven by hunger, he wrote, he began the life of a sojourner whose baggage had to be sent across the Yangzi River. In Yangzhou, he took up a tutoring job in a wealthy household, and here his perception of what native home meant shifted. He directed his homesickness to his native mountains (*gushan*), which appeared to be at once close by—just across the Yangzi River in Dantu—and too far to return to, as if lying a thousand miles away.[26] His self-identification as a scholar appeared to be affiliated with Dantu too—which, he claimed, fit poorly with the commercial milieu of Yangzhou. Proud of his scholarly interest in Han debates on commerce contained in *On the Trade of Salt and Steel* (Yantie lun; ca. 1 BCE), he nonetheless denounced trade while representing himself as knowing nothing about trading principles and living a secluded life distant from the market. And yet, he asked, why not take his sojourning place as his native home (*sang yu zi*) as well? His host treated him with much respect, and Osmanthus flourished in his residence—a token of the host's status or cultural aspirations. The host Bao Gao referred to was Xu Chaojiu (ca. 17th c.), a Huizhou merchant-poet who lived in Yangzhou and actively engaged in cultural projects there.[27] In a long rhapsody composed in 1735, Bao Gao specified that, after failing an exam in Nanjing earlier that year, he accepted Xu's invitation to live in the Xu household of Osmanthus Trees (Guiguan).[28]

Spatial registers abundant in Bao Gao's autobiographical verse destabilize home into shifting claims of belonging. What counts as native place is deliberately vague—straddling the Bao family's former home in Huizhou, Bao Gao's current home in Dantu, and the place where he frequently sojourned, Yangzhou. Bao Gao invites his readers, in this case former study mates in Dantu, to feel his perplexity and displacement along his life journey.

Genealogical projects for identifying the origins of Huizhou lineages and building up the lineages' histories began in the Ming. Records about the Bao lineage first appeared in the Ming *Xin'an mingzuzhi* (History of the illustrious lineages of Xin'an [Huizhou]), which traced its origin to Shangdang (Shanxi) during pre-Qin times (before 3 BCE). The lineage moved across the vast area encapsulated under the name Qingzhou (around Shandong and Hebei), but took on a Xin'an identity during the Eastern Jin (317–420). Descendants populated She and Qimen Counties.[29] Bao Gao's son Bao Zhizhong rephrased this history poetically: "Branches growing from Shangdang are like woods by waters, Seals divided in Xin'an maintain crucial familial ties" (Zhifen Shangdang you shuimu, fupou Xin'an liu daijin; 支分上黨猶水木，符剖新安留帶襟). To these poetic lines he added a note: "The Bao lineage originated from Shangdang and, since our ancestor Mr. Hongwen served as the prefect for XuanShezhou, descendants began to settle in this area" (Baoshi benchu Shangdang, shizu Hongwen gong wei XuanShezhou cishi, zisun shi jia yan; 鮑氏本出上党，始祖宏文公為宣歙州刺史，子孫始家焉).[30] To describe the branches that moved on to Dantu and Pinghu (Zhejiang), he used images of swan geese flying in separate directions: "A single swan goose flew by the moon of Jingkou, a pair landed on the north of the Level Lake" (Yiyan dufei Jingkou yue, shuanghong chuiluo Pinghu yin; 一雁獨飛京口月，雙鴻吹落平湖陰). The swan goose is a standard metaphor for siblings.[31] To these lines he added another note: "My home is in Jingkou, and [Bao] Xuelin's home is in Pinghu." Bao Zhizhong addressed the poem to his kinsman Bao Xuelin, and he specified that his purpose was "to trace common origins and roots" (*suyuan zhiben*; 溯源知本) by inscribing a painting about their native Bao village.[32]

Separation from home or from other ancestral lines provided the incentive for diasporic families such as Bao Zhizhong's to seek cohesion or common origins and thereby retrace, or retrospectively build, their lineages' history. As the Bao genealogy reveals, the line that moved to Dantu was thin, from Bao Gao's family alone. Moreover, none of the early migrants in this family had any success in the civil service exams. The fact that Bao Yi and Bao Gao, both professional painters, tried to earn their living by catering to the art market of Yangzhou sheds further light on the precariousness of their settlement. Bao Gao soon realized that a career as a painter was not what he truly wanted. He began to establish a reputation as a poet and scholar and succeeded in drawing the attention of Yangzhou luminaries, including the Lianghuai salt control censor Yin Huiyi (1691–1748). Yin and others enthusiastically recommended him for career advancement, but without much success. Bao Gao's biographers glossed over this fact by suggesting that he was too proud to pursue fame or status. Nonetheless, one biographer pointed to his ambiguous sojourning status (*jiji*) as a liability. Bao Zhizhong offers more glimpses into the problem. Impressed by Bao Gao's writing, the magistrate in Yangzhou was about to recommend him to the education-intendant censor when news came that Bao Daru had just passed away. At this point, "those who were jealous [of Bao Gao's talent] further used his sojourning status as an excuse [to obstruct Miao's recommendation]" (Maoji zhitu, fuyi jiji weici; 媢嫉之徒，復以寄籍為詞). After fulfilling the mourning requirements, Bao Gao succeeded in entering the state school. Unfortunately, however, he did not succeed in the subsequent provincial-level exam and gave up hope of pursuing an official career.[33] This trajectory was typical of—in Elman's words—the "lesser elites" whose number grew as one of the "unintended consequences" of meritocracy: an enormous pool of educated men who had failed the civil service examination had to put their classical education and linguistic talent to use in nonofficial occupations.[34] In Wei Shang's distinction between official elites and cultural elites, the elite identity of the latter group was shaky. It was not so much their status as their accomplishments that made them "bearers of values and culture."[35]

An early verse by Bao Gao, "Laments" (Ganyu; 1726), compares tensions in his life story to orchids suffering from rampant weeds and cites the "difficulty of anchoring roots." Bao Gao points to the dangers in his rootless life, providing a clue to what Bao Zhizhong indicated as the jealousy he had encountered: "Is there not a place to anchor roots? I suspect that disasters arise from this particular spot" (Tuogen qi wusuo? chuci yi huoduan; 託根豈無所? 處此疑禍端). The verse ends with the voice of a traveler lamenting his protracted journeys (Jiezai jilüren, zhizhu buneng can; 嗟哉羈旅人，躑躅不能餐).[36] Orchids, as used in literary conventions stemming from Qu Yuan (ca. 340–278 BCE), were a standard metaphor for the scholar-official suffering from jealousy. In the verse that followed, Bao Gao represented himself as an ill-fated scholar living among hills and roaming in sorrow by the woods and valleys.[37]

Hills and valleys drew from Qu Yuan, but the hills recurring in Bao Gao's poetry took on unambiguously local features. Hills viewed from a tower named Tower to See Hills (Jianshan Lou) evoke various local Dantu cultural traditions. Mi Fu's misty hills, though characterized by a style too abstract to reveal anything specifically local, were said to represent the Dantu landscape. Bao Gao imaginatively captured the grandness of this landscape by portraying "tens of thousands of hills" enveloped in clouds tinged with their verdancy. Or, more literally, the hills were what the clouds transformed into in their sudden diffusions (Kongzhong lüyun hu posui, sanzuo qianshan wanshan cui). He further echoed Mi Fu's calligraphy "Chengshi shanli," a celebration of a hermit culture close to the city and marketplace, by specifying the tower as being in the marketplace but facing the hills (Junlou zaishi bu zaishan, queyu zhushan cui xiangdui; 君樓在市不在山，卻共諸山翠相對). Most of all, he cast the Three Hills, the signature local landscape, as being easily identifiable by their geographical relations to each other and to the Yangzi River. Although hills in Dantu typically rise to no more than a few hundred feet, in Bao Gao's representation they turned into mountains reaching the height of rainbows or upholding the heavens with their great masses. The owner of the tower also owned these grand vistas. When he sat in leisure, it seemed as if he could put the mountains and rivers on display as a work of art next to his couch and tea table. When he chanted or wrote poetry, storms in the mountains and the torrents of the river raged under his fingers.[38]

Identified as Bao Gao's native mountains, the landscape told a story of mobility and displacement—as in a verse addressed to Wang Jinchen, affinal kin and a Huizhou native. While Wang Jinchen takes a tour from Huizhou to Dantu, Bao Gao is departing from Dantu to Yangzhou "again" (Fu zhi Guangling)—indicating how frequently he shuttled between the two places. He praises Wang in light of Xie Lingyun (385–433), whose tours won him undying literary fame, and enumerates the routes and riverways that Wang crossed to reach Runzhou (another alternative name for Zhenjiang). Here at Mount Beigu, Wang shifts between living the hermit life of a fisherman and partying at the Tower of Multiple Views on the heights. Bao Gao identifies from the tower the sites he had himself frequented, using the voice of Wang Can (177–217) to lament his repeated separation from these sites. What a pity, he writes, "by the mountains and rivers in my native land I feel like a guest" (Guxiang shanshui fan ruke; 故鄉山水反如客).[39]

Wang Can's classic work, "Rhapsody on Climbing to the Top of a Tower" (Denglou fu), provides an origin for what recent scholarship calls sojourners' literature in China. The growing popularity of this sojourners' literature testifies to the increasingly dynamic relations between people and place. By the Qing, it had become stereotypical to cite Wang Can in expressing yearning for one's native place.[40] In the original line, Wang Can expressed admiration for the place he sojourned at while pointing out that it was not his native place (Sui xinmei er fei wutu; 雖信美而非吾土). By a twist, however, Bao Gao's comparison of his own verse to Wang Can's classic piece puts in question the very idea of native place: does it refer to Xin'an (Huizhou), which his friend Wang Jinchen departed from and which he identifies elsewhere in his poetry as his native home? Or did it rather refer to Runzhou (Dantu), where his friend is enjoying the many beautiful sites while he himself is about to leave for Yangzhou? Bao Gao further enhances the sense of displacement by stating that he feels like a guest even when (or perhaps especially when) he is in his native place. In short, what can be ascertained about his verse is no more than the sense that neither Huizhou nor Dantu offers him a secure place identity at this moment.

Among the Three Hills, Mount Jiao had a peculiar attraction related to its massive cliff-polishing carvings, with the "Yiheming" appearing at the center. The rock bearing the "Yiheming" had long been lost in the Yangzi River. Retrieval of part of the rock by the Zhenjiang prefect Chen Pengnian (1663–1723) in 1713 caused an immediate sensation. Local elites exalted the remaining carvings as the foundation of Chinese calligraphy. Cliff carvings or stone inscriptions soon proliferated in emulation, symbolizing Dantu's cultural revival as reflected in the fate of the rock lost underwater and subsequently retrieved. Carvings and inscriptions then spread beyond Mount Jiao to cover the entire local landscape.[41]

A long verse by Bao Gao dramatizes the retrieval of the "Yiheming" as a story about local martial heroes wielding swords through torrents and taking back from the mouths of dragons the writings left by the immortal. Zhu Liting, to whom Bao Gao addresses the verse, had assisted the prefect in locating the inscriptions and the historical sources about their hermit author. From Bao Gao's account, Zhu invested heavily in cultural projects to earn fame. He built a tower of a hundred feet to store rubbings from the inscriptions, commissioned a painting (*Guanbei tu*) of himself observing the inscriptions, and circulated it among elites. Bao Gao composed the verse as a tribute to Zhu's painting. In hyperbolic terms, he adds that the incompleteness of the inscriptions is itself a testimony to their importance: even the moon and the heaven can be amended, according to legend, and yet the viewers of the inscriptions would always be aware of the impossibility of retrieving the original rock in its entirety.[42] Bao Gao was thus essential to the events that made a legend out of the "Yiheming." He also authored a work of evidential research on the inscriptions.

The fame attached to the local Dantu landscape was moreover framed in relation to Bao Gao's frequent travels. While in Yangzhou, he would look longingly across the Yangzi River to what he now referred to as his native mountains. While in Dantu, he would think of the gatherings he had in Yangzhou and thereby set the two places in competition. A verse dated 1735 captures these sentiments. Drinking alone at a wine shop in the southern suburbs of Dantu, he wrote on the wall about the banquets in Yangzhou:

Nine out of ten days in Guangling are spent on banquets,
From dawn to dusk grand halls are filled with talents.
Chefs moving their knives can instantly tell [which are good to
serve],
Wine and meat are sufficient for a thousand guests.
The host gives a toast and guests roar in cheers,
Though served in respect, I alone sit in silence—
Feeling uneasy like a wild deer entering the city;
While worrying that lambs would ruin vegetables in my garden.[43]

Thus he dreamed of the fine gatherings in his native mountains when grass turned green in the "south of the [Yangzi] River" (Dongfeng chuilü Jiangnan cao, mengxiang gushan youshi hao). In contrast to the extravagance of Yangzhou, at these gatherings guests enjoyed no more than tea brewed from spring water by the pine trees and served in small cups. He then goes into detail about the quietness of his excursion in the southern suburbs of Dantu. Unable to find his friends, he has to pawn his clothes to buy wine. Although he realizes he will soon leave home again in pursuit of wealth and status, he asserts that he will use his earnings to invite friends over for simple meals in a cottage he will build by the hills (*jielu*).[44]

Between 1726 and 1739, Bao Gao composed over 160 poems on the Dantu landscape.[45] His works of "contemporary-style poetry" (*jinti shi*) are even more explicit about naming the sites. While a close examination of these naming practices is beyond the scope of the present discussion, a pattern developed therein is clear: personal sentiments drive exhaustive accounts of the local sites and their historical references. At the heart of his poetry was the problem of locating home, despite Bao Gao's repeated emphasis on where his native land or native mountains were. The "homeless swan goose" compellingly evoked these sentiments, viewed from the top of Mount Beigu.[46]

Most often, the sense of displacement derived from the idea of looking into the distance from the heights is inspired by Wang Can's "Rhapsody on Climbing to the Top of a Tower" (Denglou fu). In Bao Gao's poetry, the heights take on specific names of local hills or towers. The poetic voices lamenting displacement allude richly to sojourners' poetry. Poems from his later years associate climbing to the heights unambiguously with thoughts about his native land and native people (Feishi guren bing gutu, denggao nabu si qiran). He refers directly to Wang Can when paying a compliment to his friend Wang Wenzhi—a Dantu native sojourning in Yangzhou—and suggests that the two Wangs are comparable in talent. At the same time, he gives voice to his own displacement, as well as the irony that he is lamenting his sojourning status from what he calls his native land (Fancong wutu chang yanliu; 翻從吾土悵淹留).[47] This lament casts doubt on the very idea of native land.

In 1738, Bao Gao connected the title of his poetry collection *Haimen ji* to the example of the *Huaihai ji* by Qin Guan (1049–1100). It was an unmistakable effort to define his personal identity as a poet through a local cultural identity, which he also personally shaped.[48] When sending a copy to Yin

Huiyi, he indicated that he had been compiling a history for Mount Jiao and, more broadly, for the Three Hills (Sanshan Zhi). Thus, his personal identity also drew from his scholarly interest in shaping local cultural history.[49] In the ensuing decades, Bao Gao continued to travel frequently across the Yangzi River and produce voluminous poetic works on the Dantu landscape. In his last few works, dated in the spring of 1764 and 1765, he celebrated his bond with Mount Jiao of over four decades and welcomed his friends from Yangzhou to his "humble cottage" (*wolu*) by the hill. Again, the phrase *wolu* connoted the precarious life of a traveler or sojourner—even though it had become something close to a humble home over the decades.[50]

These voluminous works set the pattern for writings by the Bao descendants. Bao Zhizhong quoted the Song master poet Su Shi (1037–1101): "Wherever my heart is at peace is my home."[51] And yet, he would look longingly at his native mountains during travels for exams or on various posts after succeeding in the exams. Bao Wenkui gave himself the style name Yeyun (Clouds Wandering in the Wilderness) and used this style name as the title of his personal collection. In an autobiographical verse, he asked why the wandering clouds could not return to their "native mountains."[52] He formulated the problem of locating home as an explicit question: "I climb onto the heights and see a thousand miles ahead—but where is my home?" (Denggao jian qianli, hechu shi wujia?).[53]

"Home Mountains": A Daughter's Claim to Ownership

The Bao sisters joined in writing their family history as aspiring women poets. A sequence of autobiographical poems by Bao Zhilan, titled "Expressing My Feelings" (Ganhuai), invoke Bao Gao's laments over his rootless life and suffering from jealousy but reframe them within a family history of attaining cultural renown (*qingxiang ye*). She celebrates Bao Gao's adherence to virtue, in contrast to descendants of other eminent lineages (*shijia zi*) who boast of their extravagance. She then bemoans her lack of opportunity to become heir (*si*) to such renown. Time and again she visits the Tower for Making Instructions and Selections (Kexuan Lou), which she specifies as Bao Gao's private library (Xian Zhengjun cangshulou ming; 先徵君藏書樓名), by now a token of her family heritage. And yet, her ambivalence about fame keeps her from inscribing her name on any piece of paper circulating beyond the inner quarters (Shenju xi xingzi, weiken ti cunzhi; 深居惜

姓字，未肯題寸紙).[54] The problematics of a daughter's claim to family legacy lie primarily in the ritual and legal principle that determined descent and inheritance through the male line (patriline). Kathryn Bernhardt identifies "daughters and wives in the absence of men" as the two categories of women who best illustrate changes in women's inheritance rights over time. For example, daughters who had no brothers lost the entitlement to their family properties laid out in the Song legal system when the early Ming government mandated nephew succession.[55] Culturally celebrated examples of daughters transmitting crucial Confucian texts as part of their families' privileged learning included Fu Sheng's daughter (ca. 2nd c. BC) and Lady Song (ca. 4th c.; awarded the title Expositor of Civilization)—both of whom lacked brothers.[56]

When Bao Zhihui made her entrance into this family history, she was unequivocal about fame: she had "the audacity to aspire to fame as a poet across Nan Xu" (shiming ganwang zhu Nan Xu; 詩名敢望著南徐). She expressed this wish on her thirtieth birthday, an occasion for reflecting on her life course and remembering her late parents and siblings (the swan geese separated from each other). Whereas Bao Gao had looked up to Nan Xu (Zhenjiang) from the perspective of a "scholar from a poor land," Bao Zhihui purported to rely on his heritage to cultivate the art of poetry and attain fame in Nan Xu:

SELF-ACCOUNT ON MY THIRTIETH BIRTHDAY

Three decades passed in an instant,
My parents have long been separated in death.
Dates for swan geese to gather or separate are hard to predict,
Talents in the younger generation, I hope, will not fall short of their
    ambitions.
My footsteps have reached the capital,
Would I have the audacity to aspire to fame as a poet across Nan Xu?
Having neglected my studies in recent years,
I shall steal a moment to read my father's books.[57]

三十初度自述

卅載韶華過隙駒，雙親早謝鹿門車。雁行聚散期難定，驥子聰明願莫虛。
游蹤舊曾經上國，詩名敢望著南徐。年來學殖多荒落，偷取餘閑讀父書。

The explicitness of Bao Zhihui's expression of literary ambition distinguished her from the other family members. According to Bao Wenkui, Bao Zhihui was preoccupied with refining the art of poetry, to the extent that she exhaustively read through collections from the private libraries of both her natal and marital families. In contrast to what was usually attributed to exemplary wives of this time—for instance, their devoted service to their families—Bao Zhihui did not start to manage household affairs until after she reached middle age (*zhongnian yiqian, weichi jiazheng*; 中年以前，未持家政), years after she married Zhang Xuan.[58] During one of the many gatherings held at the couple's home, Bao Zhihui's new poetic works were said to pour out ahead of all others'—like the rains pouring down outside, which provided the theme for poetic compositions on this occasion.[59]

The naming practices the Bao descendants used to articulate their cultural affiliations took a significant twist in Bao Zhihui's poetic works. Parallel to her wish to attain fame in Nan Xu was her desire to claim ownership of the prestige attached to the local landscape:

WATCHING THE THREE HILLS OF JINGKOU FROM A RIVER JOURNEY, COMPOSED TOGETHER WITH GEZHAI [ZHANG XUAN]

Torrents surge across the west winds toward the turbid sea,
The window on my boat opens a view onto the rising sun.
Black clouds by the ferry look like tamed elephants in sleep,
Verdant hills in the mirror—a pair of hair buns [of a young girl]—
shift over waves.
Sounds of bells from the upper realm reach down with falcons,
Shadows of pagodas in the midstream race with tides.
Every site on my home mountains is pleasant for a life growing old together,
No need to drive a cart to Mount Lumen.[60]

江行望京口三山同舸齋作

濤卷西風海色昏，篷窗洞啟看朝暾。渡頭馴象眠蒼靄，鏡裏雙螺動翠痕。
上界鐘聲隨鶻落，中流塔影帶潮奔。家山處處堪娛老，莫道驅車向鹿門。

As the title of the poem specifies, it presents a panorama of the Three Hills of Jingkou viewed from a boat sailing on the Yangzi River. The ferry in line

FIGURE 5. Zhang Yin, a section of *Jingkou sanshan tu* (1827). Used by permission of the Palace Museum of Beijing.

3 refers to the West Ferry (Xijin) leading to Mount Beigu, and the "verdant hills in the mirror ," to Jin and Jiao, the two islands rising from the middle of Yangzi River. Jin and Jiao were also known for their Buddhist temples and pagodas—hence the references to sounds of Buddhist bells and reflections of pagodas in the torrents, in lines 5 and 6. The poem predates Zhang Yin's painting *Picture of Three Hills in Jingkou* (Jingkou sanshan tu; 1827 [fig. 5]), a panoramic view of the Three Hills of Jingkou as the signature local landscape. Bao Zhihui claimed this landscape of Dantu as her home mountains, near which she and her husband would seek ideal companionship and the hermit life together.

The phrase *jiashan*, or "home mountains," derives from Bai Juyi's (772–846) poetic works. Bai uses it to refer to mountains one could characterize as home, either literally or by establishing cultural or affective bonds. In one example, Bai responds to the Tang official and general Pei Du's (765–839) wish to live a hermit life like Tao Qian's or Xie Lingyun's, by dismissing Tao's and Xie's residences as being too humble or remote (Taolu pilou nakan bi, Xieshu youwei buzu pan; 陶廬僻陋那堪比，謝墅幽微不足攀). Instead, the thirty-six peaks of Mount Song (Henan) have long kept Pei Du company and become his home mountains (Hesi Songfeng sanshiliu, changsui Shenfu zuojiashan; 何似嵩峰三十六，長隨申甫作家山).[61] For Bao Zhihui, similarly, the Three Hills of Jingkou provide lifelong company. In close proximity to a landscape repeatedly celebrated by poets and painters, the Bao descendants among them, the hills are far from being too remote or humble to qualify as her home. She asserts that there is no need to seek an ideal life anywhere else—not even on Mount Lumen (Hubei), a site favored by hermits from at least the Tang on.[62]

The poem was written at a time when Bao Zhihui orchestrated a range of spatial imagery to demarcate the cultural setting of the home she shared with Zhang Xuan. Her allusion to Mount Lumen repeats almost verbatim lines from an earlier sequence of poems she had composed in celebration of a newly built thatched cottage: "This cottage provides ample pleasure for a life in old age, what need is there to go to Lumen?" (Jici kan yulao, hexu xiang Lumen; 即此堪娛老，何須向鹿門). In that earlier sequence, she claimed to have transplanted to her new cottage plum trees from Nanjing and orchids from Suzhou—images symbolizing refined tastes and a hermit life in the cultural heartland (Gu mei yi Baixia, xiangcao mai Wuzhong; 古梅移白下，香草買吳中). By doing so, she suggested, she was able to strike a perfect balance between crafted and natural design (Yeyi rao shengqu, jingying qia huagong; 野逸饒生趣，經營洽化工). Her new home thus designed acquired a beauty equal to that of Yang Xiong's (53–18 BCE) house or Bai Juyi's garden, and she anticipated a life of companionship and a shared interest in wine and books (Zhujiu qi tongshang, cangshu hao gongwen. Yiqu Yangzi zhai, wumu Baijia yuan; 貯酒期同賞，藏書好共溫。一區楊子宅，五畝白家園。).[63] Thus what Bao Zhihui claimed as her home mountains was an expansion of these earlier spatial images.

Most of all, Bao Zhihui cast her cottage in the light of a tower located at the top of the woods (Gekai qunmumo; 閣開群木末). The phrase *mumo* comes from Qu Yuan and was adopted as the name of a tower on Mount Beigu after the Song era. The Tower at the Top of the Woods (Mumo Lou) had by this time become a famed site through repeated poetic representations by Bao Gao and others. Bao Zhihui once wrote how, when climbing Mount Beigu with Zhang Xuan, she saw the torrents of the Yangzi River raging as if just beneath her feet while hearing their sound on the "top of the woods" (Zudi jingtao mumo wen; 足底驚濤木末聞). In appropriating the historical and cultural references of the tower for her cottage, Bao Zhihui merges her home mountains and her new home into one spatial image.[64]

To further recall Bao Gao's verse about the Tower to See Hills, the owner of the tower also "owned" the vistas as if he could put them on display by his couch and tea table. Bao Zhihui developed techniques for portraying the local landscape for herself to make such claims. Take the example of her favorite theme, as indicated by Bao Wenkui, about watching rain from her studio:

WATCHING RAIN FROM THE STUDIO OF PURE JOY WITH MY NEPHEW HONGQI AND [MY HUSBAND] GEZHAI, USING THE RHYMES OF "ER XIAO"

Winds fill in the mountain tower and instantly dispel summer heat,
Clouds swirl as if splashing ink and darken all layers of the heavens.
Mists descend onto islets in the distance, where the river and the sky
  converge,
Lightning and thunder rumble across the vast space.
Floods roar, I suspect, in valleys close by,
Shrouded in vapors, I cannot tell dusk from dawn.
It's not too difficult for my fine guests to accept my invitation and
  stay–
Broken bridges are disappearing from the flooded plain.[65]

清娛閣同鴻起姪、舸齋看雨, 得二蕭

風滿山樓暑頓消，片雲翻墨黯層霄。煙低遠渚江天合，電掣長空霹靂驕。
澎湃只疑鄰磵壑，溟濛渾莫辨昏朝。不須投轄留佳客，漠漠平原沒斷橋。

From an early age, Bao Zhihui wrote admiringly of her sister Zhilan's studio, a tower located "halfway between the rivers and clouds" (Banzai shuiyun jian; 半在水雲間). The studio was named the Tower Where Clouds Rise (Qiyun Ge). Perched on the heights (*pinggao*), it allowed her to incorporate in one sweeping view what was close by in vivid detail and what lay in the distance—namely, leaves glittering with dew and hills covered in mist (Congye ming weilu, qingyan mo yuanshan; 叢葉明微露，輕煙抹遠山). It further provided a bird's-eye view of the river (Hedi gaoge wai, renzuo xiaoting zhong; 河低高閣外，人坐小庭中).[66] Similarly, when Bao Zhihui wrote about watching the storm from her studio, she made clear that it was a view from the heights by designating her studio as the "tower on the hill" (*shanlou*). From the tower she was able to see how the storm—in dramatic terms—brought together the heavens and the Yangzi River (*jiangtian he*) and flooded the land at the foot of the hills. The visual effect of the clouds and mist is reminiscent of Mi Fu's style, indicating the integration of a local cultural tradition into the view. She concludes by reaffirming her ownership of the tower, and hence the views it accords her, by addressing her "fine guests."

Juxtaposed with the views commanded by her tower are those framed in relation to her tower or assimilated into her home space. During a storm, she would leave her window open all day to see a waterfall nearby (Jingri kaixuan kan xuanpu; 竟日開軒看懸瀑). After the storm had passed, the shade of trees rolled down like a curtain, while peaks fading into mist stood just outside (Lüyin ruwo yilou xuan, louwai qifeng banhua yan; 綠蔭如幄一樓懸，樓外奇峰半化煙). On fine summer days, hills in the distance stood "on display" within her window frames, and torrents in the Yangzi River raged as if among the trees by her studio (Xiuyuan chuangjian lie, taojing shuli fan; 岫遠窗間列，濤驚樹裏翻).[67]

As Bao Zhihui's younger sister Zhifen wrote when visiting the couple's other studio on the heights, the Yinlü Shantang, the studio offered a cozy space to "collect mountains" (Gexiao ai cangshan; 閣小愛藏山) and take in drizzles and mists for viewing within the space shaped by the window frames (Zhaofei jian mu'ai, shoulan ru chuangjian; 朝霏兼暮靄，收覽入窗間).[68] Local landscape portrayed in this light became a private art collection. Guests joined as connoisseurs at the couple's studios, which figured variously as "mountain halls" (*shantang*), "mountain towers" (*shanlou*), "towers on the heights" (*gaoge* or *xuge*), or the "thatched cottage" (*maowu*) overlooking mountains and rivers. Luo Qilan (1756–after 1813), the other leading female disciple of Yuan Mei, paid several visits and wrote about the mountains lying just in front of the rolled-up window screens of Bao Zhihui's studio (Shanheng gaoge goulian zuo; 山横高閣鈎簾坐).[69] The all-encompassing verdancy of trees by Luo's description conveyed a visual effect of the tower situated among the mountain masses (Gaoge linshan wanlü nong; 高閣臨山萬綠濃). In response, Bao Zhihui referred to such verdancy as "spilled paint of dark green," and thereby converted the landscape into a landscape painting (Louwai shanguang podai nong; 樓外山光潑黛濃).[70] Family studios, thatched cottages among them, typically served as sites for elites' status performance during this time, but what distinguished Bao Zhihui's case was her conscious effort to turn these sites into vantage points from which to "own" the local landscape and invite guests to join in this creative process.

Claims of cultural ownership took root during the Tang era, and it was no coincidence that Bao Zhihui alluded to Bai Juyi in developing techniques for portraying and "owning" the landscape. Stephen Owen spots a "new interest in ownership and possession" among the mid-Tang poets. The idea was conceptualized in terms of the exclusion of and superiority over the others, or the "common," to formulate personalities of "singularity." A singular poet or a group of exceptional men would take imaginative and poetic possession of a territory while reminding the legal owner of the impermanence of possession. Bai Juyi would stake a claim to a splendid landscape as the "person who loves the mountain." Inherent in these claims were the formulation of individual style for display and the acquisition of cultural capital for the aggrandizement of the poets and their posterity.[71] Xiaoshan Yang attributes such assertion of individual style to mid-Tang politics. Bai Juyi constructed a political critique by contrasting true aesthetic possession with legal ownership: garden estates that aristocrats of Luoyang and Chang'an owned but rarely visited, or knew how to appreciate, were reflections of their excessive lifestyles and symbols of the deterioration of public order.[72] For Bao Zhihui, however, Bai's political undertones gave way to the new imperatives of a diasporic Huizhou family's search for place identity and a daughter's claim to the family's cultural heritage. Views from her family estates allowed her to take aesthetic possession of a local Dantu identity.

Aesthetic possession of spaces of all kinds created anchoring points for a family history by far dominated by the problem of locating home. Climbing to the heights continued to be an occasion for lamenting separation from family members. But unlike Bao Gao, who drew from Wang Can and sojourners' literature to express displacement, Bao Zhihui wrote the heights into spaces for aesthetic reflection and ownership. As much as she continued naming the sites—and characterizing her efforts as "searching for magnificent views across the Three Hills" (Sanshan sou shengji; 三山搜勝跡),[73] she also found the opportunity to attach Bao Gao's legacy to the site. At a cave on one of the hills, for example, she purports to discover a painting by Bao Gao. It is an enlightening moment when it dawns on her that painting and poetry have a mythical correspondence in competing for the viewer's attention (Shizhi huayushi, shenmiao xinhujing; 始知畫與詩，神妙心互競). The rain under Bao Gao's brush strokes, she writes, call forth a thunderstorm at the foot of the hill (Linli bisuodao, leiyu shangenying; 淋漓筆所到，雷雨山根應). Correspondingly, an awe-inspiring view of the storm enters her poetic lines: rains pour down and look as though "dragons and snakes had risen from a pond by the cave, in broad daylight" (Wanwan longshesheng, tanying baizhouying;

宛宛龍蛇生，潭影白晝映).[74] Through such mythical correspondence, she also seems to suggest a solution to what her sister Zhilan had perceived to be the problem of becoming heir to Bao Gao's legacy.

As for other Bao family members, the naming practices allowed Bao Zhihui to develop affective ties with the sites while exerting a formative influence on local identity. A key difference lay again in the fact that, for Bao Zhihui, these were affective ties with what she repeatedly claimed as anchoring points. On her fiftieth birthday, in 1806, she composed a "linked verse" with Zhang Xuan from the Silver Peak (Yinfeng) and expressed her joy that she was able to grow old together with him in the company of their home mountains (Cisheng xi gong jiashan lao; 此生喜共家山老).[75] The last poem she left (1810) was about all the fun she shared with her sister Zhilan in climbing to a pavilion at the top of their home mountains (Jiachu tingkong zuishangceng, Jiashan muchi kuaitongdeng; 佳處亭空最上層，家山暮齒快同登).[76]

Concurrent with Bao Zhihui's assertions to cultural anchoring, moreover, was her wish to inscribe an undying reputation onto the landscape:

IN MEMORY OF MY ELDER BROTHER LUNSHAN [BAO ZHIZHONG], COMPOSED IN SONGLIAO PAVILION #3

All across the Three Hills were inscribed these extraordinary lines;
Spirits can still be called forth as I chant the lines aloud.
[Note: My late father and my elder brother Lunshan left the largest
number of poetic lines on the Three Hills.]
I wish to polish cliffs and yet find my wrists weak;
Would I have the audacity to leave my name together with theirs, for
the next hundred years?[77]

松寥閣感舊追悼論山兄 其三

三山奇句題將徧，朗誦精靈尚可呼 先君暨論山兄三山留句最多。我欲摩崖嗟腕弱，留名敢望百年俱？

No evidence suggests that Bao Gao engraved any of his poetic lines onto the Three Hills, despite his interest in the *moya* or cliff-polishing tradition. Nonetheless, here Bao Zhihui celebrates Bao Gao's and Bao Zhizhong's poetic lines about Dantu's signature landscape as symbolic engravings that attest to their undying reputation. Echoing her aspiration to fame articulated over two decades before, on her thirtieth birthday, she expresses her ambition to attain a literary immortality equal to theirs. To recall Richard Strassberg, travel writings from the Tang onward inscribed landscapes increasingly with encounters among place, nature, history, and perceptions of the self. Literary and cultural legacies accumulated from inscribed texts through time.[78] In Bao Zhihui's case, these were encounters between accumulating family legacies, localist cultural initiatives, and her ambition for leaving her own literary legacy for posterity.

The Bao family of poets was active during a period of phenomenal expansion of both the Huizhou diaspora and women's literary activities and networks during the mid-Qing. Bao Zhihui's affiliation with Yuan Mei's group of female disciples has generally been perceived to illustrate the latter trend. In this chapter, I discuss the intersections of the two trends by examining how her family's changing claims of belonging and anchoring catalyzed her literary creativity.

Creating anchoring points suggested—paradoxically—detaching home from a fixed geographical location and opening possibilities for imagining its cultural affiliations. As Bao Zhihui wrote to her friends, the women poets from Wang Wenzhi's family, "The Peach Spring becomes home, if you have lived by it for a long time" (Taoyuan jiuzhu jiwei jia; 桃源久住即為家).[79] For the Bao and Wang families, movement across the Yangzi River went in opposite directions, but anywhere that provided a haven to migrants comparable to the Peach Spring qualified as home.

Alternatively, what home suggested to Bao Zhihui was a feel, or a perception of what figured as home: "Feeling at home when staying as a guest is being at home" (Keli neng'an jishi jia; 客裏能安即是家).[80] Bao Zhihui and Zhang Xuan were known for their shared interest in traveling, and this line refers to a stay by the West Lake during a journey to Hangzhou and Suzhou in 1801. Earlier, they had commissioned a painting of "sailing together across mists and waves" (*yanbo gongfan*; 煙波共泛) and inscribed the painting with their joined compositions.[81] The trip to Hangzhou and Suzhou finally fulfilled their "long held wish to sail across mists and waves" (*yanbo suyuan*; 煙波夙願).[82] Again, "mists and waves" draws from Wang Can's lament over separation from home. According to Shang Wei, the phrase signals the questioning of human destination in the famous adaptation made by the Tang poet Cui Hao (704?–54): Cui found nowhere to return among the expanses of mists and waves of the Yangzi River, by the Yellow Crane Tower (Huanghe Lou).[83] Bao Zhihui, however, integrates "mists and waves" along her journey into quite the opposite interpretation of human destination, borrowing from a widely quoted line by the Song master poet Su Shi, "Wherever my heart is at peace is my home" (Cixin anchu shi wuxiang; 此心安處是吾鄉). Recent scholarship has posited that Su Shi's line inspired a "diaspora consciousness" characterized not by lamentation but rather by feeling at home in one's "spiritual home."[84] In Bao Zhihui's case, Su Shi's line enables her to at once phrase mobility in terms of feeling at home and make even broader claims to cultural heritage. In the words of her nephew Yeyun (Bao Wenkui), her journey with Zhang Xuan through "mists and waves" created an even greater cultural impact on the "arena of poets" than the act of polishing cliffs would (Heyong moya ti xingshi, zaochuan jiahua man shitan; 何用摩崖題姓氏，早傳佳話滿詩壇).[85]

Bao Zhihui continued accumulating cultural bonds with landscapes (and hence the prestige attached to them) through her journeys with Zhang Xuan to the Jiangnan heartland. A recent study of her poetic works about these journeys interprets them as examples of how women of this time found an opportunity to venture beyond the inner quarters.[86] While this remains a useful interpretive framework, reading the poetic works in the totality of a family history dominated by the problem of anchoring roots or locating home reveals them to be very much about cultural anchoring and ownership.

Such claims were backed by wealth. As Stephen Owen shows, commerce and acquisition shaped a pervasive awareness of ownership during the Song. It was in response to the Song state measures against the private wealth of powerful merchants, and the ensuing factional politics, that Sima Guang (1019–86) authored the "Account of My Solitary Happiness Garden," staking claims of ownership and "militantly celebrating private property."[87] In the present case, literary production addresses not political controversies over control of wealth but rather the imperatives created by mobility and the conversion of wealth into cultural power. The Bao family was not among those Huizhou merchant families whose wealth and influence reached the pinnacle at this time. Nonetheless, in Bao Zhihui's case, we witness how a daughter's self-claimed heritage of her natal family's cultural legacies married with the wealth of a merchant family from Jiangxi. With shared cultural aspirations, the Bao and Zhang families re-created the cultural and literary landscapes of Dantu.

3

Traversing the Nine Lands

Hui and She boast their dazzling literary talents.
文光璀璨聚徽歙。

—*Jin Zike*

By the Twenty-Fourth Bridge in twilight,
Green waves and spring waters are again boundless.
二十四橋斜照裏，綠波春水又無邊。

—*He Peifen*

THE EARLIEST CONCEPTION of Jiuzhou or Nine Lands (otherwise translated as Nine Regions) was central to the legendary sage king Yu's (fl. 2100 BCE?) envisioning of a revenue and tribute system covering regions later known as China. In the widely cited chapter "Yugong" (Tribute of Yu) from the Confucian canon *The Book of Documents*, the demarcation of the Nine Lands recognized Yu's great achievements in flood control and was intended to designate, on the basis of the produce from the demarcated lands, what revenue and tribute to collect and by which routes to reach the capital. Descriptions of the geographical features of the lands and the river channels connecting them thus served to integrate the lands into a political order, as captured by the phrase *jiuzhou youtong* (lit., "thus the Nine Lands are unified"). Though exactly what regions constituted the Nine Lands continued to be contested, the concept was accepted in the ensuing ages as a general demarcation of the administrative regions of the state.[1] In a broader sense, the concept also represented efforts to understand the cosmological order, in which China figured only as one of the Nine Lands.[2]

It is beyond the scope of the present discussion to provide an even cursory survey of the geographical and cartographic knowledge springing from the early conception of the Nine Lands, but studies of two later trends help contextualize what I perceive to be a heightened awareness of the Nine Lands in writings examined here. First, for the Huizhou merchants who busily traversed the empire during the late imperial era, geographical knowledge became essential. The merchants' route maps and guides in Yongtao Du's study provided thorough directions that allowed writers and readers alike "to have the territories of the Nine Regions [i.e., the realm] as if it is in the palm of one's hand."[3] Du emphasizes the agency Huizhou merchants exercised in ordering space, particularly by prioritizing commercial needs that did not fully align with the statist definition of the Nine Lands as a political order.[4] My interest lies more in the extent to which mobility and accessible geographical knowledge stimulated the Huizhou merchants' claim to an all-encompassing view of the world they inhabited and traversed. The phrase *zhizhang*, or "[holding in] the palm," was part of a stock expression for knowing something so well one could hold it in one's palm to point out the details (*liaoruo zhizhang*). Moreover, the phrase had been used to refer to maps at least from the Song on. Maps titled *Zhizhang tu* (Pictures [of places] in the palm) and *Xialan zhizhang* (Viewing distant places in the palm) established a parallel between viewing maps and mastering knowledge about the world they delineated.[5]

Second, such knowledge needs to be understood in connection with the unprecedented interest in and development of cartography during the Qing period. Benjamin Elman shows how, on the one hand, Qing cartography gained momentum in proportion to the Qing empire's geographical ambitions. New surveying techniques brought by the Jesuits enhanced accuracy and scale in mapmaking, producing new maps for the Qing rulers to use as political and ideological weapons along the Manchu-Russian frontier, in Central Asia, and in a global context of colonial expansion involving France, the Qing, and Russia.[6] On the other hand, cartography piqued the interest of Qing literati in what Benjamin Elman calls an inward intellectual turn in *kaozheng*, or evidential research, namely, the domestication of new (Jesuit) knowledge for native topics. With their emphasis on rigorous analysis and the painstaking search for evidence, *kaozheng* scholars expected the kind of enhanced accuracy found in mapmaking for scholarly inquiries spanning classicism, geography, and mathematical astronomy. Their empirical focus

FIGURE 6. *DaQing yitong tiandi quantu* (1890?). Courtesy of the Library of Congress, Washington, DC.

also put studies of geography to practical use, such as in land reclamation and hydraulic works.[7]

Perhaps the simplest way to illustrate how these trends—the Huizhou diaspora, the accessible geographical and cartographical knowledge, and the spatial consciousness of the age—crisscrossed in unexpected ways lies in the epigraph to this chapter. An author who inscribed the poetry collection of He Peifen (fl. early 19th c.), a woman poet whose family had triple Huizhou-Guangdong-Yangzhou roots, quoted from the Jiaqing emperor to glorify Huizhou: "Hui and She boast their dazzling literary talents." The line is from a sequence of verses the Jiaqing emperor composed for the *Huangyu tu* (Pictures of the imperial entourage), a collection of maps of the Qing empire commissioned by the Kangxi emperor. In the verses, Jiaqing celebrated the cultural achievements made in the areas Kangxi had incorporated in his map to celebrate the Qing unification of the land.[8]

In the surge of interest in cartography during this time, maps with enhanced accuracy were produced side by side with those in more indigenous forms and for a variety of purposes. The *Sancai yiguan tu* (Maps of the three powers unified; 1722), for example, includes a hybrid sequence of maps emphasizing all at once human-cosmos correspondences, the Qing's universal rule, and what Elman would call the "cosmographs" of heaven, earth, and star charts.[9] For comparison, *DaQing yitong tiandi quantu* (fig. 6) is a late Qing readaptation of the cosmograph of heaven and earth. Though its title points to the Qing's universal rule, it was painted on a fan and thus figured more as an object of connoisseurship than a political assertion.[10] The coexistence of maps of such variety and hybridity, I believe, allowed room for imagination and appropriation. For the author who inscribed Peifen's poetry collection, the Jiaqing emperor's poetic line reflected most of all the Huizhou impact at its peak, and he elaborated on the achievements of "our She" (*wuShe*) in every respect. In particular, he suggested that it was time to recognize female talents from Huizhou.[11] For He Peifen and her family of poets (fl. early 19th c.), imagination and appropriation took other forms.

The He Family: Huizhou, Guangdong, and Yangzhou

Sometime around 1815, the patriarch He Bingtang (ca. 1770–?) took up a post in the salt administration in Yangzhou.[12] During the following two decades, he wrote tirelessly about his gatherings with elites in the city, and his collection of poetic manuscripts documented these gatherings in detail. The title of his collection, *Drafts from the Studio of Paulownia Blossoms* (Tonghua shuwu shicao), captured the nature of these gatherings as, unsurprisingly, efforts at cultural emulation. The phrase "paulownia blossoms" alluded to the Orchid Pavilion tradition. The Tang poet Cui Hu (772–846), for example, associated the time when "birds played with paulownia blossoms" (Niao nong tonghua ri; 鳥弄桐花日) with Orchid Pavilion gatherings.[13]

The phrase at the same time had geographical references not specific to Yangzhou. It was synonymous with a kind of blossom with a dark red color found in the south (*nanzhong tonghua you shenhongse zhe*).[14] Botanical sources identified it as indigenous to Guangdong.[15] As a poetic allusion, the birds associated with paulownia blossoms had geographical references too. Numerous literary and geographical sources identified the bird as the paulownia blossoms phoenix (*tonghua feng*), a tiny bird that fed on the dew of paulownia blossoms in Sichuan (the word *phoenix* indicates how much it was valued by the people in Sichuan).[16] He Peiyu, second daughter to He Bingtang, nonetheless asserted that *paulownia blossoms phoenix* was an alternative name for a kind of bird indigenous to Guangdong (Yuechan Shouxiang niao, yiming Tonghua feng; 粵産收香鳥，亦名桐花鳳).[17] In short, paulownia blossoms, as included in the name for He Bingtang's studio and collection of poetic manuscripts, shed light on the family's cultural and geographical affiliations.

The He family originated from She County in Huizhou. He Bingtang spent nearly three decades in Guangdong. He was about forty-five when he moved to Yangzhou in 1815. He had a son, who died young in Guangdong. His three daughters, Peifen, Peiyu, and Peizhu, were born in Guangdong and continued living there for a few years after he moved to Yangzhou. As a family of poets, He Bingtang and his daughters were active in the elite society of Yangzhou during the 1820s and 1830s.

Guangdong figured as a familiar destination for migrants during this time, despite its geographical location on the southern Qing frontier. The migrants included those who had taken up jobs as subofficials or secretaries in the local administration since the early Qing. In Steven Miles's study, they were among the producers of local Guangdong culture. What Miles calls "a cultural politics of place" played out when the eminent scholar Ruan Yuan transplanted his literary and scholarly practices to the Xuehai Tang Academy in Guangzhou during the 1820s and made it a new scholarly and cultural center in South China. Initially marginalized literati from the Pearl River delta then embraced these practices as a means of securing their position in metropolitan Guangzhou and reshaping the relationship between Guangzhou and its delta hinterland.[18]

Little information survives concerning He Bingtang's family or social status in Guangdong: he may have served in no more than minor posts in the local administration, given that he was assigned to a minor post in the Lianghuai salt administration in Yangzhou in 1815. His life was thus not among the most obvious success stories of Huizhou descendants. Also, the timing of his new assignment seemed quite ironic. The rise of the Xuehai Tang Academy came later, whereas Yangzhou in the early nineteenth century was already reeling from its failing salt administration and failures of flood control that damaged the Grand Canal.[19]

The second epigraph provides a telling example of the cultural inspiration this Huizhou-Guangdong diasporic family found in Yangzhou. The quotation is from a series of poems by He Peifen. The series, and the He family's literary production embedded in wide-ranging elite networks, signaled new waves of cultural emulation centering on Yangzhou even during the waning years of the city's heyday of salt wealth. A newly acquired literary language enabled He Bingtang and his daughters to create their cultural identities retrospectively and use Yangzhou as the nexus connecting imaginaries of space and place arising from their migration and travel history. My analysis of these literary works by the He family must then begin with Yangzhou:

He Bingtang, *Tonghua shuwu shicao*, manuscript, ca. 19th c.
He Peifen, *Lüyunge shichao*, 1841, 9 *juan*
He Peifen, *Lüyunge shiyu*, 1841, 1 *juan*
He Peiyu, *Ouxiangguan shichao*, 1849, 8 *juan*
He Peiyu, *Hongweiguan xueyin gao*, manuscript, ca. 1865.[20]
He Peizhu, *Jinyun xiaocao fu Lihua meng*, manuscript, ca. 19th c., 7 *juan*[21]
He Peizhu, *Hongxiangke xiaocao*, manuscript, ca. 19th c., 2 *juan*
He Peizhu, *Zhuyan lanxue zhai shichao*, ca. 1821–50, 1 *juan*

Moving to Yangzhou

Although later exalted by his daughters as being dedicated to the art of poetry, He Bingtang did not seem to value it much before he moved to Yangzhou. In the *Drafts from the Studio of Paulownia Blossoms* he incorporated exclusively poetic drafts dated after 1815. Shortly after arriving in Yangzhou, he expressed his wish to obtain a small place in local elite society in a couplet: "How many sky-scraping trees are there by the West of Bamboo? Wrens should be allowed to take a sprig on them" (Zhuxi duoshao lingxiao shu? yingxu jiaoliao jie yizhi; 竹西多少淩霄樹，應許鷦鷯借一枝).[22] By this time, writing about the sites and elite gatherings in Yangzhou had become routine. He Bingtang and his daughters soon acquired a poetic language to document their busy social lives at the sites. Thus the significance of Yangzhou to this family of poets lay in providing at once a physical location for their literary activities and a poetic language as a form of elite membership. Tobie Meyer-Fong reveals how, by the Qianlong period, poets already routinely wrote about the pleasures in Yangzhou. Lu Jianzeng's grand lustration festival event in Yangzhou in 1757 was characterized by pose and artifice, rather than the nostalgia that defined Wang Shizhen's cohort of early Qing poets.[23] This routine poetic language created an efficient way for newcomers like the He family to find their "small place" in Yangzhou.

To what extent did women poets such as the He sisters make themselves culturally visible in Yangzhou? Their poetry collections incorporated 271 poetic responses to over fifty women, and 210 to over fifty men, indicating their active participation in cultural events. A recent study examines how the He family maintained their native-place Huizhou ties in Yangzhou while entering key networks in Yangzhou and beyond. Examples included poets or family ties in the salt trade, Yuan Mei's female disciple Zhang Yuzhen (1766–1820) who lived in Yangzhou, the literary communities of Chen Wenshu and Kong Luhua (Peifen and Peiyu managed to become disciples of both Chen and Kong), and Yan Tingzhong's (1795–1864) literary events and projects in emulation of Ruan Yuan.[24] This chapter focuses on their poetic production, particularly how writing about Yangzhou gave rise to a heightened sense of their cultural affiliations and identities.

A few examples suffice to illustrate the recurring pattern in He Bingtang's poetry on Yangzhou. His allusion to the city's history as Wucheng (Weed-Covered City) differed dramatically from similar references in the early Qing poets. Whereas the phrase's connotation of war trauma allowed the early Qing poets to write about the war and devastation of their own time, it suggested to He Bingtang nothing different from the other alternative name of the city, Guangling. He used the names indistinguishably to refer to a flourishing place that even "Emperor Yang, coming from the west, would like to take as his home."[25] He expressed his New Year's wish (dated between 1826 and 1828) to wear his "shoes for seeking fragrance" (*xunfang ji*) and "tread on every site by the city's lakes and hills, and the Twenty-Fourth Bridge."[26] Having done exactly that, he wrote on New Year's Day of 1829, "Since old times the West of Bamboo has been known for beautiful flute tunes. I would not wear waxed shoes to seek fragrance [at the site] too often."[27] He returned to the Weed-Covered City theme sometime after his sixtieth birthday, composing five poems in a series on excursions to five specific sites: Labyrinth (Milou), Cockfight Terrace (Douji tai), Moon Temple (Yueguan), Thunder Pond (Leitang), and Crooked Jade Hook (Yugouxie). His imitation of the nostalgic tone of the early Qing poets in evoking historical references about these sites barely veils his excursions as efforts to "seek fragrance again and revisit the beauty's home."[28] Another poem written around this time serves as a succinct conclusion to his poetic production in celebrating Yangzhou as the "place for one to spend the best possible life."[29]

For his daughters, learning to write meant putting these poetic themes about Yangzhou into new configurations. A typical case was a poetic exchange titled "Spring Willows of the Weed-Covered City, with Rhymes from the 'Autumn Willows' by the Hermit Yuyang [Wang Shizhen]." The combination of the "Weed-Covered City" theme with Wang Shizhen's popular "Autumn Willows" poems moved farther from the city's war memory. Wang had originally composed this poetic sequence in Jinan in Shandong, but the poetic responses he inspired continued well into the years when he served in Yangzhou. The autumn willows became an emblem of Yangzhou—rather than Jinan—as Wang and his emulators wrote Yangzhou into a city of willows. Wang's densely allusive, nostalgic, and ambiguous poetic language was open to multiple interpretations and allowed the early Qing poets to infuse an array of sentiments into the willow image.[30] Here, by converting the autumn willows into spring willows, the He sisters recast Yangzhou as the city of willows continuing to flourish nearly two centuries after Wang's time, in renewed cultural trends. Peifen's lines on the boundless spring waters and waves by the Twenty-Fourth Bridge in twilight are highly evocative of these trends. Peiyu merges the spring willows with Wang's other popular poetic sequences on spring excursions and, in a twist, relates this season for literati gatherings to training daughters to become female talents like Xie Daoyun. Peizhu uses a range of personified images of the spring willows as young women with refreshing beauty. These young women, she clarifies, are not the same as those who accompanied the Sui emperor.[31]

The following selection illustrates in more detail how Peifen and her sisters played this poetic game:

SPRING WILLOWS OF THE WEED-COVERED CITY, WITH RHYMES FROM THE "AUTUMN WILLOWS'" BY THE HERMIT YUYANG [WANG SHIZHEN], COMPOSED WITH MY SISTERS HUANBI [PEIYU] AND ZHIXIANG [PEIZHU] #3

Golden willow branches spread out like a dancing gown,[32]
Level Hill remains what it used to be, but the dancer is different.
Young leaves take on a new hue in the warm breeze,
Light green [on the leaves] starts to even out in drizzles.
Butterflies dream of orioles and flowers in spring,
Partridges fly by [remains of] pavilions from the Six Dynasties.

The jade flute and Qiang reed convey no message,
The forlorn Fanchuan [Du Mu] must have felt disappointed.[33]

燕城春柳用漁洋秋柳韻，同浣碧芷香兩妹作 其三

金縷鬖髿學舞衣，平山如舊昔人非。嫩黃乍染風絲暖，淺碧初勻雨點稀。
三月鶯花蝴蝶夢，六朝臺榭鷓鴣飛。玉簫羌笛無消息，惆悵樊川興已違。

A few hallmarks of Yangzhou and Wang Shizhen can be easily identified in the lines about the dancer or courtesan, Level Hill, and flute tunes. The last couplet echoes Wang's lines: "Listen not, facing wind, to the three tunes on the flute, the anguish and rancor of Jade Pass is finally hard to parry."[34] To make it more explicitly about Yangzhou, Peifen associates the flute tunes with the Tang poet Du Mu, author of the best-known poetic works about Yangzhou. The reference to bygone times of the Six Dynasties similarly indicates an exercise of combining Wang Shizhen's nostalgia with Yangzhou's historical past. However, among the vague references echoing Wang, the willows stand out to suggest a change: their young leaves turning green in the warm spring breeze breathes new life into the Weed-Covered City.

Thus did the He sisters learn poetic composition and write about how they received training from their father.[35] Yangzhou and its sites supplied material for such training. Writing about the sites was often phrased straightforwardly as searching for something to transform into poetry. As the author of an inscription for Peiyu's poetry collection commented, the He sisters "never tire of writing the secluded sites by the West of Bamboo into poetry" (Zhuxi jiachu zhen youjue, xieru shipian bu yanduo; 竹西佳處真幽絕，寫入詩篇不厭多.[36]

Mastery of this poetic language in time allowed the He sisters to move agilely between poetic personas and position themselves in various relations to the sites. Spring excursions provided occasions for them to claim inheritance of the Orchid Pavilion tradition, in the role of literati drinking wine and playing literary games: "Who shall now continue the grand gathering at the Orchid Pavilion? [We] pour a ladle of wine into [the cups floating in] a winding channel" (Lanting shengshi jin sheiji? qushui diliu jiu yipiao; 蘭亭勝事今誰繼，曲水低流酒一瓢).[37] To take an excursion was also to have a full range of sensory experiences of the spring by the Red Bridge bustling with visitors in painted barks.[38] In a more explicitly autobiographical voice, Peifen puts on her beautiful clothes and mingles with groups of beautiful women by the water. The next day she takes yet another excursion in the company of *linji* (ladies from next door).[39] Peiyu, in particular, describes in meticulous detail how she dressed up for the occasion as a beautiful woman herself and gathered with her *nüban* (female friends) to visit Labyrinth and Crooked Jade Hook. These sites had originally been part of the Weed-Covered City theme but were now covered with spring flowers:

AN ACCOUNT OF THE QINGMING FESTIVAL, COPIED FROM MY VERSE COMPOSED DURING THE THIRD LUNAR MONTH

. . .
Labyrinth used to boast its ethereal scenery,
Flowers are now in bloom at this beautiful site.
Spring waves reflect the shadow—
Of the hidden orchid on its slender stem.[40]
Fine willow branches roll down by Crooked Jade Hook,
In drizzles the spring has come to the homes of swallows.
Dressed in fineries, [we] walk along the lanes,[41]
Without knowing that sunset already glows on window screens.
All kinds of earthly flowers compete to bloom,
And show off their beauty throughout the spring.[42]
Pear blossoms alone have a pure style,
Like unadorned beauties smiling in the breeze.
Viewing the blossoms, I hold the sprigs dear to my heart,
I have been old friends with these renowned flowers.[43]

. . . . . . 迷樓舊説神仙境，竝蒂花枝呈麗景。春波照出鏡中人，一朶幽蘭瘦秋影。柳絲低畫玉鈎斜，細雨春生燕子家。拾翠采香行淺徑，不知斜照下牕紗。紛紛凡卉爭春色，吐艷呈嬌過寒食。惟有梨花顏獨清，笑倚東風紅不得。看花我更惜華枝，我與名花本素知。 . . . . . .

Flowers and spring beauty (*chunse*) no doubt evoke courtesan culture. But unlike He Bingtang, who specified the purpose of his excursion to Labyrinth as pleasure seeking—to "revisit the beauty's home"—Peiyu cast hers as an event for women. The affinity she describes with the flowers reminds us of the He sisters' choice of blossoms for their style names, which famously fed into the plot of Peizhu's play, *Dream of Pear Blossoms*.[44] Elements of female companionship and social mingling in poetry by the He sisters also foregrounds a Yangzhou revisited in a light different from that represented by the woman poet Xú Deyin. In Xú's effort to carve out a separate cultural space for herself, she had consigned the "seductive beauties" to a Yangzhou culture increasingly dominated by wealth and pleasure seeking (see chapter 1).[45] She had, moreover, referred to the "ladies from next door" as far from being refined enough to be proper companions: "The ladies from next door cannot tell the joy in mountains and forests [i.e., the hermit's life], no wonder they've missed the beauty of morning mists and sunset glow" (Linji bushi shanlin qu, gufu zhaoyan yu wanxia; 鄰姬不識山林趣，辜負朝煙與晚霞).[46]

Yangzhou and Imaginaries of Space and Place

A poetic language about Yangzhou not only allowed the He family to establish their ties with the city but also stimulated them to retrace their various geographical affiliations. The willows by the Red Bridge and the luminous moon of Yangzhou, for example, functioned as memory triggers for He Bingtang to recall the decades he had spent in Guangdong: "How would I bear looking back and recalling the pearl maidens? [I sojourned in Guangdong for almost thirty years]" (Nakan huishou yi zhuniang? [Yu xiyou Lingbiao ji sanshinian]).[47] During those earlier decades, and even after he moved to Yangzhou, He Bingtang traveled frequently from post to post. His wife's fortieth birthday signaled a moment for him to retrace what he called "a life of duckweeds" and deplore separation from his family: "At the time I served in Yangzhou, whereas my family still stayed in Guangdong."[48] By the late 1820s, he had "traversed the Nine Lands" without fearing the toils of the road, and his footsteps had covered "thousands of mountains" (Budan fengyan lijiuzhou, mangxie tabian wanshanqiu; 不憚風煙歷九州，芒鞋踏遍萬山秋). More precisely, of the eighteen provinces of the empire he had traveled to fourteen.[49] A long journey to Gansu and Sichuan around 1826–28 prompted him to commission a painting of himself in the style of a Daoist wandering freely across these mountainous areas. The journey led him to recall the days when he had sailed in the seas by Guangdong.[50]

The "ancient She" (*guShe*), on the other hand, indicated his place of origin and was used for self-identification in his collection of poetic manuscripts. His daughters in turn incorporated it in their self-identification as women poets:

"He Peifen the Lady Scholar from the ancient She" (GuShe nüshi He Peifen); "He Peiyu from the Ancient She" (GuShe He Peiyu); "He Peizhu the Lady Scholar from the Peak of Celestial Capital [Mount Huang]" (Tiandu nüshi He Peizhu). The prestige attached to the "ancient She" can be attributed to the Qing cartographical projects and their political and cultural implications, but in defining the prominence of places, the He sisters' priorities lay elsewhere.

He Peifen indicated that she had never visited Huizhou even as she spoke admiringly of it as *guyuan* or *yujia* (native home): "My native home, the ancient She, has magnificent mountains and rivers. It is a pity that I have never been there because I was born in Guangdong" (Yujia guShe shanshui jijia, er shengyu Lingnan xiwei yidao; 余家古歙山水極佳，而生於嶺南惜未一到).[51] There was no indication that she, or her sisters, associated with any women poets in Guangdong. It was not until ten years after they moved to Yangzhou that they made the acquaintance of Huang Zhishu (1792–1853), a woman poet from Guangdong who had married into a family in Yangzhou.[52] Peiyu, however, reimagined the sites in Guangdong as "places to search for [material for] poetry" (*xunshi di*) during her teenage years; their difference from sites in Yangzhou made it "impossible to explain them to the young women from the Wu [Jiangsu and Zhejiang]" (Shuoyu Wuniang zong buzhi; 說與吳娘總不知). Wearing her "shoes for seeking fragrance"—a term picked up from He Bingtang's excursions to sites in Yangzhou—she left her footprints frequently at secluded places in Guangdong where, she wrote, "cranes were the first to respond to the lines we [Peiyu and her cousions] composed" (Shicheng tuokou he xiancai; 詩成脫口鶴先猜). Indigenous features pervaded Peiyu's memories of Guangdong, but these features alone did not create a distinct cultural identity. It was the poetic language she acquired in Yangzhou that created an identity retrospectively for her and her cousins as female talents comparable to Xie Daoyun and Bao Linghui (ca. 5th c.).[53] As Stephen Owen suggests, "Beginnings take on their full meaning only retrospectively: you first have to know what it was that was begun."[54] This was as true for writing a literary history as for formulating the history of a family of poets, such as in the present case.

Mount Luofu, a landmark in Guangdong, figured prominently in the He family's memories. According to local histories, Luofu had originally been named Penglai, the legendary land of immortals.[55] He Bingtang drew on his memory of Luofu when describing his travels in Sichuan.[56] For Peiyu, Luofu appeared in her "dreams of seeking immortals." Likewise, she described the other two landmarks—Dongqiao and Xiqiao—as peaks she had visited in her excursions as a "wandering immortal."[57]

MEMORIES OF LINGNAN #1

Orioles learned to chirp as gently as parrots [learned to speak],
The Island for Picking Kingfisher Plumes thrived in the spring sun.[58]
Yongshuh trees enveloped the household of the dragon daughter,
Among the peach blossoms emerged boats of the Dan fishermen.[59]
In the prime of spring sea turtles rose on tides,
In quiet night dragons swam in the sea.
Tunes of the jade flute floated by four hundred peaks,
Seeking immortals, I dreamed of visiting Mount Luofu.[60]

憶嶺南 其一

金衣學語雪衣柔，滿目韶光拾翠洲。榕樹綠圍龍女户，桃花紅出疍人舟。
春深玳瑁乘潮上，夜靜鼋鼉駕海遊。四百峰頭吹玉笛，尋仙曾夢到羅浮。

In this retrospective light, Guangdong furnishes the imagination of this family of poets with the indigenous and the fantastical. Their glorification of Guangdong as an immortal fairyland at the same time places it at the periphery in relation to Yangzhou, which they envision as the cultural center. Memories like these echo Peiyu's highly imaginative verse on Mount Taihua, a landmark in Shaanxi. The verse is a variation on a poetic exercise practiced by the He sisters. As requested by He Bingtang, the sisters inscribed his commissioned painting on his travels in Gansu, Shaanxi, and Sichuan and incorporated Mount Taihua to describe the mountainous features of these areas.[61] Peiyu then rewrote He Bingtang's travels into her own dream about climbing to the top of Mount Taihua. In what she conjures up as "an alternative cosmos divided into heaven and earth" (Bieyou tiandi kai hongmeng; 別有天地開鴻濛), she listens to the female immortal Maonü playing the zither and feels the magic power the melodies exert on the environs. The first stroke on the zither brings forth the ethereal sound of the wind, and the second stroke brings tens of thousands of lotuses into bloom in a legendary jade well. Spaces shift dramatically as the female immortal completes her performance:

From Mount Luofu rises the melody of the "Plum Blossom Tunes,"
With the wind it reaches the female immortal Magu's butterfly skirts.
Looking up and down, I freely traverse the boundless spaces between
 the sea and the sky,
How can this heart of mine find peace in the world of red dust?
In my lingering dream I hear winds shaking phoenix trees—
And take them to be zither tunes.[62]

……羅浮梅華三弄出，吹滿麻姑蝴蜨裙。海闊天空自俯仰，此心肯作紅塵想？夢回風撼碧梧桐，泠泠猶誤琴聲響。

Peiyu instantly crosses the thousands of miles separating Mount Taihua from the signature site of her birthplace, Mount Luofu, for the performance of another female immortal, Magu. What was intended as a poetic exercise on her father's travels in Shaanxi thus turns into a celebration of her own free movement across vast spaces, in the style of a wandering immortal in her dream. Her use of the term *fuyang* reveals in particular how she envisages the cosmic order through a poetic act and consciously places herself in that order. The term *fuyang* (alternatively, *yangfu*, "looking up and down") comes from the divinatory and visual terminology of the *Book of Changes* and had been incorporated into musical and lyric rituals. Thomas Noel retraces the history of a lyric tradition spawned by this term—"a poetics of looking"—which bridged vision with the patterns inherent in the natural world and the human apprehension of cosmological knowledge.[63] Classic works by Cao Zhi (192–232) and Tao Qian (365?–427), for example, illustrate how the poetic act of looking up and down allowed poets to transcend spatial boundaries and perceive the grandeur of the universe.[64] And in later landscape poetry, poets typically used this poetic act to generate interactions between individual sites, panoramic cosmos, and inner emotion.[65] Here, by "looking up and down," Peiyu wrote the signature sites from her family's travel and migration history into her free traverse of and interaction with cosmic space.

Finally, Peizhu—the youngest sister, who was said to be the cleverest at literary games—incorporates in one sweeping view these imagined and real spaces. In her play *Dream of Pear Blossoms*, the female protagonist, Du Lanxian (Peizhu herself), joins the two female immortals Pear Blossom and Lotus Flower (Peifen and Peiyu) in the celestial realm. From the Jade Terrace she identifies sites and places in the land underneath:

(Female characters taking a walk together [in the celestial realm]) (Lanxian) Take a look: here are Ying Island, Jade Tower, Fortified Terrace, and Weak Water. Is that not the Emerald City? This is precisely the Kingdom of Fragrance. [The mountains] Luofu, Taihua, Emei, and Mount Huang look as if I could hold them all in my palm. . . . (Female characters singing together) (To the Melody of *Nan yuanlinhao*) . . . looking to the endless mountains and rivers in the homeland, we walk all across the Jade Terrace. Together we point to the mists rising from the Nine Lands in the distance; together we point to the mists rising from the Nine Lands in the distance.[66]

……（作同行介）你看，這是瀛洲，這是玉宇，這是強臺，這是弱水。那邊可不是碧城？這璧正是香國。羅浮、太華、峨眉、黃山，都在指掌間矣。……（同唱）【南園林好】……望鄉關山連水連，把一座瑤臺行遍。遙共指九州煙，遙共指九州煙。

Plays on words can be identified among these names of places with mixed geographical and mythological references. Ying Island, or Yingzhou, was believed to be one of the three islands where immortals lived: Penglai, Fangzhang, and Yingzhou.[67] Penglai was an alternative name for Mount Luofu. Emerald City or Bicheng referred at once to the land of immortals and the landscapes of Guangdong.[68] It was also the style name of Chen Wenshu, mentor to Peifen and Peiyu. Fortified Terrace, Weak Water, and the Kingdom of Fragrance are way out in the distance, marking the end of the land.[69] Luofu, Taihua, Emei, and Mount Huang are landmarks in the He family's migration and travel history. (Mount Emei was among the sites in Sichuan that He Bingtang had traveled to, and Mount Huang was incorporated into Peizhu's style name.) Together they compose the Nine Lands, or the world as perceived by Peizhu. This world, she seems to indicate, comprises the "endless mountains and rivers in the homeland" that the female characters pointed to from the Jade Terrace. Yangzhou does not stand out as a landmark, but it is where the female protagonist will return when she wakes up from her dream. As the story goes, Lanxian is a cross-dressing lady scholar from Yangzhou who discovered her karmic bonds with the female immortals through her dreams.

In a literal sense in the play, the vantage point from the celestial realm allows the female protagonist to see the world as if she could hold its sites in her palm. The vantage point is evocative of that offered by a map, if we recall the parallel established between viewing maps and mastering knowledge about the world they delineate. A Qing picture, "Palm Verse about the Nine Lands," for example, demonstrates how the world can be "held in one's palm": writing the names of the Nine Lands on the palm is a way to learn the locations of the regions. Maps then follow to delineate the geographical features of these regions, and the sites Peizhu refers to can be identified among them. Pictures like this suggest close links between human apprehension of the world and cartographical production during this time.[70]

Previous scholarly debates have revolved around Lanxian's cross-dressing and ambiguous gender identity.[71] A recent study suggests that the play is a clever literary game that draws on the *Peony Pavilion* tradition and works by Qing women playwrights as if there were two competing storylines. The female protagonist constantly shifts between a storyline that emphasizes amorous feelings and one that emphasizes female bonding, thereby creating shifting effects in her gender identity and bonds with other women.[72] Viewed in light of the play's end, the game is also very much about drawing on the family's literary interest in sites and spaces and opening possibilities for imagining its multiple place affiliations. Here again we find the contrast between Yangzhou as home in reality and other locations as places for roaming and imagination. By contrast, in the late Ming play *Yuanyang meng* (Dream of mandarin ducks)—a crucial source of inspiration for Peizhu's play—the reunion of female characters in the immortal world bears no specific geographical reference other than Mount Zhongnan, with its connotations for Daoist roaming.[73]

Though writing about sites and places had become stereotypical by this time, the He family of poets used literary language for cultural anchoring, writing their family history into broadening views of a cosmic order interwoven with their multiple place affiliations. Yongtao Du emphasizes how the Huizhou merchants' route maps and guides developed their own criteria for defining prominence, which led to "a powerful alternative view of the realm . . . as an interconnected network of commercial venues."[74] In the case of the He family, literary production generated an alternative view of a cosmic order that foregrounded their own place in it. To think in terms of women's enhanced cultural visibility, what greater visibility can be attained than through Peiyu's and Peizhu's spatial claims, namely, their free traverse of and thorough knowledge about that cosmic order?

The He family's literary creativity and expanding networks gave rise to an illusion of Yangzhou in its prime. As historical sources reveal, salt wealth had started drying up, and the area suffered from problems of water control in the early nineteenth century.[75] He Bingtang referred to floods and his duty in disaster relief, in addition to his tireless efforts at networking and celebrating Yangzhou's cultural sites.[76] His contemporary, the much better known poet Gong Zizhen (1792–1841), expressed a sense of the apocalyptical change awaiting the Nine Lands: "All life in China's nine regions depends on the thundering storm, thousands of horses all struck dumb—deplorable indeed."[77] The He sisters' poetry collections came out in 1841–49. Except for a few surviving correspondences, they left no trace about their lives during the military upheavals and cataclysmic social changes characterizing the latter half of the nineteenth century.

4

Rectifying the Native Land and "All under Heaven"

Twelve dragon's guests spread out [on the Huizhou ink cake];
[The calligrapher dips the brush in the ink] and the force of the brushstrokes turns into clouds.
龍賓羅十二，下筆氣成雲。

—*Wang Ying*

First set aside charitable land, and then, charitable schools. That way lineage members will be provided with a stable means of survival and hence have peace of mind and perseverance. This was how the sage ruled All under Heaven.
先立義田以養，後立義學以教，既有恆產，復有恒心，王者治天下之道也。

—*Wang Ying*

THE CRISIS OF the early nineteenth century had been brewing in the very prosperous eighteenth century. The 1790s, Philip Kuhn eloquently argues, were already feeling the consequences of inflation, corruption, and a government increasingly inadequate for its tasks. The population explosion that had borne testimony to the prosperity of the Qianlong reign became a prime mover for further trouble: deforestation driven by overcrowding and ecological disaster resulting from land shortages. The pressure of immigrant farmers in border regions gave rise to interethnic conflict that began to destabilize Qing rule. Much of China's deepening crisis in the first half of the nineteenth century was a domestic situation inherited from the previous century as part of the "flow of its internal history," Kuhn emphasizes. Statecraft thinkers and activists had been grappling with domestic exigencies on many fronts and with questions of the political participation necessary to address them prior to the Opium War and the foreign domination in its aftermath. Mounting tension over the opium trade and foreign challenges in the 1820s and 1830s provided further stimuli for what had already been a prevalent preoccupation with statecraft and political action.[1]

Wang Ying (1781–1842), a woman poet and scholar with Huizhou-Yangzhou roots, wrote in 1838 about a crisis that she sensed to be affecting "All under Heaven" even from the perspective of those "deep in the inner quarters." The immediate context was the Qing opium ban, and she explicitly attributed the crisis to the pernicious effect of the opium trade from overseas (*waiyang*).[2] Nonetheless, the problems she described bore traces of a worsening financial situation she had written about elsewhere concerning her native land, Huizhou, and it was certainly not opium alone that was on her mind. The two chapter epigraphs indicate a time span of two to three decades in which she became aware that her native land, previously enveloped in cultural glory, was in trouble, and that measures for rectifying its trouble were broadly applicable to the crisis besetting "All under Heaven."

The first epigraph is from Wang Ying's poem on a Huizhou ink cake. It dates from the beginning of the nineteenth century (around 1801–6), during the first few years of her marriage to a Yangzhou salt merchant, Cheng Dingtiao (?–1816).[3] A commercial specialty from Huizhou, ink cakes gained popularity among the Qing elites as cultural tokens similar to what Dorothy Ko terms the "craft of *wen* (culture, literature, civility)."[4] Circulated as gifts in the Huizhou merchants' luxurious networks described in Yulian Wu's study, Huizhou ink cakes crossed geographical and cultural boundaries and cemented elite bonding among Huizhou, the Jiangnan heartland, and the Qing court.[5] The "dragon's guests," a culturally loaded term for ink cakes, alluded to a tale about the Tang emperor Xuanzong (685–762), who spotted tiny ink spirits gathering on his ink cake and introducing themselves as the "twelve dragon's guests." The allusion's assimilation into dragon patterns designed for the Qing imperial collections further enhanced the cultural values attached to this commercial product.[6] Wang Ying's poem appeared as she was drawing on various cultural resources to retrieve the renown enveloping Huizhou, her native land and that of her family.

The second epigraph is from an essay Wang Ying authored in response to questions from the Cheng kin regarding lineage welfare. The essay can be grouped into a corpus of writings from 1810–34 (specific dates unavailable), when Wang Ying lived in the Cheng lineage's native village of Huaitang in She County, Huizhou. In her essay, Wang Ying addresses the economic deterioration of the village day by day (Huaitang zhiqiong, rishen yiri). Such deterioration, she warned, foreboded equally ill for those born with kind-heartedness and those deviating from the ancestors' path. What she found particularly appalling was young people's lack of cultivation due to deteriorating means: all abandoned books whether for the purpose of practicing trade or otherwise. When it came to abandoning books, she further cautioned, the deterioration of *fengsu renxin* (local customs and people's hearts) was irrevocable. The essay resonated with other writings that represented her native home as being quite the opposite of the model Confucian place, for which Huizhou had been renowned since the late Ming.[7] Seeking remedies for the economic and moral trouble afflicting her native home enabled a political vision in which a small village provided lessons for a realm as expansive as "All under Heaven."

The term *All under Heaven* in its simplest sense indicated geographically what was demarcated into the Nine Lands,[8] but the terms and their synonyms grew in convoluted relation to a political and cultural order later known as China or a broader realm of which China constituted a part. Mark Lewis and Mei-yu Hsieh trace the etymology of *All under Heaven* to a few early occurrences in the *Book of Odes* and the *Book of Documents* and identify the Warring States period as the time when the term first gained prominence as the name of a political and territorial unit defined by a common set of cultural ideals. The geographical extension of the term into the universal realm in philosophical discussions of this time anticipated a vast multiethnic empire spanning territories of the former Zhou and its neighboring regions. In their analysis, the Han polity figured as the first multiethnic and multicultural empire governed by one supreme ruler and built on state-to-state alliance strategies in east Eurasia. And it was this Han polity that "gave a specific political sense to the vague and moralizing notion of Tianxia [All under Heaven] that had figured in political philosophy."[9]

More pertinent to my discussion here is its conception in the locality-state relationship in the late imperial period, as encapsulated in Wang Yangming's (1472–1529) famous precept, "The grandeur of the 'all-under-Heaven' is a collection of counties and prefectures; if every county and prefecture is put in good order, 'all-under-Heaven' is certainly going to be in good order."[10] There, in less contested ways, the idea signifies the polity (China) composed of localities. Yongtao Du cites Wang Yangming's precept in interpreting the perceived prominence of Huizhou among localities.[11] My discussion concerns the emphasis Wang Yangming placed on good governing (*zhi*) and its implications for studies of statecraft (*jingshi*; lit., "ordering or governing the world") in Wang Ying's time. The experiment Wang Yangming carried out in formulating the ideal local community as a building block for the polity inspired the Qing statecraft reformer Chen Hongmou (1696–1771). William Rowe's study of Chen's reforms of rural leadership and ritual institutions in Jiangxi throws much light on the dynamics among the lineage, the local township (*xiang* or *xiangli*) community, and the Qing polity.[12] This chapter examines how Wang Ying made her foray into statecraft thinking by engaging in lineage affairs and seeking remedies for her native land.

Wang Ying and the Wang Family's "Craft of *Wen*"

Wang Ying has attracted scholarly attention as a salt merchant's wife and a virtuous mother with Huizhou-Yangzhou roots. To a great extent, this book was inspired by her life.[13] She was the daughter of Wang Sunzhi (fl. 18th c.), a Huizhou descendant who was widely connected with Yangzhou elites. She grew up in Yangzhou and received a fine education before marrying the salt merchant Cheng Dingtiao at the age of twenty-one. In 1810 Cheng Dingtiao moved their family back to the Chengs' native home in Huaitang village, where she lived for over two decades. Cheng Dingtiao died of illness in 1815, and she pooled family resources to fund their son Cheng Bao's (1805–60) studies and, later, successful career path as a government official. In 1834 she moved to Cheng Bao's residence in Beijing, where she spent the rest of her life. Thus Wang Ying had primarily three residences: Yangzhou in 1781–1810, Huizhou in 1810–34, and Beijing in 1834–42. Following her death in 1842, Cheng Bao collected her works and had them printed as personal collections of poetry and prose under the titles *Ya'an shuwu shiji* (Collection of poetry from Ya'an's [courtesy name of Wang Ying] studio) and *Ya'an shuwu wenji* (Collection of prose from Ya'an's studio). Cheng Bao also circulated a painting glorifying Wang Ying as a virtuous widow teaching her son by an autumnal lamp in 1828–40 and collected inscriptions by 120 authors, including eminent government officials, elites in the Jiangnan heartland, and the large Huizhou-Yangzhou community. In 1844 Cheng Bao published them as a collection, *Qiudeng kezitu tiyong ji* (Collection of inscriptions for picture of [Wang Ying] teaching her son by an autumnal lamp), along with a collection of writings by over fifty authors in memory of Wang Ying, *Ya'an shuwu zengyan lu* (Writings in honor of Ya'an's studio).[14]

There is some controversy over Wang Sunzhi, Wang Ying's father. The *Yangzhou huafang lu* by Li Dou recorded him as a She County descendant and a multitalented man. He was a calligrapher specializing in the *lishu* (clerical script), a craftsman who made exquisite chime clocks, and a collector of rubbings.[15] There are also indications that the powerful merchant Jiang Chun hosted him as his patron and sent chime clocks he made as gifts to the imperial house.[16] Wang Ying, however, cast her father in a different light:

> My late father Mr. Sunzhi . . . had friends who were all known to be eminent figures of our time. His poetic style descended from Chen Si [Cao Zhi], and in writing classical prose he learned from Han Yu. As a calligrapher, he specialized in the Qin and Han scripts and was also good at emulating Wang Xizhi's style. Words about him as recorded in the *Yangzhou huafanglu* are not entirely true. I once read a volume of his calligraphy works of the "combined script" and composed a poem to record the truth. My husband received instructions from my father and collected rubbings from the Jin era to practice calligraphy.[17]

Wang Ying specifies that what the *Yangzhou huafang lu* highlights as Wang Sunzhi's skill as a craftsman does not accord with what she sees as her father's cultural attributes. She places him instead in the most illustrious lineages of poets, essayists, and calligraphers in Chinese history. The occasion on which she authored this brief biographical sketch was a purchase her husband Cheng Dingtiao made in the spring of 1811 with *zhongzi* (a huge amount of money): the *Dingwuben Lanting*, a highly valued Song dynasty copy of Wang Xizhi's calligraphy masterpiece on the Orchid Pavilion gathering. She writes in addition about her knowledge concerning the Dingwu copy and about her younger brother Wang Jinyuan, who, according to her, had inherited her father's talent.[18] Hence, writing about the purchase became an occasion for displaying at once her natal family's cultural legacy and her husband's cultural identity as a collector and a calligrapher, which he had acquired after receiving instruction from her father. In her poem on the Huizhou ink cake, the calligrapher takes center stage by dipping his brush in the ink and producing masterful brushstrokes. His brushstrokes turn into clouds. It is the calligrapher wielding the brush who establishes connections between what she evokes as the Huizhou luster and what she asserts as her natal family's legacy.

Versatile men like Wang Sunzhi moved agilely among disparate cultural fields and networks.[19] Their world also overlapped increasingly with the literary communities in which female talents were active. The central figure in Yangzhou at this time, Ruan Yuan, was affinal kin to Jiang Chun and referred to Wang Sunzhi as a friend.[20] Wang Ying was connected with the women poets in Ruan Yuan's family through Zhang Yin, who was lauded as the best woman poet in Yangzhou following Xú Deyin. Wang Ying was a student of Zhang Yin and her husband Huang Wenyang around the time when Ruan Yuan invited the couple to teach the brother of his wife, Kong Luhua.[21] Grand Academician Cao Zhenyong (1755–1835) referred to Wang Sunzhi as a good friend and a prodigious writer whom he had known since childhood. Cao Zhenyong was from the most powerful Huizhou lineage during the Qing. The Caos' memorial arch remains a major landmark in their native She County today.[22] Ruan Yuan and Cao Zhenyong together awarded Wang Ying's son Cheng Bao the *jinshi* degree in 1833.[23]

Among Wang Sunzhi's and Ruan Yuan's common ties was Jiang Fan (1761–1831), the esteemed scholar from a Huizhou merchant's family that owned medicine shops in Suzhou and Yangzhou. Jiang Fan's sister Jiang Zhu (1764–1804), a well-studied woman poet, was affiliated with female disciples of Ren Zhaolin (?–1796) and Yuan Mei. As an instructor herself, Jiang Zhu taught over one hundred students in Suzhou.[24] Wang Ying addressed Jiang Fan as a *fuzhi* (friend of her father).[25] Jiang Zhu inscribed Wang Sunzhi's portraits, representing him as a *yiren* and *qishi* (extraordinary person) living by the clouds over the "thirty-six lotus peaks" of Mount Huang, the signature landscape of Huizhou. In one scenario she describes, Wang Sunzhi closely resembles a Daoist immortal living where even the birds cannot reach and capable of taming tigers. In another, the space he inhabits includes splendid halls, flourishing plants symbolic of the longevity of his parents, exquisite banquets and musical performances enjoyed with his kin, and collections of books that free him from earthly concerns. His world, Jiang Zhu suggests, can be distinguished from both the mountains and forests of the recluse and the terraces and pavilions of the official; the joy inherent in this in-between world can only be fully appreciated by an extraordinary person like him (Bushi shanlin yu taige, cizhong lewei shaoren zhi).[26] The fluidity of Wang Sunzhi's identity matches her own. In Jiang Zhu's inscriptions for her self-portraits, she characterizes herself as a "master of illusions" without fixed form (Zishi huanshi wu dingxiang), with the freedom to "play in a sea of ink" to create changing selves (Mohai zongheng ren youxi).[27]

The Cheng Family: Wealth, Trade, and Risk

Few records describe Cheng Dingtiao's family background, but according to Wang Ying, Cheng Dingtiao's father kept a diary from childhood until he was eighty. Thus she located key sources for retrieving both her natal and marital families' legacies. The epilogue she wrote for this diary recaptures, in moral terms, the immense wealth her late father-in-law had amassed:

> My late father-in-law Mr. Fengzhi was known all across our native county for his generosity and moral cultivation. In childhood he started to keep a diary and, from the first day to the last every year, he would reflect on his conduct by noting down at night what he had done during the day. . . . Early on Mr. Fengzhi had managed the salt trade for a Mr. Wu in Fengxi village [She County] and had made a fortune through his diligent work and frugal habits. He opened big stores in Wuchang, Hunan, Yangzhou, and Suzhou, and purchased estates and lands in his native village [Huaitang]. Word spread that he was the richest person in our native county. Later, the Wu family suffered financial loss, and Mr. Fengzhi used his own funds to help them, even using the estates and lands he had purchased to pay their debts. Mr. Wu wept and could not bear to take them. In the end he declined, telling his son and grandson, "Mr. Cheng has never for a single moment deceived or betrayed me. You should always keep in mind his remarkable moral integrity, and never forget [his help]."[28]

As a biographical account of a merchant, the epilogue can be traced to what Qitao Guo describes as the "discursive formation" of Huizhou lineage institutions from the late Ming on, in particular genealogies and biographies that celebrated the merchants' kinship-centered virtues.[29] The epilogue suggests Wang Ying's intention to preserve and publish at least selections from her late father-in-law's diary and thereby publicize his virtues—though for some reason the diary was never published. The epilogue also provides valuable information about the Cheng family history, such as the scale of their business and the moral reputation their fortune generated.

The Tongzhi local gazetteer of Yangzhou includes a brief biography of Wang Ying's husband Cheng Dingtiao as a scholar-turned-merchant who showed a broad-ranging interest in the classics, arithmetic, tactics, and medicine. Their son Cheng Bao died defending Hangzhou against the Taiping aggressions in 1860.[30] The only surviving text by Cheng Dingtiao is a collection of instructions that he addressed to Cheng Bao as well as to his nephews (*Xun zizhi ji*). These instructions were primarily concerned with cultivating the self and important human ties by reflecting on Confucian precepts, such as those by Fan Zhongyan (989–1052), Sima Guang (1019–86), Zhu Xi (1130–1200), Cheng Yi (1033–1107), and Lü Kun (1536–1618). It is clear from a few entries that these instructions date from 1806–9, around the time Cheng Dingtiao practiced the salt trade in Guangzhou (Henan). He mentioned that he had long been away from home (Yu kejiu bugui). Writing admiringly of Wang Ying's erudition, managerial skills, and "acumen and courage like a man's" (Shiyuan er nengduan, linran you zhangfu qi; 識遠而能斷，凜然有丈夫氣), he entrusted her with the supervision of Cheng Bao's studies.[31] Wang Ying collected these instructions after Cheng Dingtiao's death in 1816 and asked Cheng Bao to print them in 1824, at the Shoucai Tang (Hall of Harmonized Colors) in their native village in Huizhou.[32]

While conducting business in Guangzhou, Cheng Dingtiao expressed his pride in skillfully dealing with the salt bandits (*sixiao*): he was able to provide moral guidance to some while dispensing punishment to others, and many gave up their illegal business as a result. This entry figured as one of his instructions and moral legacies to Cheng Bao.[33] Wang Ying's letter to him dated around this time nonetheless reveals the perils he had stepped into:

> Letter to My Husband
>
> Yesterday our servant Cao De returned home and I inquired in detail how the business was running. [From him] I learned that Guangzhou is one of the places from which salt bandits originated, and that these bandits committed all kinds of atrocities. They took people's lives at

will and abducted those serving in the salt administration. You have appeased them by doing them favors and have intimidated them by using force. [It is an admirable achievement that] you have been able to move these bandits to tears while also winning trust and respect from the administration.

Having reflected on the situation, however, I feel deeply disturbed. It falls on worthy officials to bring benefits to others and transform bandits into good people, and it is up to generals to take measures against bandits and let them feel fearful [of the consequences of their atrocities]. You have taken it upon yourself to fulfill the duties of the officials and generals while you are not in position to do so—are you sure what you have done is for the good of all? As Zhuangzi said, the shaman would not overstep his duty to act on behalf of the chef. And as it was sung in old ballads, "You cannot cut open eyes and ears for Hundun; all things follow a natural order."[34] These bandits are vicious by nature and are beyond the transformative power of virtue. You cannot possibly expect favor or force to achieve the desired effect all the time. Once they make trouble again, the administration will likely put the blame on you. The benefits, if any, are disproportionate to the potential responsibilities and dangers involved in these matters, and measures must be taken for unpredictable hazards.

Our son Bao has just entered school and has won high praise from Uncle Yucheng—why not come back home and teach him? You will find it a land of happiness by itself. Please do not "step into thorns wearing torn robes."[35] These words warrant careful deliberation.[36]

Wang Ying's letter paints a vivid picture of the perils in the salt trade during this time as experienced by one of the richest Huizhou merchant families. Salt smuggling was not new to Qing rule, but the problem became ever more severe during the Jiaqing and Daoguang reigns. Legal cases from this time indicate not only its unprecedented rampancy but also the complicated relations among salt smugglers, salt merchants, and the salt administration. The smugglers ranged broadly from those at the bottom of the social strata—vagrants, peasants, and laborers driven to desperation by poverty—to large, organized societies of armed bandits (*xiao*) who posed an increasing threat to Qing rule. Smugglers sometimes included even salt merchants and corrupt salt officials who made illegal profits from the trade. Alliances between various parties were common, and Wang Ying indicates that these alliances did not always achieve desired effects.[37] Cheng Dingtiao, as Wang Ying points out, had put himself in a very delicate relation with the bandits and the administration by making alliances with both parties while using Qing force to intimidate the bandits. Most of all, the actions he took overstepped the authority of officials and generals and were bound to incur blame or even unpredictable hazards. Elsewhere Wang Ying praised Cheng Dingtiao for his heroic spirit (*yingxiong qi*) driven by a sense of justice and his generosity in offering help to others—attributes that had been frequently used on Huizhou merchants since the late Ming.[38] But here she suggests that it is precisely such attributes that have entangled him in danger. A sequence of poems she sent to Cheng Dingtiao during this time reinforce the message of her letter, cautioning in particular against the use of military force and reminding him that "the Confucian gentleman knows how to dodge the blade [of the enemy]" (Junzi bi fengduan). Disaster, she emphasizes, often arises from complacency (Huo mei sheng deyi).[39]

Following Wang Ying's advice, Cheng Dingtiao left the web of interests and conflicts in Guangzhou and returned to Yangzhou in 1809, and to Huizhou in 1810. His business had dwindled even before he left Guangzhou. In 1812 he departed for Yangzhou again, but business did not improve before his sudden death in 1816.[40] It would seem that his earlier actions in Guangzhou had incurred financial consequences as well. Wang Ying wrote about their declining means in terms of Cheng Dingtiao's disdain of wealth and enthusiasm in delivering on promises to friends (*qingcai zhong rannuo*; 輕財重然諾), repeating an admonition from his father that he needed to think of reserves and provision for his old age.[41] Years later, when Cheng Bao won the *juren* degree in 1828, she cast Cheng Dingtiao during his last years as an aging hero running into dead ends precisely because of these admirable moral principles (Qingcai zhongyi sanshi zai, rimu tuqiong kongzishang; 輕財重義三十載，日暮圖窮空自傷). Yangzhou, once their home, only attested to the uncertainties in the life of a sojourner (Piaoling lüji Hanjiang shang; 飄零旅寄邗江上).[42] Biographers of Wang Ying later glossed over their changing family fortunes, pointing to Cheng Dingtiao's generosity in giving away his wealth, which led a family equal to untitled nobility (*sufeng*) to suffer sudden financial loss.[43]

The Native Land: Huaitang

Huaitang (lit., "pond by japonica trees") was the native land that Wang Ying referred to in 1810, when she and her natal kin in Yangzhou tried unsuccessfully to persuade Cheng Dingtiao not to move back to his native village of Huaitang. The village did not necessarily lack the kind of ideal teacher her son had in Yangzhou, she believed, but its rural environment limited his educational opportunities.[44] She wrote about Huaitang again later that year, when the town finally came into sight at the end of her river journey from Yangzhou (Guxiang kan jianjin).[45] In 1818 Wang Ying sent her son Cheng Bao back to Yangzhou to study with her natal kin.[46] She herself continued to live in Huaitang until 1834.

The Cheng lineage had settled in Huaitang during the Song dynasty. The village was located in western She County, surrounded by over thirty other villages in this densely populated area.[47] Ziyang Hill lay a few miles to the southeast, by the Lian River. It was said to be the ancestral place of the founding neo-Confucian philosopher Zhu Xi. Huizhou descendants Cao Wenzhi (1735–98), Bao Zhidao (1743–1801), and Cheng Guangguo (ca. 18th c.) took the initiative to rebuild the ancient Ziyang Academy on the hill during the Qianlong reign. The gate of the academy bore the calligraphy of Cao Wenzhi.[48] Because of Huaitang's mountain vistas, a school at the village was named Sanfeng Jingshe (Academy by Three Peaks).[49]

Huaitang today is known for the many luminaries and moral exemplars associated with it. A Song memorial arch still stands at the village entrance, and a Ming memorial arch stands at its center (fig. 7). Its neighboring villages, Tangyue in the south and Choushu in the north, boast the largest number of memorial arches from the Qing. Those in Tangyue are within walking distance from Huaitang. The surviving memorial arches are only one-tenth of those in Wang Ying's time. As in other parts of Huizhou, the social success of Huaitang residents has been attributed to the propitious location and layout of the village, particularly the nine centripetal roads symbolic of nine dragons guarding the center of the village.[50]

Wang Ying took an active interest in writing about the environment she found herself in, as well as the local customs defining human-place ties in her native land. At the entrance to Huaitang lay Lion Hill (Shishan), and she learned of a magic spring from the hill that cured many diseases (fig. 8).[51] Near its neighbor, Tangyue village, stood Dragon Hill (Longshan). Accord-

FIGURE 7. An early Ming memorial arch in Huaitang village, March 2023. Photo by Fang Liu.

ing to her, a legendary duke from the Tang dynasty was worshipped as a deity on the hill, and his favor extended to all six counties of Huizhou.[52] Close to streams, too, Huaitang had eighteen ponds with large yields of fish. She describes in detail the village customs regarding fishing while cautioning against greed in drying up the ponds to enhance profits.[53] She criticizes an especially popular local custom in Huizhou (Huisu), which she calls *fengjian* (geomancy, the practice of finding auspicious grave sites). Commonly known as *fengshui* (lit., "winds and water"), this popular practice had complicated underpinnings in Qing society and legal practice, due to mounting disputes over land and natural resources driven by economic and demographic change.[54] Wang Ying condemns local geomancy practitioners for leading people away from the correct moral path and dismisses the belief in auspicious grave sites as serving people's selfish ends rather than filial piety.[55]

In an even more critical tone, she associates the geographical features and natural disasters of Huaitang with dragons (*jiao*): "Huizhou is surrounded by thousands of mountains and, when springs flow out of the valleys, dragons often come out and cause disasters. This summer, it rained incessantly for five days, and the dragon water from the neighboring village flooded Huaitang.

FIGURE 8. Lion Hill, Huaitang village, March 2023. Photo by Fang Liu.

At first it rose to the village roads, and in a few days reached the house floor. People who owned towers survived, and those who did not lost their lives."[56] "Dragon" or "dragon water" signifies flooding. Huaitang suffered severe floods in 1821 and 1832, which destroyed Wang Ying's entire collection of calligraphy, books, and ancestors' manuscripts, and caused grave loss of life in the area. She gave sensational accounts of the horror of "dragons" rising from deep valleys (Laojiao qi youhe) and raging across mountains (Qunshan ren tengyue). Taking refuge at the top of her tower, she witnessed how instantly people were engulfed in "dragons' dens."[57] Her repeated use of the dragon terminology draws from the *Book of Rites*, which set summer as the season for "killing dragons and hunting crocodiles" (*fajiao qutuo*)—that is, taking proactive measures against floods.[58] She makes an incisive comment by attributing Huaitang's disasters to the lack of such proactive measures and to the fact that fishermen only desired profits from hunting crocodiles—which made the ancient rites nothing more than empty talk (Guzhi jin xushe; 古制今虛設).[59] It was in Huaitang that Wang Ying spent her most productive years writing on local and family issues.

Locating Family Legacies in Towers and Ancestral Halls

The Wang and Cheng family histories retold thus far, it should be clear, were very much the result of Wang Ying's persistent efforts in excavating and building her family's cultural legacy. A great variety of biographical writings can be found in her collections.[60] Her detailed representation of the virtues of merchants and their wives, as well as their family strategy of alternating between trade and Confucian learning, indicate her active engagement with prevalent discourses on Huizhou lineages' ethics and institutions.[61] Two biographical accounts she authored for her female kin foreground women's acumen and family strategies as crucial to the success of their families.[62] For my present discussion, the key is how she located her family legacies at specific estates and ancestral halls in Huaitang.

In the autumn of 1811, soon after she celebrated her husband's purchase of the Dingwu copy of Wang Xizhi's calligraphy, Wang Ying retrieved from a tower in the Wangs' native home manuscripts left by a Wang ancestor who had died a martyr during the Ming-Qing dynastic transition. The epilogue she authored for a collection of these drafts described how she searched and copied the ancestor's "manuscripts" (*shouze*)— literally, "traces left by the hand," a term commonly used to commemorate what had personally been written down by an ancestor. She specified these manuscripts as the origin of her natal family's virtues, such as loyalty and filial piety.[63] In another instance, the Chengs' private library, Weijing Shuwu (Studio for Tasting the Classics), was a relic of her natal and marital families' combined heritage. She recounts the erection of the library in the voice of the only surviving custodian who had knowledge of the legacy it housed, and who was passing on that knowledge to later generations. In particular, according to her, the library bore the calligraphic inscriptions of her father Wang Sunzhi and a successful Cheng descendant, which had created dazzling effects on the architecture and made quite a sensation in local society (*lunhuan tenghui*; *yishi shengshi*).[64]

In important ways, ancestral halls housed family and lineage heritage and institutionalized the family and lineage's power over the descendants in the form of "ancestral instructions." Wang Ying foregrounds the Shoucai Tang—where she asked Cheng Bao to print Cheng Dingtiao's collection of instructions—as a Cheng ancestral hall bearing important ancestral instructions:

The *Book of Rites* reads, "Sweetness is in harmony with other flavors, and white is in harmony with all colors. Hence it is easy for a man of moral integrity to learn the rites."[65] The sage said, "When painting, apply white the last."[66] This is because white is in harmony with all colors. When my late father-in-law Mr. Xingliu had a new house built, he chose to name its hall Harmonized Colors because he wanted future generations to realize how he had embedded the [moral significance] of white in the hall's name. When you have the opportunity to attain an eminent position, you should devote yourself to serving the state, so you have the "essence of white" in your heart. If such opportunities do not avail themselves, you can accumulate good deeds while living in the countryside, and you would be able to convey a legacy of pure white to later generations. *Those of you who come to the hall should always bear this in mind. . . .*

Laozi said, "Acknowledge the white, but remember the black."[67] Zhuangzi said, "[Look into that closed room,] the empty chamber where brightness is born! Fortune and blessing gather where there is stillness."[68] These were figures of speech they used to express their intent. The descendants of my late father-in-law have only noted how generous he was in helping others, or how actively he used his skills [in practicing trade], *and have therefore misinterpreted his instructions.* They have put their efforts in external things [instead of moral cultivation], falsely pursued the reputation for having hamonized colors, *and missed the whole point about the phrase.* Are they not in essence like the examinees who stick to the surface meaning of an exam question and digress from the preceding texts? *How can they be viewed as having properly followed ancestral instructions*! In the past, Zixia was enlightened about the rites when discussing paintings [with Confucius]. *I would be content if the Cheng descendants harbor no doubts about what I have said here.*[69]

受采堂記

《記》曰："甘受龢，白受采，忠信之人，可以學禮。"聖人所謂"繪事後素"，白受采也。先舅杏六公新屋落成，獨名其堂曰"受采"，意中隱藏一"白"字，以待後世子孫自悟。達而在上，致身報國，則精白乃心也；窮而在下，積善居鄉，則清白傳家也。登斯堂者，常持此心勿失。

. . . . . .

老子云，“知其白，守其黑。”莊子云，“虛室生白，吉祥止止。”此物此志也。為子孫者，徒見樂善好施，才力開展，誤體遺意，致力于外，是鶩“受采”虛名，失“受采”本色。與舉業家拘縛題面、脫略上文神理何異？惡足為善承祖訓邪！昔子夏因繪事一言悟及禮，後子姪輩能不疑余言斯得矣！

Wang Ying repeatedly drew attention to her privileged knowledge and interpretation of the ancestral instructions from her late father-in-law, thus establishing herself as the spokesperson for the Cheng ancestor. Hence, the ancestral hall stood as the Cheng family institution for her to address the descendants. Despite the apparently clichéd messages in the first half of the account, Wang Ying passed on important lessons that revolved around harmony. That is, the Confucian etymology of *white* embedded in the phrase *shoucai* emphasized the ability to create harmony or uniformity among different colors.[70]

As it turns out in the second half of the account, the key message lies in the esoteric connotations of *white*. Wang Ying's quotation from Laozi pairs white and black to represent opposition, echoing lines from the same stanza in the *Daode jing*: "Acknowledge the male, but retain the female" (Zhi qi xiong, shou qi ci) and "Acknowledge honors, but remember humility" (Zhi qi rong, shou qi ru). The stanza originally conveyed a political message about reaching the unity underlying oppositions. By controlling the excess of the dominant male quality and preserving the submissive female quality, those in authority in a state or a family would be able to find a solution to division and opposition, or a way "back to original simplicity, harmony, and unity."[71]

Wang Ying's quotation from Zhuangzi further reveals the danger inherent in such division, or in opposite ways of ruling the state. As the story goes, Yan Hui consulted Confucius on plans for converting the tyrant of Wei and saving the Wei people from chaos. Confucius dismissed Yan Hui's plans as bound to fail, on the basis that rulers, let alone tyrants, always "fought to win the argument." Confucius was blunt: "You will probably go and get yourself executed, that's all." The way to go forward, Confucius suggested, lay in stillness: "You may go and play in his [the ruler's] bird cage, but never be moved by fame. If he listens, then sing; if not, keep still." Such stillness could only be achieved through emptiness of the mind, a state in which one can listen with one's spirit rather than the ears.[72] Annotators of Zhuangzi interpret such stillness as the emptiness and brightness of the mind, comparable to an empty chamber where bright light (whiteness) shines in and brings fortune and blessing. In other words, the story emphasizes practical strategies for avoiding the danger of provoking a tyrant, as well as the sensory delusions likely generated in the process. One should not, for example, be deluded by what one may perceive as fame or success.[73]

From these esoteric allusions Wang Ying goes a step farther to admonish the Cheng descendants against imitating what her late father-in-law was known for, namely, his generosity in helping others and active use of his skill in trade. Such fame and success are external to the Chengs' welfare; she asserts over and again that they have been falsely interpreted as her late father-in-law's legacy. Rather, she concludes, it was the enlightening message from Confucius that her late father-in-law had in mind: creating harmony among differences.

The term *zuxun* (ancestral instructions) as used by Wang Ying was alternatively known as *jiaxun* (household instructions). It had by the mid-Ming period become an established convention for patriarchs to set down instructions for their descendants. As a moral legacy, these instructions served pedagogical and ritual purposes. Composing or reading them out at ancestral halls was itself a ritual act. According to Charlotte Furth, household or ancestral instructions were profoundly shaped by tensions in household economy and partible inheritance—in the sense, for example, "that patriarchs identified moral success as a family with the corporate solidarity of the joint *chia* unit and directed their warnings against those forces that would threaten its continuity before or after their own deaths." Perceived threats such as extravagance and irresponsibility of family members often gave rise to patriarchs' expression of concern in family instructions over the limits of their economic power.[74] Moreover, according to William Rowe, family rules at both household (*jiaxun*) and lineage (*zonggui*) levels emerged with growing frequency during the late imperial period. They became a form of self-policing and collective responsibility within the lineage, interweaving moral transformation (*hua*) with behavioral discipline, family and ancestral ritual, and what was expected to be ritually stimulated affection among kin.[75] Tensions and self-policing were very much part of what underlay Wang Ying's reinterpretation of ancestral instructions. Her writings about two other ancestral halls are illuminating.

The Benren Tang (Hall of the Roots of Benevolence) was the ancestral hall for the lineage branch from which Cheng Dingtiao's family descended. In "Da Beren Tang zuren ji" (Account of how I responded to my kin from the Hall of the Roots of Benevolence), Wang Ying specifies where this branch fits in the Cheng lineage through a brief lineage history since the Song period (fig. 9).[76] The Cheng lineage has quite a number of ancestral halls, she writes. Each of the four large branches (Zhengfu, Jiufu, Shangfu, and Xiafu) has its overall ancestral hall (*zongci*) and branch ancestral halls (*zhici*). The issue is first of all with the Benren branch's overall ancestral hall, namely the Benren Tang.

The name Benren, according to Wang Ying, is in itself an explicit ancestral instruction on the importance of adhering to the "roots of benevolence." But wealth has led the Cheng descendants away from their roots:

> The Hall of the Roots of Benevolence was wealthier than all other ancestral halls of the Cheng lineage branches, and every year, its harvests of rice and grain were several times greater than those of the other ancestral halls. The hall established ten rules, stating in general that our ancestors went through much hardship to earn the hall properties and that descendants should remain frugal for their long-term benefit. It has by now happened that fewer experienced lineage members can be found to manage the properties. [The current managers] have pawned lands without proper reason, and have stolen from the collective wealth for their own private gain. The hall has in recent years lost much of its wealth and is suffering financial straits.[77]
>
> ......惟本仁堂富甲三府，每登穀與麥 ，勝它祠數倍。堂設規條十則，大概謂祖宗創業艱難，後人宜節用為長久計。伺以老成漸少，經理失人，無故質田，假公肥己。近年不但不富，且貧矣。

Moreover, financial problems have alienated kin. Wang Ying goes on to describe how disputes have arisen between her and the other Cheng descendants over some funds that her son Cheng Bao was eligible to receive from the hall as a reward for his success in civil service examinations. She clarifies to inquiring lineage members that she has not received and would never request the funds. Somewhat ambivalently, she also clarifies that it has long been a rule set by the hall to reward successful examinees in the lineage branch. In any case, her clarifications fail to prevent the troublemakers

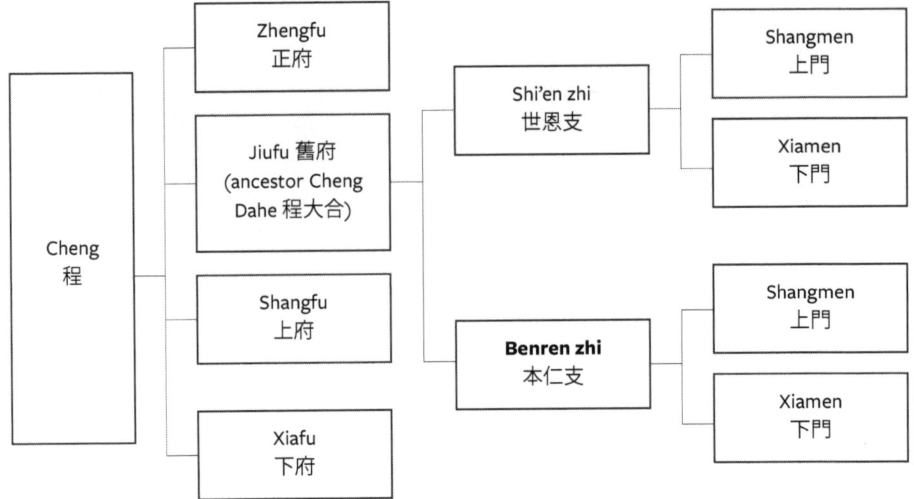

FIGURE 9. The Cheng lineage in Huaitang in the nineteenth century. The highlighted Benren branch (branch of the "roots of benevolence") is the lineage branch from which Cheng Dingtiao's family descended.

(*haoshizhe*) from spreading rumors, first about her supposed plans to use the funds for celebration and commemoration, and then about her hypocrisy in declining the funds. In conclusion, Wang Ying offers benevolence as a solution to the disputes. In the same way that benevolence helps the sage rule "All under Heaven," she tells a lineage member, benevolence would ensure the lineage's prosperity over the long term.[78] Just as Confucius offered all-embracing goodwill (benevolence) as the solution to problems in human relations, Wang Ying hoped that such goodwill would be able to resolve disputes among kin, the key human relations envisioned by Confucius.[79]

The Leshan Tang (Hall of Taking Delight in Kindness) was an ancestral hall (*zhici*) for the Benren branch, and Wang Ying authored an account to record its renovation.[80] In this case, she suggests, the hall became itself an object of dispute between the Cheng kin and those she calls the scoundrels (*wulai*) in the village. According to her, funds for constructing the hall originally came from a court award for an ancestor, Cheng Tan. The name Leshan was intended to encourage him to lead people in his native county onto the path of kindness. As inheritable property, the hall then came into the ownership of her affinal uncles Cheng Dingtai and Cheng Ding'an, but scoundrels suddenly took it by force (*duowei jiyou*). Her eldest nephew, Cheng Xuepu, in turn drove out the scoundrels, while paying a sum of money to redeem ownership. As he was about to launch a renovation project on the hall, he came to Wang Ying and told her about the ancestral instructions left by Cheng Tan:

> "Do you, my aunt, know the origin of the name Leshan? I have learned that Mr. [Cheng] Tan left the following instructions: 'If I accumulate money, my descendants may not be able to preserve it all; if I accumulate books, my descendants may not be able to read them all. What I have in my heart for my own happiness and yet would also like to share with you all is kindness. When construction is completed, I shall name the hall Taking Delight in Kindness. Would the later generations share my wish? Would they be able to take delight in kindness? I do not know for certain, but I shall remain true to what I take delight in. If I take delight in it, and if they all are able to take delight in it too, it would not be an exaggeration to say that the hall will last for a hundred generations!'"[81]

> ……"叔母知'樂善'所由名乎？姪聞潭公遺訓有云，'吾積金，子孫不盡能守也；吾積書，子孫不盡能讀也。吾心有獨樂、欲與女曹共之者，善也。堂既成，即名'樂善'。女曹豈有意邪？女曹能樂與不？吾不知然而吾固樂之。吾樂之，女曹亦樂之，雖謂斯堂百世常存可也！'"

The much-repeated character *le*, "happiness" or "what one takes delight in," is a philosophical and literary term with rich connotations. I have translated the phrase *xinyou dule* as "what I have in my heart for my own happiness." It literally means "solitary happiness," as opposed to the idea of shared or sociable happiness promoted by Mencius as a benevolent way of ruling the state. Stephen Owen's penetrating analysis of the Song literary account "Dule yuan ji" (Account of my solitary happiness garden) by Sima Guang, revisits solitary happiness in the changing social world of the Song, which was permeated by commercial activities. Sima Guang's use of the phrase in naming his garden "flew in the face of Mengzi's 'shared happiness,'" with his unabashed celebration of private property, legal ownership, and freedom from state interference. In turn this famously self-promoting account brought Sima Guang paying visitors every year, allowing him to capitalize his happiness.[82] In the story Cheng Xuepu recounted for Wang Ying, what the ancestor Cheng Tan had taken delight in was at once solitary and shared with all Cheng descendants. It resonated with the Mencius tradition of benevolence, or kindness, but it also drew unmistakable attention to the question of ownership—namely, the ownership of the hall as a piece of inheritable property, just like the money and books that Cheng Tan could alternatively have accumulated and passed on to his descendants.

In her response to Cheng Xuepu, Wang Ying elaborates on the redemptive effect kindness would have on families undergoing the swift changes of her time. A man of humble means might become suddenly successful and boast of his power and wealth in his native county, but his household might collapse soon after he dies. It is adherence to kindness that induces blessing from Heaven; in this case, Heaven would not take away what it has bestowed on a family, at least not until after several generations. The key lies primarily in how one abides by the heavenly way (*tiandao*) in resolving conflict: "To treat with leniency those who have beguiled me, and to treat with honesty those who have calculated on gain [from me]" (Renyi toubao, wuyi kuanhou; renyi jingke, wuyi hunpu; 人以婾薄，吾以寬厚；人以精刻，吾以渾樸)."[83] Once people see the effects of this heavenly way, they will realize that kindness is truly something one should take delight in. The Cheng descendants would feel enlightened about the heavenly way upon entering the hall and spontaneously feel affection for their kin. It follows, Wang Ying concludes, that Cheng Xuepu's renovation project would rightly induce Heaven's blessing.[84]

The two accounts are essentially about financial disputes, one within the Cheng lineage and the other between the Cheng kin and other villagers. They echo Cheng Dingtiao's collection of instructions concerning the importance of maintaining cardinal ties and avoiding disputes.[85] And yet, as is clear from their rich allusions and details, Wang Ying's accounts represent disputes in a much more concrete context. Disputes described in the second account are severe: they involve the use of force and fighting over ownership of the hall. Cheng Xuepu's renovation project is itself a reassertion of ownership after he drives out the scoundrels (suggesting that he, too, resorts to force). The ambiguity of the actual solution in both cases indicates that the disputes are very much ongoing.

As Joseph McDermott richly demonstrates, internecine or intralineage conflicts over properties had plagued Huizhou since the mid-Ming. Theft and fighting had been rampant, and lawsuits had revealed problems of all kinds—disputes over money, land, graves, etiquette, family succession, and so on—which gave rise to Huizhou's "reputation for being a prefecture 'hard to govern.'"[86] Much of the trouble stemmed from the inadequacy of lineage institutions for coping with challenges arising from increasing commercial activity. Conflicts also arose from the differing goals for which the institutions had been set up, such as equitable management of resources against powerful branches' assertion of privileges.[87] As a key lineage institution, the ancestral hall had assumed ritual, social, educational, and economic roles, including serving as a lineage law court for resolving disputes. Setting up or posting rules of the ancestral hall, or *cigui*, was also an effective means of shaming misbehaving members. Financially, the ancestral hall figured as a form of collective property. While it was expected to strengthen collective activities and secure proper order in the lineage, the ancestral hall in effect fell short of reducing disagreement among members or branches. It might even create further division, when, for example, a group of lineage members chose to construct a new ancestral hall to dominate lineage governance and resources. Joseph McDermott astutely delineates the irony in the construction of ancestral halls: "No more devout way could be found to countermand the call for ancestral respect than to build another hall in honor of yet another venerable ancestor."[88]

As proposed solutions to disputes, benevolence and kindness were far from being empty or idealistic terms. Patricia Ebrey eloquently shows that the Confucian ideal of family was an amalgam of strains of thought that provided a unifying vocabulary and strategies for dealing with realities involving property and inheritance issues. Ebrey examines primarily the Song concept of patriline in complex relationship with what she calls the "ritual or *tsung* orientation" (the patrilineal descent line as described in the Confucian classics) and the "*chia* orientation" (the family as a property-owning group). And she echoes Charlotte Furth in identifying the continuities from the Song to the ensuing ages, with respect to how the Ming-Qing authors of family instructions invoked ritual ideals in advancing economy-based and *chia*-oriented aims.[89]

It was common for lineages of this time to incorporate terms suggestive of these ritual ideals into the names of their ancestral halls, but interpreted as Wang Ying did, benevolence and kindness indicated key lineage institutions targeting disputes, thus providing a form of institutional endorsement of what she represented about the disputes. The point here is not so much whether lineage institutions resolved disputes or created further division as how Wang Ying engaged with, and indeed reshaped, these institutions when settling back in her native land.

The Shoucai Tang figured precisely as one of these lineage institutions. As Wang Ying assiduously explained, the hidden message it bore was to caution the Cheng descendants against division and dispute. Even more importantly, the political terminology she drew on about rulers and the heavenly way can reveal much about how she envisioned local governance in relation to the rule of the state—or statecraft.

Local Mechanisms of Statecraft

Financial disputes were embedded in the broadening crisis of the early nineteenth century. In Huaitang, the problem struck Wang Ying primarily as young people's loss of opportunity for education. Social and geographical mobility now seemed to give way to stagnation, which she phrases as "all trapped in difficult situations" (*jiewei jingkun*; 皆爲境困).[90] While the local gazetteers continued to celebrate Huizhou's prosperity and reputation for integrity or pure-heartedness (*renxin zhihou, fengsu zhichun*; 人心之厚，風俗之醇),[91] Wang Ying found local customs to be in appalling deterioration. She identified gambling, feuds, and opium abuse as the major social evils afflicting Huaitang. Young people were being led astray by gangs (*zhu feilei*) and ignored all propriety in appearance and conduct. All day long they engaged in boisterous gatherings and scared the "Confucian gentlemen" away.[92] It was no doubt in view of these bleak realities of rural life that Wang Ying decided in 1818 to send her son Cheng Bao back to Yangzhou to receive education from her natal kin.

Wang Ying offered several mechanisms for rectifying local customs. At the beginning of her essay "She yitian yixue yi" (Discussion on setting up charitable land and school), she invokes the Song statesman Fan Zhongyan's benevolent tradition of setting up charitable land as a lineage survival strategy. Here again, benevolence suggests activist and practical measures rather than an empty Confucian ideal. In answer to a nephew's inquiry regarding lineage welfare, she advises that charitable land needs to be set up as the first priority because it would provide the material means for survival and hence the material basis for moral cultivation. Together with a charitable school—which can then be set up too—it paves the "sage's way of ruling all under Heaven" (*wangzhe zhi Tianxia zhidao*; 王者治天下之道).[93]

The term *hengchan* (lit., "lasting properties"), which Wang Ying uses to refer to charitable land, comes from the *Mencius*. By Wang Ying's time, the term had taken on complicated meanings in political economy, during which process charitable land had developed into a key lineage institution. The seventeenth-century family instructions *Hengchan suoyan* (Remarks on real estate) by Zhang Ying (1638–1708) provides important background to landholding as a long-term family strategy. Hilary Beattie situates Zhang Ying's work in the history of the formation of the Chinese elite and their kinship ties and institutions. Fan Zhongyan was a key figure who instituted charitable land as a form of inalienable trust. Ostensibly intended to provide permanent livelihood for his family, Fan's initiative fell within the Song educated elites' attempt to strengthen their social foundations by recalling the power of the Tang aristocratic clans. Concentration of ownership, commercial expansion, and population growth were among the major factors in the ensuing ages that changed the relations between landowners and the labor force, in turn generating risks for landholding. Zhang Ying's work was a response to these profound changes, as well as to the riots and revolts that had come with them. Risks notwithstanding, he insisted that landed trust was basic to maintaining elite status and family and social order.[94]

In Huizhou, setting up charitable land was among the merchant virtues celebrated for fostering kinship values, as discussed by Qitao Guo.[95] Yulian Wu's study of material culture in Huizhou during the mid-Qing describes how charitable land became part of the Huizhou merchants' material and public display of wealth, Confucian morality, and shared elite interests.[96] Thus what Wang Ying invoked as a timely relief to Huaitang's problems had developed into a key lineage institution that served multiple needs of rural life in Huizhou and the interaction between rural and urban development. Restoring this institution had important economic implications, she suggested. Along with the means of moral transformation offered by charitable schools, charitable land provided mechanisms for reducing social conflict—a topic that dominated her writing from this time.[97]

Literary societies (*wenhui*) were another important local mechanism. Despite the apparently narrow reference to literary gatherings, literary societies functioned as a social, ritual, economic, educational, and recreational organization all at once. Though founded primarily on kinship ties, such societies had expanded to all levels of Huizhou society and played an active role in lineage and local governance. Recent studies have found a rich array of sources attesting to their contribution to inculcating moral and cultural values in Huizhou throughout the Qing era.[98] According to Wang Ying, the literary society of Huaitang had long been abandoned, and it was urgent to restore its function in transforming people's conduct and maintaining social order. She listed the names of over twenty Cheng descendants who had taken the initiative to reestablish the literary society in Huaitang, as well as local elites who followed fashion and enthusiastically praised its effect on local customs. The gangs, she wrote, dissipated almost instantly in awe of a *wen* culture brought back by the literary society. The young people would soon know how to behave in a proper manner when passing by temples, for example. She concluded, "When it comes to the decline of customs, who can say that Confucian gentlemen lack the means of shaming [misbehaving people]?" (Shulun fengsu zhibi, shidafu duwu kuizhi zhishu hu; 孰論風俗之敝，士大夫獨無愧之之術乎？) [99]

These essays served an explicit purpose: to convey moral and behavioral instructions to the entire Cheng lineage (*yu tongzuren gong zhizhi*; 與通族人共志之).[100] Wang Ying was taking the lead in inculcating in lineage members the values she deemed essential to the lineage's survival and welfare. From the way she described how the Cheng kin sought her advice, it can also be surmised that she had the lineage's support. In 1834, upon her departure for the capital, she once again gave instructions to some Cheng descendants and emphasized the importance of holding on to ancestral virtues rather than allowing conflict to alienate the cohabiting generations.[101]

Contracts and legal case records discovered in Huizhou paint a dynamic picture of the practices concerning women's economic status in their families during this time. A Feng emphasizes that widowed mothers often played a dominant role in household division and in transactions regarding land and properties.[102] The implications of such a role for governance of the lineage and local community are crucial. The character *shu* ("skill," "method," or "means"), as used in Wang Ying's essay, refers to the practical skills of governance, including in particular those aimed at reducing social conflict. Problems arising from the tension between the local and the state, exacerbated by the economic crisis of the early nineteenth century, stimulated tremendous interest in skills of *jingshi* ("statecraft"; "ordering or governing the world"). Endeavors of *jingshi* thinkers and reformers crystalized in the 1826 publication *Huangchao jingshi wenbian* (Compendium of statecraft writings from the reigning dynasty).[103] In writings on ancestral rites, local customs, political acumen and tactics, and medicine, Wang Ying echoed many of the themes incorporated in the *jingshi* writings.[104] She focused on developing a political vision through local mechanisms, thereby combining lineage and local governance into the "sage's way of ruling all under heaven."

A central text in this respect is "Juguan shize" (Ten rules for officialdom; 1836), which Wang Ying completed two years after arriving in the capital, where her son Cheng Bao served on the Board of Works. (Cheng Bao earned the *jinshi* degree and was assigned to the Board of Works in 1833; Wang Ying went to live with him in 1834.)[105] In the tone of a mother dispensing moral advice, she lays down ten priority areas for an official to address:

1. People's livelihood: An official must be committed to helping people earn lasting property (*hengchan*), because those driven to desperation are likely to become bandits. He should formulate good policies to facilitate developments in agriculture and sericulture, and invest whenever he can in infrastructure such as canals and river works.
2. Policymaking and implementation in local society (*xiangli*): Any policy that may inconvenience the people should be removed or implemented with discretion. Severe punishment should be put in place for misconduct such as gambling, visiting prostitutes, opium abuse, violent feuds, and bullying. A benevolent official should be able to tell toward whom to extend his benevolence, and whom to punish relentlessly so that minor misconduct does not grow into irremediable social evils.
3. Lawsuits and criminal cases in local society: An official must review legal cases in person to prevent the secretaries from exploiting them for personal profit. He should also resolve lawsuits in a diligent and efficient manner, given how fast they accumulate. Interviewing all parties involved is the best way to discover the truth. When it comes to criminal cases, once he pins down the major culprits, he should release the rest of those involved to avoid unjust consequences for them. This is because a household entangled in these cases can easily go bankrupt and an official needs to attend to the welfare of the local community (*wei difang pei yuanqi*; 為地方培元氣) on that account. In the case of a capital crime, he should act fast in arresting the culprit and preserving evidence.
4. Local elites: When assuming a county or prefectural post, it is of paramount importance for an official to familiarize himself with local affairs by establishing ties with local elites. To begin with, he can arrange a gathering and invite them to compose essays on local governance, rewarding those who write frankly about flawed policies or people who cause

harm to the local community. He should model himself on Zhuge Liang (181–234), who knew how to maximize benefit for the people by collecting ideas and useful information. If he remains well informed, those affecting justice and dominating the local community (*xiangqu*) would not dare to approach and mislead him.

5. Mechanisms for local governance: The *baojia* system in essence relies on the use of force and coercion, and is therefore inadequate for the moral transformation of the *xiang* community. By contrast, the literary society resolves disputes by ritual and moral means. It provides rightful leadership in its close resemblance to ancient libation rites (*xiangyin*). A worthy leader of the literary society, selected from those respected for their scholarship and integrity in the *xiang* communities, can resolve disputes by implementing the community pact (*xiangyue*). In the cases of small issues (i.e., those people routinely encounter), a literary society can provide solutions on its own, without having the parties involved go to court. Twice a month the literary society leader should convey the imperial instructions to the community for the moral cultivation of the unenlightened, and local customs will soon improve.
6. Education: Transformation of local customs depends on education. It is the responsibility of an official serving in a local post to pool funds for charity schools and select those distinguished by their studies for academies. Ruan Yuan is exemplary in this respect: his academies, Exegesis of the Classics (Gujing Jingshe) in Zhejiang and Sea of Learning (Xuehai Tang) in Guangdong, have played central roles in rejuvenating *wen* culture and nurturing talent in the two provinces. Ruan Yuan's example can be applied on smaller scales in counties and prefectures to nurture local talent. Once the evil paths of the misbehaving gentry (*diaosheng liejin*) are blocked, they will not dare interfere with local governance.
7. Relation to local people: An official needs to stay close to the people so that no crooked person in the local administration will be able to ruin that relation. The best ways to achieve that purpose include encouraging good deeds and charities; rewarding those who are generous in helping others; dispensing punishment for those who leave their kin in abject poverty; applying for court awards on behalf of moral exemplars and incorporating them into local gazetteers. He should also issue government notice to encourage frugal habits and ban extravagant customs.

8. Honesty: It is crucial that an official remain honest both with the emperor and with the people. He should abide by the principle set by Zhuge Liang: "Ruling the world relies on grand moral principles, rather than small favors [with which to ingratiate others]." For example, in policy-making and construction planning, he should think of what is genuinely good for the people and avoid "ornamenting outside appearances while leaving the inside void."
9. Loyalty and empathy: An official who makes every effort to benefit the people has fulfilled the principle of loyalty. In matters that may go against existing regulations but that are nonetheless good for the people—especially when it comes to matters of life or death—he should still go to great lengths to protect the people. An official who puts himself in the shoes of others has fulfilled the principle of empathy. He should always prioritize what is in the best interests of the people, or what would be feasible for his successors, over what is convenient for himself.
10. Integrity: A good official never indulges in extravagance or allows in his administrative offices any viewing of opera, gambling, or opium abuse. He would never resort to corrupt means even when confronted with extreme paucity of resources. If he is concerned exclusively with how to benefit the local community and never spends time ingratiating himself with the powerful, his superior would find no better candidate than him to develop grand schemes.[106]

As it is with statecraft writers of this time, the influence of the statecraft reformer and Jiangxi governor Chen Hongmou is prominent in Wang Ying's essay. William Rowe's study of Chen's experiment in Jiangxi focuses on how Chen aimed at building a local community at the subcounty level of the *xiang* (township). By finding respectable rural leadership, particularly expanding the authority of lineage heads in taking disciplinary measures, Chen hoped to rein in troublesome local elites and reduce rampant lineage misconduct and the perceived litigation explosion.[107] Wang Ying's vision of the *xiang*, alternatively called the *xiangli* or *xiangqu* community, resonates with Chen's experiment in her emphasis on finding the rightful rural leadership rather than relying on the *baojia* system to restore rites, implement the community compact, and reduce conflict and litigation. The prescription for mechanisms of local governance is typical in this respect. Other parallels can be drawn regarding the importance of strengthening local communities (in her words, *wei difang pei yuanqi*) as building blocks for the polity; warnings against misbehaving local elites or those dominating the local community; and invocation of ritual and moral principles in formulating practical strategies of governance.[108]

As Rowe points out, however, Chen imagined the local community from a statist perspective. That is, Chen's primary concern was local autonomy that grew increasingly out of state control, as attested to by large corporate kinship associations and lineage misconduct such as violent feuds (*xiedou*) or abuse of collective properties. Co-opting lineage leaders as state functionaries, Chen hoped, would enable him to seamlessly integrate the activity and power of lineage organization into the *xiang* community and hence enhance state control.[109]

Wang Ying demonstrates different concerns in engaging with statecraft thinking. Her essay draws explicitly from her personal experience in Huaitang. The issue for her is first of all dysfunctional lineage and local institutions: recall her incisive comments on flood control, greed, geomancy, disputes, and economic and moral decline. Envisioning mechanisms for local governance is a way to address the problems she routinely encounters in her native land. Indeed, the very first paragraph focuses on property (*hengchan*) as the material basis for survival and moral cultivation, echoing her remedy to Huaitang's deteriorating economy and customs. Rural leadership assumed by literary societies, as posited in item 5, also highlights her version of *jingshi* thinking on implementing community pacts. Such leadership is meant not so much to tighten state control over local communities as to deal with the increasing complexity of rural society. As she repeatedly emphasizes, it is from the perspective of local people that she lays out local mechanisms for governance. It follows, then, that an official's responsibility is to benefit the local (*youyi difang*) rather than ingratiating himself with his superior.[110] Moreover, as shown in item 6, she envisions local governance in transregional contexts. As a Huizhou native growing up in Yangzhou and affiliated with Ruan Yuan's networks, she invokes Ruan's key achievements in transforming elite cultures in Zhejiang and Guangdong as being applicable to local communities elsewhere. She suggests, "Why not try these [i.e., Ruan's academies and cultural projects] on a smaller scale in a prefecture or a county?" (Hebuke xiaoshizhi yijun yiyi hu? 何不可小試之一郡一邑邪？)[111]

I have referred to the idea of local communities as building blocks for the state, embodied in Wang Yangming's famous precept, "The grandeur of the 'all-under-Heaven' is a collection of counties and prefectures; if every county and prefecture is put in good order, 'all-under-Heaven' is certainly going to be in good order."[112] It was Wang Yangming who established the *xiangyue* or community covenant in Jiangxi to fill in the local power vacuum left by the declining tax and labor service (*lijia*) system. With his emphasis on group effort in resolving disputes and hence reducing litigation, Wang Yangming and his followers hoped to use the covenant to create the ideal community for people to regulate themselves, ensure harmony and security, and increase communal solidarity. By this means they continued efforts from the Song onward to "insert an intermediary step in the order of cultivation—individual, family, state, empire—by inserting the local community between family and state."[113]

According to Yongtao Du, the appeal of Wang Yangming's idea of local community for Huizhou descendants lay primarily in its creation of a spatial order in which Huizhou—as the model Confucian place—occupied a distinct place. On the one hand, every local place was believed to contain the same microcosmic social and moral order of "All under Heaven"; on the other, a place could distinguish itself from other places by standards shared by all.[114] For Wang Ying, by contrast, the appeal lay not in bolstering her native place, but rather in drawing lessons from it to develop mechanisms and practical strategies that amounted to the "sage's way of ruling all under Heaven." Precisely because every county and prefecture figured as a microcosmic locality for All under Heaven, rectifying local community and customs enabled her political vision of how to rule the state.

With challenges from overseas (*waiyang*), the locality-state relationship took on new dynamics in Wang Ying's writing. Her 1838 essay on the opium ban starts with a veiled criticism of the Daoguang emperor: despite the emperor's conscientiousness in ruling the state and setting a good example of frugality for "All under Heaven" (*wei Tianxia xian*; 為天下先), the poverty afflicting the people of "All under Heaven" only worsens day by day (*Tianxia minqiong, rishen yiri*; 天下民窮，日甚一日).[115] The situation is comparable to that in her native place:

> The general trend across All under Heaven is not something that those staying quietly in the inner quarters can have a thorough knowledge of. *And yet, to think in terms of my native place She County*: it comprises four townships, among them the west township, which used to be known as

a trove of wealth. Since opium abuse became rampant, ignorant descendants there have turned into addicts, and all households that used to live in abundance have encountered trouble for this reason. Sometimes kinsmen in the same lineage use force against each other, and relatives impose external matters frequently [on the lineage members]. As a consequence, they become poor despite the wealth their ancestors accumulated by hard work and frugal habits, and still they do not know to take the blame for their own conduct. I have no idea if there's an end to the pernicious consequences they are suffering![116]

. . . . . . 天下大勢，非靜處閨中所能周悉。但以吾歙論，地分四鄉， 西鄉舊稱富藪。自鴉片煙盛行，遂有無知子弟，逐漸吸食，凡家道素豐，莫不因此滋事。或同族骨肉挾制，或親戚外務頻加，令祖父瘽儉所積富厚及身無故變爲窮人，仍復不自痛懲，未知受害伊胡底也!

Thus her native place (*wuShe*; "our She County") as a microcosm of the state had endowed her local experience—and, in humble terms, her limited views as a woman—with broader relevance. The new imperial edict on an opium ban, she asserts, is bound to benefit All under Heaven and her native place alike (*Tianxia xingshen, wuShe xingshen*; 天下幸甚，吾歙幸甚).[117] The point here is not whether the Qing state's failure to deal with the poverty perceived by Wang Ying arose from internal or external factors. As Philip Kuhn has shown, it was a domestic crisis compounded by foreign challenges that was shaking Qing rule in the early nineteenth century.[118] Rather, at issue here is how both locality and state become subsumed into more expansive visions of the world. In the above quotation, Tianxia and *wuShe* remain largely relevant to Qing rule. Nevertheless, Wang Ying's repeated invocation of Tianxia and *wuShe* in conjunction with other spatial entities—such as *waiyang*, Zhonghua (China; 中華), *woguo* (our state/country; 我國), and the all-encompassing Tianxia *dashi* (the general trend across all under Heaven; 天下大勢)[119]—conveys her vision of a changing world order.

Political visions such as Wang Ying's cannot be taken for granted. On the one hand, they suggest a morally acceptable, even acclaimed, way of having women's moral cultivation benefit the polity. Qing writers commonly associated women's domestic role with moral influence rippling across the family-society-state continuum.[120] On the other hand, however, women were cautioned against interfering too much in public affairs, because the very moral order granting them a political vision also required them to adhere to the distinction between domestic and public.[121] In Wang Ying's case, political visions emanated first from an interface between the domestic and the public—namely, the village of Huaitang, where family and lineage affairs intersected with local problems.

Settling back in her native place required strategies that diasporic Huizhou families had commonly employed in finding anchoring elsewhere, not least in marshaling cultural resources to build up family legacies. To a great extent, the Wang and Cheng families' legacies came into the shape they were remembered for because of Wang Ying's persistent efforts to retrieve their cultural past, or to locate it in various estates and ancestral halls. By these efforts, she established her role as the only surviving custodian of the two families' legacies—a recurring feat in this book—but in her case, this role in turn enabled her to reshape key lineage institutions and local mechanisms of governance. She was then able to make her foray into the political domain of statecraft thinking and have her local experience applied to the changing world of "All under Heaven."

5

Reimagining Huizhou across War and Devastation

To Level Hill extend the auspicious vapors from Mount Huang,
The talent they nurture in women is anything but ordinary.
平山佳氣接黃山，秀毓蛾眉豈等閑。

—*Kuang Maodi*

As the ancestor [Hu Zi] said, "The more ill fortune befell, the more leisure I had. And thus, I had the opportunity to spend all day compiling [commentaries on poetry] and sit by bright windows and clean desks reading and writing."—It would be my great fortune to do the same for the rest of my life and complete a volume [of commentaries on women's poetry].
如先公[胡仔]所云，"命益蹇，身益閒，得以編次終日，明窗淨几，目披手鈔……。" 以成一書，則餘生之厚幸矣。

—*Sun Caifu*

CATACLYSMIC EVENTS CHANGED the course of the nineteenth century. The two Opium Wars (1840–42, 1856–60) challenged Qing sovereignty and legitimacy, with political, intellectual, and socioeconomic consequences that would be felt for decades to come and into the next century. Their impact was further compounded by the Taiping War (1850–64), the "most devastating civil war in human history."[1] Costing twenty to thirty million lives, it left some of the most vibrant areas in the economic and cultural heartland of China with barely any human survivors and local infrastructure and communities in near total ruin. Rethinking the Taiping War in terms of its human consequences leads to a departure from dominant narratives in service of the shifting political powers and agendas in modern Chinese history, spurring instead an interest in the survivors' stories and the emotional implications of their loss.[2]

With fundamental challenges from both within and without came the collapse of the cosmic and political order. Even decades before the end of Qing rule in 1911, according to Wei Shang, "few of the values and cultural ideals that underpinned its ideology of state emerged unscathed."[3] But the Taiping War and its aftermath also signaled a time for cultural transformation, not least because the "collapse of Heaven," as recently studied by Huan Jin, entailed the need to make sense of war violence and apocalyptic change through literary and cultural production across genres and mediums of dissemination.[4] Writing of all kinds flourished during and after the war to preserve memories and commemorate the dead. They amounted to an "act of cultural commitment to remembering," interweaving personal loss with dynastic crisis and war atrocities in conscious emulation of the poet-historian (*shishi*) Du Fu. Works by women drew attention to the changing parameters of gender spheres in times of chaos, particularly women's self-identification in relation to the political realm and the state.[5]

Huizhou and its diasporic communities in Jiangnan were among the areas most severely affected by the war. Economic recovery and physical reconstruction took a long time and continued into the twentieth century. Even as the Huizhou merchants remained active in postwar Shanghai, a city of migrants from war-torn areas, there seemed little doubt that the decline of their economic power was irrevocable in the face of competition from new forms of commerce and enterprises emerging in the late nineteenth century. A recent study, however, excavates rich primary sources detailing efforts to revive Huizhou: in material and cultural ways, Huizhou diasporic communities contributed to the reconstruction of local Huizhou society and linked it more closely to economic and cultural developments across regions.[6]

Culturally, postwar restoration took dynamic forms unconstrained by economic factors. The Huizhou community in Shanghai was among the diverse native-place communities that flourished in the city and made it "a China in miniature"—fostering paradoxically both native-place and national loyalty.[7] But, more important, Huizhou's local customs and diasporic communities became the focus of scholarly endeavors aimed at enhancing the cultural impact of the region. What came to our knowledge of the Huizhou impact owed significantly to the scholarly projects completed during the Republican era—most of all local histories and a collection of local customs and anecdotes compiled by the Republican scholar Xu Chengyao. Xu was a Huizhou native, and the local gazetteer he compiled for She County was printed by the Huizhou native-place community (*tongxianghui*) in Shanghai in 1937.[8] It should also be noted that Guang Tiefu's (fl. early 20th c.) publication in 1936 of the first anthology of poetry by women affiliated with Anhui incorporated several sections on women poets with Huizhou origins.[9]

Cultural restoration certainly started much earlier. Tobie Meyer-Fong examines diverse cultural projects, both institutional and personal, that were launched even before the end of the Taiping War to restore shattered cultural ideals and communities in Jiangnan and beyond.[10] The first epigraph to this chapter concerns the priorities of Huizhou's cultural restoration, namely the bolstering of its cultural legacy and its (diasporic) female talents. It is an inscription for the posthumously printed personal collection of Sun Caifu (1825–81), a woman poet from a salt merchant's family with double Huizhou-Yangzhou roots. The author of the inscription praises Sun's poetic talent through the signature sites of Mount Huang and Level Hill, symbolizing her Huizhou-Yangzhou legacies. In the author's imagination, the Huizhou legacy gained prominence as an origin of the "auspicious vapors" (*jiaqi*) nurturing female talents. Since the Han dynasty, geographical writing had construed the vapors (*qi*) of water and earth as fostering winds (*feng*) or local customs, which in turn defined the moral and cultural qualities of localities. Attributes of people corresponded directly to the *qi* and *feng* of the localities where they lived. From geographical writing arose genres of local writing, reinforcing the sense of the local while supplying sources for official historiography, which produced a more universal idea of the dynasty composed of localities.[11] The inscription quoted here not only evokes the enduring sense of human traits being nurtured by local and cosmological forces; the "auspicious vapors" extending from Huizhou to Yangzhou foreground key facets of the Huizhou diaspora—geographical mobility, symbiotic ties uniting the two places, and their perceived prominence among localities. Above all, their nurturing forces are distilled in their female talent.

Sun Caifu lived through the Taiping War and its aftermath. Her personal collection, *Posthumously Collected Drafts from the Studio of Collected Writings* (Congbixuan yigao; 1887), was a thin volume that nonetheless encompassed the full extent of surviving the war and commemorating the war dead, as well as Sun being commemorated as a female talent exemplary of Huizhou's legacy. The second epigraph is from Sun's preface to her ambitious, though never completed, literary project *Collected Commentaries [on Poetry] from the Imperial Palaces and Inner Quarters* (Gonggui conghua). Immediately after the war, Sun and her husband Hu Peixi (1813–88), also a Huizhou native, launched literary and scholarly projects to champion Huizhou. The "ancestor" in her preface refers to Hu Zi (1110–70), the eminent Song dynasty scholar whom the lineage of Hu Peixi claimed as an ancestor. Claiming descent from Hu Zi enables Sun to envision what would be restorative following the collapse of the former cosmic and political order.[12] Sun's project, her wartime and commemorative writings, and writings about her constitute the earliest efforts to reimagine Huizhou and its legacy through war and restoration.

War and Cultural Affirmation

Sun Caifu was born in Yangzhou in 1825. Her father, Sun Geng (ca. 1764–?), was from the Zhang family of Xiuning County, Huizhou. By Sun Geng's generation at least, the Zhang family had settled in Yangzhou to practice the salt trade. The family adopted the surname Sun because a family member had been adopted as heir to affinal kin named Sun. Sun Geng was a candidate for a post in the salt administration in Yangzhou. Sun Caifu's biological mother, née Xun, was a concubine of Sun Geng; her legal mother was Lady Wu. Sun Geng was sixty-one when Caifu was born and was a doting father. The family lived in abundance, and Caifu was said to be provided with luxurious clothes and food (*miyi xianshi*). Moreover, Sun Geng personally taught her to read and guided her in exploring a range of subjects, including the classics, history, medicine, and astronomy. She mastered rhymes at nine and composed poetry at thirteen. She also excelled in embroidery.[13] Sun Caifu thus had the opportunity to receive the kind of education available to women in successful Huizhou-Yangzhou families—and in many gentry families of this time—and was on her way to establishing a reputation as a female talent.

And yet, her personal collection, *Posthumously Collected Drafts* from the Studio of Collected Writings, opens with a verse about her family as refugees in the "new warfare" of 1842:

COMPOSED IN THE SUMMER OF RENYIN [1842], ON MY WAY TO THE NORTH, WHEN FOLLOWING MY GRANDPARENTS AND FLEEING FROM FOREIGN AGGRESSION

All of sudden we are homeless,
Feelings well up in me as we wander around.
My mother lives by the Han River [Yangzhou],
Separated from my father, now in Haizhou [Huai'an].
Family members disperse in all directions
In the heat of new warfare.
Where would the lonesome fleabane rest?
I choke with sobs.[14]

壬寅仲夏隨侍祖慈避夷氛北上途次有作

忽作無家客，飄零百感生。母居邗水上，父隔海州城。骨肉各分散，干戈新戰爭。孤蓬何處適？飲泣不成聲。

The interval between 1842 and 1853, when Yangzhou first fell to the Taiping army, may not have encouraged the kind of literary activity or networking that the 1820s and 1830s had nourished. But as refugees returned home, Sun Caifu was able to engage in poetic exercises and exchanges with other women poets in Yangzhou. Justifying her love of poetry for its didactic capacity also looked familiar, echoing debates from the "long eighteenth century."[15] Moreover, her personal collection included a considerable number of poetic works articulating her cultural affiliations, such as the typical "Yangzhou *topoi*" in tribute to Wang Shizhen. Wang's "autumn willows" poetry had become a token of Yangzhou and its elite culture, as his densely allusive and ambiguous poetic language allowed early Qing poets to give voice to wide-ranging sentiments and spurred emulation in the ensuing centuries. To acquire this poetic language was to create a cultural affiliation with the city.[16] Sun Caifu's poetic response to a lady friend, Huang Renqiu, deftly echoes Wang's allusion to the Tang poet Bai Juyi: "The willows, like the waist of Xiaoman, dance in the wind as in old times" (Manyao yijiu wu pingting; 蠻腰依舊舞娉婷). Wang's invocation of the slender waist of Xiaoman, Bai's family entertainer, to describe the willows remained very much in the cultural imagination of Yangzhou in Sun's time.[17] In her "spring willows" poems, Sun explicitly mentions the willows as a token of the city's most famous site, the Red Bridge: "In thriving verdancy the willows grow all along [roads by] the little Red Bridge" (Yiyi lübian xiaoHongqiao; 依依綠遍小紅橋).[18]

Sometime in 1842–43, Sun Caifu lost her father and younger sister. In the late spring of 1843, she returned to what she called her native home (*limen*) in Huizhou along with Lady Wu, a Huizhou native returning from Yangzhou in the company of her daughters-in-law.[19] The repeated references to Sun's two homes in correspondence with her relatives further confirm the biographical source of her double Huizhou-Yangzhou roots. They also track her conscious efforts in asserting her place identities. She laments, for example, being separated from her family, who were "sojourning by the Han River [in Yangzhou]" while she herself was now "living by the Lian River [in Huizhou]" (Jiaji Hanjiang shen Lianshui). Where she lived by the Lian River was her native home (*limen*).[20] On her twentieth birthday, in 1844, she mourned her ill fortune in losing her father at a young age and her loneliness and separation from home (*lixiang*), meaning Yangzhou.[21]

In 1848, Sun Caifu was married to Hu Peixi as his second wife. Hu was a native of Jixi County in Huizhou, and his lineage had enjoyed a scholarly reputation since the Ming period for specializing in exegesis of the Confucian classics. According to the renowned scholar Yu Yue (1821–1907), the Hu lineage can be traced to the Song scholar-officials Hu Shunzhi (1083–1143) and Hu Zi. Hu Peixi and his cousin Hu Peihui (1782–1849) were among the leading Qing scholars of the Confucian classics.[22] Hu Peixi's uncle had been a friend of Sun Caifu's late father and helped arrange the marriage. Sun Caifu then moved from Huizhou to Hangzhou, where Hu served as a secretary. The Hu family was in great financial difficulty, but she was said to be able to personally manage the household tasks despite the luxurious lifestyle she had enjoyed in her natal home.[23]

The ensuing decades brought frequent separations and travel due to Hu's change of jobs and, in 1853–64, the Taiping War. Phrases like *kedi* (place away from home) or *taxiang* (alien land) convey dislocation and uncertainty. Losing a daughter sometime before 1851, Sun Caifu wrote about her "pitiful life in a place away from home" where she barely fit in (lit., "barely had room as large as the tip of an awl").[24] In 1851, her mother-in-law, Grand Lady Zhang, passed away in Huizhou while Sun was staying in Yangzhou. She mourned the fact that she and her husband had not been by Zhang's side due to their "life of duckweed in alien lands."[25]

A series of poems on autumn swallows stand out among her poetic works from these years for interweaving a sentiment of personal loss with historical change. These poems adapt Wang Shizhen's "autumn willows" poetry, but with a tone emphatically different from her earlier poetic exercises on autumn willows or spring willows. Above all, Sun converted Wang's vague nostalgia into explicit allusions to dynastic crisis.[26] Poem #2 is typical:

AUTUMN SWALLOWS, WITH RHYMES FROM "AUTUMN WILLOWS" BY WANG YUYANG, #2

The moonlight cast over my bed last night was like frost,[27]
Swallows chattered as they flew across the wild pond.
They used to find shelter in the golden chamber,
But changing fortunes have rendered the fan useless in the autumn.[28]
New sorrows go with the swan geese flying to the southern frontiers,
Old dreams are lost in thoughts of the kingdoms of salt wealth.[29]
Do not seek your former companion behind the vermillion gate,
Since autumn, weeds have taken over the Memorial Arches of Grand Feats.[30]

秋燕四首 用王漁洋秋柳韻

床前昨夜月如霜，幾度呢喃過野塘。棲止曾將金作屋，炎涼已覺扇藏箱。
新愁訴向衡陽雁，舊夢空思海國王。莫向朱門尋故侶，秋來草沒大功坊。

Swallows as a poetic trope stood for changing fortunes during dynastic transitions. Sun compared the swallows in her poetic series to those from the "Lane of Black Robes" (Wuyi Xiang), an allusion to the aristocratic Wang and Xie families during the Six Dynasties period (Poem #1). As these families fell into oblivion in the Tang dynasty, the swallows ended up in commoners' homes.[31] For Sun Caifu, this trope conveys the swift changes in her own time: "Views of the spring, though in its prime have utterly changed" (Poem #3). In more explicit ways it alludes to historical trauma: "Since autumn, weeds have taken over the Memorial Arches of Grand Feats" ("Qiulai caomo Dagong Fang," Poem #2). The overgrown arches replace Wang Shizhen's allusion to the Lane of Lasting Prosperity (Yongfeng Fang) and the romantic sentiments associated with it. As used by the Tang poet Bai Juyi, this lane in the eastern Tang capital of Luoyang had been known for flourishing willows, which suggested to Bai the alluring beauty of his family entertainer, Fan Su. Wang's allusion to Bai gives rise to nostalgia that is, in Waiyee Li's words, "tied to a general sense of mutability, with a hint of failed romance."[32] By contrast, the Memorial Arches of Grand Feats (Dagong Fang) as used by Sun Caifu are tokens of the Ming imperial recognition of its founding general, Xu Da (1332–85), erected on either side of Xu's residence in the Ming capital, Nanjing. The overgrown arches signify the fallen dynasty, hence the autumn swallows' loss of their former shelter in a powerful family. Dated 1851–54, Sun's poetic series does not so much echo the sentiments of Ming loyalism often characterizing early Qing poetic responses to the autumn willows topos as speak to what was becoming an unprecedented crisis in the present dynasty.[33] After its first decisive victory over the Qing army in early 1851, the religious clique led by Hong Xiuquan (1814–64) declared the founding of the Taiping Heavenly Kingdom—"an act tantamount to secession," in Tobie Meyer-Fong's words—and began wreaking great havoc as it seized major ports and cities along the Yangzi River.[34]

In early 1853, as Sun Caifu visited her natal family in Yangzhou, the Taiping forces took Anqing (Anhui), and Yangzhou was among the next targets. Hu Peixi, then in Hangzhou, found the means to evacuate her from Yangzhou on the day of the city's fall.[35] Sun Caifu later recalled how they fled: "Heading to the south of the [Yangzi] river I looked to the north, / among the beacon fires that lit up the sky lay Yangzhou" (Yuxiang Jiangnan wang Jiangbei, mantian fenghuo shi Yangzhou; 欲向江南望江北，滿天烽火是揚州).[36] Hu Peixi provides more detail:

> On the twenty-third day [of the second lunar month of the year Guichou, April 1, 1853], before the dawn, we suddenly heard a lot of noise, and people yelled, "They're coming! They're coming!" Men and women started running, and the lines of people trying to get out of the city were endless. In haste we boarded a boat, and hardly had we reached the Goddess Temple before we learned that the city had fallen on this very day. The ferry to Zhenjiang was blocked, so we took the route to Tongzhou and arrived in Hangzhou by the route to Suzhou. People thought we had survived by heaven's blessing.[37]

The fall of Nanjing, Yangzhou, and Zhenjiang in 1853 were remembered with great horror: "The accumulated bones add up to a mountain, and the flowing blood forms a river."[38] After their narrow escape, the couple lived a precarious life, moving from place to place. Over the years Hu tried to pick up temporary employment along the way. He recalled, "We had an extremely uncertain life. The places we stayed at included, in Zhejiang, Hangzhou, Shaoxing, Zhuji, Huzhou, Longyou, Shouchang, Haiyan, Xiushui, Shimen, Quzhou, Jiaxing, Jiashan, and Wukang; in Jiangsu, Yangzhou and Liyang; in Hunan, Wugang and Baoqing."[39] By 1860, the Taiping troops had taken most of Anhui and Zhejiang. The couple then moved to Wugang in Hunan, where Hu Peixi took up a post in the Qing army in 1862. During these times of great uncertainty, Sun Caifu often had to grab their young children in her arms and flee at the first sign of Taiping aggression.[40] She wrote about their dislocation while sojourning in Zhuji (Zhejiang), again using the trope of swallows that had lost their shelter: "Where can the swallows come up with plans for making their nests?" (Hechu choumou ying yanlei? 何處綢繆營燕壘).[41]

What distinguishes Sun Caifu's wartime writings from other recently discovered personal accounts of the Taiping War is her focus on cultural affirmation: her favored strategy for writing and surviving the war is to embed trauma and uncertainty in poetic topoi that affirm the cultural ties with which she had affiliated herself and which she found anew in flight from war. Though correspondence in poetry may seem strange when we realize that her very survival was under threat, Sun rejoiced in her ability to connect and empathize with friends. A female friend, Song Shenghe, had been circulating a painting. Sun wrote in the poetic inscription she mailed to Song, "No rice remains at all to feed the starving scholar; but I am left with scraps of paper to send to the faraway Luan [Song Shenghe, style name Luanyin]" (Yiwu yuli gong jifeng, shengyou canjian tuo yuanluan; 已無餘粒供飢鳳，賸有殘箋託遠鸞).[42]

A few examples reinforce the apparent discrepancy between Sun's cultural affirmation and the looming presence of war. A female friend, Zhang Cifen, requested Sun's inscription on a fan with a painted image of the Goddess of Luo River. The occasion suggests to Sun the karmic bonds between her and the goddess, as a painting of the goddess that had been lost in the war now came back to her through her friend's fan.[43] Activities such as inscribing paintings and exchanging poetry survived even in the heat of war. Seeing off Zhang Cifen, Sun writes about how Zhang's expected family reunion reminds her of her separation from her own family caused by imminent war: "Year after year I watch beacon fires lit in Jiangnan" (Niannian fenghuo wang Jiangnan; 年年烽火望江南.[44] For a lyricist she praised for having inherited the style of the Ming loyalist poet Chen Weisong (1625–82), she inscribed song lyrics collected and circulated during the war, characterizing them as political commentary on chaotic times comparable to the era of the Three Kingdoms.[45] When an official, Deng Yizhi, departed to join the Qing troops in Jiangxi, Sun composed a farewell poem on behalf of her son and expressed her wish that Deng's feats would one day match those of the early Tang general who had the famed Pavilion of Prince Teng (Tengwang Ge) built in Jiangxi. By then, she hoped, Deng would have allowed a young talent like her son to follow the example of Wang Bo's (650–76) masterpiece on the site, in which Wang celebrates the site in terms of early Tang political and military glory and expresses his ambition to accomplish feats of his own.[46] In such instances, cultural affirmation took on the weightiness of survival itself, providing the means for refugees such as Sun and her family and friends to amend their lives and communities in the face of chaos and disintegration. Moreover, in determining which part of their prewar cultural life deserved to be preserved during the war, they were already establishing the terms for cultural restoration in the midst of the prolonged war.

In 1862, Sun Caifu lost her second son, who was only five years old.[47] In a Buddhist dirge she later wrote for him, Sun referred to these years (1857–62) as "a tumultuous time of battles and hundreds of hardships" (*raorao bing'ge, beigeng baiku*; 擾擾兵戈，備更百苦).[48] Later that year, again in flight, Sun Caifu and her family boarded a boat for Hunan. She cast their life as refugees succinctly in a couplet: "Three thousand miles we treaded away from home, all day long I am tormented by separation from my family" (Kelu sanqianli, lihuai shi'ershi; 客路三千里，離懷十二時).[49] The war seemed never-ending:

EXPRESSING MY FEELINGS ON A BOAT, IN FLIGHT FROM WAR AND ON MY WAY TO HUNAN WITH MY HUSBAND #2

West winds blow throughout the night,
Swan geese are scattered to the end of the sky.
Warfare is spreading all over the land,
Siblings have strayed away.
In departure I shed tears before the lamp,
Thoughts of home crowd into my mind in sleep.
May you [Hu Peixi] serve well in the troops,
Every day I shall hope that you fulfill your ambition.[50]

偕外子避兵入楚舟中述懷 其二

一夜西風急，天涯雁影飛。干戈方滿地，弟妹各離群。別淚燈前灑，鄉愁枕上紛。戎行須努力，早晚盼青雲。

While in Hunan, Sun Caifu believed that the swallows she had written about at the beginning of the war had been following her to her cottage by the Xiang River in Hunan. The trope helps her document the course of the war and dynastic crisis in spatial terms tied to her personal vicissitudes. This time she ends her poem on an uplifting tone, envisaging a new spring on the way (*bieyouchun*). She suggests that the swallows are only temporarily trapped in mud and have great prospects [for finding shelter in the home of the earl] (Mandao fenghou wu guxiang, zanjiao zongji hun fanchen; 漫道封侯無骨相，暫教蹤跡溷凡塵).[51]

It was not until 1865, after the Taiping forces had been wiped out, that the couple returned to Zhejiang, where Hu Peixi found temporary jobs in Jiaxing and Jiashan Counties. In 1869, as a reward for his military service in Hunan, Hu Peixi was assigned to a post in the prefectural school of Ningguo in Anhui.[52] There they spent the rest of their lives in restored peace. Sun wrote, "I have the joy of seeing peaceful times when my hair turns gray" (Baitou xijian taiping nian).[53] Their celebration of the end of the war took the form of a poetic act suggestive of the height of prewar elite culture: Sun emulated the domestic poetic community in the Qing novel *Dream of the Red Chamber*, which had broad resonances in reality for prewar Qing elite families. She picked a topic from the poetic series on chrysanthemums composed by the characters in the novel. Each family member had a chance to honor the flower with wine and crabs, as in the novel.[54] Chrysanthemums, as a stock expression of triumph over adversity in tribute to the poet-hermit Tao Qian (365?–427), were a fitting metaphor for Sun and her family as survivors of the war—and for the restoration of their domestic poetic community.[55] The cultural implications of Sun's writing about war and survival provided an important context for her postwar cultural production.

Commemoration: A Women-Focused War History

Across war-torn regions along the Yangzi River, local gazetteers recorded ongoing reconstruction projects into the Republican era. It would not, however, be possible to restore everything that had been destroyed. Even before the war ended, commemorative projects in honor of the war dead functioned as symbolic restoration for survivors coping with loss and rebuilding their communities.[56] Song Shenghe, the female friend whose painting Sun Caifu had inscribed, had died in 1861, when Hangzhou fell to the Taiping army. Her tragic death features prominently in Sun's postwar writing in memory of a community of female relatives and friends:

> LADY SONG WAS WIFE TO MR. WANG XICHA FROM LIYANG [JIANGSU], HER NAME WAS LUANYIN, SOBRIQUET SHENGHE. IN THE YEAR XINYOU [1861], HANGZHOU FELL. LADY SONG WALKED TO THE GUAN BRIDGE AND DROWNED HERSELF IN THE WATER.
>
> Friendship like that between Guan and Bao is rare,
> Resentment over dying in the water will not fade.
> Every year on the Hanshi festival, over the roads of Hangzhou—[57]
> Deep in the night the will-o'-the-wisp rises at the Guan Bridge.[58]
>
> 溧陽王西垞大令室宋宜人，諱鸞音，字笙和，辛酉杭城失守，宜人步至觀橋投水以殉。
>
> 管鮑論交已寂寥，葬身魚腹恨難消。年年寒食錢塘路，磷火宵深上觀橋。

Sun envisions the ghostly light of Song's spirit reappearing every year at the site of her suicide to dramatize how she is emplaced at, or bound to, the site. At the same time, Sun also imagines Song's grief over dying in the water: her body was consumed by fish and did not receive a proper burial, and thus lacked proper emplacement. This contrast between physical displacement and spiritual emplacement becomes a powerful statement on war, female martyrdom, and remembrance.[59]

Sun's mourning poem for Song is among the twenty-five poems grouped under the title "Thinking of My Friends from the Inner Quarters" (Guizhong huairen shi; 閨中懷人詩). At first glance the title may give rise to an impression that Sun was writing in the entrenched boudoir style, where a female voice typically laments her separation from her lover. But the short preface Sun wrote for this poetic sequence unequivocally focuses on female bonding over wartime experience:

I suffered from many hardships, and while I drifted in alien lands, chance brought me into contact with many worthy ladies wherever my footsteps reached. In leisure time, I composed a poem for each of the ladies, and so far I have collected twenty-five of them. Why should anything like this [poetry] be valued at all? It is just my way of expressing my feelings about separation over time. I have written down my babble as a record of my affection for my family and friends.[60]

The stock reference to poetry as a vehicle for expressing feelings is crucial here: poetry embodies a shared cultural past that connects Sun with a community of female relatives and friends. Poems in Sun's series become metapoetic when they refer to a primary function of poetry as a means for bonding and expressing profound mutual appreciation, as in the couplet "If we in the golden chambers are allowed to call ourselves friends who truly understand each other [*zhiji*], please send me poetry instead of letters" (Jingui tangxu cheng zhiji, moji yushu zhi jishi; 金閨倘許稱知己，莫寄魚書只寄詩).[61] The war cannot erase the shared cultural past embodied in poetry, even though the war has destroyed lives, eminent families, and tokens of civilization (*jijin leshi*).[62] As in the comparably calamitous times during the Ming-Qing transition, the very act of writing poetry suggests a means to rescue from oblivion what has been destroyed.[63]

The poems in Sun's poetic series cover all facets of the affective bonds Sun has had with those included there. They bring up quotidian details that will not fade from memory. They mourn bonds that have been severed by war. Or they retrace the comfort that friendship brings to Sun's life as a war refugee and the sustaining moments she finds in the shelter her friends have offered. For each woman, Sun uses the poem title as identification: an affinal aunt surnamed Zhou (Zhoushi gumu);[64] a younger sister with whom she loses contact when fleeing from war (Ermei, shi bibing Taizhou);[65] a female friend identifiable by name and place of origin (She Zheng Zi'an nüshi; Lanxi Xu Lengxiang nüshi; Shangyu Zheng Yuyin nüshi).[66]

Some of the longer titles provide more specific biographical information and details of Sun's bonding with the women: "Grand Lady Wang of Liyang [Jiangsu], Wife to Mr. Miao with the Posthumous Title of Courageous Martyr, Extended Her Generous Help to Me while I Was Staying Temporarily in Yuezhou [Zhejiang]"[67] or "Lady Liu of Baoqing [Hunan], Mother of Deng, Took Care of Me with Her Daughter-in-Law when I Gave Birth to My Son

Chuan during My Temporary Stay in Baoqing Prefecture. She Was Just Like Family and in Leisure Time Invited Me to Share Stories about Hangzhou as She Admired the Splendid Views of the West Lake." In the latter poem, Sun phrases her gratitude to her friend thus: "Wrens were graciously allowed to take a sprig" (Jiaoliao zanjie yiqizhi), suggesting that she took refuge provided by her friend.[68]

War memories found poignant expression in mourning poems. In addition to the poem for Song Shenghe, Sun wrote about how the entire family of a female friend who had once lived close by was gone:

THE LADY WAS WIFE TO MR. DU XIAOSHAN OF JIAXING, ASSISTANT TO THE COUNTRY MAGISTRATE. THEIR FORMER HOUSE WAS LOCATED IN THE JIAXING CITY NEAR THE MEMORIAL HALL FOR FAN LI [536–448 BCE], BY WHICH I ONCE LIVED IN A RENTED HOUSE. AFTER THE CATASTROPHE, THE LADY'S ENTIRE FAMILY WAS GONE.

When I rented a humble hut by the Memorial Hall of Fan Li,
People vied to praise the couple for their unrivaled affection.
Where are their towers and pavilions from those past times?
At tombs of the starving ghosts, cuckoos cry for their unvindicated deaths.[69]

嘉興杜小珊主簿室，孺人，舊宅在嘉郡城內，與范少伯祠相近，余嘗僦居於此。經難後，孺人全家俱盡。

少伯祠邊寄一椽，爭誇眷屬是神仙。舊時樓閣今何在？鬼餒墳頭叫杜鵑。

Individually, each poem functions as a brief biography of the woman Sun Caifu has bonded with. Read as a whole, the poetic series integrates the wartime experiences and life paths of the twenty-five women, which cross with Sun's at different points, into a war history. As Hu Peixi later comments, in composing this poetic series Sun echoes Du Fu, the master poet-historian who documented the turmoil during the An Lushan Rebellion (755–63): "As she looked back at the entertainment quarters lying in ruins [borrowing Du Fu's line], her brushstrokes expressed her feelings for friends [she composed a volume of poetry titled "Thinking of My Friends from the Inner Quarters"]."[70]

Thus Sun's poetic series represents an effort to emulate Du Fu's "cultural commitment to remembering" through poetry.[71]

The twenty-five biographical accounts that emerge from Sun's poetic series at once imitate and change the basis of commemoration made officially available by government-led projects, not least the biographies of martyrs that filled the pages of local gazetteers after the war. Which lives were worthy of being remembered was determined, as Tobie Meyer-Fong astutely notes, by the need to rehabilitate the legitimacy of rule put in question by the war. Hence an insistent narrative of loyalty enshrined the war dead as martyrs for the dynasty. Concurrent with this dynastic narrative were multiple local efforts to assert different bonds with the dead or redeploy institutions of commemoration for personal expressions of loss.[72] In contrast to official narratives of martyred women—often categorized as "chaste and righteous"[73]—Sun's poetic series was deeply personal, emphasizing affective bonds framed in a shared cultural past. Not all the women in her poetry are specified as martyrs of the war, moreover. Sun suggests that her affective bonds with these women are themselves worthy of being remembered as war history.

The elegies that Sun Caifu authored further illuminate the priorities of her commemorative writing. In a long elegy dedicated to Song Shenghe, Sun uses emotionally charged language in the Chuci (lyrics of the Chu) style attributed to Qu Yuan (340–278 BCE). Allusions to Qu Yuan inevitably evoke the loyal official confronting the calamities she specifies as being caused by the Taiping bandits (Yuekou). For her purposes, however, this language enables the venting of great pain, as befits its original use for lamentation embedded in the shamanistic and elegiac traditions of the quest of spirits.[74] In pain Sun retraces her bond with Song, their separations and reunion during the war, and the shock and agony that come with the tragic news of her friend's death. She not only compares their friendship to that between Guan Zhong (723–645 BCE) and Bao Shuya (?–644 BCE), as in her earlier poem, but defines it explicitly as the female version of the ideal bond between two gentlemen who truly appreciate each other (*jinguo zhi zhiyin*; 巾幗之知音).[75] Furthermore, although Sun quotes the tale of a female exemplar in mourning Song Shenghe, her elegy diverges from official narratives of martyred women in its interpretation of moral courage. She does not cast Song's courage in terms of women dying to preserve their chastity or following their husbands in death during the war. Rather, she employs a language of heroism to compare Song's courage to that of a warrior whose unfulfilled wish is to die on the battlefield, with her corpse wrapped in horsehide (*tong mage zhi weiguo*; 痛馬革之未裹).[76] Sun Caifu's woman-focused war history, then, emphatically resets the basis of commemoration from loyalty and martyrdom to women's wartime experience and bonding, especially focusing on the heroic courage conveyed through what may be called "cross-voicing."[77]

Huizhou Legacies and Women's Poetry in the Postwar Restoration

Sun Caifu and Hu Peixi launched literary and scholarly projects immediately after the war to champion Huizhou in the post-Taiping order. Best known were Hu's scholarly projects aimed at restoring the Confucian rites. Huizhou, as the "model Confucian place," was integral to Huizhou identity, and claims to Confucian learning had helped Huizhou merchant households fashion their scholarly reputation since the Ming.[78] For Hu Peixi, the Hu lineage's expertise in exegesis of the rites was useful in the post-Taiping restoration on several levels: the revival of Huizhou's cultural prestige, its scholarly communities, and diasporic families like his own; as well as, at least symbolically, restoration of a collapsed ritual and ideological order serving the needs of the dynasty, whose legitimacy had been gravely shaken by the war.

Hu's extensive *Bibliography of Works from the Jinzi Hu Lineage of Jixi* (Jixi Jinzi Hushi suozhu shumu) showcases major scholarly achievements made by Hu descendants since the Song dynasty, predominantly their work in Confucian learning.[79] The purpose, as he specifies in the preface, is to preserve the titles of what had been scattered or lost during the war so that Hu descendants would not lose track of the learning traditions defining their origin (*yuanyuan suozi*). Hu published his bibliography and selected works by Hu descendants in the Hu lineage's publication series.[80] There is also an annalistic biography (*nianpu*) of the Song official Hu Shunzhi, which Hu Peixi and his cousin Hu Peihui jointly compiled. This annalistic biography emphasizes Hu Shunzhi's loyalty to the Song court and casts him as an important ally of Yue Fei (1103–42), the general remembered for protecting the Song from Jurchen invasions.[81] This emphasis on loyalty no doubt aligned the annalist biography with post-Taiping restorative projects. The Hu lineage genealogy, published in 1907, formally recognizes these scholarly works as the lineage's cultural legacy by incorporating them in its "Yiwen" (belles lettres) section.[82]

Earlier, Sun Caifu had expressed her ambition to complete a literary project that drew inspiration from Hu Zi, son of the Song official Hu Shunzhi. Hu

Zi had been widely acclaimed for his *Commentaries [on Poetry] Collected by the Hermit Fisherman by Tiao Stream* [Huzhou, Zhejiang] (Tiaoxi yuyin conghua).[83] In 1865, shortly after she moved from Hunan to Zhejiang, Sun Caifu wrote a preface for her project *Collected Commentaries [on Poetry] from the Imperial Palaces and Inner Quarters*:

> The ancestor Mr. Tiaoxi collected facts from commentaries on poetry, historiographical writings, and miscellaneous accounts since the Song Yuanyou reign [1086–94] and took what could be used to illuminate poetic works and enhance people's learning to compile two volumes of the *Commentaries Collected by the Hermit Fisherman*, which included one hundred *juan* in total. Since our [Qing] dynasty incorporated it into *The [Complete Collection of the] Four Treasuries*, it has been circulating among scholars and poets. I have had the fortune to immerse myself in this illustrious heritage and have closely followed and emulated it. In leisure time, I, along with my husband Ziji [Hu Peixi], read through the commentaries on poetry and biographical accounts from the Southern Song until our time and selected those concerning women poets into a collection. The format of the collection follows in general the precedent set by the late master [Hu Zi], and it is titled *Collected Commentaries [on Poetry] from the Imperial Palaces and Inner Quarters*. I do not have the audacity to claim that this collection continues the ancestor's intent. It is just for the perusal of those in the inner quarters.
>
> In the year Gengshen of the Xianfeng reign [1860], we suffered from the Taiping aggressions and, in flight from war, lost all our books, including the drafts of this collection. Now, fortunately the bandits are being eliminated, and we are beginning to plan for our return home. I am thinking about shutting our door to guests and resuming our former project. As the late Mr. Tiaoxi said, "The more ill fortunes befell, the more leisure I had. And thus, I had the opportunity to spend all day compiling [commentaries on poetry] and to sit by bright windows and clean desks reading and writing."—It would be my great fortune to do the same for the rest of my life and complete a collection [of commentaries on women's poetry].
>
> Authored on the Day of the Beginning of Autumn, Year Yichou of the Tongzhi reign [1865], by Sun Caifu, wife to the twenty-fourth-generation descendant of Mr. Tiaoxi.[84]

先苕溪公取有宋元祐以後詩話及史傳、小説所載事實，可以發明詩句及增益見聞者，纂為《漁隱叢話》前、後集，共一百卷。國朝采入四庫，久已流佈藝林。芙幸沐清芬，私深鑽仰，暇日與外子子繼披閱南宋以迄我朝諸公詩話、傳記，見有涉婦女者，輒為摭錄，其體例略仿先公之舊，名曰《宮闈叢話》。非敢云繼先志，第以備閨閣中之觀覽而已。

咸豐庚申，遭粵匪之難，流離遷徙，書籍散亡，舊稿盡佚。今幸寇氛漸淨，言旋故鄉，尚思與外子子繼杜門卻掃，重理舊業。如先公所云，"命益蹇，身益閒，得以編次終日，明窗淨几，目披手鈔......。" 以成一書，則餘生之厚幸矣。

同治乙丑立秋日苕溪二十四世孫婦孫采芙識。

Though little other information about the *Collected Commentaries* survives, Sun Caifu's succinct preface provides important glimpses into how she envisioned postwar cultural restoration after the war ended. What comes to our immediate attention is Sun's claim to Hu Zi's collection of poetic commentaries as unequivocally a family and lineage legacy. She is able to stake her claim by identifying Hu Zi as an ancestor at the beginning of her preface (the "ancestor Mr. Tiaoxi"), and herself as wife to a descendant of Hu Zi ("wife to the twenty-fourth-generation descendant of Mr. Tiaoxi") at the end of the preface. She also characterizes the *Collected Commentaries* as a family project in emulation of Hu Zi's legacy, for which she and her husband have collected sources together. The relaunching of a family project so defined and devastated during the Taiping War is emblematic of the postwar restoration of the family and its legacy.

Parallel to the family's restorative project was restoration in a broader sense, as embodied in Hu Peixi's scholarly endeavors. But Hu Zi's collection of poetry commentaries did not pertain to what Hu Peixi celebrated as his lineage's expertise in the Confucian classics, nor did it fit into the narratives of loyalty dominating post-Taiping cultural and commemorative projects. Thus Hu Zi's legacy did not have much to do with the restoration of ritual or ideological order that was a priority following the Taiping War. Sun Caifu's shift in tone in stating her intention to emulate Hu Zi is revealing.

The motivation underlying the *Collected Commentaries* when Sun Caifu first started the project mostly had to do with the cultural prestige of Hu Zi's collection of poetic commentaries, attested to in particular by its integration into the literary and scholarly orthodoxies of the *Four Treasuries*. In emulating Hu Zi, Sun Caifu emphasizes her immersion in his heritage and admiration for it: "I have had the fortune to immerse myself in this illustrious heritage and have closely followed and emulated it." She refrains from endowing her project with an overly weighty purpose: it is not to continue the ancestor's project but rather to provide casual reading for women ("It is just for the perusal of those in the inner quarters").[85] Relaunching the project after the war, however, Sun links it to the ill fortune Hu Zi has experienced and defines it as the purpose of the rest of her life. The ill fortune becomes apparent in her quotation of Hu Zi's preface to the second volume of his collection. There Hu Zi begins by referring to a tumultuous time:

> I have been agonizing over a tumultuous time since I became an adult. For twenty years I lived in leisure, and I shut my door to guests by the Tiao Stream. There was nothing I needed to attend to, so I started collecting commentaries on poetry authored by worthy scholars since the Yuanyou reign [1086–94].[86]
>
> 余丁年罹於憂患，投閑二十載，杜門卻掃於苕溪之上，心無所事，因網羅元祐以來群賢詩話……

The time when Hu Zi "became an adult" was around 1127, a traumatic year in which the Jurchens captured Emperors Hui (1082–1135) and Qin (1100–61), and the Northern Song (960–1127) collapsed. The following decades witnessed conflict at the Southern Song (1127–79) court over the response to Jurchen aggression. Hu Shunzhi was embroiled in conflict between the general Yue Fei and the prime minister Qin Gui (1090–1155) and died in prison.[87] The leisure Hu Zi referred to was a euphemism for a failed career during a time of dynastic crisis and political conflict. His collection of poetic commentaries therefore had far broader implications than a diversion. A recent study points out that Hu Zi's collection set an important precedent for poetic commentaries to play a role in formulating the history of Chinese poetry by canonizing poets and embedding their creative lives in historical and cultural trends. His canonization of Du Fu, in particular, drew from the parallel between the crisis of his time and the An Lushan Rebellion, which Du Fu had recorded in his role as poet-historian.[88] Hu Zi quotes from one of his contemporaries:

> I did not find it [poetry by Du Fu] well crafted when I read it in normal times, but after I personally experienced war, death, and chaos, I realized

when I chanted it out how marvelous it was in addressing its time and speaking to people's hearts.[89]

平時讀之，未見其工；迨親罹兵火喪亂之後，誦其詩，如出乎其時，犁然有當於人心，然後知其語之妙也。

Sun Caifu saw herself in the role of Hu Zi, spending all day reading and collecting commentaries on poetry in a clean and peaceful space for the rest of her life. Clearly, she was not simply resuming a project cut short by war, but rather establishing a parallel between Hu Zi's time and her own. Hu Zi's description of Du Fu's poetry, which also applied to his own collection of poetic commentaries, was applicable to Sun Caifu's literary project too: "addressing its time and speaking to people's hearts." Literary projects like these were restorative because they functioned not only to document history but also to retrieve a shared cultural past from tumult and devastation. It can further be argued that, in relaunching her project, Sun Caifu transformed Hu Zi's legacy into a poetic history emphasizing women's participation in a shared cultural past.

Because Sun Caifu never completed her ambitious project and no drafts survive in extant versions of her personal collection, I cannot speculate on whether her project canonized women poets in the way that Hu Zi canonized (male) poets.[90] Nor do I intend to surmise from her preface exactly what roles she assigned to women in the history of Chinese poetry. My interest lies rather in identifying the two priorities she had in envisioning what was restorative following the collapse of the former cosmic and political order: a place-based (Huizhou) family and lineage legacy, and a women-focused poetic history. In the former respect, there was a notable change in strategy in making use of her family legacy. I have argued that a poetic trope in tribute to Wang Shizhen, in turn emblematic of the place identity and cultural affiliation of her natal family, helped her document the course of the war and dynastic crisis in spatial terms tied to her personal vicissitudes during the war. For restorative purposes, by contrast, it was Hu Zi's legacy that served her best. In this respect, *Collected Commentaries* significantly changed the scope of her literary and cultural production. But several factors connected the project to her earlier writings: her self-appointed role as a poet-historian, her emphasis on women-focused history, and the singular importance of cultural production to survival, commemoration, and postwar restoration.

Being Commemorated

The publication of *Posthumously Collected Drafts* from the Studio of Collected Writings in 1887 signaled a time when Sun Caifu herself became a subject of commemoration. A volume of poetic inscriptions preceding her writings celebrate her exceptional talent.[91] The first epigraph provides only one example of the inscriptions that exalted her posthumously as a female talent exemplary of the cultural legacy of Huizhou (and its symbiotic place, Yangzhou). A volume of correspondence between her and her family and relatives, appended at the end of her writings, highlighted familial roots that similarly invoked her cultural affiliation with Huizhou and Yangzhou.[92] Yet another volume of biographical and elegiacal essays followed, providing details of Sun's life that her own writings did not mention and glorifying her prodigious talent and exemplary qualities as wife and mother.[93]

These commemorative writings in Sun's honor to a great extent diverged from, or simplified, her sophisticated messages about war, commemoration, and women in assimilating her into the glorification of Huizhou and its female talent. Still, they offer an opportunity to consider the links connecting Sun's life and afterlife to broader cultural trends across war and restoration. Yu Yue, the author of a biography of Sun Caifu intended for incorporation in the Hu family genealogy (*jiacheng*), informs the reader of what brought him to Sun's knowledge:

> In the spring of the Fifth Year of the Guangxu reign [1879], I mourned for the death of my late wife Lady Yao and composed "One Hundred Sorrows." When my mourning poems reached Xuanzhou (Anhui), Ziji [Hu Peixi] took them to Lady Sun, who read them and wept. She said to Ziji, "If I die, would you mourn for our affection in the way that Mr. Quyuan ["Curved Garden," style name of Yu Yue] did for his wife?" Alas! Life and death are predetermined. Did Lady Sun have a presentiment of her death?[94]

"One Hundred Sorrows" (Bai'ai pian) refers to an extraordinary act of mourning: Yu Yue composed a series of one hundred mourning poems for his wife, Yao Wenyu, following her death in 1879. The series, along with Yu Yue's commentary, served as a memoir of their conjugal love and shared wanderings as refugees during the Taiping War. Yu Yue's family history, recently studied by Rania Huntington, is a sentimental account soaked in "ink and tears"—writings of mourning and commemoration. Yu Yue, who "clearly believed in the old tradition that words were one of the things that would not fade or rot," passed on family memories and afterlives for those he loved and set a family tradition of mourning by employing a plenitude of genres and materials.[95]

Sentimental histories pervaded the late imperial period, and as Weijing Lu reveals, it had by this time become fashionable to celebrate and display conjugal love as the basis of an ideal companionate marriage. Yu Yue's open display of conjugal love had drawn the attention of Sun Caifu and her husband.[96] In writing his biography of Sun Caifu, Yu Yue adopted a pen name in tribute to the grand historian Sima Qian, the "Jiushi shi Yu Yue" (Yu Yue, the historian of the foregone past). In doing so he endowed his writing with the historical and cultural weightiness that Sun and her husband clearly yearned for.

Yu Yue drew the material for his biography from elaborate descriptions of Sun Caifu's life in an account of conduct (*shizhuang*) and an elegy that Hu Peixi had written for her. These lengthy pieces were typical of what Martin Huang calls the "secularization of memory," a process by which quotidian or intimate details of the lives of ordinary people enter mourning literature. In changing the suitable subjects for commemoration, quotidian or intimate details changed the cultural construction of womanhood and manhood—the ideal qualities of women and men as gendered beings.[97] The many details Hu used to celebrate the affective bond between Sun and himself also served to craft the facets of Sun's life worthy of being commemorated.[98]

In particular, practicality and monetary management, rather than the cultural means Sun prized, were central to her plan to restore the family (*ji shijia zhi zaizao*; 冀室家之再造) following the war.[99] Her plan involved physical construction of a house and purchase of a small piece of land, for which she went to great lengths to amass four hundred taels of silver. The plan never materialized due to other pressing financial needs of Hu and his sons. Hu expressed his regret about the disputes they had over financial decisions related to the house. He described Sun's persistent efforts in executing her plan, the divide this matter introduced between them, and at the same time the profound affection Sun showed for him in tolerating disputes like this.[100] Furthermore, Sun instructed their son Rong (also named Zhaoli) to learn practical matters (*shuwu*) to ensure the family's long-term livelihood.

Her decision echoed motherly instructions found in biographical accounts of women in Huizhou merchant households.[101] While she believed in continuing the Hu family's scholarly tradition, she urged Hu Peixi not to put too much hope in their sons' success in the civil service examinations. She reminded him that the opportunities for such success had long been dwindling, as evidenced by Hu's own lack of luck.[102] The fact that their son Liu (also named Zhaogu) had examination candidacy with the registered status of a merchant household (*shangji*) further indicated the connection between their household and what had become a familiar characteristic of Huizhou merchant households.[103] Sun never mentioned what became of her literary project *Collected Commentaries* after she wrote her preface in 1865. Clearly, attending to the needs of a family that had lost all its belongings during the war and that encountered hardship, illness, and disputes (which Hu regretfully attributed to his own quick temper) after the war—overweighed her literary ambition.[104] Her generosity in sharing whatever savings she was able to put aside from Hu's meager earnings with those similarly suffering the consequences of the war increased their financial straits.[105] In Hu's words, "The innate brilliance of her mind was wasted on onerous household tasks and hardships day after day" (Yi tianji qingmiao zhi xinxiong, ri xiaomo yu laoku huannan *zhihzong*; 以天機清妙之心胸，日銷磨於勞苦患難之中).[106] An increasing recognition of women's domestic managerial skills and contribution in terms of female virtue allowed Hu to write these details—along with complicated messages about their affective bonds—into Sun's exemplary life history as wife and mother.[107] Recall that the biographical and elegiac essays were meant to supply material for the family's genealogy, as Yu Yue stated. Sun's life portrayed therein was intended to be enshrined as part of the Hu family history.

No sources have been located so far for the Hu family genealogy, and the Hu lineage's genealogy published in 1907 follows the more conventional format of genealogies in including only the achievements of its men.[108] Nevertheless, the *Posthumously Collected Drafts*, which included Sun's writings as well as commemorative writings for her, was published shortly after Hu Peixi published his bibliography showcasing the Hu lineage's scholarly achievements, and at the same Hu lineage publishing house, Heritage Tower (Shize Lou). Recorded as a title in the Shizelou Congkan (Publication Series from the Heritage Tower), Sun's collection has been integrated into the Hu lineage's heritage.[109] In turn, the Hu lineage's publication series, recorded by numerous entries in Huizhou local gazetteers, contributed to what is remembered as Huizhou's scholarly tradition.[110] During the 1910s–1930s, when the modern scholar Hu Shi (1891–1962), a Jixi native, explored the possibility of launching a publication series bolstering Jixi's scholarly traditions, it was Hu Peixi's publications that first came to his mind.[111]

The imaginaries of space and place examined thus far in this book grew out of the Huizhou diaspora and its implications for human-place ties, transregional mobility, the relationship between localities, and human apprehension of a cosmic and political order. By the time Sun Caifu began to write poetry, the women writers examined in this book had deftly written these trends into their cultural identity or drawn on them to engage with a changing world. It was no wonder that familiar poetic topoi affirming cultural affiliations with Huizhou and Yangzhou recur in the writings examined in this chapter. When the Taiping War and its aftermath radically reshaped relationships between the local and the imperium and among localities, it became urgent to reconstitute human-place ties and cultural identities.[112] Sun's use of a Huizhou legacy for restorative purposes and her assimilation into the glorification of Huizhou resonated in different ways with post-Taiping cultural trends.

Women's poetry in the seventeenth and eighteenth centuries was implicated in contests of localism, as well as becoming a hallmark of the cultural achievements of the High Qing imperium.[113] In addressing the question of why talented women were not a problem in the nineteenth century, Susan Mann cogently argues, "The debates about learned women that flared up at the end of the eighteenth century had subsided, and the 'woman problem' (*funü wenti*) that dominated elite discourses of the early twentieth century had yet to surface."[114] The case of Sun Caifu further attests to the way the exaltation of female talent served the needs of the post-Taiping era, a development that has barely begun to draw scholarly attention. For Sun's literary project, women's poetry suggested the possibility of retrieving from tumult and devastation a shared cultural past aligned with her priorities in writing wartime experiences and memories. For the effort to reconstitute local cultural identities, the prominence of localities—Huizhou and Yangzhou in this case—found evidence in their female talents. In both respects, it can also be argued that women's poetry as exemplars of localism and High Qing cultural achievements found new uses in the postwar cultural revival.

Other factors were at work in shaping Sun Caifu's afterlife, particularly through Yu Yue's mediation. I have drawn from biographical and elegiac essays for Sun as background to my discussion of her writings, but these essays are themselves worthy of attention, not least because they illuminate the intersections between family histories and discourses of sentimentality and female exemplarity, all with changing emphases.

6

Projecting Utopia/Dystopia

> I did not find it [poetry by Du Fu] well crafted when I read it in normal times, but after I personally experienced war, death, and chaos, I realized when I chanted it out how marvelous it was in addressing its time and speaking to people's hearts.
> 平時讀之，未見其工；迨親罹兵火喪亂之後，誦其詩，如出乎其時，犁然有當於人心，然後知其語之妙也。
>
> —*Hu Zi*

> There is no end to what I have long felt in my heart. Why don't I give voice to all I feel in my heart through [my novel] *Heroic Beauties*? . . . What I feel most strongly about is nothing but the darkness in our women's sphere.
> 吾心之感久矣，無已，其舉吾心之所感，而托鳴於《俠義佳人》乎？……最烈者，則莫若吾女界之黑暗也。
>
> —*Shao Zhenhua*

THE *COMMENTARIES [ON Poetry] Collected by the Hermit Fisherman by Tiao Stream* (Tiaoxi yuyin conghua; discussed in chapter 5) allowed Sun Caifu to establish a parallel between Hu Zi's time and her own. Its legacy seemed to reach even farther than the post-Taiping restoration. A late Qing woman novelist referred to herself as a "lady scholar from Jixi, inquiring about the fisherman" (Jixi wenyu nüshi; 績溪問漁女史), indicating her link to the fisherman hermit Hu Zi when writing during the tumultuous aftermath of the First Sino-Japanese War (1894–95), the Boxer Uprising (1899–1901), and the Russo-Japanese War (1904–5).[1] She has been identified as Shao Zhenhua (fl. early 20th c.), whose natal family was from Jixi. Her novel, *Heroic Beauties* (Xiayi jiaren), is a rare example of a late Qing novel authored by a woman.[2]

Shao Zhenhua published the two volumes of her novel in 1909 and 1911, respectively, in Shanghai, where new commercial publishing enterprises flourished. Each volume includes twenty chapters.[3] Recent studies discuss the novel in relation to late Qing publishing culture related to novels by women (or under female pen names).[4] Ellen Widmer contrasts them with the earlier *Honglou meng ying* (Shadows of the *Dream of the Red Chamber*; 1877) and suggests that these few late Qing novels, including *Heroic Beauties*, marked the debut of female novelists, who were less inhibited about identifying themselves as such. Possible factors contributing to the end of this inhibition included the novels' common focus on reforms related to women, the influence of foreign women writers, and increased publishing opportunities for women during this time.[5] Huang Jin Chu's recent study conducts detailed analyses of *Heroic Beauties* along with three other late Qing novels by women. Huang draws attention to the thematic richness of the novel, which suggests that Shao embraces a diverse range of reformist ideas about gender equality. Huang also emphasizes its progressiveness in giving voice to women's oppression while pointing out that the novel's reservations about new-style marriage show its "conservative tendency"—though often out of practical consideration.[6]

Heroic Beauties falls into what David Wang calls a "hybrid genre," combining knights-errant chivalric fiction with scholar-beauty love romance. Both genres are embedded in long genealogies of traditional Chinese fiction. Their unification in late Qing fiction set a precedent for the radicalism at the turn of the twentieth century, in which revolutionary and romantic sentiments were combined in the service of a larger social cause. It is remarkable, Wang finds, how radical intellectuals of the time found in chivalric heroism the classical equivalent of their revolutionary cause and how chivalric female characters from the earlier novels, in particular, changed roles to become revolutionaries and assassins. Such radicalism found expression in two prominent examples: *Flower of the Women's Prison* (Nüyu hua; 1904) and *The Stones of Goddess Nüwa* (Nüwa shi; 1905). Both novels feature chivalric-women-turned-revolutionaries who join women's utopias or secret societies that promote sisterhood, misandry, and violence and aim to overthrow both the corrupt Qing polity and the unequal system that has kept women in jail. Thus Wang establishes a parallel (or what he calls the "unlikely pair") between, on the one hand, taming women warriors by subjugating them to Confucian womanly virtues (e.g., in the late Qing novel *A Tale of Heroes and Loves* [Ernü yingxiong zhuan; 1873]) and, on the other hand, the conversion of chivalric women to patriotic and extremist movements in novels such as *Flower of the Women's Prison* and *The Stones of Goddess Nüwa*. Romantic sentiment gave way to revolutionary fervor in these latter cases.[7]

For the present study, *Heroic Beauties* provides an important final glimpse into women's changing imaginary of space and place following the decline of the Huizhou impact. Shao's close attention to place is an understudied detail that nonetheless constitutes the key structuring frame for the novel. Predicated on narrative innovations of the time—particularly the utopia/dystopia dyad, which held an unprecedented fascination for late Qing novelists,[8] this spatial frame enables political commentary that provides a deliberate corrective to the novel's radical predecessors.

Dawn Light for Women: Envisioning an Emergent National Order

To illustrate the novel's spatial frame, it is necessary to briefly summarize the plot and some of the characters. Gao Jianchen is a core figure among the novel's "heroic beauties." She is introduced as originating from Huaining, the prefectural seat of Anqing (Anhui), which gained unprecedented geographical and military importance during the Taiping War.[9] Raised as a talented traditional woman, Gao is married into a family of scholars and officials in Jiangyin (Jiangsu). Her husband, Lin Feibai, serves in the Hanlin Academy, studies in Europe, and returns to establish a society in Shanghai to devise and propagate schemes for national strengthening. Gao herself is a core member of a women's society in Shanghai, Dawn Light (Xiaoguang Hui), which parallels the society established by Lin Feibai but with a focus on women's education and social roles. Gao makes a long entrace in the opening chapters of the novel.

The story begins with a group of women traveling in the countryside and giving speeches to village women. The village is located on the outskirts of Ji'nan (Shandong), whose peculiar geographical features isolate it from the outside world. It is a "land of happiness" (*letu*), Shao Zhenhua writes sarcastically, because its insulation protects it from Boxers, foreigners, revolutionaries, and "civilized people."[10] Although, in reality, Shandong was a major source of the Boxer Uprising, the village in the novel has no contact at all with the uprising.[11] Nor does it have schools or money, thus saving the men from gambling. The village women admire small feet and willingly bind their own feet.[12] A group of women traveling to the village is sent by Dawn Light to enlighten the village women. Hua Caifan is from Hangzhou and has overseas experience before joining Dawn Light. Meng Yaqing is from Sichuan and studies in a girls' school affiliated with the group. Wang Lan is Hua's affinal kin and is from Ji'nan. Their arrival at the village creates quite a stir: Hua and Meng's western-style attire leads the xenophobic villagers to take them as ghosts. Thus, for the first time in this book, the rural ceases to figure as a landscape in which diasporic families may stake their cultural claims. Rather, as Yu Zhang argues, the countryside was emerging during the early twentieth century as a representational space for reformers and revolutionaries to highlight the gap between China's rural and urban areas. Crossing the gap constitutes a distinctly modern experience on personal, collective, and institutional levels.[13] Shao's novel captures the very moment of what Yu Zhang calls the epistemological shift in imagining the rural/urban distinction, using that distinction to engage with questions arising from China's modernizing agenda.[14]

Dawn Light is a women's society, Hua and Meng try to explain to villagers as well as the local gentry. As suggested by its name, the society aims to save Chinese women from their benightedness and let them see the dawn light of the modern world. Hua and Meng have followed the order of their society's president to travel from Shanghai to Shandong (and early on in Zhejiang) and give speeches on their enlightening scheme. In what has become a familiar story by now, women's enlightenment in early twentieth-century China included educational reforms for women and efforts to free them from patriarchal oppression. Both were integral to China's modernizing agenda. As Tani Barlow finds, women's education and liberation became primary indicators of the health and strength of the nation for modernizing nations all over the world during the twentieth century.[15] In the novel, this enlightening scheme immediately elicits critique—not from the village women but rather from Xiao Zhifen, the well-educated daughter of a local official.

One chapter is titled "A Speech on New Principle Conveys No Right or Wrong; A Discussion of Old Learning Comes Close to Satire and Attack" (Jiang xinli ruoshi ruofei; lun jiuxue sichao sima), foregrounding the contested issue of old and new forms of learning in educational reform.[16] Xiao comes from a remote area in Yunnan, has traveled with her father to his various official posts, and has studied in Japan and in the West. Her straddling of the old and new worlds suggests that her critique is not about the new principle itself, which the novel describes as Dawn Light's enlightening scheme. Rather, Xiao primarily targets Hua's concluding remarks on how Dawn Light's lofty scheme for saving Chinese women from their benightedness is driven by the Confucian ideal of benevolence. For Xiao, this lofty scheme is too poorly planned and carried out—based on a couple of members' speeches here and there—to be remotely convincing. How many people, she asks, can indeed benefit from the prospect of benevolence they promote?[17] Benevolence, according to Ban Wang, constituted an important basis for the late Qing thinkers to incorporate Confucian political and cultural resources into their new world vision. Liang Qichao, in particular, drew on this ideal to advocate Chinese self-determination among belligerent nation-states while reconciling nationalism with cosmopolitanism, which he saw as "a world order of peaceful coexistence and mutual respect among nations."[18] For the Dawn Light members in Shao's novel, benevolence can be an aid in their fight for gender equality if it includes women in China's progress toward modern civilization (*wenming*). For Xiao, by contrast, both benevolence and the new prospect of gender equality lack a substantial plan for implementation and are hence only empty ideals. Despite Xiao's humiliating remarks, the Dawn Light women admire her talent and rhetorical skill and recommend her to their society president. Xiao, however, soon departs for the United States to come to the aid of friends she has made there. The narrator then turns to the Dawn Light president, Meng Dimin, and the society she has founded.[19]

Meng Dimin is from a merchant's family in Jiangxi. Her uncle, a "capitalist" (a neologism at this time) who profits tremendously from commerce and mining and who is an enthusiastic philanthropist, gives her almost unlimited resources to build her society in Shanghai. She chooses the metropolitan center, Park Lane, for the society's headquarters. Affiliated with the society are girls' schools housed in western-style buildings she constructs in Ze-ka-wey, near the French concessions known for missionary libraries and schools. Her uncle lives near Foochow Road, a commercially and culturally vibrant area where capitalists, Chinese and foreign, have settled in large numbers. She herself chooses to live in the quiet suburbs close to Ze-ka-wey and her schools. She conducts business in her general office every other day. The telephone plays an important role in connecting her with her headquarters, her schools, and her uncle to ensure that Dawn Light runs smoothly.[20] A modern technology that China imported for the Self-Strengthening Movement during the 1870s, the telephone served a commercial purpose from the beginning. In the novel, this modern technology puts the Dawn Light president in control of the metropolitan sites crucial to her cause.[21]

At the headquarters, Meng Dimin's efforts have been successful. The girls' schools are flawless. But it has occurred to her that the biggest difficulty lies in recruiting female talent to serve in her society. Clearly more work needs to be done in propagating the society's schemes in the countryside. Even at headquarters, she realizes, members' knowledge and moral qualities are not on the same level. Meng urges Hua Caifan to convince Xiao to come back from the United States. At the same time, she accepts a new society member on recommendation. Several months later, while she waits impatiently for her new recruit, Hua and Xiao write to her at the same time to recommend Gao Jianchen. Meng immediately blames herself for failing to contact Gao: "Indeed, how am I so forgetful? How can I forget to ask her? She is my lifelong good friend. I must make a personal visit to her. I shall go tomorrow."[22] Thus Gao Jianchen makes her entrance in the novel.

Gao Jianchen enters the story as a crucial friend and timely support to Meng Dimin and Dawn Light. It is often Gao, along with her husband, who helps Dawn Light and its members overcome difficulties. In the meantime, Meng Dimin lauds Gao's intellectual and moral powers. They met in Nanjing, where their fathers served in the same administration after the Taiping capital was recaptured by Qing forces. Both have received a traditional education, in which Gao far eclipsed Meng. Meng both admires and feels quite intimated by Gao's high-minded moral principles and restrained character. The next day Meng departs for Jiangyin.[23]

Jiangyin is a major port on the Yangzi River in the traditional Jiangnan heartland. Traveling by waterway between Shanghai and Jiangyin is quite convenient, but it still takes a whole day for Meng Dimin to arrive in Jiangyin. It then takes her more than an hour to find the boulevard of sycamore trees leading to the secluded mansion where Gao lives with her husband's family. The mansion matches in every respect Meng's expectation of an eminent Qing scholar-official's residence—solidly founded, with grand architectural structures, exquisite furniture and garden, and a proper division between men's and women's spheres. An elderly concubine of Gao's father-in-law receives the female guests, while Meng is told that Gao and her husband have been invited to dine with foreign friends. It is not until the couple come back that Meng discovers that behind this mansion—across a big lawn and shielded by flourishing fruit trees—stands a quite independent western-style five-story house that accommodates the couple's core family. Conversations between hosts and guests start in spatial terms too. The concubine tries to exchange pleasantries by referring to Shanghai as a "big place" full of entertainment, and Jiangyin as a "small place" that may bore the guests. Meng is left speechless. Gao introduces her marvelous husband, Lin Feibai—who appears to Meng to be a handsome and brilliant young gentleman dressed in western suits and distinguished by a courteous and gallant style. Lin replies to Meng's question about his overseas experience that he studied in Germany for three years and in Belgium for another three years.[24]

Thus far it may well appear that the Lin family's mansion and the couple's western-style house provide a clear-cut contrast between old and new lifestyles. In particular, the couple's house symbolizes the emergent ideal of the nuclear family against the backdrop of the collapse of the kinship society in China.[25] A few years after the novel's publication, this new ideal was to become key to the New Culture advocates' reform of the Chinese family. According to Susan Glosser, for many of these advocates from 1915 on, the core family, or Western conjugal family, would enhance the family's productivity as an economic unit, and they soon tied it to China's modernizing enterprise.[26] In the novel, however, the very existence of the character Gao Jianchen forestalls a clear-cut binary of old and new. About one year after Gao and Meng met in Nanjing, Gao's father died of illness, and she returned to her natal home in Anhui. Soon afterward, she was married into the Lin family in Jiangyin. The suggestion that she does not have the same overseas experience as her husband does not prevent the couple from enjoying an ideal companionate marriage—sharing their concerns about China or dining with their foreign friends. Most of all, both Gao and Lin are distinguished by their "heroic" (*ying*) spirit.[27] Etymologically, *ying* refers to the quintessence or perfect embodiment of human character.[28] The author provides no evidence of such spirit in Lin, except perhaps that he is enthusiastic in promoting national strengthening and, like Gao, comes to the aid of their friends. But Shao spotlights Gao's acumen in finding a way forward as an example of her heroic spirit. Gao engages in a conversation on Dawn Light with candid critiques: women's enlightenment remains no more than an empty ideal unless Dawn Light comes up with a specific plan for raising women's awareness of the roles they need to play in the family and the society. Giving speeches in the countryside has proved ineffective. Neither is there any use in learning about women's benighted situation in the countryside unless Dawn Light can devise a plan for changing that situation.[29]

In these critiques Gao echoes her overseas-returned friend Xiao Zhifen. Gao elaborates on a few suggestions Xiao made and lays out a blueprint for Meng to restructure Dawn Light. Because education must take into consideration the large population of rural women, Dawn Light needs to prioritize technical studios (*gongyi chang*) to provide these women with practical livelihood skills. This practical training can be supplemented by girls' schools. The technical studios need new buildings, and the expected profits should be returned to the students. The girls' schools need additional spaces for those who cannot afford education, as well as shelters for the homeless. Specific regulations and guidelines need to be drafted to ensure effective management. Together they would contribute to China's emergent industries and education.[30] Once they achieve visible effects, Dawn Light should set up branches in the provinces and channels for communication and coordination. The speakers in the branches can then propagate what has proved effective rather than engaging in empty talk. To use a military metaphor, technical studios provide the main force of the army; girls' schools, the army's left and right wings; society branches, the rear army; speakers, the guerilla fighters with their sporadic attacks. Members with remarkable talent or skills are the artillerymen likely to have the greatest impact. Capital is, of course, essential, as it ensures the army's supplies.[31] The key here lies in thinking in terms of effects and devising a step-by-step plan to achieve those effects. This metaphor also conveys the urgency of achieving specific effects.

As the author endorses Gao Jianchen's critiques and suggestions, she also foregrounds how Gao declines Meng's invitation to take up a leadership role in Dawn Light's headquarters in Shanghai. It is impossible for a wife to leave behind her responsibility for household management. Gao asks, "Is a family without a wife still a family?"—thus raising a more general question about whether women's social roles should allow forsaking their familial roles. Gao finally agrees to provide part-time counsel and make monthly visits to Shanghai.[32]

These opening chapters can be read as the point by which the novel picks up where its precursors leave off. *Flower of the Women's Prison*, for example, features female assassins who resort to radical measures against the authorities to free women from prison. Toward the end, a key character, Xu Pingquan (lit., "endorsing or advancing equal rights"), reflects on whether there is an alternative approach. After the female protagonist Sha Xuemei and her assassin comrades are defeated by the government, Xu returns from overseas to promote women's education in China. Xu speaks admiringly of the progress made on women's rights through Sha's "destructive measures" before pondering the consequences of the continuing antagonism between the sexes. In the years that follow, Xu realizes her peaceful aims in establishing women's schools and inculcating mutual respect between men and women.[33] This ending has generated different interpretations. David Wang argues that Xu does not downplay Sha's radicalism, and the two women represent equally favored alternatives. The episode where the two friends part unhappily after their debate yields a sense that "women revolutionaries can differ and that they accept the consequences."[34] Ellen Widmer, by contrast, suggests that both the commentary on the novel and the story line confirm Xu's peaceful means as the correct path.[35] One may add that an alternative message could be that peaceful construction of an ideal system becomes possible after Sha has paved the way for it. As the epilogue opines, "Revolutions start with radical measures and end in peace" (Geming zhishi, xiancong jilie, hougui pinghe; 革命之事，先從激烈，後歸平和).[36] *Heroic Beauties* unambiguously favors Xu's path; the novel begins with propagating women's education and uses Gao Jianchen as a frequent reminder—to women reformers in the same camp—of what may turn out to be too radical or idealistic. The first time Gao serves at the Dawn Light headquarters in Shanghai, she tries to convince Meng Dimin that true heroism does not conflict with love between men and women because conjugal love is among the five cardinal human relations and the source of love for other humans. Meng is struck by the seriousness with which Gao responds to a comment she only made in passing.[37] This episode, which is crucial to Shao's interpretation of the major motifs of the novel, heroism and love, stands in stark contrast to the opening chapters of the *Flower of the Women's Prison*, in which Sha Xuemei condemns male oppressors of women (or *nanzei*, "male villains") and kills her own husband as one of the oppressors.[38]

To further illustrate Gao's critique of empty ideals, the novel includes an episode about another girls' school, this time located in Jiangyin, which is a backwater in terms of girls' schools. The founder of a local girls' school, Bai Huiqin, has a background similar to Xiao Zhifen: she has studied overseas since a young age and has traveled widely to her father's official posts. She is determined to promote women's education when she moves back to her native home in Jiangyin. The school is housed in the Bai family estates because Bai Huiqin has not been able to find the funds to construct a school. She also struggles to find volunteer teachers for her ambitious curriculum, which includes English, Chinese, gymnastics, music, painting, handicrafts, games, history, geography, mathematics, physics, and chemistry. An elderly lady who once took in female students—a traditional teacher of the inner chambers—is soon found to be inadequate for Bai's curriculum. Bai and Gao become friends during the process. Though Gao graciously offers to teach geography and arithmetic for free, connects Bai with a missionary's wife and daughter who agree to help teach English and music, and even contributes funds to the school, she cautions her friend against building a school on enthusiasm only; long-term financial support must be secured. Gao asks, "How can you count on everyone serving the school on a volunteer basis?" A greater problem concerns the students. Parents in Jiangyin are reluctant to send their daughters to school; even when they are persuaded to do so, students drop out all the time. In addition, students frequently encounter hostility and harassment. In a harassment case, the principal of a boys' school in the neighborhood accuses Bai's students of crossing boundaries, both physical and social, to go out in public. Gao's advice is for the students to observe the boundaries as much as possible. Bai bursts out, "I've always admired how knowledgeable and open-minded you are, but how can you say something so stubbornly conservative and corrupt? This is absolutely unacceptable! I shall have nothing to do with you from now on."[39]

A modern reader might easily take Bai's side. Indeed, the spatial boundaries constraining Chinese women were part of the "stubbornly conservative and corrupt" views hindering China's progress toward becoming a modern nation. Here, the author nonetheless takes Gao's side, giving Gao a more rational voice to calm Bai down and suggest strategies for the school to survive. What Gao has in mind are the ingrained customs that lead people to spread rumors about women who are seen in public or in the company of men, and that inculcate in men arrogance and a sense of superiority over women. At this point, it is more urgent to fight for women's right to an education than for other rights, such as entering public spaces. Even female teachers can easily become targets of harassment or rumor, and the school's reputation would be ruined if Bai failed to take extra precautions. Having convinced Bai, Gao then uses her husband's family connections to have the harasser punished without creating further sensation.[40]

Bai's school soon faces another crisis. A female student returning from Hong Kong has been newly hired to teach at the school but turns out to lack the claimed qualifications and is unable to teach properly. Even worse, she is addicted to gambling. While Bai spends time away from the school to attend to her sick mother, the new hire takes students to gamble day and night. The local administration arrests the new hire and the students, and the school has to close down under the social pressure caused by the scandal.[41] The first volume of the novel ends with Gao hastening back from Shanghai to rescue the school after she attends a meeting at Dawn Light and helps plan its development.

What Gao experiences in Shanghai seems intended as a contrast to the girls' school in Jiangyin. Dawn Light is never short of resources. The author leads us—through Gao's eyes—through the modern buildings and facilities for the girls' school affiliated with it and into a grand gathering of Shanghai officials, elites, educators, and foreigners at its headquarters. The organization has no doubt made a positive impact on the public and is developing on the track envisioned by its talented female leaders.[42] Indeed, it is a utopia for women, except when the president, Meng Dimin, finds that the new hire who claims to have studied in Japan does not have solid training in the subjects she teaches and is causing trouble. Thus this ideal system encounters exactly the same problem as does an ill-equipped girls' school in a backwater in Jiangsu. Moreover, Meng's brother, a student returned from overseas, insists that he has the right to take concubines, and the family disputes he incites distract Meng from her tasks. The author thus sets the characters in debates on issues of equality and freedom in light of the problems they face.[43] In particular, the author allows Gao Jianchen to shuttle between Shanghai and Jiangyin and thus obtain a broader picture of the problems besetting girls' schools. Gao's critique often suggests the author's favored perspective on the pitfalls to avoid in finding the way forward.[44]

The Spatial Frame: Narrative Innovation as Political Commentary

By the end of the first volume of *Heroic Beauties*, it has become clear that the author pays close attention to spatial settings. The neologism *nüjie* (women's sphere), which Shao Zhenhua uses in her preface, multiplies into specific settings in which reforms for women play out in their full complexity. As an emergent imagined community or collective identity for Chinese women, this women's sphere turns out to be fraught with contention.[45] The very reformers who are entrusted with bringing dawn light into the women's sphere are constantly reminded of their flawed plans. Bringing them into interaction with other social groups in various settings constitutes the key structuring device of the novel.

For the modern reader, it is easier to see metropolitan Shanghai as the hub of educational reforms for women. Shao Zhenhua may indeed have been referring to historical changes in Shanghai when creating *Dawn Light*. As Nanxiu Qian's study of the late Qing female reformer Xue Shaohui (1866–1911) shows, Xue and her coterie of reform-minded women founded the first women's periodical, *Chinese Girls' Progress* (Nü xuebao), in Shanghai during the 1898 reform, and it soon drew public attention and became a forum for debates on women's rights and education. The grand gathering at Dawn Light in Shao's novel closely resembles the first meeting of the Women's Study Society, held on December 6, 1897, which Qian calls the spearhead of the "multi-faceted 1898 Shanghai campaign for women's education." Shao's description of the girls' school affiliated with Dawn Light also echoes that opened by the Women's Study Society in 1898 in Shanghai.[46]

Another important factor is at work: the city as a miniature of all of China, formed paradoxically through the native sentiments of immigrants. As Bryna Goodman describes, throughout the late nineteenth and early twentieth centuries, Shanghai hosted a growing population of immigrants fleeing war or famine in their native places or pursuing economic opportunities in the city. The diversity of their native-place communities and customs changed the city's social structure and urban environment. At the same time, the scope of these native-place communities—interurban networks and even national networks—allowed them to become involved in national issues and imagine a national identity, resulting in what Goodman calls the "diversity of China in one locality."[47] The rise of Shanghai looms in the background of Shao's novel when minor characters refer to it as a place to get rich following the Taiping War.[48] But more importantly, it is the ideal location for a women's society with ambitious schemes of national scope. The diversity of its population is reflected in the diversity of backgrounds of the Dawn Light members. In particular, Jiangxi as native home to the textile merchants in Shanghai is visible in the native-place background of the Dawn Light president and her capitalist uncle.[49] Precisely at a time when China's textile trade was in crisis due to the domination of foreign capital and industry, Shao projected in response a utopian vision of China's thriving manufacturing industry backing a women's society with nationwide engagement in gender equality and modernization.[50]

With the rise of Shanghai, the former Jiangnan cultural heartland becomes the hinterland. Suzhou and Changzhou, for example, have lost their former luster as the cradle of cultural elites and female talent. As mentioned in the novel, people in these places seem especially backward and uncultivated.[51] More broadly, this is the countryside, which Dawn Light tries to penetrate from the very beginning. As Yu Zhang explains, the rural-urban distinction began to emerge at this moment as "an artificially created hierarchy of the industrial, progressive center over the agrarian, underdeveloped periphery."[52]

Jiangyin is less familiar and stands somewhere between these shifting centers and peripheries. By inserting Jiangyin into an emergent national order, Shao Zhenhua asserts her vision of the direction this order should be taking. Jiangyin is located in the Jiangnan heartland but is not as prominent as Suzhou or Changzhou. And yet, it has its own resources—embodied in the novel as the influence of a scholar-official's family combined with European knowledge and lifestyle, which take the material shape of the Lin family's solidly built mansion and the young couple's five-story western-style house behind the mansion. Gao Jianchen has no qualms about capitalizing on the family's connections—Chinese or foreign—in devising strategies for her friends' schools to survive. A place like Jiangyin, then, is well positioned to draw on its various resources to find a way forward.

Anhui matters to this order too. Huaining, as mentioned earlier, had assumed unprecedented political and military significance during and after the Taiping War. In the novel, Gao's family background and her solid training in traditional learning suggest that Huaining has also acquired cultural significance. It would even seem that it has replaced Huizhou in producing a core figure like Gao. It is no coincidence that geography is the first subject Gao offers to teach in the girls' school in Jiangyin, indicating her awareness of place and a larger order, and the cultural legacy or knowledge underlying such awareness. Gao would have been a fitting spokesperson for the "Huizhou impact," if Huaining had not by this time assumed a more important position in Anhui and nationally. But Huizhou does not die out. Shao only plays a different game by invoking Hu Zi's legacy and hence inserting Huizhou into the picture as her own cultural background.

The novel's spatial frame provides a setting for the characters to engage in dialogue and debate. Chen Pingyuan eloquently argues that one innovation made by late Qing novelists is to borrow the format of the literati travelogue to create a protagonist on the road, and hence shift from the omniscient perspective typical of the traditional Chinese novel to the restricted perspective of the protagonist. Often, the protagonist finds himself in debates due to what he observes or experiences along the way. And there lies another innovation of the late Qing novel: adaptation of the dialogic format (*duihua ti*) found in the Han-dynasty political treatise *Yantie lun* (Treatise on salt and iron; 81 BCE) into a narrative device. Usually, dialogue or debate is conducted between two leading characters, and the defense made by one character in response to the critique of the other communicates the novel's political agenda. An ensuing flaw is that the critique often appears superfluous, and the defense is only too easily justified.[53]

Female protagonists on the road suggest the enhanced freedom women had in traveling—and for that matter, the freedom female novelists had in imagining traveling.[54] Useful as it is to examine how women's travel expanded their understanding of the world, in Shao's case the point lies more in how narrative innovation by late Qing novelists enabled her to develop a sophisticated device for communicating political commentary. The protagonist on the road multiplies into the core characters in Shao's novel, and she places them at different locations, sets them on the road, shifts between their perspectives, and brings them together for debates. The many people and events they encounter or hear about along the way provide a clue to understanding what are said to be the many side plots separate from the main plot.[55] These side plots bring to the fore issues enthralling late Qing thinkers and reformers that stimulate the debates constitutive of the main plot. In particular, Gao Jianchen, as Shao's spokesperson, has the job of critiquing idealized systems or simplified solutions. Her suggestions serve not so much to provide a definitive solution as to alert her friends to pitfalls in their search for solutions. In addition to reversing the order of significance between the critique and the defense, I argue, the debates in Shao's novel creatively adapt the political genre established by the *Yantie lun* and combine it with platonic dialogue. For the Chinese reader, platonic dialogue—debate over key ethical, political, and epistemological questions initiated by Plato in imagined settings—first appeared in Thomas More's *Utopia* (1516), which was introduced to China in the early twentieth century. More borrows platonic dialogue, but unlike Plato, who draws the reader into a discussion to reach a conclusion, More allows his interlocutors to remain open to different ways of thinking.[56]

Involving multiple characters in the debates of *Heroic Beauties*—and allowing them to maintain difference in collaborative causes—conveys the novel's message about open-mindedness.

The imagined settings for the debates in the novel evoke the utopia/dystopia dyad in late Qing fiction. As defined by David Wang, utopia was the "fantastic removal of the unpleasant," whereas dystopia was its "dark counterpart" or "countertext." Part of the literary reform centering on the political novel (the "new fiction") as a medium of enlightenment, this dyad projected ideals and their reversals in staking out fictional resolutions to China's historical and modernizing problems.[57] In what Wang calls "unprecedented spatial-temporal environments," the dyad often conjured up a futuristic world in which fantastic vehicles—such as balloons, submarines, and spaceships—carried out for the characters previously unimaginable adventures that revived or ruined China.[58] Shao Zhenhua's play on these imaginary settings, however, had an explicit contemporary relevance. At least three examples of utopia/dystopia appear in the first volume of *Heroic Beauties*. The village in Shandong is a dystopia symptomatic of Chinese women's benightedness, but it is ironically introduced as a utopia protected from uprisings. The women's society that sends members to enlighten the village, by contrast, is closest to an ideal system but is no less ironically represented as a utopia that has no plans for implementing its enlightening scheme. The girls' school in Jiangyin is the worst version of this utopia—founded on idealism only and deteriorating into a dystopia because of its incessant crises and scandals.

Wucheng: The Utopia/Dystopia in "Nowhere"

The second volume can be summarized as Dawn Light's expansion in spatial terms: toward the latter half of the volume, we become aware of a branch in Hangzhou and, by its end, another branch to be set up in Beijing.[59] The rapidly evolving international order also becomes a conspicuous concern, revolving around elements such as an impending war that threatens China's survival, the characters' connections with the Korean nationalist movement against Japan, and patriotic causes backed by overseas Chinese.[60] The overall narrative is repetitive, as debates continue in settings similar to those in the first volume. Wucheng, however, stands out as a unique setting, and the chapters organized around it (28–31) are central to an even more elaborate play on the utopia/dystopia dyad.

Wucheng is "nowhere" in comparison to the familiar cities or places that appear frequently in volume 1. Even the countryside of Ji'nan is easier to locate. The reader is only given the sense that it is somewhere in the Jiangnan area, when, in volume 2, Meng Dimin, Gao Jianchen, and their friends accept an invitation to visit a private garden there. Meng departs from Shanghai, and it takes one day to arrive at Wucheng by waterway. She mentions that she will have the chance to visit Hangzhou on her way. Gao and Lin decide to depart from Suzhou, having used their connections to solve yet another problem for their friends there.[61] These clues indicate that Wucheng is connected by waterway to Hangzhou and Suzhou. The owner of the garden, Kou Dichen, is originally from Tongxiang (Zhejiang); his family has changed its registered residence to Wucheng. The two place names appear to be a pair: "wu" and "tong" constitute the Chinese name for sycamore trees. Only much later in the novel is it mentioned that, like Tongxiang, Wucheng is part of Jiaxing prefecture.[62] While this clue locates Wucheng somewhere in the backwaters of Zhejiang, nowhere in the Zhejiang local gazetteers is the place name Wucheng to be found. Wuzhou in Guangxi was often referred to as Wucheng in Guangxi local gazetteers and elsewhere.[63] It may not be a coincidence, then, that the place name is a homophone of "no city" in Chinese.

The owner, Kou Dichen, and his wife, Meng Danru, have quite remarkable backgrounds. Kou studied in the United States since he was young and received his degree from a college in New York. Meng Danru is American-born Chinese. Her family is originally from Jiangxi (distantly related to Meng Dimin) and has been extremely successful in running businesses in Singapore and the United States. The family has been in New York for generations. Danru's father is said to be a highly patriotic philanthropist who has donated lavishly to Chinese societies promoting national rejuvenation, including Dawn Light. Danru graduated from a women's college in New York and is also well trained in Chinese. Dichen and Danru met in New York and returned to China after getting married. Danru fits poorly in her native land: She is not fond of bustling Shanghai, where Dichen holds a position as a school principal. But neither has she been able to cope with the complicated family relations of the Kou family in Wucheng, particularly with the women from older generations such as concubines and unmarried sisters-in-law. To provide her a good home, Dichen has purchased one hundred *mu* of land on the outskirts of Wucheng in hopes of building an "enterprise" (*shiye*)—a neologism that refers broadly to manufacturing and mining industries and commerce based on these industries. What he has actually built is the private garden that the novel now focuses on.[64]

The garden is enclosed by walls and surrounded by a stream. The couple have planted willows and peach trees along the stream and all kinds of fruit trees in the garden. At the center stands a three-story western-style house, which they have named Villa by Clear Ripples (Qingyi Bieshu).[65] By the time they invite their friends to the garden, they have lived there for seven years. The villa allows them to enjoy their ideal companionship at a distance from their complicated extended family, without being accused of severing familial ties. It replicates, on a larger scale, Gao Jianchen's core family living in a western-style house across the grounds from the Lin family mansion. The guests include Meng Dimin and a few Dawn Light members; the Gao and Lin couple and their three children; Xiao Zhifen, who has returned from the United States and joined Dawn Light; and later, Xiao's fiancé and a friend from the United States. Hence the gathering in the garden showcases its various ties with the outside world.[66]

In a way echoing the Grand Prospect Garden in the Qing masterpiece *Dream of the Red Chamber*, the Clear Ripples garden boasts thriving plants of all kinds, ponds, rocks, and pavilions. The guests are led through sections of the garden carefully divided by lanes and bamboo fences, so that they do not exhaust the view of the "one hundred *mu*" at first sight and can instead appreciate the variations in garden design. But unlike the Grand Prospect Garden, the west side of the Clear Ripples garden serves an explicitly economic function: yielding agricultural and livestock products as food supplies for the family. Danru proudly tells her friends that there is never any need to purchase food supplies from outside.[67] Later, she reveals to her friends that the fruit trees—plum trees, in particular—are part of a plan to build an "enterprise." On each *mu* of the garden grow 240 plum trees, totaling twenty-four thousand, and the gathering was intended for the guests to see the plum trees in bloom. Every year, each plum tree yields twenty plums of the best kind, totaling 480,000 plums. They can be made into eighty thousand plum cans. The plan is to purchase machinery to manufacture cans and set up a company in Shanghai to establish business channels. The annual net profit is expected to total three thousand silver dollars, not to mention that other garden products, such as bamboo shoots and lotus seeds and roots, can be canned to generate profits as well.[68]

Danru's business plan reflects a time when can manufacturing companies grew rapidly in the United States and Europe and signaled new commercial opportunities for China. These opportunities appealed to reformers and revolutionaries who called for China to establish its own manufacturing industries, especially in light of the increasing domination of foreign investment in China during the decade preceding the 1911 revolution.[69] Thus the Clear Ripples garden at once figures as an enclave evoking the Grand Prospect Garden—as well as the Peach Blossom Spring, as suggested by the peach trees along the stream—and caters to the need to develop China's manufacturing and commerce. Readers of *Dream of the Red Chamber* may recall the economic potential of the Grand Prospect Garden: Jia Tanchun, the reform-minded character, assigns plots of land in the Grand Prospect Garden to the female servants and holds them responsible for the yield from the garden, which she hopes will offset the Jia family's daily expenses. However, Tanchun's reform is only intended for self-sufficiency, and it soon collapses under the Jia family's power struggles.[70] By contrast, Gao Jianchen characterizes Meng Danru as an "entrepreneur" (*shiye jia*, a neologism coined from *shiye*).[71] And Danru's business plan is backed by the capital of her family's business branches in Singapore and the United States, even though the garden's yields seem moderate by far.

The garden provides a base for guests to observe and reform local customs in Wucheng. Again echoing the Grand Prospect Garden, boundaries between the idealized enclave and the polluted outside world—or between what Ying-shih Yü famously terms the utopian world and the world of reality in *Dream of the Red Chamber*—easily become blurred.[72] A young girl with bound feet who appears in the garden turns out to be a niece of the Kou couple. The curiosity the girl incites among the guests leads Danru to remark that local customs are impossible to change. She pointedly condemns women in Wucheng as knowing three things only: binding feet, painting faces, and committing adultery. The extent of Wucheng's depravity is shocking, she tells her friends, but by now she has seen too much to feel shocked. For example, a family would return a bride on the basis that she has had no affairs, so clearly she has no sexual appeal. As if to prove Danru's point, several local women enter the garden, staging farces in a row about their family scandals before Danru and her guests and pleading for their help. The novel then turns to these scandals: a bought wife abused by the husband's mistress; a son set up by a nephew who commits adultery with the mother; a wife driven out by the husband's mistress and seeking a job as a maid; a young woman in a gentry family slandered by her maid and driven to death by her father; a crazy woman accusing Dichen of abandoning her (it turns out that she has been driven crazy by an unfaithful husband and abusive in-laws). Scandals set the characters in discussion. While it may seem that the author is here echoing a concern common in Qing novels—the transgressiveness of sexuality as a threat to familial and social orders—Gao Jianchen leads the discussion in different directions. First, she asks, shouldn't men and women be regarded as equal in terms of abiding by the rule of faithfulness in marriage? She then draws attention to the atrocities inflicted on the female victims in the episodes. Although her friends and she herself have much more freedom than these women, Gao asks, is such freedom determined by birth and hence a matter of pure luck?[73] In short, blurred boundaries between the garden and outside Wucheng allow the author to engage her characters—and readers—in ethical and political issues of contemporary concern. Again, as the author suggests, attitudes toward female sexuality cannot be reduced to a simplified model of progressive or conservative tendencies.

Chapters later, the author even transforms the Grand Prospect Garden into a scandal. At a setting near the Dawn Light branch in Hangzhou, Gao Jianchen encounters a distant relative from Anhui who has married into a big family in Hangzhou. The scion of that family, A Bao—a lascivious character parodying Jia Baoyu, the male protagonist of *Dream of the Red Chamber*—cannot keep his hands off his female cousins and the young maids, all in the name of free love. He ruins their reputations by violating the proper boundaries between female and male spheres, much in the way Baoyu lives among his female cousins in the Grand Prospect Garden. The only young woman who stands up to A Bao's sexual advances suffers slander and vicious treatment by the entire household. Gao Jianchen and the Dawn Light members then come to her rescue by offering her a teaching position.[74] In *Dream of the Red Chamber*—as Ying-Shih Yü reminds us—an ethical order prevails in the utopian world of the Grand Prospect Garden, and Baoyu is the ultimate arbiter of that order. That is, the position each young girl occupies in that order hinges on her proximity to Baoyu.[75] For Louise Edwards, that order reflects the gender hierarchy that *Dream of the Red Chamber* reproduces, despite the long-held view about the novel's progressiveness in elevating women's status.[76] In *Heroic Beauties*, the author condemns precisely this gender hierarchy by parodying Baoyu's relationship with his female cousins, and hence sets the utopian world of the Grand Prospect Garden in stark contrast to her utopia at Clear Ripples.

The author also sets her characters moving back and forth across the boundary between the Clear Ripples garden and outside Wucheng. The characters venture out of the garden for firsthand experience of the depraved Wucheng, then retreat into the garden for ideal friendship and debates over reformist schemes. The dialogic format of the first volume continues, and the garden's spatial boundary becomes the axis it now revolves around. Allusions to the contrast and erosion between the two worlds in *Dream of the Red Chamber* recur throughout, but they always bring into relief the contemporary concerns Shao Zhenhua intends her novel to speak to. In particular, Danru's guests now see an opportunity to expand her business plan for the Clear Ripples garden to the rest of Wucheng.[77]

The commercial area of Wucheng lies to the east of the garden. As Danru leads her guests there, they find it to be almost in an economic depression, with barely any commercial activity or customers. Farther away lie woods and villages. They soon engage in debates with the village people regarding hygienic problems and superstitious practices, and it is here that they discover Wucheng's commercial potential: sericulture. Xiao Zhifen explicitly defines sericulture as a new manufacturing industry, or *shiye*, and urges the village women to abandon their former practice of praying to gods or relying on geomancy to raise good silkworms. Rather, she asserts, "Raising silkworms is specialized knowledge in manufacturing industries."[78] It requires knowledge about the silkworm eggs, temperature, humidity, and above all, specially designed rooms for the silkworms. These rooms need good ventilation, hygienic protocols, and equipment for monitoring temperature and humidity. Xiao informs her audience that Japan has built such rooms whereas China has not yet done so. In contrast to such specialized knowledge, Xiao further explains, geomancy is based on superstition, and the sites supposed to be propitious in geomancy turn out to be good for the health only because they follow hygienic rules. No religion, indigenous or foreign, can be relied on in this respect. To this long speech Meng Dimin responds with a business plan: she offers to purchase a piece of land next to the Clear Ripples garden to build Japanese-style sericulture rooms and invites Danru, in view of her business acumen, to manage this enterprise. Schools are also to be built to teach sericulture skills to the village people. Practical matters such as drafting regulations and guidelines for management, hiring teaching staff from Japan, recruiting Japanese-language interpreters, and propagating sericulture in the neighboring areas are to be worked out in due course, as suggested by Gao Jianchen and others.[79] Thus a new space founded on specialized knowledge expands the Clear Ripples garden's business potential, in addition to expanding its physical boundary, and thus provides a remedy for Wucheng's economic depression. This project is envisioned as part of Dawn Light's plan for developing women's education with specialized knowledge, including sericulture and medicine.

Silk-reeling was among the foreign-dominated industries in China that drove reformers and entrepreneurs at this time to modernize China's own industries. In Nanxiu Qian's study, the modernization of sericulture was among the featured topics of the periodical *Chinese Girls' Progress*, founded by Xue Shaohui and her coterie of reform-minded women. One of the illustrations features a woman using a microscope—with the English word *Microscope* imprinted on the microscope—to monitor the growth of silkworms.[80] Clear Ripples' plan to build sericulture rooms and schools further echoes an earlier novel, *Women's Rights* (Nüzi quan; 1907), which calls for women's participation in *shiye*, including sericulture. Indeed, Shao Zhenhua lets her characters implement a detailed plan that *Women's Rights* lays out for a utopian Chinese Women's Society (Zhonghua Furen Hui).[81] Hygiene and medicine—like commerce and industry—were key components of China's modernizing enterprise in the early twentieth century. What Ruth Rogaski terms "hygienic modernity" captures the moment in the aftermath of the Boxer Uprising and the foreign occupation of the treaty port city of Tianjin when state intervention in health regulation and public hygiene took hold in China.[82] *Heroic Beauties* responds to this moment too, but instead of promoting state intervention, the novel imaginatively ties hygiene and medicine to entrepreneurship, knowledge and resources from abroad, educational reforms for women, and the social commitment of a group of women. A particular advantage of Meng Dimin's plan is that it will bring Dawn Light and Clear Ripples into collaboration. This suggests the growing influence the two are about to have together, across places ranging from metropolitan Shanghai to Wucheng—"no city" or nowhere.

"No city" draws the reader into a space that derives from utopia/dystopia and their Chinese equivalents as used in late Qing fiction. To return to More's *Utopia*, More coined the term *utopia* in New Latin to signify "no place."[83] Yan Fu's (1854–1921) Chinese translation of the term as "wutuo bang" (烏托邦)

was literal. Another popular Chinese translation, "wuyou zhixiang" (烏有之鄉), meant exactly the same: there was no such place.[84] The implication is that the perfect society or political system cannot be actualized. Nor does the idea offer any social panacea meant to be effective or feasible in reality.[85] Rather, "the work [*Utopia*] encourages taking a new view of social and political problems by seeing alleged (and strange) solutions to them and challenges readers to try to find out what they approve or disapprove of and why."[86]

Late Qing novelists found a convenient equivalent of the idea of utopia in the classic Chinese political allegory of Peach Blossom Spring. Liang Qichao's unfinished fictional trilogy included one volume titled *Peach Blossom Spring*. Better known in this trilogy was Liang's unfinished novel on a futuristic utopia for China, *The Future of New China* (Xin Zhongguo weilai ji; 1903).[87] Wang Miaoru, the author of *Flower of the Women's Prison*, was said to have completed a novel titled *A Legend about a Small "Peach Blossom Spring"* (Xiao Taoyuan chuanqi).[88] To these Shao Zhenhua added allusions to the two worlds of the *Dream of the Red Chamber*. As we have seen, the two worlds across the spatial boundary of the Clear Ripples garden are as interpenetrable as that across the Grand Prospect Garden. More importantly, much as the utopian world of the Grand Prospect Garden was founded on the site of the filthy Jia mansions,[89] Shao's two worlds suggest the same "no place." The utopian garden is the dystopian Wucheng.

The point here lies in more than puns that easily combine Chinese and Western cultural resources in imagining China's path to modernity and gender equality. In differentiating female utopias in late Qing fiction from their prototypes (e.g., the women's kingdom in the Ming novel *Journey to the West*), David Wang emphasizes once again their radicalism or "aggressive feminism." The Floral Blood Party, an all-woman secret society in The Stones of Goddess Nüwa, figures as a shocking example because the women assassinate corrupt male officials by the hundreds, and worse, its modern procreative technology that extracts sperm from men incites imagination about "worms that suck the bone marrow [of human beings]." Wang astutely observes that such aggressive feminism is far from complimentary and smacks of male anxiety.[90] Shao's Wucheng, then, must also be read as a response to male anxiety about aggressive feminism. The characters gathering at Clear Ripples, female *and* male, are capable of thinking and debating about alternatives to what was believed by their prototypes to be the only solution to China's problems. It is in this sense—rather than in projecting a perfect system or panacea—that Wucheng is Shao's Utopia.

The late Qing novel *Heroic Beauties* is a sophisticated response to the literary and political trends enthralling Chinese reformers at the tumultuous turn of the twentieth century. I have mainly deciphered this response through the novel's key structuring frame predicated on late Qing narrative innovations and imaginatively refashioned out of a utopia/dystopia dyad. This spatial frame captures the radical shift of center and periphery in an emergent national as well as international order as a way to engage with questions arising from China's modernizing agenda. But more importantly, by inserting backwaters and nowhere into this spatial frame, Shao Zhenhua challenges the reader to ponder utopian visions for China and its women and men, and hence take a step back from radical progressiveness or paths to modernity and gender equality. The novel remains open-ended, not only because it was cut short by the 1911 revolution.[91] The seismic changes following the 1911 revolution may indeed have made much of the debate among the characters no longer relevant. But had Shao completed a third volume, as she promises at the end of volume 2, either the foreseeable expansion of Dawn Light or its proclaimed plan for collaborating with Clear Ripples would hardly have offered a panacea or definitive solution to the new scenarios of the post-1911 revolution era.

It seems a long way from Anhui to nowhere, from laying claim to Hu Zi's legacy to responding to yet another tumultuous age. While the Huizhou diasporic communities marshaled resources to promote Huizhou and its outward-looking legacy in the early twentieth century, Shao Zhenhua assimilated inspiration old and new to take her worldview—her knowledge of the world and her approach to the changes taking place in it—beyond the Huizhou impact.

Epilogue

IT SHOULD BE obvious that the Qing women's writings now being uncovered in abundance responded to the world in which they were produced, rather than constituting an isolated terrain of their own. In terms of examining these writings in the totality of their world, what world was more tangible than the one the female authors traversed and claimed as an integral part of who they were, through explicitly spatial registers? This book begins with Huizhou as a place identity and its transregional impact beyond a place. Women's world-creating visions catalyzed by the Huizhou impact lead to discussions bearing on place studies, studies of transregional movement of people and changing human-place ties, and cross-disciplinary studies of spatiality and literature. Conversely, once an interplay is established, reframing these studies in light of women's literary and cultural production seems inevitable. The two symbiotic places Huizhou and Yangzhou differ from what has previously been known about them: both can be remapped into a cultural landscape characterized by women's enhanced visibility, as key factors enabling women's spatial and cultural claims. Other places discussed in connection with shifting centers and peripheries, the all-encompassing Tianxia, and the collapsed and restored order, as viewed by women call for more exploration of the spatial and gender relations played out on them.

Huizhou family publications in which the women's writings examined in this book were embedded suggest an archive of cultural aspirations prioritized by the largest premodern diasporic communities in China.[1] Finding ways to speak meaningfully about a selection of these publications—while many more are being excavated in reprinting and digitizing projects—has been one of my aims in this book. Any newly retrieved archives of sources may be approached in two ways: being mined for information, or else being examined as themselves products of various claims and scrutinized for the mechanisms underlying those claims. The information yielded by the sources discussed in this book includes place politics, localist projects, transregional networks, lineage building, conflicts and governance, and war and restoration. As far as these cases are concerned, family histories preserved therein lie largely outside genealogies, the primary discursive as well as material means for constructing family and lineage histories.[2] More than documenting the otherwise obscure facets of family histories, family publications—as the most valued form of cultural production—legitimatized the various claims staked out in them. They exerted control over the uncertainty and complexity inherent in the spatial restlessness of the age in ways that cannot be overlooked: by creating affective bonds ("roots") and engaging with local communities and power dynamics, sometimes in direct response to competing or conflicting interests. Acquiring a poetic language that may have become stereotypical proved to be an efficient means for achieving that purpose. Venturing into unfamiliar genres broke new ground in employing family legacies and resources for broader engagement. Needless to say, the spatial and cultural claims that female family members prioritized and that rarely made their ways into genealogies found expression in family publications.

Finally, questions of place identity spoke to changing ideals of femininity in the cultural mentality of the time. Part of this project arose out of my curiosity, as a reader of the Qing masterpiece *Dream of the Red Chamber*, concerning the double home of its talented and glamorous female protagonist, Lin Daiyu. Under the name Lin Daiyu of Gusu [Suzhou]—Suzhou being the birthplace of her father—Daiyu departs from Yangzhou to reach the Jia mansion in the capital and, after a few years, returns to Yangzhou and Suzhou for her father's burial.[3] The male protagonist, Jia Baoyu, is curious about the local customs and landscapes of her hometown, Yangzhou, and teases her for being the genuine treasure in the household of the salt control censor Lin.[4]

Suzhou continued to be the cradle of female talent during the novel's time, whereas Yangzhou figured as the place identity of the late Ming figure Xiaoqing, one of Daiyu's best-known prototypes. Versions of the Xiaoqing legend that cast her as a "thin horse" sold into a wealthy household match precisely the Yangzhou known for its glamorous courtesans and concubines.[5] What seems quite inexplicable is that this figure should acquire attributes unbefitting her status in the Qing novel: Daiyu's father has high family status not only by heritage but also through his success in the civil service examination and subsequent appointment to the salt administration in Yangzhou. Other familiar attributes include Daiyu's exceptional talent and her education in the classics, which she received from an instructor her father hired for her—qualities that enable her to outshine her peers, both female and male. Her boudoir in the Grand Prospects Garden is comparable to the best studio of a scholar.[6] It has become clear to me, in light of the research conducted for this book, that Yangzhou provided an alternative home to female talents like Xú Deyin. Their presence figured as a source of inspiration for the Qing novel in ways perhaps even more significant than the Xiaoqing legend. Status, as mentioned at the beginning of this book, was an important factor underlying the two sides of Yangzhou with respect to its women, but even status needed not understood in absolute terms. The fluidity of place identity and social status took the form of the apparently unlikely conjunction, in one character in the novel, of cultural ideals retraceable to an earlier age and those in florescence in the novel's time.

APPENDIX 1

Sites Related to Bao Zhihui's Homes and Home Mountains

Name of site	Number of appearances and page numbers	Function indicated, or key lines quoted from the poem
Hongjiao guan 紅蕉館	3 times 1.2b–4b, 9b, 2.11a–b	Studio in Bao Zhihui's natal home; site for family gatherings and reunions
Shipu ting 詩譜亭	2 times 1.8b–9a, 2.12a–b	Bao Gao's studio symbolic of family legacy; site for family gatherings and reunions; "Jiacang dujian yu xianze" 家藏蠹簡餘先澤
Qingyu ge 清娛閣	7 times 1.14a, 2.10a–b, 3.3a, 4.16a–b, 4.19b, 6.4b–5a, 6.7b	Bao Zhihui's studio in her marital home; site for family and elite gatherings
Caotang 草堂 Xiaoyuan 小園	5 times 2.6a–b, 2.7a–b, 3.1b, 3.8b–9a, 3.11a–b	Bao Zhihui and Zhang Xuan's estate; site for family and elite gatherings
Shantang 山堂	12 times 3.5b–6b, 3.7a, 3.9a–b, 3.10b–11a, 4.5a–6a, 4.12a, 4.12a–b, 4.12b–13a, 6.6a, 6.7b–8a, 6.9a, 6.9b	Zhang Xuan's studio; site for family and elite gatherings
Baihe daoyuan 百鶴道院	1 time 1.1a–b	Daoist monastery; related to the legend of the "Yihe ming"

Name of site	Number of appearances and page numbers	Function indicated, or key lines quoted from the poem
Lingjiang ge 淩江閣	3 times 1.10a, 2.5a, 6.2a–b	Expressing feelings for siblings traveling or sojourning outside Dantu; family excursion; "Cidi jingguo sishi nian" 此地經過四十年
Honghe shanzhuang 鴻鶴山莊	2 times 1.10b–11a, 2.5a–b	Hermits' retreat; related to the legend of the "Yihe ming"; birthday celebrations for Bao Zhihui's grandmother-in-law Lady Wu
Zhongxiang yuan 眾香院	1 time 1.11a–b	Excursion with Bao Zhihui's mother-in-law Lady Xue; site for elite gatherings with Wang Wenzhi
Beigu shan 北固山	1 time 1.14b	Excursion with Zhang Xuan; a panoramic view from the top of the hill; invoking historical references
Jingkou sanshan 京口三山	1 time 2.14b	River journey with Zhang Xuan; a panoramic view of the Three Hills; "Jiashan chuchu kan yulao, mo-dao quche xiang Lumen" 家山處處堪娛老，莫道驅車向鹿門
Zhulin si 竹林寺	1 time 2.16a	Buddhist temple; hermits' retreat; excursion with Zhang Xuan
Lindong ting 臨東亭	1 time 3.3a	A pavilion overlooking the Yang-zi River; excursions with family members; "Guting wanqing li cangmang" 孤亭萬頃立蒼茫

Name of site	Number of appearances and page numbers	Function indicated, or key lines quoted from the poem
Dingmao qiao 丁卯橋; Danyang dao 丹陽道; Huayang dao 華陽道; Damao feng 大茅峰; Qianyuan guan 乾元觀; Xixin chi 洗心池; Xianren qiao 仙人橋; Jima dong 績麻洞; Baiyun guan 白雲觀; Huayang dong 華陽洞; Chuiyun dong 垂雲洞	1 time 3.12a–14b	Excursions to Mount Mao, Jurong county; related to the legend of the "Yiḫe ming"; "Sanshan sou shengji" 三山搜勝跡; "Shiji su Huayang, yanxia dongtian gu" 事跡溯華陽，煙霞洞天古; "Wowen fudi qishi'er, diyi Huayang wu bozhong" 我聞福地七十二，第一華陽無伯仲
Bagong dong 八公洞	1 time 3.17a–b	Site related to Bao Gao's legacy; "Shizhi hua yu shi, shenmiao xin hu jing" 始知畫與詩，神妙心互競。
Beigu shanlou 北固山樓	1 time 6.1b	Tower on Mount Beigu; site for gathering with Luo Qilan; "Jiashan yijiu ren hezai" 家山依舊人何在
Jiyu wubo ge 積雨無波閣	1 time 6.13a–14a	Site for gathering with Luo Qilan; "Banzuo jin mingyuan, jiangshang gu Runzhou" 班左今名媛，江山古潤州
Yinfeng 銀峰	1 time 6.15a–b	Site for Bao Zhihui's excursion with Zhang Xuan, in celebration for her fiftieth birthday; "Cisheng xigong jiashan lao" 此生喜共家山老
Suanshan chanyuan 蒜山禪院	1 time 6.19b	Buddhist temple on Mount Suan (alternative name Yinfeng); hermits' retreat; excursion with Zhang Xuan

Name of site	Number of appearances and page numbers	Function indicated, or key lines quoted from the poem
Ganlu si 甘露寺	1 time 6.20a–b	Located on Mount Beigu; excursion and joint composition with Zhang Xuan; invoking historical references; "Jiangshan diyi tui sidi" 江山第一推斯地
Jiaoyan 焦巖	1 time 6.20b–21a	Excursion with Bao Zhilan; responding to poems inscribed onto the rock by Wang Wenzhi; "Yufu tianfeng haotaoqu, zhiwu qiju jixianren" 欲賦天風海濤曲，知無奇句繼先人
Songliao ge 松寥閣	1 time 6.21a–b	Tower on Mount Jiao symbolic of family legacies; site for mourning Bao Zhizhong; "Sanshan qiju ti jiangbian" 三山奇句題將徧; "Wo yu moya jie wanruo" 我欲摩崖嗟腕弱
Jiachu ting 佳處亭	1 time 6.21b–22a	Excursion with Bao Zhilan; "Jiashan muchi kuai tongdeng" 家山暮齒快同登

APPENDIX 2

Selected Original Texts Summarized in the Chapters

THE FOLLOWING SELECTED original texts provide a sense of the richness of what I call "premodern diaspora writing" produced by the Huizhou descendants. Readers will also be able to locate the original linguistic context for some of the summarized contents or quoted lines in chapters 2 and 3.

Poetry by Bao Gao and Bao Wenkui (Chapter 2)

An autobiographical verse by Bao Gao presents a typical case of a personal story embedded in a highly mobile family history:

廣陵桂館寓齋寄京口諸同學[1]

南徐昔名藩，豈惟好山水。州郡多高門，僕本寒鄉士。故家歙東潭，亦已久居此。周迴省邱墓，款曲喻鄰里。弱冠接時賢，心慕文章美。甫從操觚學，謬竊搢紳齒。父党間造門，良朋嘗萃止。經參元向席，賦竝卿雲軌。逸響奮風騷，墮緒尋圖史。亦為少年戲，蒲酒聊爾爾。饑來驅我出，江上寄行李。流寓廣陵城，交遊富人子。結駟憲非病，衣狐由不恥。雖披《鹽鐵論》，終闇貨殖理。性拙謝逢迎，經旬不入市。所憎去已遠，所歡來當邇。故山近相望，一水渺千里。主人敬愛客，種桂遍階戺。攀枝聊淹留，曷如桑與梓？

For Bao Gao, hills viewed from a tower named Jianshan Lou (Tower Where to See Hills) evoked various local Dantu cultural traditions:

見山樓即席醉歌[2]

空中綠雲忽破碎，散作千山萬山翠。君樓在市不在山，卻共諸山翠相對。東南山勢排長虹，西山一片撐鴻濛。北山突峙倚天塹，石帆直指滄海東。誰裁半幅吳江水，更掛高高碧窗裡。樓上仙人終日閑，坐攬江山列床几。有時放吟還疾書，山雨江濤奔腕底。……

Phrased as Bao Gao's "native mountains," the landscape tells a story of mobility and displacement in a verse addressed to Wang Jinchen:

復之廣陵留別汪近晨[3]

君從新安來，我向廣陵去。歸船及南風，五月一相遇。五月南風揚子津，茫茫復作渡江人。與君笑語苦未了，江干卻立話情親。江東諸謝才華勝，阿大中郎共標映。中間小謝思更清，十歲成詩康樂並。弱冠好文復好游，吳山越水遠行舟。盤渦七十二灘險，富春山多逢處留。錢江八月波濤壯，回棹蜻蛉向湖上。秋菊寒泉薦水仙，棲鴉流水聞菱唱。南浮震澤下姑蘇，行行卻抵丹陽湖。潤州客居無可樂，北固山前閑釣魚。舉手鱸魚四十九，得意滿酤京口酒。多景樓高會眾賓，晚召鄒生與枚叟。座中末至余最羞，江天斜照賦登樓。衡才直等金三品，重義何論銀一流。海門蒼蒼隱煙樹，石壁松寥讀書處。我舊棲遲向此山，聞君方欲將舟去。愛君五色絢爛驚世駭俗之文章，秋鷹天馬無比方。山雞照影不敢顧，人言此是雛鳳凰。旦暮雲霄看搏擊，下帷更愛焦岩寂。鐘鼓山堂鸛鶴驚，海天風雨魚龍集。見此君文變益奇，獨予行路心增悲。故鄉山水反如客，佳處不得相追隨。追隨不得傷懷抱，橫大江兮揚桂櫂。別後秋期無幾時，遇君當在金陵道。

A verse by Bao Gao dramatizes the retrieval of the "Yiheming" carvings on polished cliffs as a local Dantu legend:

觀碑圖歌為祝荔亭作[4]

蛟龍不識字，偷齧神仙書。焦巖水落見碑版，志士往往搜其餘。我聞長沙老子滄州客，千尺長絙挽穹石。鋃鋙割波壯士怒，直奪蛟龍口中物。奪歸祕室立重扃，黑夜時復驚雷霆。中間奇字七十二，字字俱作風濤形。君本長沙佳弟子，不惜黃金換青史。搆作齊雲百尺樓，擘破剡溪千丈紙。山之麓、江之沮，斯碑復出誰功歟？移山神力君與俱，長沙逝後識此無？多君示我觀碑圖，惜哉全本久摧剝。人間摹勒非真書，真書世眼那能辨？但從完好求肌膚。吁嗟乎！月可脩、天可補，媧皇石、吳剛斧。華陽仙去隺不歸，茲銘缺落終千古。

The luster attached to the local Dantu landscape is framed in relation to Bao Gao's frequent travels to Yangzhou:

乙卯三月，陳仲公治具相邀游春，期會城南酒肆。侵晨有客叩門，趣予同行，予方未寤。比至，虛無人，久遲卒不見至。際晚，取酒獨酌，醉中率爾賦得二百八十字，書之壁上，以俟異日一笑[5]

廣陵十日九遊譏，高堂日暮羅英彥。饔子揮刀立能辨，漿酒霍肉千夫膳。主人奉爵眾賓歡，僕居上座默不言。頗慙野鹿入城市，復愁羔羊踏菜園。東風吹綠江南草，夢想故山游事好。都籃茶具盛美潔，松下泉甘瓷琖小。歸家寒食耽冶遊，北門風雨涼如秋。前一日遊北郭呂氏園，值大雨。故人陳遵好事者，詰旦期我城南陬。……獨往城南不見人，柳花滿店空流水。上山採薇暮苦飢，罏頭因典布單衣。野老深憐作詩瘦，故人笑殺食言肥。人生俯仰百難遂，不獨今晨良宴會。來日驅車還出門，急須致身富與貴。料理俸錢餉朋輩，結廬便學邃庵邃。客來筍蕨出山厨，下箸一餐飽乃快。邃庵楊公石淙別業在鴻鶴山下。

Bao Gao's sense of displacement derived from the idea of looking into the distance from the heights, as inspired by Wang Can's "Rhapsody on Climbing to the Top of a Tower" (*Denglou fu*):

登北固同旭昭[6]

迢迢別嶺赴長川，隱隱層樓極遠天。形勝江山餘一 . . . [missing character]，滄桑俯仰又千年。鯨鯢秋色來巴蜀，鴻雁邊聲落薊燕。非是故人並故土，登高那不思凄然。

Bao Wenkui, who gave himself the style name Yeyun (Clouds Wandering in the Wilderness), composed an autobiographical verse on this theme and asks why the wandering clouds could not return to their "native mountains":

野雲行[7]

野雲孤飛何所止？一去無端忽千里。少微真人舉手招 處州地處少微， 竟入千山萬山裡。山中何有有白雲，朝飛暮返何紛紛。野雲徘徊傍岩壑，白雲騰笑非其群。吁嗟處州何可處，夕畏長蛇朝畏虎。野雲之來亦良苦，寥落終年竟誰語？有時痛哭還放吟，邊人只謂雲無心。世間閑雲亦自有，野雲不願空山守。願隨甘霖潤枯槁，願為劍氣干斗牛。奈何鬱鬱居此間，不敢高飛出林藪。噫吁嘻！野雲亦自有故山，胡為朝出暮不還？逝將乘風破巨浪，影動紫金浮玉間。故人焦先有茅屋，門對蓬萊雲滿目。江山大好不歸來，野雲野雲何處宿？

Bao Wenkui phrases the problem of locating home into an explicit question:

秋日即事有懷同里諸子次張舸齋姑丈見寄四首元韻 其四[8]

遊子豈無志，人生亦有涯。登高見千里，何處是吾家？髩發先秋改，關河入夢賒。蕭條誰可與？落日數歸鴉。

Bao Wenkui represents Bao Zhihui's new poetic works as "pouring out" ahead of all others, like the rains "pouring" outside:

清娛閣看雨仝舸齋茝香姑母分韻[9]

雲挾龍醒卷碧霄，片時高閣暑全消。江飛白練光淩亂，山墮蒼煙影動搖。小徑屢聞風折竹，前村應是漲平橋。試看一雨過三日，點筆新詩更湧潮 謂姑母詩先成。

Poetry by the He Family (Chapter 3)

For the He sisters, learning to write meant picking up the poetic themes about Yangzhou and putting them in new configurations. A typical case was their poetic exchange modeled on Wang Shizhen's "Autumn Willows" poetic series:

蕪城春柳用漁洋秋柳韻，同浣碧芷香兩妹作[10]

何佩芬

輕盈疑是綠珠魂，鏡裏樓臺畫裏門。暮雨垂青窺眼角，春山含翠妬眉痕。二分璧月人千里，萬樹桃花水一村。留得絳仙螺子黛，淡濃須共美人論。

穠華滿眼已無霜，眠起依依照鑑塘。板渚波柔牽畫舫，邗溝風軟拂征箱。長條攀折愁公子，小字娉婷憶女王。薄暖輕陰寒食路，一枝紅繪杏花坊。

金縷鬖髿學舞衣，平山如舊昔人非。嫩黃乍染風絲暖，淺碧初勻雨點稀。三月鶯花蝴蝶夢，六朝臺榭鷓鴣飛。玉簫羌笛無消息，惆悵樊川興已違。

温柔慣惹女兒憐，高髻玲瓏翠綰煙。解語已輸花綺麗，含情聊伴草芊綿。鶯梭燕剪忙佳日，緒態蠻腰占妙年。二十四橋斜照裏，綠波春水又無邊。

燕城春柳用漁洋山人秋柳韻[11]

何佩玉

一縷纖纖倩女魂，春風乍拂小橋門。鬢籠細雨梳青影，眉譜輕煙暈碧痕。盤馬客行花外路，聽鶯人立水邊村。錦帆寂寞隋隄冷，金粉叢殘忍再論。

萬樹何曾著曉霜，微雲香雨臥橫塘。搓成弱線穿羅幕，畫出嬌波借鏡箱。詩句祗今傳謝女，笛聲從古愛桓王。天涯又是清明節，細草繁花苜蓿坊。

燕翦雙拋織翠衣，三千殿腳事全非。夕陽紅漾花光亂，春水青環月影稀。金縷曲中香未散，玉鉤斜畔絮初飛。誰能遣此温柔致，欲綰離人願總違。

寶兒憨態更堪憐，學畫鴉黃淡似煙。夢醒瓊花空色相，歌殘玉樹尚纏綿。雞臺事業非前日，螢苑風光感昔年。十里珠簾爭捲處，如絲曾覆翠闌邊。

燕城春柳疊用漁洋秋柳韻四律[12]

何佩珠

長堤宛轉媚花魂，一帶深圍古寺門。青到眼梢流美盼，翠生眉尾露纖痕。煙輕水軟迷前渡，杏白梨紅畫小村。枝弱鶯兒棲不定，柔情如許好同論。

梅片初飛白似霜，漫疑風絮點芳塘。玉簫吹斷無雙地，金線填成第幾箱。照影自應憐月姊，含情曾否侍花王。蜀岡西去紅橋外，誰問當時碎錦坊。

隋宮曾拂美人衣，煬帝風流事已非。雕粉牆陰春雨細，泥金亭畔畫船稀。翩翩紫燕初調語，穀穀黃鴉正學飛。秀色三分青一抹，莫嫌眉樣與時違。

腰肢瘦削易生憐，殘月斜欹一笠煙。少女和風多細膩，社公微雨太連綿。買春空炫黃金色，學舞初窺碧玉年。百尺垂絲收不起，鞦韆架側杏花邊。

Unlike He Bingtang, who specified the purpose of his excursion to Labyrinth as pleasure-seeking, Peiyu casts hers as an event for women:

清明日即事 補錄三月作[13]

何佩玉

幽夢模糊香霧裏，碧牕鸚鵡催人起。爲言今日是清明，花滿雕欄絢紅紫。初換春衫怯曉涼，鏡匳微展明螺光。晨霞掩映鬥雙頰，脂粉着衣生軟香。梳成雲髻蘭膏透，倦態低徊玉釵溜。笑靨從教桃李爭，修眉肯學春波縐。簾捲鞦韆小院中，鴉鬟小妹語東風。游絲飛絮盡無力，偏向虛簷罥落紅。見說千家試新火，樓臺十里輕煙鎖。韶光旖旎畫難成，鬥草西園鬟雙𩯭。才過冷節嫩晴天，蹴鞠還分白打錢。學舌雛鶯啼暖日，牽絲侍女汲新泉。裊裊垂楊吹不住，王孫歸路知何處。紅羅先繡鳳頭鞋，女伴相招踏青去。踏青先上寶兒墳，屧印香泥碧有痕。淺淺蘼蕪顏色好，絳仙眉黛最銷魂。迷樓舊說神仙境，竝蒂花枝呈麗景。春波照出鏡中人，一朵幽蘭瘦秋影。柳絲低畫玉鉤斜，細雨春生燕子家。拾翠采香行淺徑，不知斜照下牕紗。紛紛凡卉爭春色，吐艷呈嬌過寒食。惟有梨花顏獨清，笑倚東風紅不得。看花我更惜華枝，我與名花本素知。分付封姨莫狼藉，爲祈青帝好扶持。歸來深院重門閉，一寸苔茵弄新翠。刺繡初挑鳳尾紋，學書未寫蠅頭字。閒情時復寄龍腰，珠箔玲瓏寶篆銷。四面簾垂清晝永，茶煙吹綠上芭蕉。

The willows by the Red Bridge and the “luminous moon” of Yangzhou function as memory triggers for He Bingtang to recall the decades he spent in Guangdong:

虹橋秋柳次趙艮甫明經韻 其一[14]

何秉棠

隋堤宛轉路茫茫，漸覺陶衣門徑荒。明月二分瓊樹冷，西風萬里玉關涼。數聲蟬噪隨流水，幾點鴉棲帶夕陽。縱使細腰猶解舞，那堪回首憶珠娘 予昔遊嶺南幾三十年。

Indigenous features pervade Peiyu’s memories of Guangdong:

憶嶺南[15]

何佩玉

金衣學語雪衣柔，滿目韶光拾翠洲。榕樹緑圍龍女户，桃花紅出蛋人舟。春深玳瑁乘潮上，夜靜黿鼉駕海遊。四百峰頭吹玉笛，尋仙曾夢到羅浮。

消夏花田景最宜，燈光摇漾碧玻璃。荔奴椰子盛荷葉，蜆妹魚姑唱竹枝。壓擔素馨香作串，堆盤新藕雪成絲。髫年摘豔尋詩地，説與吴娘總不知。

越王臺上好秋光，珠女珠兒話夕陽。野蟹領孫行稻隴，沙魚分子出茭塘。畫闌豔破紅蕉雨，玉碗清浮白蔗漿。一枕夢回涼意滿，又聽深巷賣檳榔。

嚴冬和靄似春朝，衣熨吴綿襯軟綃。林有柑橙群鳥樂，天無霜雪萬花驕。竹雞過雨啼幽塢，桐鳳收香挂綺寮 粵産收香鳥亦名桐花鳳。 尚記遊仙清興好，東樵浮翠接西樵 東西樵皆峰名。

The poetic language Peiyu acquired in Yangzhou retrospectively created an identity for her and her cousins as female talents comparable to Xie Daoyun and Bao Linghui:

憶嶺南章氏諸表姊[16]

何佩玉

沉香浦暖禁煙初，小扇輕衫出錦車。枝結珊瑚鮫客網，鏡開翡翠蚌人居。晚風蔞葉鳴鵯鵊，春水桃花上鱖魚。往事依稀勞夢想，羅浮山色近何如。

最憐生小荔枝鄉，愛擘輕紅十八孃。粉鏡曉梳蝴蝶髻，羅衾宵爇鷓鴣香。閒翻錦字緘珠密，細數燈花覺漏長。莫更登樓頻極目，碧雲無際海天蒼。

窈窕文窗不染埃，尋芳屐每印蒼苔。芭蕉果熟和煙摘，茉莉香清帶露開。話到同心花亦笑，詩成脱口鶴先猜。謝娘鮑妹無消息，愁倚春風憶玉臺。

點點輕陰倦繡幃，紅棉作絮不勝衣。閒情拋豆鸚哥小，野味充厨蜆子肥。千縷漸看青鬢減，十年愁與素心違。夢魂若逐東風去，記取伊人住翠微。

As requested by He Bingtang, the He sisters inscribed his commissioned painting on his travels in Gansu, Shaanxi, and Sichuan, incorporating Mount Taihua to describe the mountainous features of these areas:

家君命題隴蜀遊圖三首[17]

何佩芬

煙蘿繞徑碧紛紛，風景圖成却俗氛。數騎曉迎峰頂日，一鞭晴轉隴頭雲。青猿收果穿林去，白鹿銜花與客分。最愛夕陽斜照處，杜鵑紅到薛濤墳。

翠嶂明流路鬱紆，千條垂柳拂吟鬚。山花山鳥留詩境，秋水秋雲入畫圖。龍嶺停驂看瀑瀉，鳳坡攬轡聽禽呼。一官白首勤王事，不憚馳驅萬里途。

太華岧嶤蜀道通，子規啼徧淡煙中。浣花溪上春波綠，濯錦江頭夕照紅。人向群山登鳳嶺，雲隨匹馬度蠶叢。歸來細檢諸遊草，更愛峰巒畫不窮。

Peiyu rewrote He Bingtang's travels into her own dream of climbing to the top of Mount Taihua, and her free traverse of and interaction with the cosmic space:

夢登太華絶頂，聽毛女玉姜彈琴，醒後作歌記之[18]

何佩玉

丹崖翠碧何玲瓏，芙蓉千朵涵虚空。離離星斗似可摘，別有天地開鴻濛。青鸞導雲間，白鶴趨前路。瑶草香迴環，半染三霄露。翩然忽遇古仙姝，皓齒修蛾姑射如。玉鍊顏兮嚲雙髻，青蘭倒影紅霞裾。餐我紫莖綠葉之華芝，飲我五雲百花之醽醁。靜援朱絲白雪之瑶琴，妙奏瀟煙湘雨之仙曲。一彈松風謖謖天外來，再彈玉井萬柄蓮花開。三彈四彈月將夕，惟見一抹銀河洗。秋碧雪瀑翻空卷，玉龍涼雲，劃破青山脊。斂環一笑香繽紛，抗手欲招雲中君。羅浮梅華三弄出，吹滿麻姑蝴蝶裙。海闊天空自俯仰，此心肯作紅塵想？夢回風撼碧梧桐，泠泠猶誤琴聲響。

CHINESE CHARACTER GLOSSARY

Bao Daru 鮑大儒
Bao Gao 鮑皋
baojia 保甲
Bao Wenkui 鮑文逵
bao wusheng 保吾生
Bao Yi 鮑彝
Bao Zhifen 鮑之芬
Bao Zhihui 鮑之蕙
Bao Zhilan 鮑之蘭
Bao Zhizhong 鮑之鐘
Beigu 北固
bieji 別集

caogu xue 操觚學
Cao Wenzhi 曹文埴
Cao Zhenyong 曹振鏞
Chanzhi si 禪智寺
Chen Ruizhu 陳蕊珠
Cheng Bao 程葆
Cheng Dingtiao 程鼎調
chengshi shanlin 城市山林
Chudi zhizhang zhitu 楚地指掌之圖

Dantu 丹徒
Dingwuben Lanting 定武本蘭亭
Dongqiao 東樵
Douji tai 鬥雞臺
Du Lanxian 杜蘭仙
duowei jiyou 敓為己有

fajiao qutuo 伐蛟取鼉
fangzhi 方志
fuyang 俯仰

fengjian 風鑑
fengsu renxin 風俗人心

Gao Jianchen 高劍塵
Gaoyang 高陽
geli 格力
Guangling 廣陵
Guangzhou 光州
gujia 故家
gushan 故山
guShe 古歙

hanxiang shi 寒鄉士
hengchan 恆產
He Bingtang 何秉棠
He Peifen 何佩芬
He Peiyu 何佩玉
He Peizhu 何佩珠
Hu Peihui 胡培翬
Hu Peixi 胡培系
Hu Shunzhi 胡舜陟
Huayang Yiheming kao 華陽瘞鶴銘考
Huaihai 淮海
Huaitang 槐塘
Huang Wenyang 黃文暘
Huang Zhirou 黃之柔
Huangyu tu 皇輿圖
Huang Zhishu 黃之淑
Huizhou 徽州

jiacheng 家乘
jiake 家刻
Jiang Chun 江春

Jiang Fan 江藩
Jiang Zhu 江珠
jiangtian he 江天合
Jiangyin 江陰
Jianshan lou 見山樓
Jiao[shan] 焦[山]
jiashan 家山
jielu 結廬
jiji 寄籍
jijin leshi 吉金樂石
Jin[shan] 金[山]
jinshen chi 搢紳齒
Jingkou 京口
Jingkou sanshan tu 京口三山圖
Jingkou wenxian lu 京口文獻錄
Jingjiang 京江
jingshi 經世
Jiuzhou 九州
jiuzhou youtong 九州攸同
Jixi 績溪

Kexuan lou 課選樓
Kong Luhua 孔璐華

Leitang 雷塘
liewei 獵微
lijia 里甲
limen 里門
Lin Feibai 林飛白
linji 鄰姬
liuyu shiren 流寓詩人
lunhuan tenghui 輪奐騰輝
Luo Qilan 駱綺蘭
Luofu 羅浮

Ma Yueguan 馬曰琯
Ma Yuelu 馬曰璐
Meng Danru 孟澹如
Meng Dimin 孟迪民
Mi Fu 米芾
Milou 迷樓
Mingyue lou 明月樓
miyi xianshi 靡衣鮮食
moya 摩崖
Mumo lou 木末樓

Nan Xu 南徐
Niansi qiao 廿四橋
nüjie 女界

Pinghu 平湖

Qimen 祁門
qingxiang ye 青緗業
Qiyun ge 起雲閣
Qingzhou 青州
Qiuliu shi 秋柳詩
Qujiang ting 曲江亭

Runzhou 潤州

sang yu zi 桑與梓
shangji 商籍
Sanshan zhi 三山志
Shao Zhenhua 邵振華
She 歙
shiye jia 實業家
Shize lou 世澤樓
shouma 瘦馬
si 嗣
sixiao 私梟
sufeng 素封
Sui gong 隋宮
Sun Caifu 孫采芙

Taihua 太華
Tangmo 唐模
Tianxia 天下
Tongbao Hanlin fang 同胞翰林坊
Tongxiang 桐鄉

Wangji lieguo zhizhang zongtu 王畿列國指掌總圖
Wangji zhizhang zhitu 王畿指掌之圖
Wang Tingzhang 汪廷璋
Wang Shizhen 王士禎

Wang Sunzhi 汪損之
Wang Ying 汪嫈
Weijing shuwu 味經書屋
weisu 違俗
wolu 蝸廬
Wucheng 梧城 (sycamore city)
Wucheng 無城 ("no city")
Wucheng 蕪城 (weed-covered city [Yangzhou])
Wu Qi 吳綺
Wu Tan 吳譚
Wu Wu 吳吳
wuShe 吾歙
Wuzhou 梧州

Xialan zhizhang 遐覽指掌
xiangqu 鄉曲
xiangxian 鄉賢
xiangyin 鄉飲
xiangyue 鄉約
xiedou 械鬥
Xijin 西津
Xiqiao 西樵
Xiuning 休寧
Xiuyuan 休園
Xú Deyin 徐德音
Xú Xuling 徐旭齡
Xǔ Mingxian 許明賢
Xǔ Peihuang 許佩璜
Xǔ Shican 許士粲
Xǔ Xinrui 許信瑞
Xuanwen yifan 宣文懿範
xueyin gao 學吟稿
xunfang ji 尋芳屐
xunshi di 尋詩地

Yangzhou 揚州
Yantie lun 鹽鐵論
yeru xigu 業儒習賈
Yeyun 野雲
Yinfeng 銀峰
Yinlü shantang 飲綠山堂
youyi difang 有益地方
Yu Yue 俞樾
Yuanyang meng 鴛鴦夢
"Yugong" 禹貢
Yueguan 月觀
Yugouxie 玉鈎斜
yuyan fanfu 魚鹽販負

"Zhang Sheng dabuzhuang" 張升大布莊
Zhang Xuan 張鉉
Zhang Yin 張崟
Zhenjiang 鎮江
Zheng Dongli 鄭東里
Zheng Maojia 鄭懋嘉
Zheng Weiguang 鄭為光
Zheng Xiaru 鄭俠如
Zhengjun 徵君
zhu feilei 諸匪類
zhuniang 珠娘

NOTES

INTRODUCTION

1. For pioneering English scholarship, see Ho, "The Salt Merchants of Yang-Chou"; and Ho, *The Ladder of Success*. More recently, see Zurndorfer, *Change and Continuity in Chinese Local History*; Qitao Guo, *Ritual Opera and Mercantile Lineage*; and Qitao Guo, *Huizhou*; McDermott, *The Making of a New Rural Order in South China*, vol. 1; McDermott, *The Making of a New Rural Order in South China*, vol. 2; Du, *The Order of Places*; Yulian Wu, *Luxurious Networks*.
2. For pioneering studies, see Ko, *Teachers of the Inner Chambers*; Mann, *Precious Records*. Also see the digital library for Ming and Qing women's writings built by Grace S. Fong, available at https://digital.library.mcgill.ca/mingqing/search/index_eng.php.
3. Fu Ying, MingQing *Anhui funü wenxue zhushu jikao*, 405–563.
4. On the issue of agency, see Qitao Guo, "Engendering the Mercantile Lineage."
5. Ho, *The Ladder of Success*.
6. Elman, *Civil Examinations and Meritocracy*, 4.
7. Ho, "The Salt Merchants of Yang-Chou," 168. Chinese scholars are excavating a repertoire of sources concerning the Huizhou merchants' social and cultural impact on the Jiangnan heartland. See, for example, Wang Zhenzhong, *Ming-Qing Huishang yu Huai-Yang shehui bianqian*, 58–119; Tang Lixing, *Suzhou yu Huizhou*.
8. See Hegel, *Reading Illustrated Fiction in Late Imperial China*, 132–33. Most famous among these book carvers and craftsmen were the Huang and Liu families from She County in Huizhou.
9. The Jiangnan heartland included the prefectures of Suzhou, Songjiang, Changzhou, Jiaxing, Huzhou, and occasionally Zhenjiang. For Yangzhou's ambivalent Jiangnan identity, see Ko, *Teachers of the Inner Chambers*, 21. For Yangzhou as a center of a "transregional and transdynastic" elite culture during the early Qing era, see Meyer-Fong, *Building Culture in Early Qing Yangzhou*.
10. For the definition of the High Qing era, see Mann, *Precious Records*, 3, 20–23. Also see Wu's (*Luxurious Networks*, 4–6) brief introduction of the Huizhou salt merchants as a unique social group during the High Qing.
11. Du, *The Order of Places*, 5–6.

12. Wu, *Luxurious Networks*, 3.
13. See Steven Miles's use of the term *diaspora* in a limited manner to conceptualize cultural bonds, networks, and dispersion, rather than as forced separation from homeland or collective trauma commonly associated with the Jewish and African diasporas. Miles, *Chinese Diasporas*, 10–13.
14. Du, *The Order of Places*, 1.
15. Zurndorfer, "Book review: *Ritual Opera and Mercantile Lineage*."
16. Finnane, *Speaking of Yangzhou*, 231.
17. Qitao Guo, *Ritual Opera and Mercantile Lineage*, 75; Miles, *Chinese Diasporas*, 46–50.
18. Mann, *Precious Records*, 202.
19. Lu, *True to Her Word*.
20. Soja, *Thirdspace*, 1–2. For a review of the spatial turn, see for example, Gunn, "The Spatial Turn."
21. Luo, "Theories of Spatiality and the Study of Medieval China," 218.
22. David and Wilson, *Inscribed Landscapes*, vii–viii. See also, for example, Cosgrove and Daniels, *The Iconography of Landscape*; Massey, *Space, Place, and Gender*; Thomas, *Time, Culture, and Identity*; David and Wilson, *Inscribed Landscapes*. On worlding, see Heidegger, *Poetry, Language, Thought*, 44–45.
23. Clark, Finlay, and Kelly, *Worldmaking*, 2.
24. "Yugong"; Wang Deheng, *Zhongguo fangzhi xue*, 4–5; Wang Chengzu, *Zhongguo dilixue shi*, 16–32.
25. Wang Deheng, *Zhongguo fangzhi xue*, 3–8, 23, 79.
26. Strassberg, *Inscribed Landscapes*, 12, 36–44.
27. Harrist, *The Landscape of Words*.
28. Owen, *The End of the Chinese "Middle Ages,"* 27, 33.
29. Xiaoshan Yang, *Metamorphosis of the Private Sphere*, 3; also see 2–4, 11–90.
30. Owen, *All Mine!* Also see the innovative use of spatiality in understanding the history of emotions in Chinese literature and culture in Lam, *The Spatiality of Emotions in Early Modern China*.
31. Wang (*Spatial Imaginaries in Mid-Tang China*, 2) defines spatial imaginaries as the imagination and representation of spaces in terms of how or whether they were inhabited by people. For Wang's discussion of Liu Zongyuan's landscape essays, see 98–108, 195–209, 235–45, 313.
32. Fong, "Feminist Theories and Women Writers of Late Imperial China," 105–6. Fong (109) quotes the following from Maureen Robertson as a pioneering effort to address the applicability question: "To the objection that critical concepts not derived from the Chinese tradition are in this context inappropriate, the answer must be that patriarchy and the gender arrangements that lead to a problematic relationship between women and their representation in language, and between women and writing, are not unique to the 'West.'"
33. Massey, *Space, Place, and Gender*, 2.
34. Ebrey, *The Inner Quarters*, 25. Man Xu recently suggested in *Crossing the Gate*

that the gap between the ideal and the reality during this time can be much bigger than previously believed.

35. Ko, *Teachers of the Inner Chambers*, 21. Ko also argues that women's loyalty to their native places often fragmented their networks.
36. Yanning Wang, *Reverie and Reality*.
37. Mann, "The Virtue of Travel for Women in the Late Empire," 70.
38. See, for example, Moyer, *Woman Rules Within*; Hu Siao-chen, *Churu mimi huayuan*, 7–64; Yuefan Wang, "Garden, Gender, and Memory," 30–56.
39. Widmer, "Gentility in Transition," 21–44.
40. I use the term in its usual sense as human apprehension and interpretation of the universe of beings, derived from the German word *weltanschauung*. For an extensive study of the concept of worldview in Western theological and philosophical traditions, see Naugle, *Worldview*, esp. 58–60.
41. Du, *The Order of Places*. For the rise of local institutions and their centrality to the "making of a new rural order" in Huizhou, see McDermott, *The Making of a New Rural Order*, 2 vols.
42. Also see Du's use of a similar term, *spatial order*, in "Locality, Literati, and the Imagined Spatial Order," 409.
43. For example, see Tingyang Zhao, *All under Heaven*.
44. Saussy, *The Making of Barbarians*, 2–4.
45. For example, see Ban Wang, *Chinese Visions of World Order*.
46. Geng Chuanyou, "Shiyu de pianli he chonghe," 161–62. For Geng's reprinting and digitizing project, launched in 2021, see the news release at https://rwc.ahu.edu.cn/2021/1111/c10366a273727/page.htm. Thus far I have been unable to locate outcome from the project, but Geng's 2019 article can be read as formulating the foundation for his project.
47. For printing as a means of decentering cultural power, see Chow, *Publishing, Culture, and Power*.
48. Geng Chuanyou, "Shiyu de pianli he chonghe," 163–66.
49. Robertson, "Literary Authorship by Late Imperial Governing-Class Chinese Women."
50. In terms of including marginal figures, see, for example, Matthew Sommer's latest study of transgender histories in China, *The Fox Spirit, the Stone Maiden, and Other Transgender Histories from Late Imperial China*. For the now expanding field of studies on women and gender in China, see Yates and Cai, "Bibliography of Women and Gender in China (2018–2022)."
51. Fong, *Herself an Author*, 10.
52. See, for example, Jiang Xiaoping, "Nüxing shuxie yu qing'ai yuejie"; Feng Erkang, "Qingdai Huizhou cainü de wenxue chuangzuo shenghuo." Also see Xiaorong Li's 2025 study ("Gender, Genre, and Locality," 230–57) on the earliest anthologizing project on Anhui women by the Republican scholar Guang Tiefu and Guang's efforts in writing these women into local history and cultural memory.

53. See, for example, Feng Erkang, "Qingdai Huizhou xianyuan de zhijia he shengcun shu"; Feng Erkang, "Qingdai Huizhou xianyuan chuse de shehui lishi jianzhi." These two articles can also be found in *Feng Erkang wenji*, 150–60, 161–72. Feng (*Feng Erkang wenji*, 4) specifies that he draws the material from Fu Ying's sourcebook. For a summary of studies covering various facets of women's lives in Huihzhou, see Tao Liangqin, "Jinnian lai Huizhou funüshi yanjiu zongshu."
54. McDermott, "The Chinese Domestic Bursar"; Mann, "Dowry Wealth and Wifely Virtue."
55. Xie Xin, "*Fuchu ji* Huishang xianxiang yanjiu."
56. See, for example, the question addressed in a recent dissertation on Huizhou genealogical projects: Xin Yu, "Publishing at the Grassroots," 15–18.
57. I am grateful to the participants of the workshop "China Seen from a Locality" for these stimulating questions.
58. Du, *The Order of Places*, 23–26.
59. For the idea of authenticity as a claim of identity, see Duara, "The Regime of Authenticity." For such claims concerning native-place ties, see Duara, "Local Worlds." For the collapse of order during the Taiping War and cultural restoration and transformation in its aftermath, see Meyer-Fong, *What Remains*; Jin, *The Collapse of Heaven*.
60. For references to thin horses, see Altenburger, Wan, and Bordahl, *Yangzhou, A Place in Literature*, 4–5. For a translation of a Chinese essay on thin horses, see 381–405.
61. Finnane, *Speaking of Yangzhou*, 217, 222.
62. Finnane, *Speaking of Yangzhou*, 214.
63. Finnane, *Speaking of Yangzhou*, 217.
64. Mann, *Precious Records*, 6, 202.
65. Dai Jian, *Qingchu zhi zhongye Yangzhou yule wenhua yu wenxue*, 249; Shi Mei, "Qingdai Jiangsu funü wenxian de jiazhi he yiyi," 482–501.
66. Ruan Yuan, *Huaihai yingling ji*, Preface 1a. For a detailed discussion of such homogeneity, see Ma Tengfei and Luo Shijin, "Qingdai 'Huaihai wenxue quan' jiqi shixue puxi."
67. Dai Jian, *Qingchu zhi zhongye Yangzhou yule wenhua yu wenxue*, 249.
68. Ruan Yuan, *Huaihai yingling ji*; Wang Yu and Ruan Hen, *Huaihai yingling xuji*; Wang Yu, *Jiangsu shizheng*.
69. Ruan Yuan, *Huaihai yingling ji*, "Fanli" 1a–b.
70. On Wang Shizhen and the Red Bridge gatherings, see Meyer-Fong, *Building Culture in Early Qing Yangzhou*, 25–74; esp. 58–63 for these gatherings as *xiuxi* (spring lustration ritual) in tribute to the Orchid Pavilion tradition. For related studies, see Chang, "Wang Shizhen (1634–1711) and the 'New' Canon"; Jiang Yin, *Wang Yuyang yu Kangxi shitan*; Waiyee Li, *Women and National Trauma*, 61–99; Yan Zhixiong, *Qiuliu de shijie*.
71. Ho, "Salt Merchants of Yang-Chou."

72. Ruan Yuan, *Guangling shishi*. Records about Wu Qi appear throughout the collection: 1, 12–13, 43–44, 56, 92–94, 101, 106–8, 121, 127, 142.
73. Quoted in Fu Ying, *MingQing Anhui funü wenxue zhushu jikao*, 452.
74. Ruan Yuan, *Guangling shishi*, 131–32. Also see Fu Ying, *MingQing Anhui funü wenxue zhushu jikao*, 405, 481; Xu Chengyao, *Sheshi xiantan*, 34, 136, 358, 360, 625, 913. For the poetic language describing the city's sudden reversals of fortune, see Meyer-Fong, *Building Culture in Early Qing Yangzhou*, 10. For poetic traditions about the Tower of the Luminous Moon, see Gu Luan, *Guangling langu*, 26.
75. Fu Ying, *MingQing Anhui funü wenxue zhushu jikao*, 465. Ruan Yuan's two other literate concubines were Liu Wenru (1777–1846) and Xie Xue (?–1837). Liu's works did not survive in a personal collection. For Xie's collection of poetry, see Xie Xue, *Yongxu ting shicao*. For a discussion of female talents from Ruan Yuan's family, see Wei, *Ruan Yuan*, 243–57.
76. See, for example, Finnane, *Speaking of Yangzhou*, 221–22.
77. Tang Qingyun, *Nüluoting gao*. For Ruan Yuan's cultural projects centering on the tower, see Meyer-Fong, *Building Culture in Early Qing Yangzhou*, 77, 114–18.
78. See, for example, Dai Jian, *Qingchu zhi zhongye Yangzhou yule wenhua yu wenxue*, 274–94, 335–46; Song Qingxiu, *Qingdai Jiangnan nüxing wenxue shilun*, 219–31.
79. For a study of the Xuehai Tang and the place politics revolving around it, see Miles, *The Sea of Learning*. For Tang Qingyun's poem on the Xuehai Tang, see Tang Qingyun, *Nüluoting gao*, 6.11b–12a.
80. For the status of courtesans and concubines during the late Ming, including changing cultural values of the era that elevated the status of educated courtesans, see Zurndorfer, "Prostitutes and Courtesans." For a study of the entertainer-concubine in light of changing family and gender relations during the Song and Yuan periods, see Bossler, *Courtesans, Concubines, and the Cult of Female Fidelity*.
81. For an introduction to Wang Ying's life and works, see Binbin Yang, *Heroines of the Qing*, 8–9, 130–34. For the making of family history in her writing, see Yang Binbin, "Funü zhushu yu Huishang jiazu tuibian."
82. For the decline of Huizhou salt wealth, see, for example, Ho, "The Salt Merchants of Yang-Chou," 130; Finnane, *Speaking of Yangzhou*, 16–17. For recent studies that excavate sources about the expansion of the Huizhou diasporic networks and communities in the nineteenth and early twentieth centuries, see, for example, Zhang Xiaopo, *Lüwai Huizhou ren yu jindai Huizhou shehui bianqian yanjiu*.
83. Geertz, *The Interpretation of Cultures*, 3–30.

1. ANCHORING IDENTITIES

Epigraphs: Xú Deyin, "Xinqing," in *Lüjingxuan shichao*, 5.3b. For an introduction to Xie Daoyun (ca. 4th c.) and her fame as the "model par excellence of a woman poet" in Chinese history, see Idema and Grant, *The Red Brush*, 136–44. Xú Deyin, "Ku da'er Peihuang jianshi xiao'er Xinrui," in *Lüjingxuan xuji*, 8b–9a.

1. For a history of the Huizhou merchants in Yangzhou, see Finanne, *Speaking of Yangzhou*, 43–68, 236–64.
2. Chang, "Wang Shizhen (1634–1711) and the 'New' Canon," 307. Alternatively, Waiyee Li terms Wang's poetic style "a poetics of indirectness." For a detailed analysis of this poetics and its dense web of allusions, see Waiyee Li, *Women and National Trauma*, 61–75.
3. For the early Qing literary communities in Yangzhou formed through Wang Shizhen's autumn willows poetry, see Waiyee Li, *Women and National Trauma*, 75–96.
4. Meyer-Fong, *Building Culture in Early Qing Yangzhou*. Discussions of the use of places as sites for self-representation in autobiographical works from the late imperial era are also useful to my readings below. See De Weerdt, "Places of the Self."
5. Jiang Yin, *Wang Yuyang yu Kangxi shitan*; Yan Zhixiong, *Qiuliu de shijie*.
6. Feng Erkang, "MingQing shiqi Yangzhou de Huishang jiqi houyi shulue," 243–44.
7. For the collection of data, see Zhu Wanshu, *Huishang yu Mingqing wenxue*, 124–25. Zhu (124) cites Feng Erkang's assertion that the data in Yangzhou amounted to 286 from the late Ming to the mid-Qing. Also see Yongtao Du's (*The Order of Places*, 161–200) detailed discussion of reforms on household registration during the Ming and Qing eras.
8. Yanfeng, *Qinding chongxiu liangZhe yanfazhi*, *juan* 24, "Shangji 1," 7a; *juan* 25, "Shangji 2," 13b–14a. For the quotations here, see *juan* 24, "Shangji 1," 1a–b.
9. See, for example, Yun Zhu, *Guochao guixiu zhengshiji*, 6.2b.
10. For Xú Deyin's connection with the Banana Garden Poetry Club, see Zhao Houjun, "Qingchu Qiantang nüshiren Xú Deyin jiqi zuopin lunxi." For the Banana Garden Poetry Club, see Ko, *Teachers of the Inner Chambers*, 234–37. Also see Idema and Grant, *The Red Brush*, 471–95.
11. For an introduction to the "second high tide" of women's writing culture during the Qing, see Idema and Grant, *The Red Brush*, 567–77.
12. See, for example, Zhao Jishi, *Kangxi Huizhou fuzhi*, 13.48b; He Yingsong and Fang Chongding, *Jiaqing Xiuning Xianzhi*, 9.14b.
13. For quick references, see Fu Ying, *MingQing Anhui funü wenxue zhushu jikao*, 489–91. An autobiographical poem by Xú Deyin ("Kuzi shuhuai bashou," in *Lüjingxuan xuji*, 9b) indicates that she was born in Yangzhou. A translation and analysis of the poem follows.
14. Yuan Mei, *Suiyuan shihua*, 58.
15. For comments on Zhang Yin, see, for example, a poem by the woman poet Wang Ziyi (ca. 19th c.) included in Zhang Yin, *Lüqiu shuwu shichao*, 100a. For comments on Zhu Lan, see Fu Ying, *MingQing Anhui funü wenxue zhushu jikao*, 502.
16. In chronological order: Wang Qishu, *Xiefang ji*, 4.8b–15a; Ruan Yuan, *Huaihai yingling ji*, 298–301; Ruan Yuan, *Guangling shishi*, 128–29; Ruan Yuan and Yang

Bingchu, *Liang Zhe youxuan lu*, 10.2b–3a; Wang Yu, *Jiangsu shizheng*, 162.18b–22b; Yun Zhu, *Guochao guixiu zhengshiji*, 6.2b–4b; Cai Dianqi, *Guochao guige shichao*, 3.11a–15b; Xu Chengyao, *Sheshi xiantan*, 214–17; Guang Tiefu, *Anhui mingyuan shici zhenglue*, 119–20. See additionally Chen Wenshu's (1771–1843) valorization of the female talents of "our Hang[zhou]," including Xú Deyin: Zhao Houjun, "Fu: Yiwen, Yishi, Jiping," 121.

17. See Meyer-Fong's and Steven Miles's discussions of the regional and the transregional in Ruan Yuan's scholarly and literary projects. For example, Ruan Yuan compiled the *Huaihai yingling ji* to celebrate a genealogy of literary achievements in his native Yangzhou area while confirming its status as a cultural center in Jiangnan. Meyer-Fong, *Building Culture in Early Qing Yangzhou*, 120–27. When Ruan Yuan transplanted his evidential scholarship to Guangdong, initially marginalized literati from the Pearl River Delta embraced his scholarly practices as a means of securing their position in Guangzhou and reshaping the relationship between Guangzhou and its delta hinterland; Miles, *The Sea of Learning* (see pp. 17–19 for identity accretion and reinvention during the process).
18. Zhao Yin'gu, *Gaoyang sizhong ji*, reprinted in 1746 as *Jiangdu Xǔshi jiaji*. For collected biographical and historical sources about the Xǔ family, see Xu Chengyao, *Sheshi xiantan*, 212–17.
19. This fact attested to the fluidity of Huizhou identity. For convenience of discussion, I will refer to the family as Huizhou descendants in Yangzhou. For the rise of Huizhou merchants in Yangzhou during the late Ming, as well as the symbiotic relationship between Huizhou and Yangzhou, see Finnane, *Speaking of Yangzhou*, 57–68.
20. The ancestral shrine is named Hall for Promoting Righteousness (Shangyi Tang). The bridge is named Gaoyang Bridge (Gaoyang Qiao) to honor the lineage's Gaoyang origin. The arch, ancestral shrine, and bridge are all located in Tangmo village. The shrine for local worthies is mentioned in Zhao Hong'en, *Qianlong Jiangnan tongzhi*, *juan* 159 (from the Erudition database on Chinese local gazetteers).
21. Xǔ Tianqiu, *Biyushanfang shichao*, preface by Xú Deyin, 1a–b. There is no indication in her preface concerning exactly who reprinted and edited this new edition of the *Xǔshi jiaji*.
22. Xú Deyin, *Lüjingxuan xuji*, 21a. For records about Ma Yueguan, see Li Dou, *Yangzhou huafanglu*, 86–89; for records about Wang Tingzhang, see p. 350.
23. Ko, *Teachers of the Inner Chambers*, 38.
24. See Li Bai, "Qiuxi shuhuai," in Li Bai, *Li Bai ji jiaozhu*, annotated by Qu Tuiyuan, 3:1401–4. See Li's related poem about seeking refuge in Anhui: "Bidi Sikongyuan yanhuai," 1404–6.
25. See related poems and annotations in Li Bai, *Li Bai ji jiaozhu*, annotated by Qu Tuiyuan, 2:546–57.
26. See, for example, Xǔ Chengjia, "Wucheng huaigu," "Jihai xiaqiu zayong," "Qiren," "Shu Liang Zhigong zhaibi," "Song Zhuyin xiong zhiren Shaoxing,"

"Song Qin Liuxian taishi fu Jingzhou he Deng Xiaowei yun," in *Lieweige shiji*, 1.2a–5a. Citations from this collection are based on the 1707 edition. For a discussion of how early Qing poets drew from the An Lushan Rebellion to write about the war and devastation of their own time, see Wai-yee Li, *Women and National Trauma*, 82.

27. For a translation of the poem by Du Mu (803–52), see Owen, *An Anthology of Chinese Literature*, 631.
28. Xǔ Chengjia, "Wucheng huaigu," in *Lieweige shiji*, 1.1a–2a.
29. Meyer-Fong, *Building Culture in Early Qing Yangzhou*, 25–74, esp. 66. Also see records in Li Dou, *Yangzhou huafanglu*, 221.
30. See, for example, Li Dou, *Yangzhou huafanglu*, 220–21, 224; Xǔ Chengyao, *Sheshi xiantan*, 212–14.
31. Xǔ Chengjia, "Qixi Chanzhi si song Wang Ruanting xiansheng beishang jihe liubie yun," in *Lieweige shiji*, 1.11a–b.
32. Xǔ Chengjia, "Jinan Wang Ruanting xiansheng teshou Shidu chengzeng," in *Lieweige shiji*, 2.7b–8a.
33. Ruan Yuan, *Guangling shishi*, 15.
34. See Xǔ Chengjia's essays and poems in Zheng Qinghu, *Yangzhou Xiuyuan zhi*, 1.7a–8b, 2.29a–31a, 3.4a–5a, 3.13a–14b, 6.16a–20b, 7.15a–b, esp. 2.31a; and essays by Xǔ Mingxian and Xǔ Chengyuan, 5.31a–32b.
35. On the Zheng family's social success in late Ming Yangzhou, see Finnane, *Speaking of Yangzhou*, 62–68; Meyer-Fong, *Building Culture in Early Qing Yangzhou*, 30–31.
36. Zheng Qinghu, *Yangzhou Xiuyuan zhi*, *juan* 8.
37. Xǔ Chengjia, "Duzhuo huai jia Qingyu Shiyu," "Jia Qingyu xiong xie Yushan Wenhou beishang jing Guangling chushi dujiang shi suohe," "Huang Kunwu taishi tong jia Fangcheng Tianyu wangji Suying ting," "Du Wu Mingqing xiansheng ji jian xian Wenmu gong xu youjian xiansheng wei xian Wenmu jiacheng xu shuai'er youzuo," in *Lieweige shiji*, 1.14b, 17a, 18b, 2.11a–b. See also records about Xǔ Guo and Xǔ Qingyu in Xǔ Chengyao, *Sheshi xiantan*, 5, 24, 104, 223, 278, 676, 680, 1051.
38. Xǔ Chengjia, "Bai fumu," in *Lieweige shiji*, 3.6a. For the Wang family's learning preserved in a blue chest, see Shen Yue, *Songshu*, 6:1624.
39. Xǔ Yingnian, "Liewei caotang guhuai ge," in *Huaishu shichao*, 1.1a–b.
40. See Du Fu, "Caotang jishi," "Caotang," in Du Fu, *Du Gongbu shiji jizhu*, annotated by Zhu Heling, 323, 434–36.
41. Ruan Yuan, *Huaihai yingling ji*, 82–85; Ruan Yuan, *Guangling shishi*, 36, 102, 107.
42. Li Baotai and Chen Guanguo, eds., *Jiaqing Ganquan xian xuzhi*, *juan* 10 (from the Erudition database on Chinese local gazetteers).
43. For Xú Xuling's official titles, see He Yingsong and Fang Chongding, *Jiaqing Xiuning Xianzhi*, 11.34a. Xú Xuling was promoted to position of vice minister of works in 1684 and was soon reappointed to be director-general of grain

transport. He passed away in the latter post in 1687. See Qian Shifu, *Qingdai zhiguan nianbiao*, vol. 1, 563; vol. 2, 1366–68. Other major posts he occupied before 1684 included junior chamberlain of the court of imperial sacrifices, censor-in-chief of the Left, and governor of Shandong; see Zhao Erxun, *Qing-shi gao*, "Liezhuan" 60 (from the Erudition database). See as well the preface by lady Lou in Xú Deyin, *Lüjingxuan shichao*, 1a. On the migration of the Xiuning descendants to Hangzhou and the broader Zhejiang area during the late Ming, see Finnane, *Speaking of Yangzhou*, 59.

44. See Chen Wenshu's comments in Zhao Houjun, "Fu," 121. For "bright moonlit nights" associated with Yangzhou, see Owen, *An Anthology of Chinese Literature*, 630, in particular the translation of references as "mingyue erfen": "Take all this world's bright moonlit nights, divide them in three parts, and the two most breathtaking are the city of Yang-zhou." "Plum blossoms" in Chen Wenshu's celebration of Hangzhou culture most likely referred to the cultural legacy of Lin Bu (967–1028), a hermit living among plum trees on the Hill in Isolation (Gushan) of Hangzhou. Xú Deyin construed it as part of her natal cultural legacy in her poetic works: "Lisheng zhi penjing si yuniao dunwang jilü yinzuo shishi," "Yongwuhuanshi he Lin Yaqing yun," "Chudu liubie Lin Yaqing furen," in *Lüjingxuan shichao*, 2.5a, 7b, 13a–14b.
45. Lou Canxia, preface to Xú Deyin, *Lüjingxuan shichao*, 1a.
46. Xú Deyin, "Chunri yuanju shimu zuo," in *Lüjingxuan shichao*, 1.14b–15a.
47. See, for example, Shen Deqian, *Guochao shi biecaiji*, 750. For studies of companionate marriages during the late imperial period, see Ko, *Teachers of the Inner Chambers*, 179–90; Lu, *Arranged Companions*.
48. Xú Deyin, "Guo Tinghua shuwu," in *Lüjingxuan shichao*, 1.7a.
49. Xú Deyin, "He Lisheng chunyou shu suojian," "Xiaoqi Liewei caotang shu suojian," "Kuyu tan," "Xinqing," in *Lüjingxuan shichao*, 1.14a–b, 3.6b, 4.5a, 5.3b. It may be relevant here that Xie Daoyun, with her distinguished family background, was said to have greatly despised her husband and treated him and his younger brother as her intellectual inferiors. See Idema and Grant, *The Red Brush*, 138–39.
50. The phrase *jinfen* originally referred to "gold powder" used in women's cosmetics and became a stock metaphor of extravagance and sensuality. See *Ciyuan*, 3158. I translate Xú Deyin's poetic line more literally as "By walls painted in gold dust stands the home of Xie Daoyun."
51. Xú Deyin, "Chunxiao mancheng," in *Lüjingxuan shichao*, 1.4b.
52. Xú Deyin, "Ti jiuju haitanghua xia," in *Lüjingxuan shichao*, 3.3a.
53. Ruan Yuan, *Guangling shishi*, 128–29.
54. Xú Deyin, "Caotang chunji shi Xiaozhai jiushi zhi zhi xi er youzuo," in *Lüjingxuan shichao*, 3.3b.
55. Shen Deqian, *Guochao shi biecaiji*, 750.
56. Xú Deyin, "Xiaoqi Liewei caotang shu suojian," in *Lüjingxuan shichao*, 3.6b.
57. Xú Deyin, "He Lisheng chunyou shu suojian," "Xiti suojian youyin," in *Lüjingxuan shichao*, 1.14a–b, 5.3a–b. The term *shicui* or "gathering kingfisher plumes"

comes from the "Luoshen fu" by Cao Zhi (192–232). Owen, *An Anthology of Chinese Literature*, 196.

58. Xú Deyin, "Fude zishi xunchun qujiaochi wei Jinchang Wuyuan zuo youxu," in *Lüjingxuan shichao*, 3.7b–8b.
59. Xǔ Yingnian, "Hongqiao chunfan yi Yuren hechu jiao chuixiao qizi weiyun" #5, in *Huaishu shichao*, 1.11b. This alludes to a well-known metaphor used in "Pipa xing" (Song of the lute) by Bai Juyi. See Bai Juyi, *Bai Juyi ji jianjiao*, annotated by Zhu Jincheng, 2:685.
60. Xú Deyin, "Yufan Hongqiao yong Yuren hechu jiao chuixiao weiyun" #5, in *Lüjingxuan shichao*, 5.2b.
61. Xǔ Yingnian, "Hongqiao chunfan yi Yuren hechu jiao chuixiao qizi weiyun" #7, in *Huaishu shichao*, 1.11b.
62. Xú Deyin, "Yufan Hongqiao yong yuren hechu jiao chuxiao weiyun" #7, in *Lüjingxuan shichao*, 5.3a.
63. For Du Fu's thatched cottage on the west bank of the Rang, see Du Fu, "Kuizhou ge shi jueju" #5, "Muchun ti Rangxi xinlin caowu wushou," "Zi Rangxi jingfei qie yiju dongtun maowu sishou," in Du Fu, *Du Gongbu shiji jizhu*, annotated by Zhu Heling, 522, 616–17, 675–77.
64. Xú Deyin, "Qiuhuai shiwu shou" #1, in *Lüjingxuan shichao*, 4.10a.
65. For Du Fu's poem on the abandoned woman wearing green sleeves, see Du Fu, "Jiaren," in Du Fu, *Du Gongbu shiji jizhu*, annotated by Zhu Heling, 204–5.
66. Xú Deyin, "Qiuhuai shiwu shou," in *Lüjingxuan shichao*, 4.10a–12a.
67. Xú Deyin, "Huanqi xieyang lü bingyin," in *Lüjingxuan shichao*, 5.4b–5a (my emphasis).
68. Xú Deyin, "Huanqi xieyang lü bingyin," in *Lüjingxuan shichao*, 5.5a.
69. The poetic sequences of Bo Shaojun (d. 1626) and Qian Shoupu (c. 1801–69) lamenting the deaths of their husbands provide valuable examples of how this poetic genre became a vehicle for expressions of private emotions, records of family life, and more public commemoration. See Fong, "Private Emotion, Public Commemoration"; Idema, "The Biographical and the Autobiographical in Bo Shaojun's One Hundred Poems."
70. Xú Deyin, "Ku xianbi Lou Taigongren sishi shou," in *Lüjingxuan shichao*, 4.1a–5a.
71. On the use of interlinear notes in poetry as an increasingly common means of life-writing, see Fong, "Private Emotion, Public Commemoration," 23.
72. This alludes to the story of Yu Dingguo's (?–40 BCE) father. See Fan Ye, *Hou Hanshu*, *juan* 88 (from the Erudition database).
73. Liu Xiang, *Lienü zhuan*, *juan* 2 (from the Erudition database).
74. Xǔ Yingnian, "Waigu Donghai Lou Taifuren wanci," in *Huaishu shichao*, 3.9b–10b.
75. The first few titles in Xú Deyin's sequel indicate that she moved to her son's official post in Henan in around 1733. Xú Deyin, "Ru da'er Quanhe cuixie," in *Lüjingxuan xuji*, 1b–3b.
76. Ruan Yuan, *Guangling shishi*, 8; Xu Chengyao, *Sheshi xiantan*, 214–17.

77. Xú Deyin, "Ku da'er Peihuang jianzhi xiao'er Xinrui," in *Lüjingxuan xuji*, 8b–9a.
78. That is, he was appointed to an official post after passing the civil service exam.
79. Xú Deyin uses the widely cited example of Liu Zhongyin's (?–864) mother to describe her own experience of raising and educating her sons. See Ouyang Xiu, *Xin Tang shu*, *juan* 163, "Liezhuan" 88 (from the Erudition database).
80. Fong, "Private Emotion, Public Commemoration," 22; Idema, "The Biographical and the Autobiographical," 235.
81. Xú Deyin, "Kuzi shuhuai bashou," in *Lüjingxuan xuji*, 9a–11b.
82. There are several mountains named Lingjiu or Vulture. Here it probably refers to that located in Jiangxi, since Xú Deyin records her grandfather's journeys in Jiangxi. Xú Xuling's filial behavior is also recorded in Ji Zengyun, *Yongzheng Zhejiang tongzhi*, *juan* 158 (from the Erudition database on Chinese local gazetteers).
83. This refers to his service in the Lianghuai salt administration. See my earlier introduction to his appointments. "Huai Yang" refers to areas along the lower Huai and Yangzi Rivers.
84. The phrase "qi wu di" in the original text can be interpreted as "residence of the censor." It alludes to the poem "Chang'an guyi" by Lu Zhaolin (ca. 7th c.). See Peng Dingqiu et al., *Quan Tang shi*, vol. 2, 518–19.
85. This may refer to the Kangxi emperor's first journey to the Jiangnan region in 1684. See Zhao Erxun, *Qingshi gao*, "Benji" 7 (from the Erudition database).
86. This refers to Xú Xuling's appointment as director-general of grain transport in 1685 and his death in 1687. See my earlier introduction to his appointments.
87. This alludes probably to the popular story about the king of the ancient Shu longing for his native land after death.
88. This refers to the fact that Xǔ Yingnian earned the *jinshi* degree in 1700. See my earlier introduction about the Xǔ family.
89. Here Xú Deyin is drawing on the stories of Wang Xizhi (303–61) and Emperor Xuanzong (685–762) as examples of ideal matches. "Fanghui" in the original text refers to the courtesy name of Chi Yin (313–84), Wang's brother-in-law. See Zhang Pu, *Han Wei liuchao yibai sanjia ji*, *juan* 59 (from the Erudition database).
90. Xú Deyin, "Kuzi shuhuai bashou," in *Lüjingxuan xuji*, 9a–10a.
91. Xú Deyin, "Kuzi shuhuai bashou," in *Lüjingxuan xuji*, 10a.
92. See Ko's (*Teachers of the Inner Chambers*, 285) discussion of Huang Yuanjie (ca. 17th c.) as an eminent example in this respect.
93. Xú Deyin, "Kuzi shuhuai bashou," in *Lüjingxuan xuji*, 10a.
94. Xǔ Yingnian, "Wanqing youyi Lüjing xuan," in *Huaishu shichao*, 4.13a.
95. Xú Deyin, "Qingming jishi," in *Lüjingxuan shichao*, 5.4a.
96. Li Baotai and Chen Guanguo, *Jiaqing Ganquan xian xuzhi*, *juan* 10. On Ban Zhao and Lady Song, see Idema and Grant, *The Red Brush*, 17–42, 52–54.
97. Zhao Houjun, "Fu: Yiwen, Yishi, Jiping," 121.
98. Shen Deqian, preface to Xú Deyin, *Lüjingxuan xuji*, 2a.

99. Xú Deyin, "Zeng Shen Guiyu shaozongbo," "Shen zongbo yugao nanhuan zuoci zhihe," "Wen shaozongbo you Tiantai yishi daijian," "Shaozongbo wangguo bilu chuzeng shoushu Xuanwen yifan sidazi tang'e jianzeng fuci fengxie," "Fengxie Zhuang zhongcheng jizeng bian'e ershou," in *Lüjingxuan xuji*, 12b, 14a–b, 16a, 20a–b, 21a. For lady Song's title as the Expositor of Civilization (Xuanwen Jun), see Idema and Grant, *The Red Brush*, 54.

100. Shen Deqian, preface to Xú Deyin, *Lüjingxuan xuji*, 1a–2b. Shen included poetic works by Xǔ Yingnian in his anthology for Qing poets and praised the couple's ideal companionate marriage (*Guochao shi biecaiji*, 750). The reason he did not incorporate Xú Deyin's works derives from his editorial principle of including only those poets who had passed away by the time of his anthologizing project. He believed that a poet's achievements could be judged in a definitive way only posthumously. Xú Deyin lived much longer than her husband.

101. Xǔ Chengyao, *Sheshi xiantan*, 614. For Ruan Yuan's family background, see also Meyer-Fong, *Building Culture in Early Qing Yangzhou*, 115.

102. Zheng Xing, *Yuan Mei nianpu xinbian*, 46, 100–102, 270, 282–83, 286–88, 302, 416, 431, 471–72, 590, 604–5. See also Li Dou, *Yangzhou huafanglu*, 243.

103. The literary activities of Yuan Mei's female disciples in Yangzhou merit a separate study. For the present discussion, see the poems by Luo Qilan and Bao Zhihui that refer to these activities: Luo Qilan, *Tingqiuxuan shiji*, 4.3a–6b, 12b–14b, 18a–b, 5.1a–b, 3a, 15a–b, 6.3a; Bao Zhihui, *Qingyuge yingao*, 2.1b–2b, 6.16a–18b.

104. Yuan Mei, *Suiyuan shihua*, 58.

105. Zhao Houjun, "Fu: Yiwen, Yishi, Jiping," 113–14, 119.

106. Xú Deyin, "Xiegu Jingting liangjun daike xuji shiyi xiezhi," in *Lüjingxuan xuji*, 21a. For records about the Ma brothers, see Li Dou, *Yangzhou huafanglu*, 86–89; for records about Wang Tingzhang, see p. 350. For those who passed the *Boxue hongci* exam in 1736, see Ruan Yuan, *Guangling shishi*, 8. Also see discussion of the Ma brothers in Finnane, Speaking of Yangzhou, 253–61.

107. Xú Deyin, "Nifu Zhuxi ting," in *Lüjingxuan xuji*, 21b. Her efforts are recorded in Li Dou, *Yangzhou huafanglu*, 5. For a translation of Du Mu's poem related to the "Bamboo West," see Owen, *An Anthology of Chinese Literature*, 632.

108. Li Dou, *Yangzhou huafanglu*, 240–41; Ruan Yuan, *Guangling shishi*, 36; Xú Deyin, "Ti Cheng Lingyan Xishan chuidiao tu," in *Lüjingxuan xuji*, 12b.

109. Xú Deyin, "Guo Heshi Dongyuan," in *Lüjingxuan xuji*, 12a; Li Dou, *Yangzhou huafanglu*, 315, 324.

2. OWNING THE LANDSCAPE

Epigraphs: Bao Gao, "Beigu qiuwang" #2, in Bao Gao, *Haimen shichao*, 4.1b; Bao Zhihui, "Bingyin Eryue Nianqiri tong Gezhai li jiangshang zhu daoyuan deng Yinfeng lianju," in *Qingyuge yingao*, 6.15a–b. It was a linked verse Bao Zhihui composed with her husband Zhang Xuan (1756–?). Bao Zhihui adds a note to the line quoted here: "This is my fiftieth birthday."

1. Elman, *Civil Examinations and Meritocracy*, 4.
2. Li Dou, *Yangzhou huafanglu.*
3. For the geographical reach of the Huizhou merchants, see Du, *The Order of Places*, 50–57.
4. For records about Guazhou, including Wang Anshi's lines, see Gu Luan, *Guangling langu*, 2. For Jingkou and Jingjiang, see Shi Weile and Zhu Lingling, *Zhongguo lishi diming dacidian zengdingben*, 1725, 1727.
5. Yan Qilin and Cheng Jian, *Jingkou wenhua*, 2–10. Also see Bao Tian-zhong, preface to *Kangxi Dantu xianzhi*; reprinted as "Kangxi zhi xu" in He Shaozhang, Feng Shoujing, and Lü Yaodou, *Guangxu Dantu xianzhi*, 1b. Bao Tianzhong was then serving as the county magistrate of Dantu. For the latest study of Zhenjiang in global contexts in the nineteenth and early twentieth centuries, see Xin Zhang, *The Global in the Local.*
6. Jingjiang, or Jing River, was an alternative name for the Yangzi River as it flowed by Mount Jing and hence, like Jingkou, was used as a synecdoche for Dantu.
7. For example, see Mao Meng, "Luelun Zhenjiang Baoshi wenhua shijia ji zhuyao shiren shizuo," 61–63. Jiangnan referred broadly to the lower Yangzi delta, south of the Yangzi River. The Jiangnan heartland included the prefectures of Suzhou, Songjiang, Changzhou, Jiaxing, Huzhou, and occasionally Zhenjiang. For a brief social history of Jiangnan, as well as its amorphous cultural identities, see Ko, *Teachers of the Inner Chambers*, 19–21.
8. Yuan Mei, *Suiyuan nüdizi shixuan*, 4.18a–21a.
9. See the various biographical sources collected in Fu Ying, *MingQing Anhui funü wenxue zhushu jikao*, 410, 412, 413, 418. Also see entries in the local gazetteer: He Shaozhang, Feng Shoujing, and Lü Yaodou, *Guangxu Dantu xianzhi*, 33.35b–38a, 33.45b–46a, 34.30b, 38.25a–b. For the joint collection of the Bao sisters, see Bao Zhilan, Bao Zhihui, Bao Zhifen, *Jingjiang Baoshi sannüshi shichao.*
10. Xu Chengyao, "Yiwenzhi," in *Shexian zhi*, 15.17a. Also see Anhui Tongzhi Guan, "Yiwenkao gao," in *Anhui tongzhi gao* (from the Erudition database on Chinese local gazetteers).
11. Luan Kaiyin, *Jingjiang huapai*, 40. For the Yangzhou school of painters, see, for example, Yangzhou Wenxue Yishu Gongzuozhe Lianhehui and Qingdai Yangzhou Huapai Yanjiuhui, *Qingdai Yangzhou huapai yanjiuji.*
12. Bao Qingxi, *Xin'an Baoshi Chengfengpai zhipu*, juan 4 and 5.
13. Bao Qingxi, preface to Bao Qingxi, *Xin'an Baoshi Chengfengpai zhipu*, 3b.
14. Xin Yu, *Publishing at the Grassroots*, 24.
15. See, for example, Qitao Guo's (*Huizhou*, 111–33) description of Huizhou as the "Confucian heartland of women."
16. The editor referred in particular to the devastating effects of the Taiping War. Bao Qingxi, *Xin'an Baoshi Chengfengpai zhipu*, 2b–3b.
17. Luan Kaiyin, *Jingjiang huapai*, 9–11, 17–20.
18. Luan Kaiyin, *Jingjiang huapai*, 63–69. From comparative studies of Qing merchant groups from different regions, it is clear that the Huizhou descendants

had predominant success in achieving upward mobility. See, for example, Feng Erkang, "Ming Qing shiqi Yangzhou de Huishang jiqi houyi shulue." Here we see the economic and cultural successes of a merchant's family from Jiangxi.

19. Luan Kaiyin, *Jingjiang huapai*, 44–48.
20. Luan Kaiyin, *Jingjiang huapai*, 63–100.
21. For records about the first two titles, see Liu Dakui, "Haimen gong muzhiming," 4.42a. The third title appeared in Bao Gao's note to a poetic work dated around 1738. For the "Yiheming" and the *moya* inscriptions on Mount Jiao, see Li Xubin, *Dubei Jiaoshan*; Shanghai Shuhua Chubanshe, *Yihe ming*. Mount Jiao remains the signature landscape of Zhenjiang today.
22. Bao Zhilan, "Pingba," in Bao Zhihui, *Qingyuge yingao*, 6a–b. Bao Zhilan here referred to Bao Zhihui's journeys with her husband to the Jiangnan heartland. But as I argue below, a closer examination of Zhihui's poetic works in the totality of the Bao family's literary and artistic production reveals a predominant focus on Dantu.
23. I use a reprint edition of Bao Gao's poetry in the *Qingdai shiwenji huibian* (Compendium of Poetry and Essays from the Qing Period). The Shanghai Library has a different edition of the *Haimen shichao*, titled *Haimen chuji* (9 *juan*). I refer to it when contents cannot be found in the reprint edition.
24. Bao Gao, "Guangling Guiguan jiyu Jingkou zhu tongxue," in *Haimen shichao waiji*, 4.3a–b.
25. For "NanXu," see Shi Weile and Zhu Lingling, *Zhongguo lishi diming dacidian zengdingben*, 1916. Also see Meyer-Fong's (*Building Culture in Early Qing Yangzhou*, 8) discussion of how the Qing writers preferred ancient names of places "for their ability to evoke the atmosphere of a place as a cultural, rather than functional or administrative entity."
26. Alternatively, *gushan* can be interpreted as the "mountains I lived by previously." The character *gu* as "native" stems from its reference to a "previous" or "former" place.
27. For records about Xu Chaojiu, see Li Dou, *Yangzhou huafanglu*, 174.
28. Bao Gao, "Guishu fu," in *Haimen shichao waiji*, "Bulu" 8b.
29. Dai Tingming and Cheng Shangkuan, *Xin'an mingzu zhi*, 88–98.
30. Bao Zhizhong, "Ti Baozhuang tu wei Xuelin zuo," in *Lunshan shichao*, 10.23b. Shangdang was located in Luzhou, Shanxi, during the Sui dynasty. XuanShezhou included Xuanzhou, Shezhou, and Raozhou in Anhui during the Tang dynasty. See Shi Weile and Zhu Lingling, *Zhongguo lishi diming dacidian zengdingben*, 192, 2118.
31. Bao Zhizhong, "Ti Baozhuang tu wei Xuelin zuo." For swan goose as a metaphor for siblings, see, for example, Du Fu, "Qianxing" #1, in Du Fu, *Du Gongbu shiji jizhu*, annotated by Zhu Heling, 181. Moreover, as a migratory bird, the swan goose provided a fitting metaphor for Bao Zhizhong's "migrating" lineage.
32. Bao Zhizhong, "Ti Baozhuang tu wei Xuelin zuo." Also see records about the Bao descendants in Pinghu in Bao Qingxi, *Xin'an Baoshi Chengfengpai zhipu*, "Fubian" 1b.

33. See Liu Dakui, "Haimen gong muzhiming," 4.40b; Bao Zhizhong, "Haimen gong xinglue," 4.68b. For the education-intendant censor's responsibilities for approving students for admission to state schools, testing and classifying them periodically, and certifying those considered to be qualified to undertake the civil service exams, see Hucker, *A Dictionary of Official Titles in Imperial China*, 496.
34. Elman, *Civil Examinations and Meritocracy*, 4.
35. Wei Shang, "The Literati Era and Its Demise," 249.
36. Bao Gao, "Ganyu yishou," in *Haimen shichao*, 1.1b.
37. Bao Gao, "Wangyuan qu," in *Haimen shichao*, 1.1b–2a.
38. Bao Gao, "Jianshan lou jixi zuige," in Bao Gao, *Haimen shichao*, 1.3b–4b.
39. Bao Gao, "Fuzhi Giangling liubie Wang Jinchen," in *Haimen shichao*, 1.8b–9b.
40. Jiang Yin, "Yizhong geng zhenshi de rendi guanxi yu wenxue shengtai"; "Qingdai shixue yu diyu wenxue chuantong de jiangou."
41. Li Xubin, *Dubei Jiaoshan*, 10.
42. Bao Gao, "Guanbei tu ge wei Zhu Liting zuo," in *Haimen shichao*, 1.2b–3a. Zhu Liting was the owner of the Tower to See Hills.
43. Bao Gao, "Yimao sanyue . . . ," in *Haimen shichao*, 2.4b–5b.
44. Bao Gao, "Yimao sanyue . . . ," in *Haimen shichao*, 2.5b. The phrase *jielu* alludes to the hermit poet Tao Qian.
45. Data are collected from the *Haimen shichao*, which dates roughly to 1726–39.
46. See the epigraph. Zhongzhou as a place name was located at the convergence of the Wen and Wei Rivers in Shandong. See Shi Weile and Zhu Lingling, *Zhongguo lishi diming dacidian zengdingben*, 420. I translate it as "central island" because Bao Gao here writes about overlooking Dantu from Mount Beigu. Also refer to how Bao Gao used the swan goose as a metaphor for his precarious life. Bao Gao, *Haimen shichao*, 6.8a–b.
47. Bao Gao, "Deng Beigu tong Xuzhao," in *Haimen erji*, 209–10; Bao Gao, "Liqiu qian er'ri . . . ," in *Haimen sanji*, , 598.
48. Found in the Shanghai Library version: Bao Gao, "Jidi Hao weibian *Haimen ji* cheng wan'er xiaoshi," in *Haimen chuji*, 9.5b. Haimen belonged to the Tongzhou prefecture and was part of the Huaihai area. Bao Gao used it as his style name and the title for his personal collection. This was decades earlier than Ruan Yuan's *Huaihai yingling ji* in terms of following Qin Guan's example.
49. Found in the Shanghai Library version: Bao Gao, "Ji Yin gongzi Youchang Zhongzhou fucheng *Haimen ji* bajuan," in *Haimen shichao*, 9.14b–15a.
50. Bao Gao, "Yiyou sanyue Jiaoshan xiwu Gao Xuting kunji . . . ," in *Haimen sanji*, 708.
51. Bao Zhizhong, "Qianxing" #1, in *Lunshan shichao*, 10.24a.
52. Bao Wenkui, "Yeyun xing," in *Yeyun shichao*, 2.6b–7a.
53. Bao Wenkui, "Qiuri jishi youhuai tongli zhuzi ci Zhang Gezhai guzhang jianji sishou yuanyun" #4, in *Yeyun shichao*, 2.7b–8a.
54. Bao Zhilan, "Ganhuai wushou," in *Qiyunge shichao*, 3.1a–b. Bao Zhizhong used *Kexuan lou* as the title for the posthumously collected poetry of his mother,

Chen Ruizhu. The title "Zhengjun" referred to the hermit who declined an invitation to serve in the government. See Gong Yanming, *Zhongguo lidai zhiguan bieming dacidian zengdingben*, 697.

55. Bernhardt, *Women and Property in China*, 4–8.
56. Idema and Grant, *The Red Brush*, 52–54.
57. Bao Zhihui, "Sanshi chudu zishu," in *Qingyuge yingao*, 2.1a.
58. Bao Wenkui, "Pingba" 7b, in Bao Zhihui, *Qingyuge shichao*.
59. Bao Wenkui, "Qingyuge kanyu tong Gezhai zhang Chaixiang gumu fenyun," in *Yeyun shichao*, 3.7b.
60. Bao Zhihui, "Jiangxing wang Jingkou sanshan tong Gezhai zuo," in *Qingyuge yingao*, 2.14b.
61. Bai Juyi, "He Pei linggong Nanzhuang yijue," in Bai Juyi, Bai Juyi ji jianjiao, annotated by Zhu Jincheng, 5:2307.Bai implied here that the magnificence of Mount Song would make it more suitable as Pei's home.
62. Mount Lumen was located in Xiangyang, Hubei. See Shi Weile and Zhu Lingling, *Zhongguo lishi diming dacidian zengdingben*, 2541–42.
63. Bao Zhihui, "Gezhai gou caotang luocheng xifu sishou," in *Qingyuge yingao*, 2.6a.
64. For the first poetic line quoted here, see Bao Zhihui, "Gezhai caotang luocheng xifu sishou" #4, in *Qingyuge yingao*, 2.6b. For the second poetic line quoted here, see Bao Zhihui, "Tong Gezhai deng Beigu shan," in *Qingyuge yingao*, 1.14b. For Bao Gao's references to *mumo*, see for example: Bao Gao, "Beigu qiuwang" #4, in *Haimen shichao*, 4.2a. Bao Gao, "Mumo lou dengtiao tong Wenru zuo," in *Haimen erji*, 274.
65. Bao Zhihui, "Qingyuge tong Hongqi zhi Gezhai kanyu de erxiao," in *Qingyuge yingao*, 3.3b.
66. Bao Zhihui, "Xiaye tong Huanyun sanmei ji Wanfang dazi Qiyunge naliang," in *Qingyuge yingao*, 1.2a.
67. Bao Zhihui, "Xiari qianhuai shishou," in Bao *Qingyuge yingao*, 6.2b.
68. Bao Zhifen, "Ti Zhang Gezhai zizhang Yinlü shantang," in *Sanxiuzhai shichao*, 1.13a. By contrast, poetic works by Zhang Xuan more often served social purposes than developing techniques for portraying the landscape.
69. Bao Zhihui, "Siyue sanri Luo Qiuting guo xiaoyuan . . . ," in *Qingyuge yingao*, 2.7a–b; Luo Qilan, "Qiuting yuanchang," in Bao Zhihui, *Qingyuge yingao*, 2.7b.
70. Bao Zhihui, "Qiuting yao Lunshan xiong Wanfang zi Huanyun mei . . . ," in *Qingyuge yingao*, 3.8b–9b.
71. Owen, "Singularity and Possession," in *The End of the Chinese "Middle Ages,"* 12–33. See esp. 27–28, 33.
72. Xiaoshan Yang, *Metamorphosis of the Private Sphere*, 3; see also 2–4, 11–90.
73. Mount Mao was located in Jurong County, in the west of Dantu, but was associated with the legend of the True Hermit of Huayang and the "Yiheming" attributed to him. "Three Hills" here had a broader connotation than that defined by the geographical boundaries of the local Dantu.

74. Bao Zhihui, "Xiari guo Bagong dong jian xianzhengjun huasong xiaofu," in *Qingyuge yingao*, 3.17a–b.
75. See the second epigraph.
76. Bao Zhihui, "Jiachuting tong Wanfang zi . . . ," in *Qingyuge yingao*, 6.21b. See appendix 1 for a list of sites that appear in her poetic corpus, providing a glimpse of the scope of these affective ties and anchoring points.
77. Bao Zhihui, "Songliaoge ganjiu zhuidao Lunshan xiong," in *Qingyuge yingao*, 6.21a–b.
78. Strassberg, *Inscribed Landscapes*, 12, 36–44.
79. Bao Zhihui, "Chou Cuipingzhou Wang Ailan . . . ," in *Qingyuge yingao*, 6.16b–17a. Wang Qiong (ca. 18th–19th c.; courtesy name Ailan) was a granddaughter of Wang Wenzhi and a well-connected woman poet and anthologizer of women's poetry. For a selection of her poetry, see Wang Qiong, *Ailan shichao*. By contrast, Bao Gao compared Wang Wenzhi to Wang Can in terms of living a sojourner's life.
80. Bao Zhihui, "Hulou jishi ershou," in *Qingyuge yingao*, 5.4b.
81. Bao Zhihui, "Ziti Yanbo gongfan xiaozhao," in *Qingyuge yingao*, 3.1a–b; 3.7b–8a.
82. Bao Zhihui, "Xihu sishou," in *Qingyuge yingao*, 5.1b–2a. For her poetry on their journey in 1801, see the poems incorporated into *juan* 5 of the *Qingyuge yingao*.
83. Shang Wei, *Tixie mingsheng*, 21.
84. Zili Ma and Fan Pik Wah, "Hearts in the Hometown," 268–86.
85. Bao Wenkui, "Yeyun zengshi," in *Qingyuge yingao*, 5.2b.
86. Xiao Yanwan, *Shindai no josei shijintachi*, 81–106. For a book-length study on travel poetry by women from this time, see Yanning Wang, *Reverie and Reality*.
87. Owen, *All Mine!*, 89; see 85–105 for discussion of Sima Guang's essay.

3. TRAVERSING THE NINE LANDS

Epigraphs: Jin Zike, preface to He Peifen, *Lüyunge shichao*, 1a–3a; He Peifen, "Wucheng chunliu yong Yuyang Qiuliu yun tong Huanbi Zhixiang liangmei zuo," in *Lüyunge shichao*, 5.8a–b.

1. Wang Chengzu, *Zhongguo dilixue shi*, 16–32.
2. Shi Weile and Zhu Lingling, *Zhongguo lishi diming dacidian zengdingben*, 42–43.
3. Du, *The Order of Places*, 202.
4. Du, *The Order of Places*, 230–37.
5. The Song maps titled *Zhizhang tu* include fourteen maps of the Zhou terrain and twelve states, of which three are extant: *Wangji lieguo zhizhang zongtu* (General picture of the [Zhou] terrain and the states in the palm), *Wangji zhizhang zhitu* (Picture of the [Zhou] terrain in the palm), *Chudi zhizhang zhitu* (Picture of the Chu in the palm). See Cao Wanru, *Zhongguo gudai ditu ji Zhanguo*, maps 123–25. According to the explanatory note, *zhizhang zhi tu* was an alternative name for simplified maps. The early Qing maps titled *Xialan*

zhizhang include twenty maps drawn from a set of Ming maps of the administrative areas of the Ming empire and neighboring tributary states. See Lin Tianren, *Huangyu soulan*, 54–57.

6. Elman, *On Their Own Terms*, 200–205.
7. Elman, *On Their Own Terms*, 195–99.
8. Dong Gao, *HuangQing wenying xubian*, 45.8a. For a study of the *Huangyu tu* and its political and cultural legacies, see Bai Hongye and Li Xiaocong, *Kangxi chao Huangyu quanlan tu*.
9. Lü Anshi, *Sancai yiguan tu* (1722), in Lin Tianren, *Huangyu soulan*, 402. The idea of *sancai* came from the *Book of Changes* (*Ciyuan*, 25) and referred to heaven, earth, and humans.
10. Anonymous, *DaQing yitong tiandi quantu*, in Lin Tianren, *Huangyu soulan*, 94.
11. Jin Zike, preface to He Peifen, *Lüyunge shichao*, 1a–3a.
12. The second poem in He Bingtang's personal collection includes a note that he was serving in Yangzhou while his family stayed in Guangdong. In 1822 he wrote that he had served in Yangzhou for seven years. His sixtieth birthday fell between 1830 and 1831. See He Bingtang, "Shounei sishi chudu"; "Renwu qiuri qijia zhijiang shuaicheng silü"; and "Liushi shengchen ci Yixiang ernü yun," in *Tonghua shuwu shicao*, 1b, 4b–5a, 73b–74a.
13. Cui Hu, "Sanyue wuri pei Pei dafu fan Changsha Donghu," in Peng Dingqiu et al., *Quan Tang shi*, vol. 11, 4148. He Bingtang also compared himself to Cui Hu when joining a party on boats and passing by the Red Bridge. He Bingtang, "Jin Zike zhao tongren fanzhou Taohua an kan hongbai taohua fenfu qijue liushou" #3, in *Tonghua shuwu shicao*, 1b–2b.
14. Duan Chengshi, *Youyang zazu*, *juan* 10 (from the Erudition database).
15. See, for example, Ji Han, *Nanfang caomu zhuang*, *juan* 1; Chen Jingyi, *Quanfang beizu*, *juan* 19 (versions from the Erudition database).
16. See, for example, Li Deyu, "Shu Tonghuafeng shan fu bing xu," in *Li Wenrao ji*, *juan* 1; Song Qi, *Yibu fangwu lueji*; Zhu Mu, *Fangyu shenglan*, *juan* 51; Cao Xuequan, *Shuzhong guangji*, *juan* 58 (versions from the Erudition database).
17. He Peiyu, "Yi Lingnan" #4, in *Ouxiangguan shichao* (8 *juan*), 2.4b–5a.
18. Miles, *The Sea of Learning*, 26–31.
19. Finnane, *Speaking of Yangzhou*, 16–17. Also see Zurndorfer, "Cities and the Urban Economy."
20. Though dated around 1865, the contents of the collection include predominantly poetic exercises from the 1820s and 1830s.
21. This collection includes *Jinyun xiaocao* 2 *juan* and *Lihua meng* 5 *juan*.
22. He Bingtang, "Huang Xiaofeng zi Lingnan jihuai qilü ershou ciyun chouzhi" #2, in *Tonghua shuwu shicao*, 2b. For the cultural significance of the West of Bamboo as a signature site in Yangzhou, see Gu Luan, *Guangling langu*, 29. The allusion to wrens derived from the *Zhuangzi* and indicated a place as small as that occupied by the bird. Zhuang Zhou, *Nanhua zhenjing zhushu*, *juan* 1 (from the Erudition database).

23. See Meyer-Fong, *Building Culture in Early Qing Yangzhou*, 69, 74.
24. Yang Binbin, "Yangzhou guixiu zhushu yu jiaoyou yanjiu xinshiye," 100–101.
25. He Bingtang, "Wucheng huaigu," in *Tonghua shuwu shicao*, 30a. For early Qing poets' use of "Weed-Covered City" to juxtapose the city's past glory with current ruin, see Meyer-Fong, *Building Culture in Early Qing Yangzhou*, 12.
26. He Bingtang, "Yuandan shibi," in *Tonghua shuwu shicao*, 42a.
27. He Bingtang, "Jichou Yuandan lichun," in *Tonghua shuwu shicao*, 58b.
28. He Bingtang, "Wucheng huaigu wuyong," in *Tonghua shuwu shicao*, 77b–78b. For records about the sites, see Gu Luan, *Guangling shishi*, 25, 27, 20, 38.
29. He Bingtang, "Zhang Fuchuan yishi jianzeng ciyun fengda" #2, in *Tonghua shuwu shicao*, 76b.
30. For references on Wang's "autumn willows" poetic sequence, see Waiyee Li, *Women and National Trauma*, 65.
31. He Peifen, "Wucheng chunliu yong Yuyang Qiuliu yun tong Huanbi Zhixiang liangmei zuo," in *Lüyunge shichao*, 5.8a–b; He Peiyu, "Wucheng chunliu yong Yuyang shanren Qiuliu yun," in *Ouxiangguan shichao*, 2.13a–14a; He Peizhu, "Wucheng Chunliu dieyong Yuyang Qiuliu yun silü," in *Zhuyan lanxuezhai shichao*, 18b–19a.
32. The phrase *jinlü* refers at once to willow sprigs and to the Tang verse "Jinlü yi" (Gown made of golden threads), hence the metaphor of the dancing gown. For records about the verse, see, for example, Ji Yougong, *Tangshi jishi, juan* 56 (from the Erudition database).
33. The phrase "jade flute and Qiang reed" is a play on words combining Du Mu's line about the "jade-white beauty" playing the flute with Wang Shizhen's reference to the Jade Pass (see note below). The Qiang reed was originally associated with the Jade Pass in Wang Zhihuan's popular verse, "Liangzhou ci." See, for example, Ji Yougong, *Tangshi jishi, juan* 26.
34. For the translation and analysis of Wang's poem, including the lines quoted here, see Wai-yee Li, *Women and National Trauma*, 65.
35. See, for example, Peifen's note to a poetic sequence: "I continue learning poetic compositions from my father even since I got married." He Peifen, "Qiuri shuhuai ci Huanbi yun," in *Lüyunge shichao*, 4.12a–13a.
36. Pang Zhonglu, "Tici," in He Peiyu, *Ouxiangguan shichao*, 1a.
37. He Peiyu, "Shangsiri yuzhong jishi fenghe Yunlanzi sishou" #3, in *Hongweiguan xueyingao*, 603.
38. He Peifen, "Hushang kan mudan" #1, in *Lüyunge shichao*, 1.2b.
39. He Peifen, "Shangsi jishi" #1, #3, in *Lüyunge shichao*, 2.6a–b.
40. Reflections in spring waves allude to the story of Xiaoqing, the ill-fated and talented concubine from Yangzhou. For the story as an inspiration for women writers during the Qing era, see Widmer, "Xiaoqing's Literary Legacy."
41. The term *shicui* (gathering kingfisher plumes), which I translate simply as "dressed in fineries," came from the "Luoshen fu" (Goddess of the Luo River)

by Cao Zhi (192–232). For a translation of the piece, see Owen, *An Anthology of Chinese Literature*, 194–97.

42. The Hanshi festival was around the same time as the Lustration and Qingming festivals and indicated the end of spring. Hence, I translate the line as "show off their beauty throughout the spring."
43. He Peiyu, "Qingmingri jishi bulu sanyue zuo," in *Hongweiguan xueyingao*, 557.
44. For autobiographical elements in the play, see Hua Wei, *MingQing funü zhi xiqu chuangzuo yu piping*, 128–53. See particularly 141–43 concerning its indebtedness to the late Ming play *Yuanyang meng* (Dream of Mandarin ducks), with autobiographical elements highlighting the affective bonds between the female author Ye Xiaowan and her sisters.
45. See, for example, Xú Deyin, "He Lisheng chunyou shu suojian," in *Lüjingxuan shichao*, 1.14a–b.
46. Xú Deyin, "Guo Tinghua shuwu," in *Lüjingxuan shichao*, 1.7a.
47. He Bingtang, "Hongqiao Qiuliu ci Zhao Genfu mingjing yun," in *Tonghua shuwu shicao*, 45b–46b. Red Bridge was alternatively named Rainbow Bridge. The term "Lingnan" referred to Guangdong, or the Pearl River delta. See Miles, *The Sea of Learning*, 5. The term *zhuniang* (pearl maiden) preceding the note about Lingnan referred to courtesans in Guangdong "flower boats" who were dressed in Jiangnan fashion. Some of these boats were known as the Yangzhou group. See Miles, *The Sea of Learning*, 62.
48. He Bingtang, "Shounei sishi chudu" #1, in *Tonghua shuwu shicao*, 1b.
49. He Bingtang, "Ci Zheng Xiaofeng pingyuan tibi," in *Tonghua shuwu shicao*, 47b.
50. He Bingtang, "Ziti LongShuyou tu," in *Tonghua shuwu shicao*, 39a–b.
51. He Peifen, "Qiuri shuhuai ci Huanbi yun" #5, in *Lüyunge shichao*, 4.13a.
52. See, for example, He Peiyu, "Xiwu Huang Gengwan nüshi," in *Ouxiangguan shichao*, 1.20a. A line indicates the time lapse: "It has been ten years since I [Peiyu] left the Pearl River." For records about Huang Zhishu, see Xian Yuqing, *Guangdong nüzi yiwen kao*, 43–44. For a recent study of women poets in Guangdong during the Qing, see Ellen Widmer and Zhao Yingzhi, "Shiba shiji de Guangdong cainü," 40–46.
53. He Peiyu, "Yi Lingnan" #2; "Yi Lingnan Zhangshi zhu biaozi" #3, in *Ouxiangguan shichao*, 2.4b–5a, 2.6b–7a.
54. Owen, *The End of the Chinese "Middle Ages,"* 8.
55. Song Guangye, *Luofushanzhi huibian*, *juan* 8. Also see Shi Weile and Zhu Lingling, *Zhongguo lishi diming dacidian zengdingben*, 1655.
56. He Bingtang, "Ziti LongShuyou tu," in *Tonghua shuwu shicao*, 39b.
57. He Peiyu, "Yi Lingnan" #1, #4, in *Ouxiangguan shichao*, 2.4b–5a. For these landmarks of Guangdong, see Shi Weile and Zhu Lingling, *Zhongguo lishi diming dacidian zengdingben*, 1655.
58. The Island for Picking Kingfisher Plumes was located in Nanhai County in Guangdong. See Ruan Yuan and Chen Changqi, *Guangdong tongzhi*, *juan* 101 (from the Erudition database for Chinese local gazetteers).

59. *Dan* referred to an ethnic group in Guangdong who made their living as fishermen. See, for example, records about the Dan families in Gui Dian, *Nanhai Xianzhi*, *juan* 2 (from the Erudition database for Chinese local gazetteers).
60. He Peiyu, "Yi Lingnan" #1, in *Ouxiangguan shichao*, 2.4b.
61. See, for example, He Peifen, "Jiajun mingti LongShuyou tu sanshou" #3, in *Lüyunge shichao*, 4.2a–b. For records about Mount Taihua, see Shi Weile and Zhu Lingling, *Zhongguo lishi diming dacidian zengdingben*, 384. Mount Taihua is better known today as Mount Hua.
62. He Peiyu, "Mengdeng Taihua jueding ting Maonü Yujiang tanqin xinghou zuoge jizhi," in *Ouxiangguan shichao*, 6.1a–b. Peiyu's verse was an imitation of Li Bai's classic piece on dreaming of visiting Mount Tianmu. See Li Bai, "Mengyou Tianmu yin liubie," in Li Bai, *Li Bai shixuan*, selected and annotated by Qian Zhixi and Liu Qinghai, 158–62. It is not entirely clear whether her reference to phoenix trees here also echoes her reference to the "paulownia blossom phoenix" as an indigenous feature of Guangdong.
63. Noel, "Rereading a Poetics of Divination."
64. Noel, "Rereading a Poetics of Divination," 280, 288.
65. Noel, "Rereading a Poetics of Divination," 294.
66. He Peizhu, *Lihua meng*, 289.
67. See, for example, Sima Qian, *Shiji*, *juan* 6 (from the Erudition database).
68. For the former reference, see Li Shangyin, "Bicheng," in *Li Yishan shji*, *juan* 5. For the latter reference, see Zhu Mu, *Fangyu shenglan*, *juan* 6 (versions from the Erudition database).
69. For Fortified Terrace, see Yue Shi, *Taiping huanyu ji*, *juan* 188. For Weak Water, see Ban Gu, *Hanshu*, *juan* 57. For Kingdom of Fragrance, see Li Fang, *Taiping guangji*, *juan* 383 (versions from the Erudition database). The jade tower has broad references.
70. Anonymous, *Jiuzhou tushuo*, in Gong Chuhan and Qi Xi, *Zhongguo xijian difang shiliao jicheng disanji*, sequence 3, vol. 94, 1–14.
71. Yan Dunyi, "He Peizhu de *Lihua meng*," 300–304; Hua Wei, *MingQing funü zhi xiqu chuangzuo yu piping*, 128–53.
72. Yang Binbin, "Yangzhou guixiu zhushu yu jiaoyou yanjiu xinshiye," 98.
73. Ye Xiaowan, *Yuanyang meng*, 398–99. Ye Xiaowan wrote the play to mourn the early deaths of her sisters and set an important precedent for imagining the reunion of female characters in the immortal world.
74. Du, *The Order of Places*, 237.
75. Finnane, *Speaking of Yangzhou*, 16–17.
76. See, for example, He Bingtang, *Tonghua shuwu shicao*, 82a; He Bingtang, "Suimu dongting zhouci oucheng" #2, "Tuci Honghuabu wen cunren shu shuizai chuangran youzuo," "Zhuanxiang Baimen zhongtu zushui mancheng qilü ershou," in *Tonghua shuwu shicao*, 44a–b, 53a, 82a.
77. Writing on the eve of the First Opium War (1840–42), Gong sensed a deepening crisis and was among the first to call for human action to galvanize China out of

what he perceived to be its stagnation. David Wang, "Chinese literature from 1841 to 1937," 564. Here I use Wang's translation of the poetic lines by Gong Zizhen.

4. RECTIFYING THE NATIVE LAND AND "ALL UNDER HEAVEN"

Epigraphs: Wang Ying, "Huimo," in *Ya'an shuwu shiji*, 1.9b; Wang Ying, "She yitian yixue yi," in *Ya'an shuwu wenji*, 1.35a.

1. Kuhn, *Origins of the Modern Chinese State*, 1, 6.
2. Wang Ying, "Xiwen jin yanpianyan ji," in *Ya'an shuwu wenji*, 2.12a–13b. For the opium ban and related historical facts brought up in the essay, see Hsu, *The Rise of Modern China*, 179.
3. For a brief introduction to Wang Ying's life and works, see Binbin Yang, *Heroines of the Qing*, 8–9, 130–34. Detailed information follows.
4. Ko, *The Social Life of Inkstones*. Ko's focus is the inkstone, but her discussion includes the Huizhou ink cake as a commercial product with cultural values similar to those of the inkstone; see, for example, 42–44.
5. Yulian Wu, *Luxurious Networks*.
6. For the tale about the "dragon's guests," see Feng Zhi, *Yunxian zaji*, *juan* 1; Lu You, *Moshi*, *juan* 2 (versions from the Erudition database). For the "dragon patterns" designed for the Qing imperial collections of ink cakes, see Ko, *The Social Life of Inkstones*, 24–30.
7. For Huizhou's reputation as the "model Confucian place," see, for example, Du, *The Order of Places*, 49.
8. See, for example, Ban Gu, *Hanshu*, *juan* 28.1 (from the Erudition database).
9. Lewis and Hsieh, "*Tianxia* and the Invention of Empire in East Asia," 31.
10. Cited from Du, *The Order of Places*, 49.
11. Du, *The Order of Places*, 49.
12. Rowe, "Ancestral Rites and Political Authority."
13. Yang Binbin, "Funü zhushu yu Huishang jiazu tuibian." Also see the "annalistic biography" (*nianpu*) that organizes some of Wang Ying's works in chronological order: Li Qiuju, "Qingdai nüshiren Wang Ying nianpu."
14. Binbin Yang, *Heroines of the Qing*, 8–9.
15. Li Dou, *Yangzhou huafanglu*, 282.
16. Xu Chengyao, *Sheshi xiantan*, 674.
17. Wang Ying, "Shu *Dingwuben Lanting* hou," in *Ya'an shuwu wenji*, 2.20a.
18. Wang Ying, "Shu *Dingwuben Lanting* hou," in *Ya'an shuwu wenji*, 2.20b.
19. Ko, *The Social Life of Inkstones*, 190–200; Yulian Wu, *Luxurious Networks*, 194.
20. Ruan Yuan, "Qiudeng kezi tuji," 3a, in Cheng Bao, *Qiudeng kezi tu tiyongji*.
21. For details, see Yang Binbin, "Funü zhushu yu Huishang jiazu tuibian," 180–85.
22. For a case study of the Cao family, see Ho, *The Ladder of Success*, 289–92.
23. Ruan Yuan, "Qiudeng kezi tuji," 3a, in Cheng Bao, *Qiudeng kezi tu tiyongji*.
24. A recent study of Jiang Fan uncovers his family's genealogy, which meticulously lists its descendants from Jingde, a county usually referred to as the

expanded Huizhou area. Jiang Fan's father, Jiang Qidong (1722–86), moved the family business to Suzhou and Yangzhou. See Qi Yongxiang, *Jiang Fan yu Hanxue shichengji yanjiu*, 8–31. For a pioneering study of the Buddhist dimensions of Jiang Zhu's poetry, see Grant, "Little Vimalakirti."

25. Wang Ying, "Jiang Zhengtang [Jiang Fan] fuzhi zhuti Qiujiang tingchao tu ji Tangren ju," in *Ya'an shuwu shiji*, 1.2b–3a. In addition, Jiang Fan's annalistic biography records the poem by Wang Ying. See Min Erchang, *Jiang Ziping xiansheng nianpu*, 597.
26. Jiang Zhu, "Ti Wang Sunzhi Chunxuan bingmao tu," "Ti Wang Sunzhi xiang," in *Xiao Weimo shigao*, 2705, 2713.
27. Jiang Zhu, "Ziti Weimo yinji tu xiaoying," "Xie Fang Qingjiang wei bu Hanmei xiaoying," in *Xiao Weimo shigao*, 2703, 2715.
28. Wang Ying, "Ba xianjiu Fengzhigong riji hou," in *Ya'an shuwu wenji*, 2.24a–b.
29. Qitao Guo, *Huizhou*, 83–102.
30. Ying Jie and Yan Duanshu, *Xuzuan Yangzhou fuzhi*, *juan* 15 (from the Erudition database for Chinese local gazetteers).
31. Cheng Dingtiao, *Xun zizhi ji*, 26b–28b. A copy of this work is held by the Anhui Library. An author of one of the prefaces (Cao Cheng, 7a–8a) mentions that Cheng Bao reprinted the work in 1844.
32. Cheng Bao, "Epilogue," in Cheng Dingtiao, *Xun zizhi ji*, 29a–b.
33. Cheng Dingtiao, *Xun zizhi ji*, 18a.
34. For the story of Hundun, see Zhuang Zhou, *Nanhua zhenjing zhushu*, *juan* 3 (from the Erudition database).
35. This means getting entangled in unnecessary trouble or concerns.
36. Wang Ying, *Ya'an shuwu wenji*, 1.19a–b.
37. See, for example, Zhang Xiaoye, *Qingdai siyan wenti yanjiu*, 91–103, 164–99; Wu Haibo, *Lianghuai siyan yu difang shehui*, 216–323.
38. Wang Ying, "Jisi qiuri jie fuzi Henan laishu jiangci Huaibei yanwu gui Hanshang ke Bao'er bingyun jin xidu Yuan Yishan shi wei jiju jicheng" #1, in *Ya'an shuwu shiji*, 2.1a. According to Qitao Guo's (*Huizhou*, 87, 100–101) discussion, similar attributes, such as "chivalrous integrity and generosity" (*xiayi kangkai*), were often used in late Ming biographies for Huizhou merchants.
39. Wang Ying, "Jicheng fuzi wushou" #5, in *Ya'an shuwu shiji*, 1.15a.
40. Wang Ying, "Song fuzi zhi Yangzhou," in *Ya'an shuwu shiji*, 2.9b–10a. She inserted a note that Cheng Bao was seven years old this year, i.e., 1812.
41. Wang Ying, "Jisi qiuri jie fuzi Henan laishu jiangci Huaibei yanwu gui Hanshang ke Bao'er bingyun jin xidu Yuan Yishan shi wei jiju jicheng" #4, in *Ya'an shuwu shiji*, 2.1b.
42. Wang Ying, "Daoguang Wuzi qiuwei Bao'er huoshou yi er shiyi shihu jijin shiyousannian yi yuangan jishi suicheng chang'ge," in *Ya'an shuwu shiji*, 3.4b–5a.
43. Liu Wenqi, "Chengmu Wang taiyiren jiazhuan," in Cheng Bao, *Ya'an shuwu zengyanlu*, "Zhuan" 1b. For *sufeng* as a lofty term coined in the late Ming to

refer to the Huizhou merchants who had accumulated immense wealth, see Qitao Guo, *Huizhou*, 98.

44. Wang Ying, "Gengwuchun fuzi guizi Guangzhou jiang yijia huiShe dadi zhizhi Yucheng zushu bing fushi zeng Bao'er liuxing," in *Ya'an shuwu shiji*, 3.9b–10a.
45. Wang Ying, "Yanling xiaofa," in *Ya'an shuwu shiji*, 2.5b.
46. Wang Ying, "Wuyin chunri ming Bao'er zhi Yangzhou yi Jinyuan dadi yu songchumen er wuhuishou shi tongku biequ yu wei wuyi jiuzhi yinci jishi," in *Ya'an shuwu shiji*, 3.1a.
47. See the map in Lao Fengyuan and Shen Botang, Daoguang *Shexian zhi*, "Pictures" 6a.
48. For an introduction of Huizhou as a model Confucian place because of Zhu Xi's influence, see Qitao Guo, *Ritual Opera and Mercantile Lineage*, 16–17. For the Ziyang Academy, see Ma Buchan, *Huizhou fuzhi*, 3.1a, 3.41b–43a. The academy stays alive today as the site for the She County High School.
49. Ma Buchan, *Huizhou fuzhi*, 2.6.
50. Field trips taken in August 2019 and March 2023.
51. Wang Ying, "Shishan," in *Ya'an shuwu shiji*, 2.11a.
52. Wang Ying, "Longshan miao," in *Ya'an shuwu shiji*, 2.10b–11a.
53. Wang Ying, "Dongri lizhong guan dayu ge," in *Ya'an shuwu shiji*, 3.9b–10a.
54. Brown, *Laws of the Land*.
55. Wang Ying, "Yuanzang," in *Ya'an shuwu wenji*, 1.13a–b.
56. Wang Ying, "Chujiao ji," in *Ya'an shuwu wenji*, 2.11a–b.
57. Wang Ying, "Chujiao tan bingxu," in *Ya'an shuwu shiji*, 3.11a–12a.
58. Zheng Xuan, *Liji*, *juan* 5 (from the Erudition database).
59. Wang Ying, "Chujiao tan bingxu," in *Ya'an shuwu shiji*, 3.11a–12a.
60. For a brief discussion of these writings, see Yang Binbin, "Funü zhushu yu Huishang jiazu tuibian," 185–99.
61. For these discourses, see Qitao Guo, *Huizhou*, 83–102.
62. Wang Ying, "Gengpu zubo yuanpei Bao taigongren wudai tongtang ji," "Junyi zushugu Hu tairuren qishi shouxu," in *Ya'an shuwu wenji*, 2.14a–15b, 2.16a–18b.
63. Wang Ying, "Shu yuanzu Zhenminggong cangao hou," in *Ya'an shuwu wenji*, 2.21a–b.
64. Wang Ying, "Da zhisun Shiquan wen Weijing shuwu ji," in *Ya'an shuwu wenji*, 2.7a–8b. Also see Wang Ying, "Zaichuan xiandabo jian Weijing shuwu bieye e wei xiandaren suoshu jianzhi shengan fushi sanzhi Xuecheng jiuzhi Xuesi," in *Ya'an shuwu shiji*, 3.15b.
65. Zheng Xuan, *Liji*, *juan* 7 (from the Erudition database).
66. He Yan, *Lunyu zhushu*, *juan* 3 (from the Erudition database). My translation here follows the annotators' interpretation. The line is otherwise translated as "Lastly, they paint upon a plain surface." See Roberts, *The Analects*, 43.
67. *Laozi*, Stanza 28. See translation in Roberts, *Dao De Jing*, 78.
68. *Zhuangzi*, ch. 4. See translation in Watson, *The Complete Works of Chuang Tzu*, 58.

69. Wang Ying, "Shoucai tang ji," in *Ya'an shuwu wenji*, 2.6a–b (my emphasis).
70. Zheng Xuan, *Liji*, *juan* 24 (from the Erudition database). Hence my translation of *shoucai* as "harmonized colors."
71. Roberts, *Dao De Jing*, 78.
72. Watson, *The Complete Works of Chuang Tzu*, 54–58.
73. See, for example, Lin Xiyi, *Zhuangzi kouyi*, *juan* 5 (from the Erudition database).
74. Furth, "The Patriarch's Legacy," 195–96.
75. Rowe, "Ancestral Rites and Political Authority," 384–85.
76. I have created a graph below according to Wang Ying's account. See Wang Ying, "Da Beren tang zuren ji," in *Ya'an shuwu wenji*, 2.2a.
77. Wang Ying, "Da Benren tang zuren ji," 2.2b.
78. Wang Ying, "Da Benren tang zuren ji," 2.2b–3a.
79. For a recent study of the Confucian concept of benevolence, see Qiyong Guo et al., "The Values of Confucian Benevolence."
80. Wang Ying, "Xiu Leshan tang ji," in *Ya'an shuwu wenji*, 2.4a–5b.
81. Wang Ying, "Xiu Leshan tang ji," in *Ya'an shuwu wenji*, 2.4a–b.
82. Owen, *All Mine!*, 15, 89–105.
83. Wang Ying, "Xiu Leshan tang ji," 2.5a.
84. Wang Ying, "Xiu Leshan tang ji," 2.5a–b.
85. Cheng Dingtiao, *Xun zizhi ji*, 1b–2a, 16b–17a, 25a.
86. McDermott, *The Making of a New Rural Order in South China*, vol. 1, 302.
87. McDermott, *The Making of a New Rural Order in South China*, vol. 1, 316.
88. McDermott, *The Making of a New Rural Order in South China*, vol. 2, 67, 65–68. Also see Michael Szonyi's (*Practicing Kinship*, 90–93) discussion of the ancestral hall as the most visible symbol of kinship organization in local Fujian societies during the late imperial period. Relevant here is his key argument that institutional structures are shaped by complex and multivalent kinship practices and strategies devised by individuals and groups.
89. Ebrey, "Conceptions of the Family in the Sung Dynasty," 220–40.
90. Wang Ying, "She yitian yixue yi," in *Ya'an shuwu wenji*, 1.35b.
91. Indeed, compilers of the Daoguang Huizhou gazetteer had the clear intention to bolster the local moral reputation. See Cheng Huaijing, preface to Ma Buchan, *Daoguang Huizhou fuzhi*, 5a.
92. Wang Ying, "Fushe wenhui ji," in *Ya'an shuwu wenji*, 2.10a–b.
93. Wang Ying, "She yitian yixue yi," in *Ya'an shuwu wenji*, 1.35a.
94. Beattie, *Land and Lineage in China*, 2–17.
95. Qitao Guo, *Huizhou*, 100.
96. Yulian Wu, *Luxurious Networks*, 138.
97. With respect to charitable schools, she praised a school run by her affinal uncle Cheng Guangqiao as an exemplary case. Wang Ying, "She yitian yixue yi," in *Ya'an shuwu wenji*, 1.35b.
98. See, for example, Zhang Xiaopo, "Qingdai Huizhou wenhui yunzuo jiqi keju gongneng."

99. Wang Ying, "Fushe wenhui ji," in *Ya'an shuwu wenji*, 2.10b.
100. Wang Ying, "She yitian yixue yi," in *Ya'an shuwu wenji*, 1.35b.
101. Wang Ying, "Jiawu rudu liushi Xuefu dazhifu Xuexun erzhifu bing zhuzhifu Shiying Shibi liang zhisunfu," in *Ya'an shuwu shiji*, 3.15b–16a.
102. A Feng, *MingQing shidai funü de diwei yu quanli*, 134.
103. Rowe, "Ancestral Rites and Political Authority," 399. Also see Lin, "Two Social Theories Revealed." For a reprint of the 1826 compendium of *jingshi* writings, see He Changling, Wei Yuan, et. al., *Qing jingshi wenbian*.
104. For a brief discussion of Wang Ying's writings on medicine, through which she develops a parallel between the treatment of illness and the ruling of the state, see Binbin Yang, *Heroines of the Qing*, 130–34.
105. Wang Ying, "Guisi Bao'er cheng jinshi xuanfen gongbu shuci jishi," in *Ya'an shuwu shiji*, 3.14a. This fact also meant that Cheng Bao did not have the kind of experience of lineage and local governance that Wang Ying wrote about in her essays.
106. Wang Ying, "Juguan shize," in *Ya'an shuwu wenji*, 1.37a–43a.
107. Rowe, "Ancestral Rites and Political Authority," 391–94.
108. For relevant discussions of Chen's Jiangxi experiment in these respects, see Rowe, "Ancestral Rites and Political Authority," 381, 391–92. For the invocation of the Confucian classics in formulating statecraft strategies, see Lin, "Two Social Theories Revealed," 24.
109. Rowe, "Ancestral Rites and Political Authority," 394.
110. Wang Ying, "Juguan shize," in *Ya'an shuwu wenji*, 1.42b.
111. Wang Ying, "Juguan shize," in *Ya'an shuwu wenji*, 1.40b.
112. Cited from Du, *The Order of Places*, 49.
113. Hauf, "The Community Covenant in Sixteenth Century Ji'an Prefecture," 40. For Wang Yangming as inspiration for Chen Hongmou, see Rowe, "Ancestral Rites and Political Authority," 388, 390.
114. Du, *The Order of Places*, 49.
115. Wang Ying, "Xiwen jin yapianyan ji," in *Ya'an shuwu wenji*, 2.12a.
116. Wang Ying, "Xiwen jin yapianyan ji," in *Ya'an shuwu wenji*, 2.12b (my emphasis).
117. Wang Ying, "Xiwen jin yapianyan ji," in *Ya'an shuwu wenji*, 2.13a.
118. Kuhn, *Origins of the Modern Chinese State*, 1, 6.
119. Wang Ying, "Xiwen jin yapianyan ji," in *Ya'an shuwu wenji*, 2.12a–b.
120. Mann, *Precious Records*, 15.
121. Yi Jo-lan, "'Tianxia zhizheng zi furen shi.'"

5. REIMAGINING HUIZHOU ACROSS WAR AND DEVASTATION

Epigraphs: Kuang Maodi, "Tici," in Sun Caifu, *Congbixuan yigao*, 1a; Sun Caifu, "*Gonggui conghua* xu," in Sun Caifu, *Congbixuan yigao*, 3.5b–6a.

1. Meyer-Fong, *What Remains*, 1.
2. Meyer-Fong, *What Remains*, 4–15.
3. Shang, "The Literati and Its Demise," 246.

4. Jin, *The Collapse of Heaven.*
5. Chang, "Women's Poetic Witnessing," 507. Also see Mann, "The Lady and the State"; Xiaorong Li, *Women's Poetry of Late Imperial China,* 115–44.
6. Zhang Xiaopo, *Lüwai Huizhou ren yu jindai Huizhou shehui bianqian yanjiu,* 8–15.
7. Goodman, *Native Place, City, and Nation,* 27, 9–38.
8. Xǔ Chengyao, *Shexian zhi*; Xǔ Chengyao, *Sheshi xiantan.* Also see Yongtao Du's ("Locality, Literati, and the Imagined Spatial Order," 409) study of local gazetteers flourishing during the Republican era.
9. Guang Tiefu, *Anhui mingyuan shici zhenglue.* Guang (189–90) records Sun Caifu as a Yizheng [Yangzhou] native, and mother to the Jixi women poets Hu Huizhu and Hu Ruizhu.
10. Meyer-Fong, *What Remains,* 135–74.
11. Chittick, "The Development of Local Writing in Early Medieval China," 50–52, 63–67. Also see Manling Luo's summary of the article in relation to recent studies on early medieval Chinese worldviews and their hidden politics in "Theories of Spatiality and the Study of Medieval China," 212.
12. A more detailed discussion in this respect is in order.
13. Yu Yue, "Sun yiren zhuan," in Sun Caifu, *Congbixuan yigao,* "Zhuan" 1a; Liu Shouhui, "Qing gugaofeng yiren Ningguofu xundao Hu xiansheng qi Sun yiren muzhiming," in Sun Caifu, *Congbixuan yigao,* "Muzhiming" 1a; Hu Peixi, "Jishi Sun yiren shizhuang," in Sun Caifu, *Congbixuan yigao,* "Shizhuang" 1a.
14. Sun Caifu, *Congbixuan yigao,* 1.1a.
15. Sun Caifu, "Yu yin ai yinyong lüwei jiaci suohe zuoci zijie," in Sun Caifu, *Congbixuan yigao,* 1.3a. For debates on women's talent and virtue in the previous "long eighteenth century," see Susan Mann, *Precious Records,* 83–94.
16. For a detailed analysis of Wang Shizhen's "autumn willows" poetry, see Waiyee Li, *Women and National Trauma,* 61–75.
17. Sun Caifu, "Huang Renqiu furen yi 'Fanggui' 'Qiuliu' ershi suohe jiyong yuanyun gefu yilü," in *Congbixuan yigao,* 1.3b. For Wang Shizhen's allusion to Bai Juyi's willow poems, see Waiyee Li, *Women and National Trauma,* 69.
18. Sun Caifu, "Chunliu," in *Congbixuan yigao,* 1.7a.
19. Sun Caifu, "Sifu," "Kumei," "Guimao muchun tongxiang Wutaifuren xie lingxi zhufuren guili fuzhou xiewang jihe gaoqing ji xiangfeng er henwan fu huanzhao yi fenxing momo cunxin buren qingbie yuanfu duanzhang liaoyi zhigan," in *Congbixuan yigao,* 1.3a, 1.4b, 1.9b.
20. Sun Caifu, "Yugui limen hou shuji shedi," in *Congbixuan yigao,* 1.10a.
21. Sun Caifu, "Jiachen eryue shibari nianjie zaixun ganfu yilü," in *Congbixuan yigao,* 1.12a.
22. Yu Yue, "Song zengshaoshi Sanshan Hugong nianpu xu," in *Chunzaitang zawen,* vol. 4, *juan* 5 (from the Erudition database).
23. Hu Peixi, "Jishi Sun yiren shizhuang," in Sun Caifu, *Congbixuan yigao,* 1a. For a biography of Hu Peixi, see Anhui Tongzhi Guan, *Anhui tongzhi gao,* "Liezhuan" (from the Erudition database on Chinese local gazetteers).

24. Sun Caifu, "Kunü jiji waizi Wulin," in *Congbixuan yigao*, 2.4a.
25. Sun Caifu, "Zhuitong xiangu Zhangtaifuren," in *Congbixuan yigao*, 2.5b–6a.
26. Sun Caifu, "Qiuyan sishou yong Wang Yuyang Qiuliu yun," in *Congbixuan yigao*, 2.6b–7a.
27. Sun is invoking Li Bai's well-known line about the frosty moonlight as an invocation of the traveler's thoughts about home.
28. Sun is comparing the fate of the swallows to that of Concubine Ban, one of the concubines of the Emperor Cheng (r. 32–7 BCE) of the Western Han. Concubine Ban was known for comparing her loss of the emperor's favor to a fan being put away in autumn. See Idema and Grant, *Red Brush*, 77–78.
29. Sun is probably alluding to what pre-Qin texts described as the kingdoms founded on enormous wealth made from salt and other products of the sea (haiwang zhi guo). See *Ciyuan*, 1803. Salt wealth also evokes Sun's family background.
30. For records of the Memorial Arches of Grand Feats, see Lu Yingyang, *Guangyu ji, juan* 2 (from the Erudition database).
31. See Liu Yuxi, "Wuyi xiang," in Peng Dingqiu et al., *Quan Tang shi*, vol. 11, 4117.
32. Waiyee Li, *Women and National Trauma*, 69; for analysis of Wang's allusion to the Yongfeng lane, see 68–70.
33. For the early Qing Ming loyalist responses to the "autumn willows" poetry, see Waiyee Li, *Women and National Trauma*, 75–96.
34. Meyer-Fong, *What Remains*, 5. It is even more likely that Sun composed this poetic sequence between 1853–54, given the fall of Nanjing to the Taiping army in 1853.
35. Yu Yue, "Sun yiren zhuan," in Sun Caifu, *Congbixuan yigao*, 1b.
36. Sun Caifu, "Guizhong huairenshi Ermei Shi bibing Qinzhou," *Congbixuan yigao*, 3.2a.
37. Hu Peixi, "Jishi Sun yiren shizhuang," in Sun Caifu, *Congbixuan yigao*, 2b. Zhenjiang was south of Yangzhou, across the Yangzi River. Tongzhou was east of Yangzhou.
38. Meyer-Fong, *What Remains*, 35.
39. Hu Peixi, "Ji wangshi Sun yiren wen," in Sun Caifu, *Congbixuan yigao*, "Jiwen" 1a.
40. Hu Peixi, "Jishi Sun yiren shizhuang," in Sun Caifu, *Congbixuan yigao*, 2b. For prose accounts of their life as refugees or Hu's temporary employments during these years, see Yu Yue, "Sun yiren zhuan," in Sun Caifu, *Congbixuan yigao*, 1b–2a; Liu Shouhui, "Qing gugaofeng yiren Ningguofu xundao Hu xiansheng qi Sun yiren muzhiming," in Sun Caifu, *Congbixuan yigao*, 1b; Hu Peixi, "Jishi Sun yiren shizhuang," in Sun Caifu, *Congbixuan yigao*, 2a–b.
41. Sun Caifu, "Yuyuan manxing shizai Zhuji," in *Congbixuan yigao*, 2.8a–b.
42. Sun Caifu, "Jiti Song Shenghe nüshi Luanyin Tianhan yizhu tu," in *Congbixuan yigao*, 2.8a.
43. Sun Caifu, "Zhang Cifen nüshi zhuti Luoshen bianmian" #1, in *Congbixuan yigao*, 2.8b–9a.
44. Sun Caifu, "Song Cifen nüshi guining," in *Congbixuan yigao*, 2.9a.

45. Sun Caifu, "Yanjun Shiqiao yi zunfu Dongli xiansheng suozhu Dongpo yufuci Zhongxiangci zhuti," in *Congbixuan yigao*, 2.9b. For a brief introduction to the stylistic features of Chen Weisong's poetry expressing sentiments of Ming loyalism, see Waiyee Li, "Early Qing to 1723," 225–26.
46. Sun Caifu, "Daicheng Deng Yizhi taishou," in *Congbixuan yigao*, 2.12a.
47. Sun Caifu, "Jimeng," in *Congbixuan yigao*, 2.9b–10a.
48. Sun Caifu, "Dao Dashi shu," in *Congbixuan yigao*, 3.5a–b.
49. Sun Caifu, "Xie waizi bibing ruChu zhouzhong shuhuai" #1, in *Congbixuan yigao*, 2.10a.
50. Sun Caifu, *Congbixuan yigao*, 2.10a.
51. Sun Caifu, "Cunju jian shuangyan," in *Congbixuan yigao*, 2.10b.
52. Hu Peixi, "Jishi Sun yiren shizhuang," in Sun Caifu, *Congbixuan yigao*, 2b.
53. Sun Caifu, "Xixue shi zhu ernü," in *Congbixuan yigao*, 2.14a–b.
54. Sun Caifu, "Yuanju chuhua qingxiang ke'ai yinfang Daguan yuan shi'er ti zhiwei xiaoshi hezhe xu bajiu chi'ao xiang huaqian yizui ye," in *Congbixuan yigao*, 2.13a. For responses from her family members, see 2.13a–14a.
55. For a translation of one of Tao Qian's masterpieces on his hermit life picking chrysanthemums by his eastern hedge, see Owen, *An Anthology of Chinese Literature*, 316. Also see Sun's related poems praising Hu Peixi's perseverance in overcoming hardships in the image of the chrysanthemum: Sun Caifu, "Shuzhai juhua shengkai waizi shixiang jiaoshiyuan zhezhi xiangyi yingzhi yishi," in *Congbixuan yigao*, 2.12b–13a.
56. Meyer-Fong, *What Remains*, 135–74.
57. The Hanshi festival, around the same time as the Qingming festival, is a time for mourning.
58. Sun Caifu, *Congbixuan yigao*, 3.4a.
59. I am indebted to Professor Manling Luo for her insights as my panel discussant at the AAS 2024.
60. Sun Caifu, "Guizhong huairen shi ershiwu shou," in *Congbixuan yigao*, 3.1a.
61. Sun Caifu, "Guizhong huairen shi ershiwu shou," in *Congbixuan yigao*, 3.1b.
62. The phrase "jijin leshi" refers literally to inscribed bronze utensils and stone steles from ancient times. In poem #14, they stand for the civilization destroyed by the war. Sun Caifu, "Guizhong huairen shi ershiwu shou," 3.3a.
63. Waiyee Li, "Early Qing to 1723," 173–74.
64. Sun Caifu, "Guizhong huairen shi ershiwu shou," in *Congbixuan yigao*, 3.1a.
65. Sun Caifu, "Guizhong huairen shi ershiwu shou," in *Congbixuan yigao*, 3.2a.
66. Sun Caifu, "Guizhong huairen shi ershiwu shou," in *Congbixuan yigao*, 3.2a, 3.2b, 3.3a.
67. Sun Caifu, "Guizhong huairen shi ershiwu shou," in *Congbixuan yigao*, 3.3a.
68. Sun Caifu, "Guizhong huairen shi ershiwu shou," in *Congbixuan yigao*, 3.3a. Notably, "Wrens taking a sprig" as a metaphor for Sun Caifu taking refuge during the war figures in contrast to He Bingtang's networking efforts in a thriving local Yangzhou society. See chapter 3.

69. Sun Caifu, "Guizhong huairen shi ershiwu shou," in *Congbixuan yigao*, 3.4a.
70. Hu Peixi, "Tici" #3, in Sun Caifu, *Congbixuan yigao*, 3b. For Du Fu's line cited by Hu Peixi, see Du Fu, "Qiuxing" #6, in Du Fu, *Du Gongbu shiji jizhu*, annotated by Zhu Heling, 531.
71. Chang, "Women's Poetic Witnessing," 507. Also see Waiyee Li ("Early Qing to 1723," 173–74) for a brief introduction to the main aspects of the *shishi* or "poetic histories," particularly the invocation of Du Fu's "Qiuxing" poems, as used by the Ming loyalist poets.
72. Meyer-Fong, *What Remains*, 135–74.
73. Meyer-Fong, *What Remains*, 143.
74. For a brief introduction of the Chuci style, see Owen, *An Anthology of Chinese Literature*, 155–56.
75. For stories about the friendship between Guan and Bao, see Lie Yukou, *Liezi, juan* 6 (from the Erudition database). The term *zhiyin* originally referred to male bonding too; Sun appropriated it for female friendship. See Lie Yukou, *Liezi, juan* 5.
76. Sun Caifu, "Diao Wangmu Song yiren wen, Wang Xicha daling shi," in *Congbixuan yigao*, 3.6a–7b.
77. For women's "cross-voicing"—their employment of a language of heroism in writing about war—see Waiyee Li, *Women and National Trauma*, 100–200. See particularly page 198 regarding women's writing about the Taiping War. Mann, "The Lady and the State," 284n5, 296–305. Also see Li Guo's (*Writing Gender in Early Modern Chinese Women's Tanci Fiction*, 191–219) recent discussion of how late Qing *tanci* fiction reconfigures war and political conflict in history by highlighting women's political activism and in the context of the female author's own personal loss during the Taiping War.
78. Du, *The Order of Places*, 19–21, 28–40. Qitao Guo, *Ritual Opera and Mercantile Lineage*, 15–19, 56–74. Huizhou was the ancestral place of Zhu Xi, founder of what was promoted as the neo-Confucian orthodoxy during the late imperial era.
79. Hu Peixi, *Jixi Jinzi Hushi suozhu shumu*. "Jinzi" refers to an honorary title of a Hu ancestor and was used to identify the lineage.
80. For these works, see, for example, Hu Peixi, *Jixi Hushi congshu shizhong*.
81. Hu Peihui and Hu Peixi, *Hu shaoshi nianpu*. Also see Yu Yue's preface to the chronological biography for Hu Shunzhi: Yu Yue, "Song zengshaoshi Sanshan Hugong nianpu xu," in *Chunzaitang zawen*, vol. 4, *juan* 5.
82. Hu Guangzhi, *Jixi Jinzi Hushi jiapu*. The genealogy is now in the collections of the Anhui and Shanghai Libraries.
83. Hu Zi, *Tiaoxi Yuyin conghua*.
84. Sun Caifu, "*Gonggui conghua* xu," in *Congbixuan yigao*, 3.5b–6a. The year Gengshen [1860] saw a major victory by the Taiping forces and their subsequent occupation of nearly all of Jiangsu. Hsu, *The Rise of Modern China*, 243.
85. Alternatively, the line can be interpreted as providing casual reading for Sun and her husband spending time together in the inner quarters.
86. Hu Zi, *Tiaoxi Yuyin conghua*, vol. 2, 1.

87. See Yu Yue, "Song zengshaoshi Sanshan Hugong nianpu xu" in *Chunzaitang zawen*.
88. See, for example, Bian Dongbo, "*Tiaoxi Yuyin conghua* Dushilun de lishi wenhua beijing jiqi neihan," esp. 48–49.
89. Hu Zi, *Tiaoxi Yuyin conghua*. vol. 2, 1.
90. Hu Peixi indicates that Sun's drafts were preserved at their home after her death. The local gazetteers of Anhui incorporated the title in its sections on local belles lettres. See Hu Peixi, "Jishi Sun yiren shizhuang," in Sun Caifu, *Congbixuan yigao*, 3b; Anhui Tongzhi Guan, *Anhui tongzhi gao*, "Yiwenkao gao" (from the Erudition database on Chinese local gazetteers). Also see Fu Ying, *MingQing Anhui funü wenxue zhushu jikao*, 380. But to date the drafts have not been located.

    Canon formation in the history of Chinese poetry is a complicated topic beyond the scope of my present study. For quick references, see Pauline Yu, "Poems in Their Place"; Chang, "Wang Shizhen (1634–1711) and the 'New' Canon." Also see Grace Fong's study of the late Ming anthologizing projects on women's poetry, which were too unselective to have canonizing effects. Fong, "Gender and the Failure of Canonization."
91. Multiple authors, "Tici," in Sun Caifu, *Congbixuan yigao*.
92. Multiple authors, "Fulu," in Sun Caifu, *Congbixuan yigao*, 1.
93. Multiple authors, "Fulu," in Sun Caifu, *Congbixuan yigao*, 2.
94. Yu Yue, "Sun yiren zhuan," in Sun Caifu, *Congbixuan yigao*, 3b.
95. Huntington, *Ink and Tears*, 195–99. For details about the "Bai'ai pian," see 12–21.
96. Lu, *Arranged Companions*, esp. 14–18, for trends regarding the open display of conjugal affection among the Qing literati. Lu (192) also points out the "striking similarity" between Yu Yue's mourning poems and poetry by You Tong (1618–1704) and Qu Dajun (1630–96) from two centuries earlier.
97. Martin Huang, *Intimate Memory*, 3–7.
98. Other biographical and elegiac essays appended to the *Congbixuan yigao* are beyond the scope of this study.
99. Hu Peixi, "Ji wangshi Sun yiren wen," in Sun Caifu, *Congbixuan yigao*, 2b.
100. Hu Peixi, "Ji wangshi Sun yiren wen," in Sun Caifu, *Congbixuan yigao*, 2a–b.
101. Hu Peixi, "Jishi Sun yiren shizhuang," in Sun Caifu, *Congbixuan yigao*, 3a. Hu Peixi, "Ji wangshi Sun yiren wen," in Sun Caifu, *Congbixuan yigao*, 2a; see chapter 4 for Wang Ying's biographical accounts of women in the Huizhou merchant households. Rong did not give up his scholarly pursuits. He is recorded as a student in the National School. Hu Peixi, "Jishi Sun yiren shizhuang," in Sun Caifu, *Congbixuan yigao*, 5a.
102. Hu Peixi, "Jishi Sun yiren shizhuang," in Sun Caifu, *Congbixuan yigao*, 4a.
103. Hu Peixi, "Jishi Sun yiren shizhuang," in Sun Caifu, *Congbixuan yigao*, 5a. See Yongtao Du's discussion of the Qing reforms on the "registered status of the merchant's household." Du, *The Order of Places*, 191–93.
104. Hu Peixi, "Jishi Sun yiren shizhuang," in Sun Caifu, *Congbixuan yigao*, 4a–b. Hu Peixi, "Ji wangshi Sun yiren wen," in Sun Caifu, *Congbixuan yigao*, 1b–2b.

105. Hu Peixi, "Jishi Sun yiren shizhuang," in Sun Caifu, *Congbixuan yigao*, 3b.
106. Hu Peixi, "Jishi Sun yiren shizhuang," in Sun Caifu, *Congbixuan yigao*, 4b. Notably, Hu Peixi (3b–4a) paints a more conventional picture of Sun Caifu as a devoted wife and mother, representing her literary project *Gonggui conghua* as a diversion.
107. For women's managerial skills and financial resourcefulness as attributes worthy of recognition, see Mann, "Dowry Wealth and Wifely Virtue."
108. In this respect the Hu lineage's genealogy differs from the Bao lineage's genealogy discussed in chapter 2. The Bao women's literary achievements were central to the editor's agenda for showcasing the lineage's cultural legacy, which in turn served to prevent the lineage's dispersion following the Taiping War. See chapter 2.
109. According to Fu Ying, Sun's collection is recorded as a title in the *Shizelou congkan* by the *Zhongguo congshu guanglu* (Bibliography for publication series in China). Fu Ying, *MingQing Anhui funü wenxue zhushu jikao*, 379. In addition to the published version of the *Congbixuan yigao*, a hand-copied version is now in the collection of the Anhui Museum.
110. Anhui Tongzhi Guan, *Anhui tongzhi gao*, "Yiwenkao gao."
111. Hu Chengye, "Hu Shi yu weijingde Jixi congshu."
112. For the changing relationships between the local and the imperium and among localities, see Meyer-Fong, *What Remains*, 152–63.
113. For women's literary communities as "icons of localism" during the seventeenth century, see Ko, *Teachers of the Inner Chambers*, 232–33. For women's poetry as the hallmark of High Qing cultural achievement, see Mann, *Precious Records*, 94–120.
114. Mann, *The Talented Women of the Zhang Family*, 196.

6. PROJECTING UTOPIA/DYSTOPIA

Epigraph: Hu Zi, "Preface," in *Tiaoxi Yuyin conghua*, vol. 2, 56; Shao Zhenhua, preface to *Xiayi jiaren*, 85.

1. Hsu, *The Rise of Modern China*, 419–39.
2. Hu Wenkai, *Lidai funü zhuzuo kao*, 401; Fu Ying, *MingQing Anhui funü wenxue zhushu jikao*, 374–75.
3. Shao Zhenhua, *Xiayi jiaren chuji*; Shao Zhenhua, *Xiayi jiaren zhongji*. Volume 1 was published under the penname Jixi Wenyu Nüshi, and volume 2 under the name Lao Shao Zhenhua. Lao was the family name of Shao's husband. Although Shao states at the end of volume 2 that a third volume is forthcoming, to date there has been no publication record of that volume. For a reprint edition, see Shao Zhenhua, *Xiayi jiaren*, 83–699. The novel was reprinted along with two other late Qing novels on women's rights: Siqi Zhai, *Nüzi quan*; Wang Miaoru, *Nüyu hua*.
4. Widmer, "*Honglou meng ying* and Three 'Women's Novels' of Late Qing"; Wu Yujuan, "Zouchu chuantong de dianfan"; Huang Jin Chu, *Nüxing shuxie de duoyuan chengxian*.

5. Widmer, "*Honglou meng ying* and Three 'Women's Novels' of Late Qing," 323–26. *Honglou meng ying* by Gu Chun (1799–1877) is the first extant Chinese novel authored by a woman.
6. Huang Jin Chu, *Nüxing shuxie de duoyuan chengxian*, 121–23, 205–8.
7. David Wang, *Fin-de-siecle Splendor*, 156–74.
8. For a brief introduction to utopia/dystopia in the late Qing fictional imagination, see David Wang, "Chinese Literature from 1841 to 1937," 453–55.
9. For a detailed discussion of Huaining's war memory and post-Taiping restoration interwoven with a young girl's personal and family histories, see Yang Binbin, foreword to *Jindai nüxing riji wuzhong wai yizhong*, 30–57.
10. Shao Zhenhua, *Xiayi jiaren*, 92. This isolated "land of happiness" is evocative of the Peach Blossom Spring mentioned in chapter 1—the classic literary imagination about a land for refugees, which was invoked time and again in writings about war and devastation. According to Owen, Peach Blossom Spring also figured as a "beguiling vision of society without a state." Owen, *All Mine!*, 15.
11. For the Boxer Uprising, see Hsu, *The Rise of Modern China*, 387–407.
12. Foot-binding was stigmatized at this time as the archetypical form of patriarchal oppression of Chinese women, which had to be abolished for China's modernizing enterprise. For a revisionist history of the practice, see Ko, *Cinderella's Sisters*.
13. Yu Zhang, *Going to the Countryside*.
14. Yu Zhang, *Going to the Countryside*, 3–5.
15. Barlow, *Women and Writing in Modern China*, 1.
16. Shao Zhenhua, *Xiayi jiaren*, 136. Implicit in China's modernizing agenda—also a familiar story by now—was the clear divide between tradition and modernity, the old and the new, in various aspects of the Chinese society. For the influx of Western ideas and knowledge subsumed under the umbrella term *new learning*, see Hsu, *The Rise of Modern China*, 420–25.
17. Shao Zhenhua, *Xiayi jiaren*, 137.
18. Ban Wang, *China in the World*, 42–44.
19. Shao Zhenhua, *Xiayi jiaren*, 161.
20. Shao Zhenhua, *Xiayi jiaren*, 162–66.
21. For the growth of metropolises in China at the turn of the twentieth century, including Shanghai, see Hsu, *The Rise of Modern China*, 430. The telephone was introduced into China in 1882. For a brief history of the telephone published in Republican China, see Xu Yingchang, *Dianhua*.
22. Shao Zhenhua, *Xiayi jiaren*, 167.
23. Shao Zhenhua, *Xiayi jiaren*, 168–69.
24. Shao Zhenhua, *Xiayi jiaren*, 169–74.
25. For the political, legal, and economic changes causing the collapse of the kinship society in China, see Hsu, *The Rise of Modern China*, 427–28.
26. Glosser, *Chinese Visions of Family and State*, 3. According to Glosser, "New Culture" advocates believed that the Western conjugal family encouraged

productivity, independence, and civic virtue through some of the basic ideas it was founded on, such as free marriage choice, companionate marriage, and economic independence from the extended Chinese family and lineage.

27. For Gao, such "heroic" spirit is coupled with her apparent aloofness, or *leng* (lit., coldness). For Lin, it is literally about his masculine beauty shining outward (*xiongzi yingfa*). Shao Zhenhua, *Xiayi jiaren*, 171, 173.
28. The character *ying* originally referred to plants that blossom without producing seeds. From the etymological origin of *blossom* derived references to *quintessence* and, later, *heroic*. See *Ciyuan*, 2637.
29. Shao Zhenhua, *Xiayi jiaren*, 175.
30. Shao Zhenhua, *Xiayi jiaren*, 176–77. For the call for China's industrial development in response to foreign investment and domination, see Hsu, *The Rise of Modern China*, 432–36.
31. Shao Zhenhua, *Xiayi jiaren*, 177.
32. Shao Zhenhua, *Xiayi jiaren*, 177.
33. Wang Miaoru, *Nüyu hua*, 756.
34. David Wang, *Fin-de-siecle Splendor*, 172–73.
35. Widmer, "*Honglou meng ying* and Three 'Women's Novels' of Late Qing," 313n26.
36. Luo Jingren, epilogue to Wang Miaoru, *Nüyu hua*, 760. Luo was Wang's husband, who authored the commentaries on her novel.
37. Shao Zhenhua, *Xiayi jiaren*, 281.
38. Wang Miaoru, *Nüyu hua*, 720–23. It is only at the end that the author celebrates the love between Xu Pingquan and her husband (759).
39. Shao Zhenhua, *Xiayi jiaren*, 287–317.
40. Shao Zhenhua, *Xiayi jiaren*, 317–19.
41. Shao Zhenhua, *Xiayi jiaren*, 320- 26.
42. Shao Zhenhua, *Xiayi jiaren*, 281–86.
43. Shao Zhenhua, *Xiayi jiaren*, 192–212, 216–62. I have quickly summarized these episodes due to limited space. For the influx of Western ideas of equality and freedom, see Hsu, *The Rise of Modern China*, 422.
44. It has been suggested that the character Gao Jianchen may reflect the novel's autobiographical aspects, particularly regarding Gao's family and marriage background. See Huang Jin Chu, *Nüxing shuxie de duoyuan chengxian*, 14–15. My purpose here is not to prove whether the novel can be read autobiographically but rather to point out that Shao Zhenhua uses Gao's critiques as favored perspectives in the debates.
45. For recent studies of the concept and its implications for a collective identity of Chinese women in the early twentieth century, see Yun Zhu, *Imagining Sisterhood in Modern Chinese Texts*, 1–34; Yun Zhang, *Engendering the Woman Question*, 49–80.
46. Nanxiu Qian, *Politics, Poetics, and Gender in Late Qing China*, 123, 123–58.
47. Goodman, *Native Place, City, and Nation*, 19.

48. Shao Zhenhua, *Xiayi jiaren*, 416.
49. For the Jiangxi textile merchants in Shanghai, see Goodman, *Native Place, City, and Nation*, 25. The Huizhou merchants in Shanghai were known for pawnshops and tea trade (30, 33), but clearly, they no longer fit Shao's imagination about the new capital and industry.
50. For the crisis of textile trade, see Hsu, *The Rise of Modern China*, 435.
51. See, for example, Shao Zhenhua, *Xiayi jiaren*, 264–75.
52. Yu Zhang, *Going to the Countryside*, 5.
53. Chen Pingyuan, *Zhongguo xiaoshuo xushi moshi de zhuanbian*, 186–203.
54. For a discussion of women's travels in four late Qing novels by women, including *Xiayi jiaren*, see Huang Jin Chu, *Nüxing shuxie de duoyuan chengxian*, 145–70.
55. Widmer attributes the novel's greater length and complexity compared to its two predecessors partly to its multiple heroines and the "side plots that only meanderingly make their way back to the main story line." Widmer, "*Honglou meng ying* and Three 'Women's Novels' of Late Qing," 316.
56. For the introduction of *Utopia* into China, see, for example, Gao Fang, "*Wutuobang* zai Zhongguo de bainian chuanbo." For the dialogic format of *Utopia*, see Sacks, introduction to Thomas More, *Utopia*, vii–viii.
57. David Wang, *Fin-de-siecle Splendor*, 270. For an overview of the late Qing literary reform, see David Wang, "Chinese Literature from 1841 to 1937," 440–45.
58. David Wang, "Chinese Literature from 1841 to 1937," 453.
59. Shao Zhenhua, *Xiayi jiaren*, 530, 572.
60. Shao Zhenhua, *Xiayi jiaren*, 383, 457, 525–27. Similar to what Haiyan Lee (*Revolution of the Heart*, 81–82) finds about the patriotism in the late Qing popular butterfly and mandarin ducks fiction, recognition of the equivalent status of the Chinese nation vis-a-vis other nations marked a momentous shift in the Chinese perception of the world order.
61. Shao Zhenhua, *Xiayi jiaren*, 456–57.
62. Shao Zhenhua, *Xiayi jiaren*, 509.
63. See, for example, Wu Jiuling and Shi Minggao, *Qianlong Wuzhou fuzhi*. A search in the comprehensive dictionary of place names in Chinese history confirms my point here: there is no place name in Zhejiang related to Wucheng. See Shi Weile and Zhu Lingling, *Zhongguo lishi diming dacidian zengdingben*, 2448–49.
64. Shao Zhenhua, *Xiayi jiaren*, 457–60. One *mu* is equal to around one-sixth of an acre. The character *ye* was from Sino-Japanese-European loanwords, such as commerce—*shōgyō—shangye*; enterprise—*kigyō—qiye*; industry—*kōgyō—gongye*. Lydia Liu, *Translingual Practice*, appendix B, 286, 288, 290.
65. Shao Zhenhua, *Xiayi jiaren*, 460. The phrase *qingyi* alludes to human labor and productive activities as represented in "The Woodcutter's Song" in the *Shijing*. For an English translation, see Xu Yuanchong, *Shijing*, 201.
66. Shao Zhenhua, *Xiayi jiaren*, 460, 483.
67. Shao Zhenhua, *Xiayi jiaren*, 461–64.

68. Shao Zhenhua, *Xiayi jiaren*, 528–29.
69. Hsu, *The Rise of Modern China*, 432–36.
70. See chapter 56 of the novel. Cao Xueqin, *Honglou meng*, 763–71.
71. Shao Zhenhua, *Xiayi jiaren*, 464.
72. Ying-shih Yü, "The Two Worlds of *Honglou meng*."
73. Shao Zhenhua, *Xiayi jiaren*, 462–79.
74. Shao Zhenhua, *Xiayi jiaren*, 535–47.
75. Ying-shih Yü, "The Two Worlds *of Honglou meng*," 144.
76. Edwards, *Men and Women in Qing China*.
77. Shao Zhenhua, *Xiayi jiaren*, 485–511. Due to limited space, here I focus on the most illustrative example, instead of going through all the episodes of the guests' experience of Wucheng.
78. Shao Zhenhua, *Xiayi jiaren*, 504.
79. Shao Zhenhua, *Xiayi jiaren*, 504–11.
80. Nanxiu Qian, *Politics, Poetics, and Gender in Late Qing China*, 142.
81. Siqi Zhai, *Nüzi quan*, 77–81.
82. Rogaski, *Hygienic Modernity*, 13.
83. Sacks, introduction to More, *Utopia*, ix.
84. Gao Fang, "*Wutuobang* zai Zhongguo de bainian chuanbo," 183.
85. Sacks, introduction to More, *Utopia*, viii–ix.
86. Sacks, introduction to More, *Utopia*, ix–x.
87. David Wang, *Fin-de-siecle Splendor*, 302–12. Also see Ban Wang's recent discussion of the world visions Liang projected in this novel and other writings: Ban Wang, *China in the World*, 40–58.
88. David Wang, *Fin-de-siecle Splendor*, 171.
89. Ying-shih Yü, "The Two Worlds *of Honglou meng*," 141.
90. Wang, *Fin-de-siecle Splendor*, 286.
91. It has been suggested that the 1911 revolution may have disrupted Shao's plan for publishing a third volume. Huang Jin Chu, *Nüxing shuxie de duoyuan chengxian*, 2.

EPILOGUE

1. I borrow the term *archive* from Maram Epstein's ("Zaisheng yuan and the Writing of Women's Culture," 169) recent study on Qing *tanci* fiction by women. Epstein uses the term to refer to the extensive records of the women writers' affective responses to the gender ideology of their time, kept in the *tanci* genre.
2. In the case of the Bao family (see chapter 2), the genealogy was compiled at a much later time and driven by different agendas.
3. See Cao Xueqin, *Honglou meng*, 35–37, 187.
4. See Cao Xueqin, *Honglou meng*, 266–67.
5. See, for example, Wu Bing, *Liaodu geng*, 272.
6. See Cao Xueqin, *Honglou meng*, 533.

APPENDIX 2

1. Bao Gao, *Haimen shichao waiji*, 4.3a–b.
2. Bao Gao, *Haimen shichao*, 1.3b–4b.
3. Bao Gao, *Haimen shichao*, 1.8b–9b.
4. Bao Gao, *Haimen shichao*, 1.2b–3a.
5. Bao Gao, *Haimen shichao*, 2.4b–5b.
6. Bao Gao, *Haimen erji*, , 209–10.
7. Bao Wenkui, *Yeyun shichao*, 2.6b–7a.
8. Bao Wenkui, *Yeyun shichao*, 2.7b–8a.
9. Bao Wenkui, *Yeyun shichao*, 3.7b.
10. He Peifen, *Lüyunge shichao*, 5.8a–b.
11. He Peiyu, *Ouxiangguan shichao*, 2.13a–14a.
12. He Peizhu, *Zhuyan lanxuezhai shichao*, 18b–19a.
13. He Peiyu, *Hongweiguan xueyingao*, 557.
14. He Bingtang, *Tonghua shuwu shicao*, 45b–46b.
15. He Peiyu, *Ouxiangguan shichao*, 2.4b–5a.
16. He Peiyu, *Ouxiangguan shichao*, 2.6b–7a.
17. He Peifen, *Lüyunge shichao*, 4.2a–b.
18. He Peiyu, *Ouxiangguan shichao*, 6.1a–b.

BIBLIOGRAPHY

PRIMARY SOURCES

Anhui Tongzhi Guan 安徽通志館, ed. *Anhui tongzhi gao* 安徽通志稿. 1934.

Bai Juyi 白居易. *Bai Juyi ji jianjiao* 白居易集箋校. Annotated by Zhu Jincheng 朱金城. Reprint, Shanghai: Shanghai Guji Chubanshe, 1988.

Ban Gu 班固. *Hanshu* 漢書. Qing Qianlong Wuyingdian edition.

Bao Gao 鮑皋. *Haimen chuji* 海門初集. 1739.

Bao Gao 鮑皋. *Haimen erji* 海門二集. Manuscript; preface 1753. Reprinted in *Qingdai shiwenji huibian*, vol. 310, 124–493. Shanghai: Shanghai Guji Chubanshe, 2010.

Bao Gao 鮑皋. *Haimen sanji* 海門三集. Manuscript, ca. 1765. Reprinted in *Qingdai shiwenji huibian*, vol. 310, 494–711.

Bao Gao 鮑皋. *Haimen shichao* 海門詩鈔. 1739. Reprinted in Qingdai Shiwenji Huibian Bianzuan Weiyuanhui 清代詩文集匯編編纂委員會, ed., *Qingdai shiwenji huibian* 清代詩文集匯編, vol. 310, 21–113.

Bao Gao 鮑皋. *Haimen shichao waiji* 海門詩鈔外集. 1739. Reprinted in *Qingdai shiwenji huibian*, vol. 310, 114–23.

Bao Qingxi 鮑慶熙, ed. *Xin'an Baoshi Chengfengpai zhipu* 新安鮑氏承鳳派支譜. 1923.

Bao Wenkui 鮑文逵. *Yeyun shichao* 野雲詩鈔. 1839.

Bao Zhifen 鮑之芬. *Sanxiuzhai shicichao* 三秀齋詩詞鈔. 1882.

Bao Zhihui 鮑之蕙. *Qingyuge yingao* 清娛閣吟稿. 1811; 1882.

Bao Zhilan 鮑之蘭. *Qiyunge shichao* 起雲閣詩鈔. 1882.

Bao Zhilan, Bao Zhihui, and Bao Zhifen. *Jingjiang Baoshi sannüshi shichao* 京江鮑氏三女史詩鈔. 1882.

Bao Zhizhong 鮑之鐘. "Haimen gong xinglue" 海門公行略. In Bao Qingxi, *Xin'an Baoshi Chengfengpai zhipu*, 4.68a–73a.

Bao Zhizhong 鮑之鐘. *Lunshan shichao* 論山詩鈔. 1832.

Cai Dianqi 蔡殿齊, ed. *Guochao guige shichao* 國朝閨閣詩鈔. 1844.

Cao Wanru 曹婉如, ed. *Zhongguo gudai ditu ji Zhanguo—Yuan* 中國古代地圖集 戰國一元. Beijing: Wenwu Chubanshe, 1990.

Cao Xueqin 曹雪芹. *Honglou meng* 紅樓夢. Reprint, Beijing: Renmin Wenxue Chubanshe, 1982.

Cao Xuequan 曹學佺. *Shuzhong guangji* 蜀中廣記. Ming edition.

Chen Jingyi 陳景沂. *Quanfang beizu* 全芳備祖. Ca. 13th c.
Chen Ruizhu 陳蕊珠. *Kexuanlou yishi* 課選樓遺詩. 1882.
Cheng Bao 程葆, ed. *Qiudeng kezi tu tiyongji* 秋燈課子圖題詠集. 1844.
Cheng Bao 程葆, ed. *Ya'an Shuwu zengyanlu* 雅安書屋贈言錄. 1844.
Cheng Dingtiao 程鼎調. *Xun zizhi ji* 訓子侄記. 1824; 1844.
Ciyuan 辭源. 1915; reprint, Beijing: Shangwu Yinshuguan, 1979.
Dai Tingming 戴廷明 and Cheng Shangkuan 程尚寬. *Xin'an mingzu zhi* 新安名族志. Annotated by Zhu Wanshu 朱萬曙 et al. Reprint, Hefei, Anhui: Huangshan Shushe, 2007.
Dong Gao 董誥, ed. *HuangQing wenying xubian* 皇清文穎續編. 1796.
Du Fu 杜甫. *Du Gongbu shiji jizhu* 杜工部詩集輯注. Annotated by Zhu Heling 朱鶴齡. Reprint, Baoding: Hebei Daxue Chubanshe, 2009.
Duan Chengshi 段成式. *Youyang zazu* 酉陽雜俎. Sibu Congkan edition.
Fan Ye 范曄. *Hou Hanshu*後漢書. Copy from the Song edition.
Feng Zhi 馮摯. *Yunxian zaji* 雲仙雜記. Sibu Congkan edition.
Fong. Grace S. "Ming Qing Women's Writings" 明清婦女著作數字計劃. *McGill Library Digital Collections*. 2014. Available at https://digital.library.mcgill.ca/mingqing/english/index.php.
Fu Ying 傅瑛. *MingQing Anhui funü wenxue zhushu jikao* 明清安徽婦女文學著述輯考. Hefei, Anhui: Huangshang Shushe, 2010.
Gong Chuhan 宮楚涵 and Qi Xi 齊希, eds. *Zhongguo xijian difang shiliao jicheng* 中國稀見地方史料集成. Sequence 3, vol. 94. Beijing: Xueyuan Chubanshe, 2014.
Gong Yanming 龔延明, ed. *Zhongguo lidai zhiguan bieming dacidian zengdingben* 中國歷代職官別名大辭典 增訂本. Beijing: Zhonghua Shuju, 2019.
Gu Luan 顧鑾. *Guangling langu* 廣陵覽古. Annotated by Wang Mingfa 王明發. Reprint, Yangzhou: Guangling Shushe, 2004.
Guang Tiefu 光鐵夫. *Anhui mingyuan shici zhenglue* 安徽名媛詩詞徵略. 1936. Reprint, Hefei, Anhui: Huangshan Shushe, 1986.
Gui Dian 桂坫, ed. *Nanhai Xianzhi* 南海縣志. 1910.
He Bingtang 何秉棠. *Tonghua shuwu shicao* 桐花書屋詩草. Manuscript, 19th c.
He Changling 賀長齡, Wei Yuan 魏源, et al., eds. *Qing jingshi wenbian* 清經世文編. Reprint, Beijing: Zhonghua Shuju, 1992.
He Peifen 何佩芬. *Lüyunge shichao* 綠筠閣詩鈔. 1841.
He Peiyu 何佩玉. *Hongweiguan xueyingao* 紅薇館學吟稿. Manuscript, 1865. Reprinted in *Qingdai Gaochaoben* 清代稿鈔本, edited by Sang Bing 桑兵, sequence 4, vol. 161, 547–637. Guangzhou: Guangdong Renmin Chubanshe, 2012.
He Peiyu 何佩玉. *Ouxiangguan shichao* 藕香館詩鈔. 1849.
He Peizhu 何佩珠. *Lihua meng* 梨花夢. Manuscript, 19th c. In Hua Wei 華瑋, ed. *MingQing funü xiquji* 明清婦女戲曲集, 267–93. Taibei: Zhongyang Yanjiuyuan Zhongguo Wenzhe Yanjiusuo, 2003.
He Peizhu 何佩珠. *Zhuyan lanxuezhai shichao* 竹煙蘭雪齋詩鈔. Lanhui Tang edition, ca. 1821–50.

He Shaozhang 何紹章, Feng Shoujing 馮壽鏡, and Lü Yaodou 吕耀斗, eds. *Guangxu Dantu xianzhi* 光緒丹徒縣誌. 1879.
He Yan 何晏, annot. *Lunyu zhushu* 論語注疏. Qing Jiaqing edition.
He Yingsong 何應松 and Fang Chongding 方崇鼎, eds. *Jiaqing Xiuning Xianzhi* 嘉慶休寧縣志. 1815.
Hu Guangzhi 胡廣植, ed. *Jixi Jinzi Hushi jiapu* 績溪金紫胡氏家譜. 1907.
Hu Peihui 胡培翬 and Hu Peixi 胡培系. *Hu Shaoshi nianpu* 胡少師年譜. 1882.
Hu Peixi, ed. *Jixi Hushi congshu shizhong* 績溪胡氏叢書十種. 1871–76.
Hu Peixi, ed. *Jixi Jinzi Hushi suozhu shumu* 績溪金紫胡氏所著書目. 1884.
Hu Wenkai 胡文楷. *Lidai funü zhuzuo kao* 歷代婦女著作考. Amended by Zhang Hongsheng 張宏生and Shi Min 石旻. Shanghai: Shanghai Guji Chubanshe, 2008.
Hu Xiaoming 胡曉明 and Peng Guozhong 彭國忠, eds. *Jiangnan nüxing bieji* 江南女性別集 Vol. 1. Hefei, Anhui: Huangshan Shushe, 2008.
Hu Xiaoming 胡曉明 and Peng Guozhong 彭國忠, eds. *Jiangnan nüxing bieji*. Vol. 4. Hefei, Anhui: Huangshan Shushe, 2014.
Hu Zi 胡仔. *Tiaoxi Yuyin conghua* 苕溪漁隱叢話. Annotated by Liao Deming 廖德明. Reprint, Beijing: Renmin Wenxue Chubanshe, 1984.
Hua Wei 華瑋. *MingQing funü xiquji* 明清婦女戲曲集. Taibei: Zhongyang Yanjiuyuan Zhongguo Wenzhe Yanjiusuo, 2003.
Ji Han 嵇含. *Nanfang caomu zhuang* 南方草木狀. Song Baichuan Xuehai edition.
Ji Yougong 計有功. *Tangshi jishi* 唐詩紀事. Qing Siku edition.
Ji Zengyun 嵇曾筠, ed. *Yongzheng Zhejiang tongzhi* 雍正浙江通志. Qing Siku edition.
Jiang Zhu 江珠. *Xiao Weimo shigao* 小維摩詩稿. Reprinted in Li Lei 李雷, ed., *Qingdai guige shiji cuibian* 清代閨閣詩集萃編, vol. 5, 2694–2719. Beijing: Zhonghua Shuju, 2015.
Lao Fengyuan 勞逢源 and Shen Botang 沈伯棠, eds. *Daoguang Shexian zhi* 道光歙縣志. 1828.
Li Bai 李白. *Li Bai ji jiaozhu* 李白集校注. Annotated by Qu Tuiyuan 瞿蛻園. Reprint, Shanghai: Shanghai Guji Chubanshe, 1980.
Li Bai 李白. *Li Bai shixuan* 李白詩選. Selected and annotated by Qian Zhixi 錢志熙 and Liu Qinghai 劉青海. Beijing: Shangwu Yinshuguan, 2016.
Li Baotai 李保泰 and Chen Guanguo 陳觀國, eds. *Jiaqing Ganquan xian xuzhi* 嘉慶甘泉縣續志. 1810.
Li Deyu 李德裕. *Li Wenrao ji* 李文饒集. Sibu Congkan edition.
Li Dou 李斗. *Yangzhou huafanglu* 揚州畫舫錄. 1795. Reprint, Beijing: Zhonghua Shuju, 2007.
Li Fang 李昉. *Taiping guangji* 太平廣記. Republican reprint edition.
Li Shangyin 李商隱. *Li Yishan shji* 李義山詩集. Sibu Congkan edition.
Lie Yukou 列禦寇. *Liezi* 列子. Sibu Congkan edition.
Lin Tianren 林天人, ed. *Huangyu soulan: Meiguo Guohui tushuguan suocang MingQing yutu* 皇輿搜覽: 美國國會圖書館所藏明清輿圖. Washington, DC: Library of Congress, 2014.

Lin Xiyi 林希逸. *Zhuangzi kouyi* 莊子口義. Ming edition.
Liu Dakui 劉大櫆. "Haimen gong muzhiming" 海門公墓志銘. In Bao Qingxi, ed., *Xin'an Baoshi chengfengpai zhipu*, 4.40a–42a.
Liu Junwen 劉俊文. Erudition 愛如生Database for Chinese Texts. Beijing: Beijing Airusheng Shuzihua Jishu Yanjiu Zhongxin. (Sources from the Erudition database are specified in the corresponding notes.)
Liu Xiang 劉向. *Lienü zhuan* 列女傳. Qing Siku edition.
Lu Yingyang 陸應陽. *Guangyu ji* 廣輿記. Qing Kangxi edition.
Lu You 陸友. *Moshi* 墨史. Qing Zhibuzu Zhai edition,
Luo Qilan 駱綺蘭. *Tingqiuxuan shiji* 聽秋軒詩集, 6 *juan*. After 1796.
Ma Buchan 馬步蟾, ed. *Daoguang Huizhou fuzhi* 道光徽州府志. 1827.
Ouyang Xiu 歐陽修 et al., eds. *Xin Tang shu* 新唐書. Qing Qianlong edition.
Peng Dingqiu 彭定求 et al., eds. *Quan Tang shi* 全唐詩. Qing Kangxi edition. Reprint, Beijing: Zhonghua Shuju, 2003.
Qian Shifu 錢實甫. *Qingdai zhiguan nianbiao* 清代職官年表. Beijing: Zhonghua Shuju, 1980.
Qingdai Shiwenji Huibian Bianzuan Weiyuanhui 清代詩文集匯編編纂委員會, ed. *Qingdai shiwenji huibian* 清代詩文集匯編. Shanghai: Shanghai Guji Chubanshe, 2010.
Ruan Yuan 阮元. *Guangling shishi* 廣陵詩事. 1799; annotated by Wang Mingfa 王明發. Reprint, Yangzhou: Guangling Shushe, 2004.
Ruan Yuan 阮元, ed. *Huaihai yingling ji* 淮海英靈集. 1798. Reprint, Shanghai: Shanghai Guji Chubanshe, 1995.
Ruan Yuan 阮元and Chen Changqi 陳昌齊, eds. *Guangdong tongzhi* 廣東通志. 1822.
Ruan Yuan 阮元 and Yang Bingchu 楊秉初, eds. *Liang Zhe youxuan lu* 兩浙輶軒錄. 1803.
Sang Bing 桑兵, ed. *Qingdai Gaochaoben* 清代稿鈔本. Guangzhou: Guangdong Renmin Chubanshe, 2012.
Shanghai Shuhua Chubanshe 上海書畫出版社, ed. *Yihe ming* 瘞鶴銘. Shanghai: Shanghai Shuhua Chubanshe, 2012.
Shao Zhenhua 邵振華. *Xiayi jiaren chuji* 俠義佳人初集. Shanghai: Shangwu Yinshuguan, 1909. Reprint, Nanchang, Jiangxi: Baihuazhou Wenyi Chubanshe, 1993.
Shao Zhenhua 邵振華. *Xiayi jiaren zhongji* 俠義佳人中集. Shanghai: Shangwu Yinshuguan, 1911. Reprint, Nanchang, Jiangxi: Baihuazhou Wenyi Chubanshe, 1993.
Shen Deqian 沈德潛. *Guochao shi biecaiji* 國朝詩別裁集. 1760. Reprinted as *Qingshi biecai ji* 清詩別裁集 (Shanghai: Shanghai Guji Chubanshe, 1984).
Shen Yue 沈約, ed. *Songshu* 宋書. Reprint, Beijing: Zhonghua Shuju, 1974.
Shi Weile 史為樂 and Zhu Lingling 朱玲玲, eds. *Zhongguo lishi diming dacidian zengdingben* 中國歷史地名大辭典 增訂本. Beijing: Zhongguo Shehui Kexue Chubanshe, 2017.
Sima Qian 司馬遷. *Shiji* 史記. Qing Qianlong Wuyingdian edition.
Siqi Zhai 思綺齋. *Nüzi quan* 女子權. 1907. Reprint, Nanchang, Jiangxi: Baihuazhou Wenyi Chubanshe, 1993.

Song Guangye 宋廣業. *Luofushanzhi huibian* 羅浮山志會編. Qing Kangxi edition.
Song Qi 宋祁. *Yibu fangwu lueji* 益部方物略記. Qing edition.
Sun Caifu 孫采芙. *Congbixuan yigao* 叢筆軒遺稿. 1887.
Tang Qingyun 唐慶雲. *Nüluoting gao* 女蘿亭稿. 1814; 1831. Reprinted in Xiao Ya'nan 蕭亞男, ed., *Qingdai guixiu ji congkan* 清代閨秀集叢刊, vol. 28, 197–452. Beijing: Guojia Tushu Chubanshe, 2014.
Wang Miaoru 王妙如. *Nüyu hua* 女獄花. 1904. Reprint, Nanchang, Jiangxi: Baihuazhou Wenyi Chubanshe, 1993.
Wang Qiong 王瓊. *Ailan shichao* 愛蘭詩鈔. In Ren Zhaolin 任兆麟 and Zhang Zilan 張滋蘭, eds., *Wuzhong nüshi shichao* 吳中女士詩鈔. 1789.
Wang Qishu 汪啓淑, ed. *Xiefang ji* 擷芳集. 1773.
Wang Ying 汪嫈. *Ya'an shuwu shiji* 雅安書屋詩集. 1844.
Wang Ying 汪嫈. *Ya'an shuwu wenji* 雅安書屋文集. 1844.
Wang Yu 王豫, ed. *Jiangsu shizheng* 江蘇詩徵. 1821.
Wang Yu 王豫 and Ruan Heng 阮亨, eds. *Huaihai yingling xuji* 淮海英靈續集. 1826.
Wu Bing 吳炳. *Liaodu geng* 療妒羹. Ming edition. Reprint, Yangzhou: Jiangsu Guangling Guji Keyinshe, 1990.
Wu Jiuling 吳九齡 and Shi Minggao 史鳴皋, eds. *Qianlong Wuzhou fuzhi* 乾隆梧州府志. 1873.
Xian Yuqing 冼玉清. *Guangdong nüzi yiwen kao* 廣東女子藝文考. Shanghai: Shangwu Yinshuguan, 1941.
Xiao Ya'nan 蕭亞男, ed. *Qingdai guixiu ji congkan* 清代閨秀集叢刊. Beijing: Guojia Tushu Chubanshe, 2014.
Xie Xue 謝雪. *Yongxu ting shicao* 詠絮亭詩草. 1818. Reprinted in Xiao Ya'nan, ed., *Qingdai guixiu ji congkan*, vol. 26, 167–376.
Xu Chengyao 許承堯. *Sheshi xiantan* 歙事閑譚. Draft, 1930. Reprint, Hefei, Anhui: Huangshan Shushe, 2014.
Xu Chengyao 許承堯. *Shexian zhi* 歙縣志. Shanghai: LüHu Tongxianghui, 1937.
Xú Deyin 徐德音. *Lüjingxuan shichao* 綠淨軒詩鈔. 1707; 1746.
Xú Deyin 徐德音. *Lüjingxuan xuji* 綠淨軒續集. 1752.
Xǔ Chengjia 許承家. *Lieweige shiji* 獵微閣詩集. 1707; 1746.
Xǔ Changling 許昌齡. *Bimoting ji* 碧摩亭集. 1707; 1746.
Xǔ family. *Jiangdu Xǔ shi jiaji* 江都許氏家集. Ca. 1746. Reprinted in Xu Yanping 徐雁平and Zhang Jian 張劍, eds., *Qingdai jiaji congkan* 清代家集叢刊, vol. 44. Beijing: Guojia Tushuguan Chubanshe, 2015.
Xǔ Tianqiu 許天球. *Biyushanfang shichao* 碧雨山房詩鈔. 1746.
Xǔ Yingnian 許迎年. *Huaishu shichao* 槐墅詩鈔. 1707; 1746.
Yanfeng 延豐, ed., *Qinding chongxiu liang Zhe yanfazhi* 欽定重修兩浙鹽法志. 1862–75. Reprint, Shanghai: Shanghai Guji Chubanshe, 1995.
Ye Xiaowan 葉小紈. *Yuanyang meng* 鴛鴦夢. In Ye Shaoyuan 葉紹袁, ed., *Wumengtang ji* 午夢堂集, 383–401. Reprint, Beijing: Zhonghua Shuju, 1998.
Ying Jie 英傑 and Yan Duanshu 晏端書, eds. *Xuzuan Yangzhou fuzhi* 續纂揚州府志. 1874.

Yu Yue 俞樾. *Chunzaitang zawen* 春在堂雜文. 1899.
Yuan Mei 袁枚, ed. *Suiyuan nüdizi shixuan* 隨園女弟子詩選. 1796.
Yuan Mei 袁枚. *Suiyuan shihua* 隨園詩話. 1790. Reprint, Nanjing: Jiangsu Guji Chubanshe, 2000.
Yue Shi 樂史. *Taiping huanyu ji* 太平寰宇記. Qing Siku edition.
"Yugong" 禹貢. In *Shangshu* 尚書. Sibu Congkan edition.
Yun Zhu 惲珠. *Guochao guixiu zhengshiji* 國朝閨秀正始集. 1831.
Zhang Pu 張溥, ed. *Han Wei liuchao yibai sanjia ji* 漢魏六朝一百三家集. Qing Siku edition.
Zhang Xuan 張鉉. *Yinlüshantang shiji* 飲綠山堂詩集. 1814.
Zhang Yin 張因. *Lüqiu shuwu shichao* 綠秋書屋詩鈔. Ca. 1796–1820.
Zhang Yin 張崟. *Taochan'ge ji* 逃禪閣集. Manuscript with preface dated 1849.
Zhao Erxun 趙爾巽. *Qingshi gao* 清史稿. 1928.
Zhao Hong'en 趙弘恩, ed. *Qianlong Jiangnan tongzhi* 乾隆江南通志. 1736.
Zhao Jishi 趙吉士, ed. *Kangxi Huizhou fuzhi* 康熙徽州府志. 1699.
Zhao Yin'gu 趙飲谷, ed. *Gaoyang sizhong ji* 高陽四種集. 1707. Reprinted in Xu Yanping 徐雁平and Zhang Jian 張劍, eds., *Qingdai jiaji congkan* 清代家集叢刊, vol. 43. Beijing: Guojia Tushuguan Chubanshe, 2015.
Zheng Qinghu 鄭慶祜, ed. *Yangzhou Xiuyuan zhi* 揚州休園志. 1773.
Zheng Xuan 鄭玄, annot. *Liji* 禮記. Sibu Congkan edition.
Zhu Mu 祝穆. *Fangyu shenglan* 方輿勝覽. Qing Siku edition.
Zhuang Zhou 莊周. *Nanhua zhenjing zhushu* 南華真經注疏. Annotated by Guo Xiang 郭象 and Cheng Xuanying 成玄英. Guyi Congshu edition.

SECONDARY SOURCES

A Feng 阿風. *MingQing shidai funü de diwei yu quanli—yi MingQing qiyue wenshu, susong dang'an wei zhongxin* 明清時代婦女的地位與權利——以明清契約文書、訴訟檔案為中心. Beijing: Shehui Kexue Wenxian Chubanshe, 2009.
Altenburger, Roland, Margaret B. Wan, and Vibeke Bordahl, eds. *Yangzhou, A Place in Literature: The Local in Chinese Cultural History*. Honolulu: University of Hawai'i Press, 2015.
Bai Hongye 白鴻葉 and Li Xiaocong 李孝聰. *Kangxi chao Huangyu quanlan tu* 康熙朝《皇輿全覽圖》. Beijing: Guojia Tushuguan Chubanshe, 2014.
Barlow, Tani. *Women and Writing in Modern China*. Stanford, CA: Stanford University Press, 1998.
Beattie, Hilary J. *Land and Lineage in China: A Study of T'ung-Ch'eng County, Anhwei, in the Ming and Ch'ing Dynasties*. Cambridge: Cambridge University Press, 1979.
Bernhardt, Kathryn. *Women and Property in China, 960–1949*. Stanford, CA: Stanford University Press, 1999.
Bian Dongbo 卞東波. "*Tiaoxi Yuyin conghua* Dushilun de lishi wenhua beijing jiqi neihan" 《苕溪漁隱叢話》杜詩論的歷史文化背景及其內涵. In Bian Dongbo, *Songdai shihua yu shixue wenxian yanjiu* 宋代詩話與詩學文獻研究, 47–80. Beijing: Zhonghua Shuju, 2013.

Bossler, Beverly. *Courtesans, Concubines, and the Cult of Female Fidelity: Gender and Social Change in China, 1000–1400*. Cambridge, MA: Harvard University Asia Center, 2013.

Brown, Tristan G. *Laws of the Land: Fengshui and the State in Qing Dynasty China*. Princeton, NJ: Princeton University Press, 2023.

Chang, Kang-i Sun. "Wang Shizhen (1634–1711) and the 'New' Canon." *Qinghua xuebao* 清華學報 (Tsing Hua Journal of Chinese Studies) 37, no. 1 (2007): 305–20.

Chang, Kang-i Sun. "Women's Poetic Witnessing: Late Ming and Late Qing Examples." In David Der-wei Wang and Shang Wei, eds., *Dynastic Crisis and Cultural Innovation: From the Late Ming to the Late Qing and Beyond*, 504–22. Cambridge, MA: Harvard University Asia Center, 2005.

Chang, Kang-i Sun, and Stephen Owen, eds. *The Cambridge History of Chinese Literature*. Cambridge: Cambridge University Press, 2010.

Chen Pingyuan 陳平原. *Zhongguo xiaoshuo xushi moshi de zhuanbian* 中國小說敘事模式的轉變. Shanghai: Shanghai Renmin Chubanshe, 1988.

Chittick, Andrew. "The Development of Local Writing in Early Medieval China." *Early Medieval China*, no. 1 (2003): 35–70.

Chow, Kai-wing. *Publishing, Culture, and Power in Early Modern China*. Stanford, CA: Stanford University Press, 2004.

Clark, Tom, Emily Finlay, and Philippa Kelly. *Worldmaking: Literature, Language, Culture*. Amsterdam: John Benjamins, 2017.

Cosgrove, Denis, and Stephen Daniels, eds. *The Iconography of Landscape: Essays on the Symbolic Representation, Design, and Use of Past Environments*. Cambridge: Cambridge University Press, 1988.

Dai Jian 戴健. *Qingchu zhi zhongye Yangzhou yule wenhua yu wenxue* 清初至中葉揚州娛樂文化與文學. Beijing: Shehui Kexue Wenxian Chubanshe, 2008.

David, Bruno, and Meredith Wilson, eds. *Inscribed Landscapes: Marking and Making Place*. Honolulu: University of Hawai'i Press, 2002.

De Weerdt, Hilde. "Places of the Self: Pictorial Autobiography in the Eighteenth Century." *Chinese Literature: Essays, Articles, Reviews (CLEAR)* 33 (Dec. 2011): 121–49.

Du, Yongtao. "Locality, Literati, and the Imagined Spatial Order: A Case of Huizhou, 1200–1550." *Journal of Song-Yuan Studies* 42 (2012): 407–44.

Du, Yongtao. *The Order of Places: Translocal Practices of the Huizhou Merchants in Late Imperial China*. Leiden: Brill, 2015.

Duara, Prasenjit. "Local Worlds: The Poetics and Politics of the Native Place in Modern China." *South Atlantic Quarterly* 99, no. 1 (Winter 2000): 13–45.

Duara, Prasenjit. "The Regime of Authenticity: Timelessness, Gender, and National History in Modern China." *History and Theory* 37 (Oct. 1998): 287–308.

Ebrey, Patricia B. "Conceptions of the Family in the Sung Dynasty." *Journal of Asian Studies* 43, no. 2 (Feb. 1984): 219–45.

Ebrey, Patricia B. *The Inner Quarters: Marriage and the Lives of Chinese Women in the Sung Period*. Berkeley: University of California Press, 1993.

Edwards, Louise P. *Men and Women in Qing China: Gender in the Red Chamber Dream*. Leiden: Brill, 1994.

Elman, Benjamin. *Civil Examinations and Meritocracy in Later Imperial China*. Cambridge, MA: Harvard University Press, 2013.

Elman, Benjamin. *On Their Own Terms: Science in China, 1550–1900*. Cambridge, MA: Harvard University Press, 2005.

Epstein, Maram. "*Zaisheng yuan* and the Writing of Women's Culture." *Journal of Chinese Literature and Culture* 10, no. 1 (2023): 169–94.

Feng Erkang 馮爾康. "Ming Qing shiqi Yangzhou de Huishang jiqi houyi shulue" 明清時期揚州的徽商及其後裔述略. *Huixue* 徽學 (2000): 1–23.

Feng Erkang 馮爾康. "Qingdai Huizhou cainü de wenxue chuangzuo shenghuo jiqi zuopin biaoda de ganqing shijie" 清代徽州才女的文學創作生活及其作品表達的感情世界. In Feng Erkang, *Feng Erkang wenji* 馮爾康文集, 173–214. Tianjin: Tianjin Renmin Chubanshe, 2019.

Feng Erkang 馮爾康. "Qingdai Huizhou xianyuan de zhijia he shengcun shu" 清代徽州賢媛的治家和生存術. *Tianjin shifan daxue xuebao* 天津師範大學學報, no. 4 (2014): 23–29.

Feng Erkang 馮爾康. "Qingdai Huizhou xianyuan chuse de shehui lishi jianshi" 清代徽州賢媛出色的社會歷史見識. *MingQing luncong* 明清論叢, no. 1 (2015): 360–67.

Finnane, Antonia. *Speaking of Yangzhou: A Chinese City, 1550–1850*. Cambridge, MA: Harvard University Asia Center, 2004.

Fong, Grace S. "Feminist Theories and Women Writers of Late Imperial China: Impact and Critique." *Journal of Chinese Literature and Culture* 9, no. 1 (April 2022): 105–30.

Fong, Grace S. "Gender and the Failure of Canonization: Anthologizing Women's Poetry in the Late Ming." *CLEAR* 26 (Dec. 2004): 129–49.

Fong, Grace S. *Herself an Author: Gender, Agency, and Writing in Late Imperial China*. Honolulu: University of Hawai'i Press, 2008.

Fong, Grace S. "Private Emotion, Public Commemoration: Qian Shoupu's Poem of Mourning." *CLEAR* 30 (2008): 19–30.

Furth, Charlotte. "The Patriarch's Legacy: Household Instructions and the Transmission of Orthodox Values." In Kwang-Ching Liu, ed., *Orthodoxy in Late Imperial China*, 187–211. Berkeley: University of California Press, 1990.

Gao Fang 高放. "*Wutuobang* zai Zhongguo de bainian chuanbo—Guanyu fanyishi jiqi banben de xueshu kaocha" 《烏托邦》在中國的百年傳播——關於翻譯史及其版本的學術考察. *Zhongguo shehui kexue* 中國社會科學, no. 5 (2017): 181–204.

Geertz, Clifford. *The Interpretation of Cultures: Selected Essays*. New York: Basic Books, 1973.

Geng Chuanyou 耿傳友. "Shiyu de pianli he chonghe—Huixue yu Zhongguo wenxue guanxi lunlue" 視域的偏離和重合——徽學與中國文學關係論略. *Xueshu jie* 學術界251, no. 4 (2019): 158–67.

Glosser, Susan L. *Chinese Visions of Family and State, 1915–1953*. Berkeley: University of California Press, 2003.

Goodman, Bryna. *Native Place, City, and Nation: Regional Networks and Identities in Shanghai, 1853–1937*. Berkeley: University of California Press, 1995.

Grant, Beata. "Little Vimalakirti: Buddhism and Poetry in the Writings of Chiang Chu (1764–1804)." In Harriet T. Zurndorfer, ed., *Chinese Women in the Imperial Past: New Perspectives*, 286–307. Leiden: Brill, 1999.

Gunn, Simon "The Spatial Turn: Changing Histories of Space and Place." In Simon Gunn and Robert J. Morris, eds., *Identities in Space: Contested Terrains in the Western City since 1850*, 1–18. Aldershot: Ashgate, 2001.

Guo, Li. *Writing Gender in Early Modern Chinese Women's Tanci Fiction*. West Lafayette, IN: Purdue University Press, 2021.

Guo, Qitao. "Engendering the Mercantile Lineage: The Rise of the Female Chastity Cult in Late Ming Huizhou," *Nan Nü* 17, no. 1 (2015): 9–53.

Guo, Qitao. *Huizhou: Local Identity and Mercantile Lineage Culture in Ming China*. Oakland: University of California Press, 2022.

Guo, Qitao. *Ritual Opera and Mercantile Lineage: The Confucian Transformation of Popular Culture in Late Imperial Huizhou*. Stanford, CA: Stanford University Press, 2005.

Guo, Qiyong, et al. "The Values of Confucian Benevolence and the Universality of the Confucian Way of Extending Love." *Frontiers of Philosophy in China* 7, no. 1 (March 2012): 20–54.

Harrist, Robert E. *The Landscape of Words: Stone Inscriptions from Early and Medieval China*. Seattle: University of Washington Press, 2008.

Hauf, Kandice. "The Community Covenant in Sixteenth Century Ji'an Prefecture, Jiangxi." *Late Imperial China* 17, no. 2 (Dec. 1996): 1–50.

Hegel, Robert E. *Reading Illustrated Fiction in Late Imperial China*. Stanford, CA: Stanford University Press, 1998.

Heidegger, Martin. *Poetry, Language, Thought*. Translated by Albert Hofstadter. New York: Harper & Row, 1975.

Ho, Ping-ti. *The Ladder of Success in Imperial China: Aspects of Social Mobility, 1368–1911*. New York: Columbia University Press, 1962.

Ho, Ping-ti. "The Salt Merchants of Yang-Chou: A Study of Commercial Capitalism in Eighteenth-Century China." *Harvard Journal of Asiatic Studies* 17, no. 1 (1954): 130–68.

Hsu, Immanuel C. Y. *The Rise of Modern China*. 6th ed. New York: Oxford University Press, 2000.

Hu Chengye 胡成業. "Hu Shi yu weijingde Jixi congshu" 胡適與未竟的績溪叢書. *Anhui shixue* 安徽史學, no. 2 (1993): 82.

Hu Siao-chen 胡曉真. *Churu mimi huayuan: Jindai nüxing xushi wenxue de qianshi jinsheng* 出入秘密花園: 近代女性敘事文學的前世今生. Hong Kong: Sanlian Shudian (HK), 2021.

Hua Wei 華瑋. *MingQing funü zhi xiqu chuangzuo yu piping* 明清婦女之戲曲創作與批評. Taibei: Zhongyang Yanjiuyuan Zhongguo Wenzhe Yanjiusuo, 2003.

Huang Jin Chu 黃錦珠. *Nüxing shuxie de duoyuan chengxian: Qingmo Minchu nüzuojia xiaoshuo yanjiu* 女性書寫的多元呈現: 清末民初女作家小說研究. Taibei: Liren Shuju, 2014.

Huang, Martin W. *Intimate Memory: Gender and Mourning in Late Imperial China*. Albany: State University of New York Press, 2018.

Huntington, Rania. *Ink and Tears: Memory, Mourning, and Writing in the Yu Family*. Honolulu: University of Hawai'i Press, 2018.

Idema, Wilt. "The Biographical and the Autobiographical in Bo Shaojun's One Hundred Poems Lamenting My Husband." In Joan Judge and Ying Hu, eds. *Beyond Exemplar Tales: Women's Biography in Chinese History*, 230–45. Berkeley: University of California Press, 2011.

Idema, Wilt, and Beata Grant. *The Red Brush: Writing Women of Imperial China*. Cambridge, MA: Harvard University Asia Center, 2004.

Jiang Xiaoping 蔣小平. "Nüxing shuxie yu qing'ai yuejie: Xiqu shi shijye zhong de *Lihua meng* jiedu" 女性書寫與情愛越界：戲曲史視野中的《梨花夢》解讀. *Minzu yishu* 民族藝術, no. 4 (2013): 132–36.

Jiang Yin 蔣寅. "Qingdai shixue yu diyu wenxue chuantong de jiangou" 清代詩學與地域文學傳統的建構. In Jiang Yin, *Shijiao yu fangfa: Zhongguo wenxueshi tansuo* 視角與方法：中國文學史探索, 549–73. Beijing: Beijing Daxue Chubanshe, 2018.

Jiang Yin 蔣寅. *Wang Yuyang yu Kangxi shitan* 王漁洋與康熙詩壇. Beijing: Zhongguo Shehuikexue Chubanshe, 2001.

Jiang Yin 蔣寅. "Yizhong geng zhenshi de rendi guanxi yu wenxue shengtai—Zhongguo gudai liuyu wenxue yinlun" 一種更真實的人地關係與文學生態——中國古代流寓文學引論. In Jiang Yin, *Shijiao yu fangfa*, 130–46.

Jin, Huan. *The Collapse of Heaven: The Taiping Civil War and Chinese Literature and Culture, 1850–1880*. Cambridge, MA: Harvard University Asia Center, 2024.

Ko, Dorothy. *Cinderella's Sisters: A Revisionist History of Footbinding*. Berkeley: University of California Press, 2005.

Ko, Dorothy. *The Social Life of Inkstones: Artisans and Scholars in Early Qing China*. Seattle: University of Washington Press, 2017.

Ko, Dorothy. *Teachers of the Inner Chambers: Women and Culture in Seventeenth-Century China*. Stanford, CA: Stanford University Press, 1994.

Kuhn, Philip A. *Origins of the Modern Chinese State*. Stanford, CA: Stanford University Press, 2002.

Lam, Ling Hon. *The Spatiality of Emotions in Early Modern China: From Dreamscapes to Theatricality*. New York: Columbia University Press, 2018.

Lee, Haiyan. *Revolution of the Heart: A Genealogy of Love in China, 1900–1950*. Stanford, CA: Stanford University Press, 2007.

Lewis, Mark E., and Mei-yu Hsieh. "*Tianxia* and the Invention of Empire in East Asia." In Ban Wang, ed., *Chinese Visions of World Order: Tianxia, Culture, and World Politics*, 25–48. Durham: Duke University Press, 2017.

Li Qiuju 李秋橘. "Qingdai nüshiren Wang Ying nianpu" 清代女詩人汪嫈年譜. MA thesis, Huaibei Shifan Daxue, 2014.

Li, Waiyee. "Early Qing to 1723." In Kang-i Sun Chang and Stephen Owen, eds., *The Cambridge History of Chinese Literature*, 152–244. Cambridge: Cambridge University Press, 2010.

Li, Waiyee. *Women and National Trauma in Late Imperial Chinese Literature*. Cambridge, MA: Harvard University Asia Center, 2014.

Li, Xiaorong. "Gender and Textual Politics during the Qing Dynasty: The Case of the *Zhengshi ji*." *Harvard Journal of Asiatic Studies* 69, no. 1 (June 2009): 75–107.

Li, Xiaorong. "Gender, Genre, and Locality: A Solicited Collection of Poetry by Notable Women from Anhui, 1936." In Manling Luo, ed., *Cross-generic Perspectives on Traditional Chinese Literature*, 230–57. Leiden: Brill, 2025.

Li, Xiaorong. *Women's Poetry of Late Imperial China: Transforming the Inner Chambers*. Seattle: University of Washington Press, 2012.

Li Xubin 李敘彬. *Dubei Jiaoshan* 讀碑焦山. Zhenjiang: Jiangsu Daxue Chubanshe, 2015.

Lin, Man-houng. "Two Social Theories Revealed: Statecraft Controversies over China's Monetary Crisis, 1808–1854." *Late Imperial China* 12, no. 2 (Dec. 1991): 1–35.

Liu, Lydia H. *Translingual Practice: Literature, National Culture, and Translated Modernity—China, 1900–1937*. Stanford, CA: Stanford University Press, 1995.

Lu, Weijing. *Arranged Companions: Marriage and Intimacy in Qing China*. Seattle: University of Washington Press, 2021.

Lu, Weijing. *True to Her Word: The Faithful Maiden Cult in Late Imperial China*. Stanford, CA: Stanford University Press, 2008.

Luan Kaiyin欒開印. *Jingjiang huapai* 京江畫派. Nanjing: Jiangsu Renmin Chubanshe, 2019.

Luo, Manling. "Theories of Spatiality and the Study of Medieval China." *Journal of Chinese Literature and Culture* 9, no. 1 (April 2022): 195–224.

Ma Tengfei 馬騰飛 and Luo Shijin 羅時進. "Qingdai 'Huaihai wenxue quan' jiqi shixue puxi" 清代淮海文學圈及其詩學譜系. *Suzhou daxue xuebao* 蘇州大學學報, no. 4 (2016): 138–45.

Ma, Zili, and Fan Pik Wah. "Hearts in the Hometown: Diaspora Consciousness and Literature of the Tang and Song." Translated by Wendy Hor. *Journal of Chinese Literature and Culture* 7, no. 2 (Nov. 2020): 268–86.

Mann, Susan. "Dowry Wealth and Wifely Virtue in Mid-Qing Gentry Households." *Late Imperial China* 29, no. 1S (2008): 64–76.

Mann, Susan. "The Lady and the State: Women's Writings in Times of Trouble during the Nineteenth Century." In Grace S. Fong and Ellen Widmer, eds., *The Inner Quarters and Beyond: Women Writers from Ming through Qing*, 283–313. Leiden: Brill, 2010.

Mann, Susan. *Precious Records: Women in China's Long Eighteenth Century*. Stanford, CA: Stanford University Press, 1997.

Mann, Susan. *The Talented Women of the Zhang Family*. Berkeley: University of California Press, 2007.

Mann, Susan. "The Virtue of Travel for Women in the Late Empire." In Bryna Goodman and Wendy Larson, eds., *Gender in Motion: Divisions of Labor and Cultural Change in Late Imperial and Modern China*, 55–74. Lanham, MD: Rowman & Littlefield, 2005.

Mao Meng 茆萌. "Luelun Zhenjiang Baoshi wenhua shijia ji zhuyao shiren shizuo" 略論鎮江鮑氏文化世家及主要詩人詩作. *Jiangsu daxue xuebao* 江蘇大學學報, no. 5 (2009): 61–63.

Massey, Doreen B. *Space, Place, and Gender*. Minneapolis: University of Minnesota Press, 1994.

McDermott, Joseph P. "The Chinese Domestic Bursar." In Masayoshi Uozumi 魚住昌良, ed., *Dentō to kindaika: Chō (Takeda) Kiyoko Kyōju koki kinen ronbunshū* 伝統と近代化: 長 (武田) 清子教授古稀記念論文集, 267–84. Tōkyō: Kokusai Kris Tokyō Daigaku Ajia Bunka Kenkyūjo, 1990.

McDermott, Joseph P. *The Making of a New Rural Order in South China, vol. 1: Village, Land, and Lineage in Huizhou, 900–1600*. Cambridge: Cambridge University Press, 2013.

McDermott, Joseph P. *The Making of a New Rural Order in South China, vol. 2: Merchants, Markets, and Lineages, 1500–1700*. Cambridge: Cambridge University Press, 2020.

Meyer-Fong, Tobie S. *Building Culture in Early Qing Yangzhou*. Stanford, CA: Stanford University Press, 2003.

Meyer-Fong, Tobie S. *What Remains: Coming to Terms with Civil War in Nineteenth Century China*. Stanford, CA: Stanford University Press, 2013.

Miles, Steven B. *Chinese Diasporas: A Social History of Global Migration*. Cambridge: Cambridge University Press, 2020.

Miles, Steven B. *The Sea of Learning: Mobility and Identity in Nineteenth-Century Guangzhou*. Cambridge, MA: Harvard University Asia Center, 2006.

Min Erchang 閔爾昌. *Jiang Ziping xiansheng nianpu* 江子屏先生年譜. Beijing: Beijing Tushuguan Chubanshe, 1999.

More, Thomas. *Utopia*. Translated by Ralph Robynson; edited by David Harris Sacks. 1556. Reprint, Boston: Bedford/St. Martins, 1999.

Moyer, Jessica D. *Woman Rules Within: Domestic Space and Genre in Qing Vernacular Literature*. Leiden: Brill, 2020.

Naugle, David K. *Worldview: The History of a Concept*. Grand Rapids, MI: William B. Eerdmans, 2002.

Noel, Thomas D. "Rereading a Poetics of Divination: Oracular Visuality and Iterations of Landscape in Wei-Jin Lyricism." *Journal of Chinese Literature and Culture* 9, no. 2 (Nov. 2022): 277–307.

Owen, Stephen. *All Mine! Happiness, Ownership, and Naming in Eleventh-Century China*. New York: Columbia University Press, 2021.

Owen, Stephen. *An Anthology of Chinese Literature*. New York: Norton, 1996.
Owen, Stephen. *The End of the Chinese "Middle Ages": Essays in Mid-Tang Literary Culture*. Stanford, CA: Stanford University Press, 1996.
Qi Yongxiang 漆永祥. *Jiang Fan yu Hanxue shichengji yanjiu* 江藩與《漢學師承記》研究. Shanghai: Shanghai Guji Chubanshe, 2006.
Qian, Nanxiu. *Politics, Poetics, and Gender in Late Qing China: Xue Shaohui and the Era of Reform*. Stanford, CA: Stanford University Press, 2015.
Roberts, Moss, trans. *The Analects: Conclusions and Conversations of Confucius*. Oakland: University of California Press, 2020.
Roberts, Moss, trans. *Dao De Jing: The Book of the Way*. Berkeley: University of California Press, 2019.
Robertson, Maureen. "Literary Authorship by Late Imperial Governing-Class Chinese Women and the Emergence of a 'Minor Literature.'" In Grace S. Fong and Ellen Widmer, eds., *The Inner Quarters and Beyond: Women Writers from Ming through Qing*, 381–83. Leiden: Brill, 2010.
Rogaski, Ruth. *Hygienic Modernity: Meanings of Health and Disease in Treaty-Port China*. Berkeley: University of California Press, 2004.
Rowe, William T. "Ancestral Rites and Political Authority in Late Imperial China: Chen Hongmou in Jiangxi." *Modern China* 24, no. 4 (1998): 378–407.
Saussy, Haun. *The Making of Barbarians: Chinese Literature and Multilingual Asia*. Princeton, NJ: Princeton University Press, 2022.
Shang, Wei. "The Literati Era and Its Demise (1723–1840)." In Kang-i Sun Chang and Stephen Owen, eds., *Cambridge History of Chinese Literature*, 245–342. Cambridge, Cambridge University Press, 2010.
Shang Wei 商偉. *Tixie mingsheng: Cong Huanghe lou dao Fenghuang tai* 題寫名勝：從黃鶴樓到鳳凰臺. Beijing: Sanlian Shudian, 2020.
Shi Mei 史梅, "Qingdai Jiangsu funü wenxian de jiazhi he yiyi" 清代江蘇婦女文獻的價值和意義. In Zhang Hongsheng 張宏生, ed., *Ming Qing wenxue yu xingbie yanjiu* 明清文學與性別研究, 482–501. Nanjing: Jiangsu Guji Chubanshe, 2002.
Soja, Edward W. *Thirdspace: Journeys to Los Angeles and Other Real-and-Imagined Places*. Cambridge, MA: Blackwell, 1996.
Sommer, Matthew. *The Fox Spirit, the Stone Maiden, and Other Transgender Histories from Late Imperial China*. New York: Columbia University Press, 2024.
Song Qingxiu 宋清秀. *Qingdai Jiangnan nüxing wenxue shilun* 清代江南女性文學史論. Shanghai: Shanghai Guji Chubanshe, 2015.
Strassberg, Richard E. *Inscribed Landscapes: Travel Writing from Imperial China*. Berkeley: University of California Press, 1994.
Szonyi, Michael. *Practicing Kinship: Lineage and Descent in Late Imperial China*. Stanford, CA: Stanford University Press, 2002.
Tang Lixing 唐力行. *Suzhou yu Huizhou: 16–20 shiji liangdi hudong yu shehui bianqian de bijiao yanjiu* 蘇州與徽州：16–20 世紀兩地互動與社會變遷的比較研究. Beijing: Shangwu Yinshuguan, 2007.

Tao Liangqin 陶良琴. "Jinnian lai Huizhou funüshi yanjiu zongshu" 近年來徽州婦女史研究綜述. *Xibu xuekan* 西部學刊, no. 4 (2020): 139–46.

Thomas, Julian. *Time, Culture, and Identity: An Interpretive Archaeology*. London: Routledge, 1996.

Wang, Ao. *Spatial Imaginaries in Mid-Tang China: Geography, Cartography, and Literature*. Amherst, NY: Cambria Press, 2018.

Wang, Ban, ed. *China in the World: Culture, Politics, and World Vision*. Durham: Duke University Press, 2022.

Wang, Ban. *Chinese Visions of World Order: Tianxia, Culture, and World Politics*. Durham: Duke University Press, 2017.

Wang Chengzu 王成組. *Zhongguo dilixue shi* 中國地理學史. Beijing: Shangwu Yinshuguan, 2015.

Wang, David Der-Wei. "Chinese Literature from 1841 to 1937." In Kang-i Sun Chang and Stephen Owen, eds., *The Cambridge History of Chinese Literature*, 413–564. Cambridge: Cambridge University Press, 2010.

Wang, David Der-Wei. *Fin-de-siecle Splendor: Repressed Modernities of Late Qing Fiction, 1849–1911*. Stanford, CA: Stanford University Press, 1997.

Wang Deheng 王德恒. *Zhongguo fangzhi xue* 中國方志學. Zhengzhou: Daxiang Chubanshe, 2009.

Wang, Yanning. *Reverie and Reality: Poetry on Travel by Late Imperial Chinese Women*. Lanham, MD: Lexington, 2014.

Wang, Yuefan. "Garden, Gender, and Memory: Shang Jinglan and Her Writings in the Ming-Qing Transition." *Journal of Chinese Literature and Culture* 10, no. 1 (Apr. 2023): 30–56.

Wang Zhenzhong 王振忠. *Ming-Qing Huishang yu Huai-Yang shehui bianqian* 明清徽商與淮揚社會變遷. Beijing: Sanlian Shudian, 1996.

Watson, Burton, trans. *The Complete Works of Chuang Tzu*. New York: Columbia University Press, 1968.

Wei, Betty P. T. *Ruan Yuan, 1764–1849: The Life and Work of a Major Scholar-Official in China before the Opium War*. Hong Kong: University of Hong Kong Press, 2006.

Widmer, Ellen. "Gentility in Transition: Travels, Novels, and the New *Guixiu*." In Daria Berg and Chloë Starr, eds., *The Quest for Gentility in China: Negotiations beyond Gender and Class*, 21–44. London: Routledge, 2007.

Widmer, Ellen. "*Honglou meng ying* and Three 'Women's Novels' of Late Qing." In Luo Jiurong 羅久蓉 and Lü Miaofen 呂妙芬, eds., *Wusheng zhisheng (III): Jindai Zhongguo de funü yu wenhua (1600–1950)* 無聲之聲(III)：近代中國的婦女與文化 (1600–1950), 301–26. Taibei: Zhongyang Yanjiuyuan Jindaishi Yanjiusuo, 2003.

Widmer, Ellen. "Xiaoqing's Literary Legacy and the Place of the Woman Writer in Late Imperial China." *Late Imperial China* 13, no. 1 (1992): 111–55.

Widmer, Ellen, and Zhao Yingzhi 趙穎之. "Shiba shiji de Guangdong cainü" 18 世紀的廣東才女. *Zhongshan daxue xuebao* 中山大學學報 49, no. 3 (2009): 40–46.

Wu Haibo 吳海波. *Lianghuai siyan yu difang shehui* 兩淮私鹽與地方社會. Beijing: Zhonghua Shuju, 2018.

Wu Yujuan 吳宇娟. "Zouchu chuantong de dianfan—WanQing nüzuojia xiaoshuo nüxing tuibian de lichen" 走出傳統的典範——晚清女作家小說女性蛻變的歷程. *Donghai Zhongwen xuebao* 東海中文學報 19 (2007): 239–68.

Wu, Yulian. *Luxurious Networks: Salt Merchants, Status, and Statecraft in Eighteenth-Century China*. Stanford, CA: Stanford University Press, 2017.

Xiao Yanwan 蕭燕婉. *Shindai no josei shijintachi: En Bai no on'nadeshi tenbyō* 清代の女性詩人たち: 袁枚の女弟子點描. Fukuoka-shi: Chūgoku Shoten, 2007.

Xie Xin 謝欣. "*Fuchu ji* Huishang xianxiang yanjiu" 《複初集》徽商現象研究. *Anhui guangbo dianshi daxue xuebao* 安徽廣播電視大學學報, no. 1 (2009): 91–94.

Xu, Man. *Crossing the Gate: Everyday Lives of Women in Song Fujian (960–1279)*. Albany: State University of New York Press, 2017.

Xu Yingchang 徐應昶. *Dianhua* 電話. Shanghai: Shangwu Yinshuguan, 1935.

Xu Yuanchong 許淵沖, trans. *Shijing* 詩經. Changsha: Hunan Chubanshe, 1993.

Yan Dunyi 嚴敦易. "He Peizhu de *Lihua meng*" 何佩珠的《梨花夢》. In Yan Dunyi, *Yuan Ming Qing xiqu lunji* 元明清戲曲論集, 300–304. Zhengzhou, Henan: Zhongzhou Shuhuashe, 1982.

Yan Qilin 嚴其林 and Cheng Jian 程建. *Jingkou wenhua* 京口文化. Nanjing: Nanjing Daxue Chubanshe, 2001.

Yan Zhixiong 嚴志雄. *Qiuliu de shijie: Wang Shizhen yu Qingchu shitan ceyi* 秋柳的世界：王士禛與清初詩壇側議. Hong Kong: Hong Kong University Press, 2013.

Yang Binbin 楊彬彬. "Funü zhushu yu Huishang jiazu tuibian: Wang Ying (1781–1842) zhushu zhong jiazushi de chengxian" 婦女著述與徽商家族蛻變: 汪嫈（1781–1842）著述中家族史的呈現. *Qingshi luncong* 清史論叢 (Dec. 2018): 173–200.

Yang Binbin 楊彬彬, annot. *Jindai nüxing riji wuzhong wai yizhong* 近代女性日記五種 外一種. Nanjing: Fenghuang Chubanshe, 2021.

Yang Binbin 楊彬彬. "Yangzhou guixiu zhushu yu jiaoyou yanjiu xinshiye—Yi He Peizhu yimen jiaoyouquan weili" 揚州閨秀著述與交遊研究新視野——以何佩珠一門交遊圈為例. *Funü yanjiu luncong* 婦女研究論叢 149 (2018): 97–108.

Yang, Binbin. "Anchoring Identities in Yangzhou: Xú Deyin (1681–after 1760) and the Re-Invention of the Huizhou Legacy." *Chinese Literature: Essays, Articles, Reviews* 44 (2022): 141–73.

Yang, Binbin. *Heroines of the Qing: Exemplary Women Tell Their Stories*. Seattle: University of Washington Press, 2016.

Yang, Binbin. "Yangzhou Revisited: Spatial Imaginaries and Women's Literature during the Qing." *Journal of Chinese Literature and Culture* 10, no. 1 (April 2023): 57–80.

Yang, Xiaoshan. *Metamorphosis of the Private Sphere: Gardens and Objects in Tang-Song Poetry*. Cambridge, MA: Harvard University Asia Center, 2003.

Yangzhou Wenxue Yishu Gongzuozhe Lianhehui 揚州市文學藝術工作者聯合會 and Qingdai Yangzhou Huapai Yanjiuhui 清代揚州畫派研究會, eds. *Qingdai*

Yangzhou huapai yanjiuji 清代揚州畫派研究集. Yangzhou: Yangzhou Wenxue Yishu Gongzuozhe Lianhehui, 1980.

Yates, Robin D. S., and Danni Cai. "Bibliography of Women and Gender in China (2018–2022)." *NanNü: Men, Women and Gender in China* 25, no. 2 (Oct. 2023): 213–343.

Yi Jo-lan 衣若蘭. "'Tianxia zhizheng zi furen shi': Shilun MingQing shidai de muxun zizheng" 天下之政自婦始：試論明清時代的母訓子政. In You Jianming 遊鑑明, ed., *Zhongguo funüshi lunji* 中國婦女史論集, vol. 9, 111–37. Taibei: Daoxiang Chubanshe, 2011.

Yu, Pauline. "Poems in Their Place: Collections and Canons in Early Chinese Literature." *Harvard Journal of Asiatic Studies* 50, no. 1 (June 1990): 163–96.

Yu, Xin. "Publishing at the Grassroots: Print Culture and Rural Society in Early Modern China." PhD diss., Washington University in St. Louis, 2022.

Yü, Ying-shih. "The Two Worlds of *Honglou meng* (*Dream of the Red Chamber*)." Revised version in Josephine Chiu-Duke and Michael S. Duke, eds., *Chinese History and Culture: Seventeenth Century through Twentieth Century*, 134–51. New York: Columbia University Press, 2016.

Zhang Xiaopo 張小坡. *Lüwai Huizhou ren yu jindai Huizhou shehui bianqian yanjiu* 旅外徽州人與近代徽州社會變遷研究. Beijing: Zhonghua Shuju, 2018.

Zhang Xiaopo 張小坡. "Qingdai Huizhou wenhui yunzuo jiqi keju gongneng" 清代徽州文會運作及其科舉功能. *Anhui shifan daxue xuebao* 安徽師範大學學報 45, no. 5 (2017): 543–50.

Zhang Xiaoye 張小也. *Qingdai siyan wenti yanjiu* 清代私鹽問題研究. Beijing: Shehui Kexue Wenxian Chubanshe, 2002.

Zhang, Xin. *The Global in the Local: A Century of War, Commerce, and Technology in China*. Cambridge, MA: Harvard University Press, 2023.

Zhang, Yu. *Going to the Countryside: The Rural in the Modern Chinese Cultural Imagination, 1915–1965*. Ann Arbor: University of Michigan Press, 2020.

Zhang, Yun. *Engendering the Woman Question: Men, Women, and Writing in China's Early Periodical Press*. Leiden: Brill, 2020.

Zhao Houjun 趙厚均, ed. "[Lüjingxuan shichao] Fu: Jiping, Yiwen, Yishi" [綠淨軒詩鈔] 附：佚文、佚詩、輯評. In Hu Xiaoming 胡曉明 and Peng Guozhong 彭國忠, eds., *Jiangnan nüxing bieji chubian* 江南女性別集, vol. 1, 111–26. Hefei, Anhui: Huangshan Shushe, 2008.

Zhao Houjun 趙厚均. "Qingchu Qiantang nüshiren Xú Deyin jiqi zuopin lunxi" 清初錢塘女詩人徐德音及其作品論析. *Guji yanjiu* 古籍研究, no. 1 (2013): 282–94.

Zhao, Tingyang. *All under Heaven: The Tianxia System for a Possible World Order*. Translated by Joseph E. Harroff. Oakland: University of California Press, 2021.

Zheng Xing 鄭幸. *Yuan Mei nianpu xinbian* 袁枚年譜新編. Shanghai: Shanghai Guji Chubanshe, 2011.

Zhu Wanshu 朱萬曙. *Huishang yu Mingqing wenxue* 徽商與明清文學. Beijing: Renmin Wenxue Chubanshe, 2014.

Zhu, Yun. *Imagining Sisterhood in Modern Chinese Texts, 1890–1937*. Lanham, MD: Lexington, 2017.

Zurndorfer, Harriet T. "Book review: *Ritual Opera and Mercantile Lineage*." *Harvard Journal of Asiatic Studies* 67, no. 1 (2007): 229–37.

Zurndorfer, Harriet T. *Change and Continuity in Chinese Local History: The Development of Hui-chou Prefecture, 800 to 1800*. Leiden: Brill, 1989.

Zurndorfer, Harriet T., ed. *Chinese Women in the Imperial Past: New Perspectives*. Leiden: Brill, 1999.

Zurndorfer, Harriet T. "Cities and the Urban Economy." In Debin Ma and Richard von Glahn, eds., *The Cambridge Economic History of China*, 546–47. Cambridge: Cambridge University Press, 2022.

Zurndorfer, Harriet T. "Prostitutes and Courtesans in the Confucian Moral Universe of Late Ming China (1550–1644)." *International Review of Social History* 56 (2011): 197–216.

INDEX

Page numbers in *italics* indicate illustrations.